Also available at all good book stores

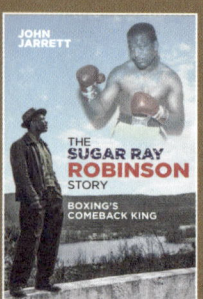
9781785315350

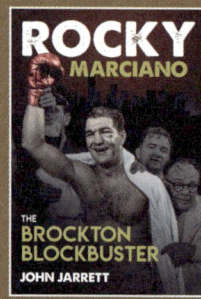
9781785313813

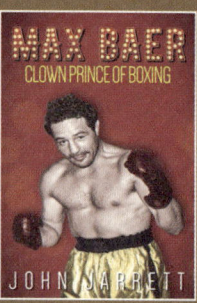
9781785312960

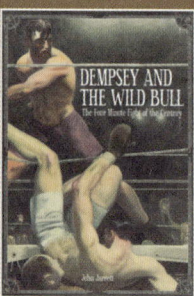
9781785310317

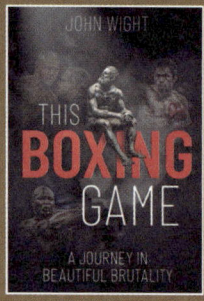
9781785316272

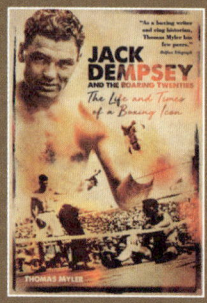
9781785316371

9781785316425

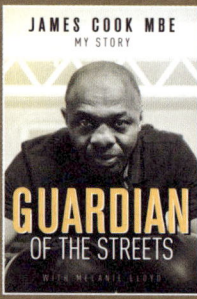
9781785314919

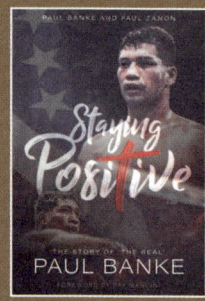
9781785315404

This is a gripping memoir which doubles up as an insightful deep dive into the world of entertainment and sports by a journalist who identified the phenomenon of MMA fighting as well as one man's journey to discover who he really is.

Halina Watts (*Sunday Mirror*)

Fiaz Rafiq and I bonded over Bruce Lee. His interview-heavy books on Lee, Muhammad Ali & Arnold Schwarzenegger and pioneering coverage of full combat 'cage' sports was impressive. Like Lee, he was a small-boned kid, and saw martial arts as an avenue. His passion became his life's work as a writer. No one else covers MMA with such insight. Now, he spins out his unlikely life story with entertaining energy, verve, sincerity and passion.

Alex Ben Block (*The Hollywood Reporter* – former editor – veteran showbiz journalist)

An inspiring story of a kid who discovered his path in life – and success – through his passion for Bruce Lee and the martial arts. Highly recommended.

Matthew Polly (*New York Times* bestselling authour)

Fiaz knows exactly how to get to the heart of every story seamlessly – and telling his own is no different. A must read for fans of combat sports, MMA and Hollywood.

Ellie Henman (*The Sun*)

He (Fiaz) studies his subjects and does his homework so much that he can't go wrong. Fiaz studies the person – like he studied about me, Bruce Lee, Muhammad Ali, Arnold Schwarzenegger, and all those guys. And he knows more about the person than the person knows about himself.

Royce Gracie (Three-time UFC champion/legend)

TO THE TOP

TO THE TOP

ENTER THE OCTAGON, THE RING AND ENTERTAINMENT

FIAZ RAFIQ

First published by Pitch Publishing, 2021

Pitch Publishing
A2 Yeoman Gate
Yeoman Way
Worthing
Sussex
BN13 3QZ
www.pitchpublishing.co.uk
info@pitchpublishing.co.uk

© 2021, Fiaz Rafiq

Every effort has been made to trace the copyright. Any oversight will be rectified in future editions at the earliest opportunity by the publisher.

All rights reserved. No part of this book may be reproduced, sold or utilised in any form or transmitted in any form or by any means, electronic or mechanical, including photocopying, recording or by any information storage and retrieval system, without prior permission in writing from the Publisher.

A CIP catalogue record is available for this book from the British Library.

ISBN 978-1 78531 885 6

Typesetting and origination by Pitch Publishing
Printed and bound in India by Replika Press Pvt. Ltd.

CONTENTS

Foreword 9
Preface 12

1. Crazy Obsessions 15
2. It's a Man's World 26
3. Feeling Despondent 36
4. The American Dream 51
5. Enter the Gracies 63
6. Returning to Los Angeles 72
7. Enter the Journalist 85
8. UFC Assignment 97
9. Realer than the UFC 108
10. The Giants 113
11. Hollywood, Here We Come! 122
12. Home Sweet Home 136
13. MMA Hits the Mainstream 143
14. Ringside & Brock 'The Beast' Lesnar 154
15. UFC 105 Encounters 162
16. Boxing Vs UFC: The Tyson-Gracie Challenge 173
17. UFC, Royals & Rich Arabs 184
18. Mike, Managers & Me 194
19. Muhammad Ali Encounters 204
20. From Martial Arts to Movie Magic 215
21. I'll Be Back 228
22. From Hospitality to MMA Chaos 239
23. Adventures in New York 252

24. Las Vegas	259
25. Canada: MMA Mad	267
26. The Massive MMA Fiasco	274
27. I'm No Terrorist	279
28. From Racism to Road Rage	294
29. Mr Rocky	300
30. Bruce Lee: Enter the Ring	310
31. Enter the Octagon	316
32. Old School Meets New	322
33. Challenging Conor McGregor	331
34. Tough Man Tales	343
35. Notorious	351
36. Meeting with an Underworld Figure	362
37. The Perils of Sports Fame	370
38. Michael, Matt & Martial Arts	377
39. A New Direction: New World	384
40. Flying High	395
41. A Tumultuous Year	409
Epilogue	419
Afterword	421
Acknowledgements	428

FOREWORD

I'VE KNOWN Fiaz for a long time, for more than 24 years to be precise, since 1996 when he first visited the Gracie Academy in Los Angeles, California as a 20-year-old and became my student. That's how far back we go. Subsequently, whenever he visited Los Angeles, he would occasionally take private lessons with me on a one-on-one basis. I don't believe in good students and bad students, but in good teachers and bad teachers. If I'm a good teacher, then a student will learn.

Despite Fiaz's long-term enthusiasm for the martial arts and Ultimate Fighting Championship (UFC), he eventually gravitated towards and forged a professional career in journalism, focusing on combat sports and entertainment in the literary world. He's been around the arts for a long time, particularly as a sportswriter dedicated to promoting the sport of mixed martial arts (MMA), professional fighters and world champions.

MMA has been labelled the fastest-growing sport in the world, and it has certainly presented endless opportunities for different businesses, gyms, fighters, fans, judges and magazines, culminating in the mainstream media taking a keen interest in what was once labelled 'human cockfighting'. Fiaz has been a part of the effort to legitimise MMA from the outset, and always helped publicise my seminars and anything I was promoting via coverage in the press.

'Hey, Royce,' he would say, when barely anyone knew about MMA. 'Is there anything you would like to promote in the magazine?' He has always supported me – I can't say enough good things about that.

Another thing Fiaz brings from martial arts is a strong work ethic. He creates work of a high calibre because he's utterly resolute in his approach. He always researches his subjects with devotion, and, by putting in the time and effort by doing his homework, he can't go wrong. Fiaz studies the person – just as he studied me, Bruce Lee, Muhammad Ali, Arnold Schwarzenegger, and all those guys – and produces commendable results.

Ever since I've known him he's invariably spoken with great pride and optimism about the late Bruce Lee. He would say to me with great conviction that if Bruce Lee, who was already researching MMA, was alive today he would have embraced Gracie Jiu-Jitsu. Fiaz devoted an inordinate amount of time to researching Bruce Lee's life and he knows everything about the man. He literally knows more about him than the late master knew about himself. I remember joking with him, saying I can't stand the fact I'm number two on his list of heroes after Bruce Lee. I told him I should be his number one.

We never fail to inject a dose of humour when we get together, especially whenever he's in Los Angeles or we're talking over the phone. He had a tendency to complain about being subjected to terrifying ordeals at the American airports because of his religious background. Consequently I used to tease him about that all the time. Recently I was showing some of my students in America one of the videos Fiaz sent me of him praying in the street. They all thought it was amusing. They were like, 'Man, that guy's crazy.' I said, 'He doesn't care, he just dropped down in the street and started praying.'

Indeed, these days it's very hard to find individuals who you can call real friends because it's not out of the ordinary for people to have ulterior motives – they are looking for something in return. True friendship is not easy to find and sustain. But Fiaz has been a good friend of mine for many years now. I know that if I need anything I can

FOREWORD

count on him day or night. I'm very pleased he's written his memoir showcasing his journey as a journalist, because having worked with, been around, interviewed and written about a plethora of fascinating figures he has compelling insights to share with the world.

Royce Gracie
UFC legend

PREFACE

WHEN I first began my career in journalism, never in a million years did I envisage that one day I would be writing my memoir. Even a few years later, when I had already had the opportunity to explore and write about the colourful lives of some of the world's biggest sporting and Hollywood action heroes, it never really dawned on me that I would share my own journey. It was only after almost two decades in my chosen career that I started to consider myself alongside other notable journalists who I saw releasing their memoirs and autobiographies – many were from the political fraternity, but a few had written their own acclaimed and award-winning combat sports-related memoirs. Matthew Polly (a Bruce Lee biographer and martial arts enthusiast) and Davis Miller (a Muhammad Ali and Bruce Lee biographer) were huge inspirations for my own writing, but also made me consider whether other people might find value in reading about my life, just as I had read about theirs.

Before embarking on the project of encapsulating my life experiences, though, I asked myself, *Why would I want to write and share my story?* This wasn't a hard question to answer, for two key reasons. Firstly, having worked closely with many famous individuals I have a great deal to share, from the anecdotes they shared in our interviews and personal conversations to the details of their lives I've never had the space to recount before. Secondly, coming from a

PREFACE

humble background where facing prejudice was a daily hurdle, I felt that my story of beating the odds to become a successful writer and reach the top could inspire others facing their own struggles.

For almost as long as I can remember, my ultimate aspiration has been to become a professional writer and author, but the forum I found to explore my craft came from another place. My voracious appetite for the written word developed alongside an almost unhealthy obsession with the fighting arts, something I pursued for much of my youth. Eventually, my interest lead me to holding the prestigious position of chief columnist and features writer for the number-one martial arts magazine, *Martial Arts Illustrated* – a post that gave me unprecedented access to many warriors and athletes, helping me to forge friendships with some historically significant names in combat sports. And, eventually, my dream of working alongside some of the UFC champions was one that I made a reality through motivation, obsession, hard work and resilience.

I was able to break into Hollywood when I came on board the now-defunct *Impact: The Global Action Movie Magazine*, and subsequently the national tabloids. When it comes to the glitz and the glamour of celebrity life, the majority of us only ever aspire to getting an autograph or selfie from our favourite stars. We never really have the opportunity to sit down with them and discuss their lives, or rub shoulders with those closest to them. For me, though, being up close and personal with these people became a part of my regular routine.

It was never a smooth ride, however. On my journey I experienced hardship, rejection, and harassment, including discrimination at American airports and a disturbing visit from the United Kingdom's Special Branch, which suspected me of being a threat to national security. Somehow, I made it through to write this book, which I started in 2015 but then shelved it, as I focused on other projects. It wasn't till five years later that I decided to finish the book. It's a fascinating odyssey in the form of a personal journey through my own coming-of-age story in which I share the struggles, triumphs and low points as a journalist, alongside hundreds of behind-the-scenes anecdotes and stories of UFC, boxing and entertainment stars and my personal experiences working with the best. I hope you enjoy the ride as much as I enjoyed the drive.

CHAPTER ONE

CRAZY OBSESSIONS

AS A young kid growing up I was profoundly influenced by the late, great Bruce Lee. The King of Kung Fu made an everlasting impression on my life. No, I didn't grow up in the 1970s at the height of the kung fu boom. I was a child of the 1980s, a decade that saw great socio-economic change due to leaps in technology and advances in globalization. The world was rife with conflict, from the Cold War, to the Falklands War, Iran–Iraq and the Soviet–Afghanistan War. Pop sensations Michael Jackson, Madonna, Prince and Wham were selling millions of records. Action heroes Sylvester Stallone and Arnold Schwarzenegger were competing for the number-one spot at the box office. And Mike Tyson was obliterating every opponent put in front of him. It was a time when larger-than-life heroes were the norm, but I became obsessed with a small, ultra-lean Chinese guy who'd died almost a decade before.

I first encountered Bruce Lee when I was ten years old. I remember the day vividly. It was 1985 and I was at a family friend's house with my brother and two neighbour friends. To keep us kids entertained the family friend's nephew slipped a videocassette of *Enter the Dragon*, Bruce's only Hollywood action film, into the chunky VCR. Back in those days there was no such thing as DVDs, let alone a streaming platform that instantly granted access to hundreds of films from Hong

TO THE TOP

Kong or China. It was the era of the classic videocassette, chunky silver-and-black video players, and going to the local video shops to scout out something that looked promising. As a matter of fact, many TVs were made out of wood, and today's teenagers would have been appalled by the size of the screen on which we had to watch Bruce's dazzling choreography. But still, what I witnessed that day was just totally mesmerising.

Never before had I been exposed to such an amazing depiction of the human body in motion. Bruce himself looked almost unreal, stripped of all fat and as lean and dangerous as the preying mantises that fight early in the film. By the finale, he's dispatching multiple fighters with deadly fists and feet, looking utterly believable, in contrast to the slow-motion choreography of most action films and the telegraphed punches of Rocky.

I was hypnotised: I had just been introduced to this phenomenon and was eager to learn more, but to my dismay I was quickly told that this diminutive-looking guy who beat the hell out of 20 fighters at once had vanished from the face of this earth. *What?* I thought to myself. *No, he can't have. I've just had the most remarkable experience of my life and you're telling me this deadly fighting machine is gone!* It was beyond belief. Sadness tinged the exhilaration I felt at seeing Bruce's balletic performance, but from that day onwards my whole life would change completely. Things would never be the same again.

Not that it was easy to get my kung fu fix. After my first introduction to this different kind of action hero, whenever *Enter the Dragon* was playing on TV, I would have to sneak down from my bedroom to watch it, as my own family hadn't yet bought a VHS player. This was problematic because this all-time classic was always on late at night at around 11pm, and had a few scenes that most parents would have doubtless thought of as inappropriate viewing – for me it was more than that because watching a movie late at night wasn't something we could do. I was supposed to be in bed by ten, and so to overcome this barrier, I would slowly sneak down the squeaky stairs to get my fix of the Little Dragon.

This was no easy task, believe me. It would take me about ten minutes to get downstairs because I didn't want to wake anyone up and get caught in the act by my parents, yet I'd want to get downstairs as soon as possible. The epic opening fight scene with Bruce and Sammo Hung, a skinny guy and a fat man battling it out in what resembled an MMA setting, was one of my favourite fights in the film. You have to understand that one of the consequences of breaking rules at home included getting a good hiding. Still, I was prepared to break the rules over and over if I had to. Another key thing I had to do to avoid getting caught was to keep the volume level low – just loud enough so I could detect what the actors were saying. Take into account that back in those days there were no remote controls, which was always a pain because you had to get up from the comfort of your seat to adjust the volume. Fortunately, I had pretty good ears, and so somehow I got away with it every single time. Whether my parents were aware that I was sneaking down or not, I will never know because they never mentioned it, or questioned me.

As I've mentioned, we never had a VCR in those days, and so, though I was itching to watch the handful of other movies Bruce had made, I had no access to them. Instead I would find solace through conversing with a friend in school who understood my Bruce Lee obsession. As others played soccer or talked about who won the game over the weekend, my friend would relate the storylines of Bruce's other films and how the kung fu master would kick arse as I eagerly hung on to his every word. I needed more Bruce. It felt like being deprived of something. I felt like a drug addict wanting to feed a habit.

Eventually, I found a way to get my fix. At weekends I would go, along with another friend who shared his enthusiasm for the martial arts master, to the house of a friend who we coaxed into sitting through the films. Renting a Bruce Lee video, which at that time cost only 50 pence, became a weekend ritual. I had specifically taken out a video club membership at a local video rental store just to do it. And if you checked my rental record, you'd find that other than *Enter the Dragon, Fist of Fury, Big Boss, Way of the Dragon* and *Game of Death*, I never rented any other film from the store. Sure, I occasionally enjoyed other Hong Kong kung fu flicks, but most if not all of these were cheesy with laughably trite scripts, compared with the intensity of Bruce's output. I'm sure the owner had become aware of the pattern because a number of times he gave me peculiar looks when I visited the store. Why they never showed these movies on TV – other than *Enter the Dragon*, Bruce's only Western effort – was beyond comprehension to me. Everyone I spoke to got fired up with an intense emotion whenever they watched this lithe Chinese man on screen. No other actor on the big screen, no matter how popular, came close to the persona this fighter possessed, a feeling that's never been replicated.

I feel that sometimes someone filters into your life and their influence is so palpable that it leaves an everlasting impression. It certainly happens with crazy Elvis fans and Michael Jackson devotees, but for me Bruce Lee felt different. He wasn't just a performer, but someone who lived his life by a certain philosophy, a certain code. I had become totally consumed and it became an unhealthy obsession, affecting every area of my life. I was a Bruce Lee convert salivating for more. I had a burning desire to learn every single thing possible about this Chinese-American. From *Enter the Dragon* onwards, for me, it was Bruce Lee 24/7 – no question about it.

I'll be honest, there have been times throughout my life when I've thought, *What if Bruce Lee had never existed? What would the world be like? What direction would my own life have taken?* I have actually thanked God, who created this man, a man who not only brought joy to my life, but to millions of peoples' lives around the globe. He was the epitome of cool, a symbol of male vigour and hope to people who couldn't hope to compete with traditional jocks. No matter what problems you were facing in life, watching Bruce was a sanctuary for you as you took delight in watching him take on endless obstacles in the four-and-half films he had churned out in the two years that made up his truncated career. We all need something in life that helps us forget our problems for a while, and for me it was Bruce.

***

Growing up, I never particularly had an affinity for reading in school. In fact, I never was inclined to study much at all. However, once Bruce Lee came along I developed an interest in literature relating directly to the martial arts. From the age of ten, I would religiously visit the local library in town with my brother and my next-door neighbour and borrow books relating to the oriental arts. Bodybuilding books – specifically the ones written by Robert Kennedy, who was a well-known Canadian bodybuilding author – also caught my attention. Eventually, I developed a voracious appetite for the written word. Being a young teenager finding a path in life, in my 'reading sessions' I took delight in the mini step-by-step pictorials more than the text. Some kids grew up reading superhero tales which helped them cope with adversity, but the antics of Batman and Superman never invoked my interest. I got my thrills from learning everything I could about my hero and martial arts when I was growing up via the medium of print.

In my second year of high school, in 1989, when I was 13, it dawned on me that martial arts magazines existed. I remember coming across *Combat* magazine and its competitor *Martial Arts Illustrated* on the shelves of WHSmith in town, and being immediately entranced by this new source of information. I would religiously save my bus fare so I could purchase the monthly *Martial Arts Illustrated*, which at that time cost £1.25. Well, I say that, but sometimes it was financially beneficial to stand there and flick through the pages, read, look at the actions pictures and shove the copy back on the shelf, often placing it in the wrong pile. This strategy was seemingly implemented by many like-minded people – at least it seemed that way from the mismatched nature of the shelves.

Bruce was more than a martial artist. His mind and intellect – he studied philosophy at the University of Washington – eventually influenced me to a great degree. He once wrote, 'Many people live only for their image. That is why whereas some have a self, a starting point, most people have a void because they are so busy projecting themselves as this or that. Wasting, dissipating all their energy in projection and conjuring up a facade, rather than centring their energy on expanding and broadening their potential.' Similarly, he told an interviewer, 'It is easy for me to put on a show and be cocky and then feel pretty cool. Or I can do all kinds of phony things and be blinded by it. Or I can show you some really fancy movement. But to express oneself honestly, not lying to oneself, that is, my friend, very hard to do.' He believed that imitation was not the path and he advised his students to find their own way and not be blinded by followers. Certainly, this concept of finding your own way was derived from the writings of the great philosophers he read about, but he implemented the philosophies into his art and teachings – and, as he advised others to do with his art of jeet kune do, added what was specifically his own.

One of the core tenets of his philosophy was to know yourself. Why would Bruce pursue philosophy? This is a question I'd wanted answered for my own personal satisfaction ever since I came across this as a young man. 'My majoring in philosophy was closely related to the pugnacity of my childhood,' Bruce once said. 'I often asked myself these questions: what comes after victory? Why do people value victory so much? What is glory? What kind of victory is glorious?' With the assistance of his university teacher, who advised Bruce when he was about to select a subject, he chose to study a subject that he believed would explain what man lives for. 'When I told my friends and relatives that I had picked philosophy, they were all amazed about to select. Everybody thought I had better go into physical education since the only extra-curricular activity that I was interested in, from my childhood until I graduated from my secondary school, was Chinese martial arts.'

CRAZY OBSESSIONS

By and by you came to realise that the late kung fu master, the man with a physique to die for and an iron fist, was an extremely intellectual human being. He perceived a direct application of philosophy to a physical art form. Furthermore, he was an ardent follower of self-help writers, Napoleon Hill and Norman Vincent Peale being two of the more prominent ones to influence him. When I learned about Bruce's reading habits I wasted no time in collecting more books from his inspirations as I strove to train my mind as much as my body in emulating the late kung fu master.

Flicking through martial arts periodicals, the adverts for clothing, equipment and tomes caught my attention as much as the photos of martial artists performing high and flying kicks. The martial arts was an industry in itself, I would soon come to realise. I got into the habit of ordering goodies from the mail-order adverts. Mind you, literature wasn't cheap and as a young teenager I didn't have a lot of money.

I would also have to have my purchases delivered to a friend's house instead of my own address. I had a tendency to keep my hobby and passion a secret, like a scared little boy. For some odd reason I found it a taboo subject to broach. In my house, even asking to stay out late could prove troublesome. We grew up in a disciplined home where extra-curricular activity was not on the menu. Telling my parents I'd become obsessed with this strange man from Hong Kong would have been like being in an Italian restaurant but asking for Chinese noodles. It seemed that other kids' aspirations were supported by their parents, but I was deprived of that privilege. This can have an indelible impact on a kid's development. It feels likes the other kids have been given an edge, a head start in a race, and you can't start your run until they're halfway to the finishing line. How are you going to triumph against someone when you're way behind because you are being held back? It's a feeling that stayed with me into my adult years, but later it would vanish.

Still, if you look at this from a more optimistic angle, if you lack support and encouragement while growing up, it can boost your motivation. And as a consequence you're determined to prevail in life. So it can work both ways. Some people have things given to them on a plate, but they lack commitment and that all-important relentless drive, and so they never make it, they never achieve their goals. Whether I had support or not, I feel I had a natural tendency and passion for pursuing what I wanted in life, sure that nothing was going to hinder my progress. No one was going to extinguish my dreams because of my sheer tenacity.

There are countless success stories about successful people who had it hard, but still had their dreams manifest into a reality through sheer force of will. These are the kind of stories and lessons that offered me inspiration. I'm a big believer in making your own destiny. I find it rather disappointing when I hear people say, 'Well, it's not going to happen to me.' In life no matter what you pursue, I firmly believe in that it doesn't matter where you come from – whether it's a small village in Asia, like the one my parents came from, or a big bustling city in the West – you've got a brain, two arms and two legs just like most others, so you can pursue something in life and achieve your goals.

* * *

Growing up, there was a small muscle store – that's how I thought of it – near my house. The magazines displayed in the window would always attract my attention when I passed, my only window to a world that I barely knew existed. *Muscle & Fitness* and *FLEX* (the Bible of bodybuilding) were the kings of the iron-pumping periodicals. Bodybuilding's most recognisable personalities and champions graced the covers of these glossy magazines, which were an inspiration to the fans and fanatics alike. With an ever increasing fervour for learning about the stars and champions of the sport of bodybuilding, I familiarised myself with the big names of the era – Lee Haney, Shawn Ray, Dorian Yates, and Lee Labrada, a small-statured bodybuilder who gave hope to others' more modest muscle-building efforts. Rachel McLish, who merits special historical significance in the sport of women's bodybuilding, Lenda Murray and Corey Everson – the latter actually appeared in Jean Claude Van Damme's *Double Impact,* in which she showcased her high-kicking martial arts skills – were the female stars.

As I immersed myself obsessively in my hobbies and cultivated a penchant for the martial arts in particular, taking things to the extreme was nothing unusual for me. I believe I was born an extreme, obsessive person. Eventually, it would become my biggest asset in life, but my obsession did get me into trouble several times. In English, for instance, I was once caught reading a bodybuilding magazine under the table once. Eventually, my teacher threatened to bring my interests to my parents' attention, which scared me more than you might think. I don't think my parents would have understood why I was reading about scantily dressed men and women in a magazine. Eventually, I was let off with a warning. Many years later I consoled myself with the fact that even the great Arnold Schwarzenegger had his fair share of arguments with his parents when he was growing up obsessed with a sport that nobody really cared about. Still, I was always careful to hide those periodicals under my bed at home.

More serious was the fact that I took to regularly sneaking a nunchaku, a small weapon, into school, which I tucked under my jumper. I was very lucky one day when I got into an altercation after English class that my friend had my pair of 'chucks'. On another occasion I beat up a boy named Craig, who had to be hospitalised because of a broken nose and ribs. The fight lasted under ten seconds as I hit him with multiple head butts and round kicks to his ribs. He couldn't do anything. Had this illegal weapon been found, there would've been grave consequences. By the way, I had all the justification for resorting to a fight and would never fight to hurt anyone unless it was for self-defence. But he had been giving me the attitude for a while and for no reason provoking me.

Martial arts and physique personalities were undoubtedly famous in their own worlds, but even the mainstream general public, who didn't follow these sports, had some sort of reverence towards these alpha males and females. At the same time, bodybuilding and its adherents more often than not received negative press from the mainstream media because of the stigma of drugs attached to the sport and its athletes. Steroids were part and parcel of the iron-pumping game, and of course still are. These glossy, colourful publications were littered with supplements and nutrition adverts, aimed at convincing readers to part with their hard-earned cash by claiming that the over-muscled athletes featured next to them used nothing else. Whether these products worked or not is another story, but those well-placed adverts certainly caught my attention.

Suddenly I was enticed into trying out natural supplements. I kept it simple. I was an advocate of vitamin C because Bruce Lee consumed 1,500 mg of it every day. We had these free purple coloured free multi-vitamin tablets prescribed from the family doctor. My whole family was on them. So, I had this pill every day thinking it would make me invincible and strong. Protein is essential in building muscle, and if you're an athlete you should consume plenty of protein, the experts claimed. Well, I did for a while, but then I stuck to natural milk, drinking three glasses daily in the vain hope of becoming a superman.

It wasn't long before I was put off supplements, or should I say 'magic pills', after I survived a near-death experience in my mid-teens. I had ordered GABA (gamma aminobutyric acid, a naturally occurring amino acid) capsules from a company via mail order, which was one of the main avenues you used to buy supplements in the days before the internet. Now they are stocked in Walmart and TESCO, but back in the day things were a lot tougher. Anyway, after gulping down some capsules they had an adverse affect. I became extremely ill. Well, worse than that. My whole body felt 'dead'. A doctor had to be called. I felt like I was on the verge of leaving this world. I had an allergic reaction to the pills, and my brain and body felt like a sponge. I was hallucinating. The doctor said I had one of the most severe allergic reactions to the capsules he'd ever seen. Well, after that unfortunate episode I took an oath that I would never take something like that again. And I never did. I was relieved enough that I was going to live. I became very wary of supplements. I valued my life more than any amount of muscle I might put on. Stories of bodybuilders dying after taking steroids had been circulated in the specialist press and it was petrifying. But I never took steroids and was never tempted to experiment at any cost whatsoever.

To be honest, although I ventured into the world of supplements, I never seriously continued taking them on a long-term basis, one reason being that they were too damn expensive. How could a kid afford them? And as for how some people could sustain their habit on a monthly basis, throwing away their hard-earned cash on the hopes of muscle, was beyond my comprehension. So, it was short-lived for me. At the time, one big company was publicising its products like no one else. The company seemed to have caught on with consumers and attracted a loyal following, even breaking into the mainstream in terms of customer base and distribution. The martial arts and bodybuilding bug had hit me hard by now. It was infectious. And nothing and nobody was going to cure this infection.

CHAPTER TWO

IT'S A MAN'S WORLD

MOST YOUNG teens played and watched soccer in our community – when I say 'community', I mean the South Indian Asian one – but hardly any teenagers hit the gym. And it would be a miracle if anyone actually pursued the martial arts of the Far East. You would be hard pressed to find an Asian kid with an interest in the oriental arts serious enough that they would even take part, let alone pursue it on a serious level. Of course, like anything, there were the exceptions.

Perhaps one of the most striking aspects of Bruce Lee is his trademark physique. This 135-pound frame is revered by his fans and I was no different as a youth, admiring his onion skin definition and razor-sharp cuts. In 1989, at the age of 13, I stepped into a weight training gym in an attempt to emulate my hero.

A lot of the gyms in those days were housed in old orange-bricked mills. These gyms would often be referred to as 'bodybuilding gyms'. Most of these facilities have become extinct now as big modern-day franchise facilities have mushroomed all over the world, but back in the day it was grim and gritty. Every Saturday morning, along with a friend, I would religiously walk to this gym for a workout. It was an old-school facility, full of big, burly, sweaty men pumping iron, with physiques which were built on years of hardcore training, proper diet and nutrition – and in some cases steroids – hitting the weights.

IT'S A MAN'S WORLD

We were just two teenage kids who thought could one day make the drastic transformation to look just like the stars we admired. Black Box's *Right on Time* would be blaring as we pumped our tiny teen muscles, inspired by the bodybuilding stars. The atmosphere was electric, aggressive but friendly.

I vividly recall that on the walls the gym had posters plastered around of Serge Nubret, Franco Columbu, Dave Draper, Bill Grant and Chris Dickerson – some of the greats I would interview decades later when I became a sports journalist.

I stuck to the iron for a long time. In my youth I contemplated whether I should take the martial arts or bodybuilding route, as far as dedicating time to a physical pursuit was concerned. It's difficult to jump between two disciplines – one can't ride two horses at the same time. Even though I continued pumping iron, martial arts was my first love – it always had been. Working with weights became a form of supplementary training. My bedroom became my training space. I'd stretch out my legs, throw high kicks and hundreds of punches into the air and try to mimic Bruce Lee. My uncle, who had moved to the United Kingdom from Paris several years earlier, was a martial arts enthusiast himself. He would teach me moves in our living room, from high kicks to painful stretches and some kung fu moves. We shared a mutual appreciation of the arts, and he became very close to me, encouraging me to further pursue the martial arts.

Moreover, as soon as I had discovered that Bruce had developed his own form of combat, which he labelled jeet kune do (literally translated as 'the way of the intercepting fist'), I was immediately drawn to it like a moth to a bulb. How could I train in Thai-boxing or karate when Bruce Lee, the man I idolised, had created his own system? This motivated me in my quest to learn more about the man. I embarked on a fascinating journey of discovery, delving into his art and those who were directly associated with it, such as his personal students. I would accumulate any information I could get my hands on about the system.

To put things into perspective, I was a small-boned kid. I often suffered from asthma and physically, I believe, a lot of kids were stronger and healthier than me. One of my best childhood friends, 'Big' Ash, was always stronger physically and a lot bigger in stature. I wasn't one of those types of people who took up martial arts because they had to, to defend themselves because they got into fights or were bullied. To be honest, I really didn't perceive the martial arts primarily as a means to defend yourself if someone attacked you. That was pretty far from my mind. To me it was about learning to fight and enjoying a hobby.

In hindsight it's funny, but when 'Big' Ash and I were making our transition into high school at age 11, we proclaimed to ourselves that we were going to be the toughest in the class, or maybe the best soccer players. We were eager to stand out and garner respect. Nope, it didn't happen – at least not for me. 'Big' Ash unleashed his potential early and did make a name for himself.

Growing up, some kids are blessed with a big mouth, something I never had. It's a double-edged sword. Being all talk can get you what you want, but often bullies or people with the gift of the gob develop a somewhat false sense of confidence. They are of the belief that they are tough, which is pure supposition, as they can 'act' themselves to the top, with intimidation often playing a key role. Lack of physical development and suffering from asthma was my worst enemy, alongside my childhood shyness. Being far too inhibited inevitably dented my confidence even further. It's believed that most shy children develop shyness because of the type of interactions they have with their parents. Parents who are authoritarian or overprotective can cause their children to be shy. I fell into this category. I would come to learn in life that if you're a diffident individual, it will have an adverse effect on your life and how people perceive you, while those who are extrovert will be seen as better people even though you might be better and more capable than them, given the opportunity. If you are sociable person you like to be around people and can easily socialise.

In general, and in particular within the community, if you exude confidence and are talkative – hold long conversations with people – you are perceived as someone who knows the world, a superior being who others feel very comfortable with, which seems to garner respect from peers and those around you. There's value placed on you. It's a system that rewards arrogance, and I was never comfortable in it.

As a kid I was involved in an average number of fights, but never got beat badly – and every single one I beat I did so with a degree of ease. Every single time it was the other kid or individual who would provoke me with attitude, as they would perceive me as unimposing. They would find out the hard way. Trouble would always come to me; I never went out looking for it. There were physically stronger kids than me. There was always the frightening prospect of losing, which to my young mind would be more mortifying than getting hurt. An overwhelming fear would grip me in the gut just to think about it. I was never afraid of getting hurt.

Eventually, I would tally up ten altercations in my youth – losing two. My first loss taught me a lesson. I learned that if you decide to fight, don't go in half-heartedly. In my early teens I decided to get into an altercation with a boy from school who had been giving me some attitude for no reason whatsoever. Because I had put another boy, who I mentioned earlier, in hospital I decided to avoid punching this boy in the face or doing serious damage, instead hitting him on his shoulder of all things. Wrong move! He took me down and totally controlled me, sitting on top of me in what modern MMA fighters call the 'mount'. Me being 'nice' in a fight led to me getting my arse handed to me. *Never will I ever do that again*, I thought to myself. In fact, this boy used to watch WWF and was quite solid.

As children we make that all-too-important transition into becoming teenagers, watching movie and sports stars dreaming to be like our heroes one day. It's such a vital time in life, and making the right choices can have a profound effect. Sometimes you are also influenced by, to whatever degree, someone you know and are in awe of. For me, I grew up in a predominately Asian community. If I'm honest, if there was anyone who influenced me it was Affy. Some other young teens growing up in our community who, by the way, won't admit to it now, also revered Affy. He was a local boy four years older than me, who was the epitome of cool and toughness and someone I looked up to. He is one of my best friends now. You could say that he was like a local celebrity in our little community. Years later I remember reading an autobiography of the unlicensed famous boxer and street fighter Lenny McLean, who said that when you could fight in school you were treated like a celebrity. He was somewhat right. In school, being tough and fighting meant respect came flooding in and you were treated like as if you were famous in your own little world. I mean, every kid wants to be liked and appreciated and is willing to do dumb things for attention, a phase we all go through.

As kids we constantly want to prove ourselves and cultivate an aura which radiates around screaming that we are unbeatable and can beat up the other kids. It is human nature and part of growing up. It's an alpha male thing. But when you're a kid and in the middle of adolescence, more often than not you do things without much thought and you regret some of them when looking back as an adult.

More importantly, when you hit your teens, you start developing as a person. Real growth and self-development starts from 13, as your body is now ready, even if your brain is a little behind. Your bones and body start to adapt, but your brain's still young. Now you're in the process of transitioning into becoming a man in the real world where it matters, and you've got to make the best of it. I don't care who you are and what you do before that. And at 18 you're an adult, and it's time to make the most of yourself. I started training at 13, so it was perfect timing on my part. I would come to learn that Bruce Lee started training at 13, too, while Arnold Schwarzenegger started training with weights at 15. Mike Tyson started boxing just before he turned 13.

Now, there are always people who perceived themselves as 'hard' when they were 12, and it's something they carry on their backs to completely define themselves for the rest of their lives. It's a mentality which is absolutely preposterous and delusional. As a matter of fact, it's amusing to me. Again, it's an attitude that was rife where I grew up, and in any community for that matter. It's thought-provoking that most people – certainly something I witnessed where I grew up – are inclined to hide their weaknesses and play down their faults, while highlighting their strengths, more often than not strengths that they don't really possess. Looking or feeling bad about themselves in front of their peers is the primary reason for concealing their true nature. They feel their pride would be dented severely if the truth was revealed. Honestly, most people are insecure and they crave acceptance, and at times they feel the need to put up a fake front. This breed is not only delusional, but they are not being truthful to themselves. Insecure people have a tendency to resort to this, but it doesn't help, as it boils down to insecurity and denial.

The problem was that some people 'talked' their way to the top of the status mountain, and being able to beat up other kids in a fight when you are a kid yourself has no real bearing on your manliness as an adult, something they would never truly learn. The all-too-familiar cock of the walk from school, when you look back in hindsight, is kind of a pathetic figure. Essentially 80 per cent of these young men fall into the fake tough-boy category. Some never had a fight, while others didn't have meaningful fights. Imagine a boxer proclaiming to be a world champion when he's only fought on a domestic level in his region, or worste still he's merely sparred or trained and never fought.

One of the foremost lessons I learned in life comes from achievers of the highest calibre – fighters in particular, but also sports athletes and other well-known personalities. I came to learn that it's OK to highlight and reveal your weaknesses openly, accept them and come to terms with them. I, as a young boy, was reluctant to expose my shortcomings, but it eventually would sink in as I understood the professional fighters' backgrounds and way of thinking. If you are secure and content, then you won't mind exposing and talking about your deficiencies. The contrast between the two types of people is so profound you'd think one is in the Premier League and the other relegated to the Sunday League, the latter being the kid or young man who called himself the 'cock' or 'tough' in school without ever having a fight, or the bully. So the lesson I learned from some of the toughest men in the world has been: never hide your deficiencies and it's OK to embrace them. When you're a kid growing up you can eventually unleash your potential and find yourself. And this is what I would eventually do as far as challenging myself went.

* * *

So, one of the most thought-provoking and intriguing things I came to comprehend was, at what level, physically and mentally, famous fighters and champions were when they were growing up. I, of course, went on to study and write about some of the most notorious fighters in the fight game, which gave me extensive knowledge of their backgrounds and childhoods. Bruce Lee started training in the wing chun kung fu system in Hong Kong at an early age, but didn't use it much. William Cheung, his close childhood friend, told me that he and fellow students rarely let Bruce fight in the infamous rooftop matches that took place when they were young. Bruce was a child actor and William said it wouldn't look good if his friend fought and his face got battered and bruised. As much as I am an ardent follower of Bruce and his legend – many sources are often biased and can more often than not be accused of highlighting the more positive sides while neglecting to elucidate the weaknesses – over the decades certain stories have circulated about Bruce being super-invincible as a teenager taking part in rooftop fights. These tales are often sugar-coated, so it's tough to tell where the truth lies.

Then there's the notion that had he not made it and gone to America he would have become a gangster. I find that implausible at best. In fact, I surmise it may be best to dismiss these thoughts altogether. Moreover, at the wing chun school there were some seniors with more knowledge and skill than Bruce. He would have had to cultivate humility.

Recognised as the biggest draw the pugilistic world has had to offer since the retirement of Muhammad Ali, the mighty Mike Tyson, who became the youngest heavyweight champion in boxing and earned the Moniker of 'Baddest Man on the Planet', was a timid kid and was a victim of bullying. He started to develop at the right age, just before he became a teenager, and by the time he was in his mid-teenage years, he was so ferocious that he'd beat you before the fight even began. 'When I read the stories about myself, people keep saying that I was a tough kid in the streets,' Tyson revealed in an interview after winning the heavyweight title. 'I used to get into a lot of fights, but they didn't know that I used to get beat up all the time. Maybe I had a lot of fights but I always got beat up. They say I was street tough, and that I used to go beating up everybody in the street. But it wasn't really like that till I started fighting in the ring, then it became a whole different story.'

Speaking of boxers, Sugar Ray Leonard once told me when and why he chose the brutal sport of boxing. 'I pursued boxing because I was such a shrimp and a non-athlete,' one of the all-time greats recounted. 'My brothers Roger and Kenny were basketball players, football players and track stars, but I couldn't match them until I started boxing. I was the type of young kid at 14 that was never really athletically inclined. They were real athletes. The same reason my brother Roger encouraged me to come down to the centre and get involved in boxing.' He went on to become pound-for-pound the best pugilist in the world.

You want other examples? Jean Claude Van Damme, a bespectacled skinny and weak teenager, transformed himself into an Adonis, earning the nickname 'Muscles from Brussels'. And I will never forget what Bill 'Superfoot' Wallace, the greatest kicker in the world and world martial arts champion, revealed once in an article I read as a teen – if there were 37 kids in his school class, he wasn't in the first 36 toughest people. Sandy Holt, who became famous in Thai-boxing circles as a national and European champion, was bullied as a youngster because he was short and small. My good friend Ronnie Green, a five-time world Thai-boxing champion and the best ever to have come out of his country in this brutally punishing sport, was a victim of bullying and racism. But after taking up the arts at 13, he was fighting professionally at the age of 17. Geoff Thompson, probably the most famous doorman in Britain and reality-based martial arts personality was bullied as a teenager and transformed himself into a fighting machine, revolutionising the martial arts. His legendary 'real approach' to street fights changed the landscape of martial arts forever.

Another close friend of mine, Joe Egan, Mike Tyson's sparring partner who earned the title of 'Toughest White Man on the Planet' from the notorious boxing legend, was also a victim of bullying as a kid. He suffered prejudice and bullying because of his Irish descent and accent. Then you have one of the best fighters ever to step into the Octagon in the brutal sport of MMA, UFC welterweight champion, Georges St-Pierre (GSP), who was another victim of bullying as a kid. From the age of 15, he was training and fighting and beating full-grown men. He told me in an interview that, 'I had a lot of anger and pride in me when I was growing up. I didn't want to tell nobody about my problems. I had pride and a big ego, so I wouldn't tell anyone because I thought they'd say I'm like a baby or a kid who cannot defend himself.' And finally, the most bizarre story I've come across on this subject was about the professional bodybuilder, Tim Belknap, who got beaten up by girls in school who used to steal his lunch money when he was in his early teens. He certainly made something of himself.

So what do all these legendary fighters, alpha males, notorious men, have in common? They had that natural potential within, and at the right developmental stages unleashed it to the max. It's all to do with timing – it's all about when it will kick in. Successful fighters have all endured hardships and obstacles in various shapes and forms. A lot of the self-proclaimed tough guys, when growing up as kids, aren't prepared to suffer – hence they are never able to unleash their potential when they become men. There is nothing of any great substance there in the first place, other than the verbal artillery and a persona. This, no doubt, is what separates the two types of men.

Sometimes a person's success exposes others' shortcomings, and when a person becomes successful, people who have known this person often change their attitude. Do you know why strangers support you more than people you know? Because people you know have a tough time accepting that you come from the same place, while they are still in the same place. 'When you become famous you don't change, people around you change,' I remember actor Dustin Hoffman saying. I think he's right. A lot of the times when you make it, you stay humble and shy away from boasting. But people you know and have known all your life or for many years, they change their attitude towards you. They start having this negative vibe and attitude towards you. It's what I call the 'near-far scenario' – most people have a tendency to appreciate someone or something which has an enigma attached to it or they see from afar. And I always wonder what reaction the world champion fighters prompt in people from their childhood, who had once perceived them through a completely different lens.

CHAPTER THREE

FEELING DESPONDENT

I WAS still at school when I came across a small black-and-white advert in a national newspaper offering a writing course. The Home Learning Course, as it was called, was offered by The Writers Bureau, and would set you back £25 – a decent amount of cash at that time. I wasted no time in filling out the little coupon, as you did back in those days, and slipping the cash in an envelope to post it. I had made up my mind to become writer. Whether I thought I would succeed or not is entirely another story. I always held the belief that I should go out and grab what I craved in life. I was determined enough, there's no doubt about it, but I'm not sure I was confident that I actually had the skills to carve out a writing career.

I eagerly waited for weeks and weeks for the coursework package to appear at my doorstep – but nothing. The Writers Bureau was based in Manchester city centre, on Dale Street. Disillusioned with the 'goods' not arriving, I decided to take a bus and pay the Bureau a visit to squeeze some answers out of them.

The office was on the second or third floor. As I walked into the dimly-lit room, it looked as if it had been ransacked, with tonnes of papers, folders and cabinets spilling out everywhere. It wasn't exactly a modern-day visually appealing setting as far as ambience goes. It resembled more of the kind of 1930s newspaper office which I had

FEELING DESPONDENT

seen in countless old black-and-white Humphrey Bogart gangster films. You could actually smell the paper.

I was greeted by a nice well-mannered lady, which was a good start. Keeping myself composed, I told her that I had ordered the writing course but was still waiting for it to appear. In those days, 14 to 28 days for delivery was the norm. Now, when you order something from the internet or over the phone, your item is likely to be despatched the same day or the next day. But back in those days, you were lucky if you received that kind of prompt service. So you had no choice but to play the waiting game.

Anyway, I provided the lady with my details and explained to her that I had placed cash in the envelope as a means of payment, only to be told you're not supposed to send cash through the post and that cheque or postal orders were the safest method of payment. Yes, my naivety. Well, as it happens, there was no record of my order. It was obvious that whoever got their dirty hands on the envelope had stolen the money and binned my order form. Protesting to my helper, I told her that someone had stolen the money and that I wasn't pleased about the situation. Still, there was nothing either of us could do about it as there was no record or proof.

She was apologetic, but that wasn't going to bring my money back nor was the company going to, out of sympathy, give me the course for free. So I had to hand over my hard-earned money again – actually, it was my life savings as I was still in school and not working or on benefits. She gave me a big turquoise cardboard box and I walked off, maintaining my polite demeanour. Next thing, I'm walking with a box glued to my chest in Manchester's Arndale shopping centre.

That box was damn heavy. I was never a heavy lifter in the gym and was somewhat frail then. Struggling and out of breath I walked into a clothing store to ask for a carrier bag, but the sales assistant declined to assist me. I'm sure she thought I was carrying a suspicious package. At the time there was no Middle East-related terrorism – even though it did exist, notably in Beirut – and the IRA would succeed in bombing the Arndale several years later. In fact, whenever the word 'terrorists' was uttered in the news back in the early 1990s, it was usually related to the IRA. So I guess she was being sagacious. Well, her attitude pissed me off and as I exited the entrance, I let out a swear word, which I assume she didn't hear.

Being a really young, aspiring, wannabe writer who often fantasised about one day having a book on the shelf with his name emblazoned across the cover, I scoured the course info, not really paying close attention to detail. However, it wasn't long before I drafted my first ever writing piece, on none other than on my hero Bruce Lee. I wrote it, or should I say 'scribbled' it, on A4 paper with a blue biro. Back in those days that's how most people wrote articles – in pen. Or they would type it out on a typewriter. At one point I purchased one, but couldn't get the damn thing to function properly. That typewriter was a pain in the ass, but I was never good with technology. I'd surprise myself if I could screw a clothing hook on the wall, never mind get a typewriter working. These days, I have no option, I must admit, but to embrace modern technology, not out of choice but necessity. But compared to most people I'm still living in the ancient times.

Drooling with excitement, I sent the scruffy hand-written piece to the *Daily Mirror* of all people. Looking back now, I was thinking big right from the start. Scribbling an article, a first attempt, you'd expect one of the major national newspapers to dismiss it and refrain from even responding. I mean, I'd have chucked it in the nearest bin. But to my great surprise I received a letter back, which I still have in my possession, dated 19 May 1993.

'Dear Fiaz, thank you for letting me see a copy of your article on Bruce Lee,' the features editor wrote in my first rejection letter, which, by the way, would be only one of very few rejections I would ever receive as I progressed in my martial arts magazine-writing career, which lasted 15 years. 'Sadly, it is not suitable for publication on this occasion and I am therefore returning it to you in the hope that you will meet with success elsewhere. Again, thank you for getting in

FEELING DESPONDENT

touch.' Although this was my first rejection in the literary world, to me it was a win to just have had a response from this prestigious red-top giant. Furthermore, it was encouraging and had a rather optimistic feel to it. I had just left school eight months earlier, so life was just beginning. It wasn't the end of the world. I could handle rejection, no problem. Bring it on! Unbeknownst to me this would be the beginning of a life-altering experience.

New research conducted more recently revealed that the most desired jobs in Britain are not what you might think. Instead of actors and musicians, it seems that an aura of prestige still surrounds the quiet, intellectual life enjoyed by authors. Being an author is the number-one mos-desired job in Britain. Men and women share preferences for the most popular jobs, and law, journalism, medicine and TV feature in both top tens. Moreover, some years ago in America a study was conducted to find the number-one profession people aspired to – and, as it happens, more people wanted to be authors than pursue any other profession.

I guess I was on the right track. Now, I knew it wouldn't be easy. Everyone knows that writing is one of the toughest professions to make a career of. If the odds of making it as a professional writer are one in 10,000, then the odds of becoming a household name is one in 100,000. And, some people would probably tell you that, the odds of being published if you write a book are one to two per cent. Those chances aren't much different from those of becoming a professional sports star, a well-known actor or a famous musician. Not only is there no guarantee of success, it's almost the exact opposite.

Speaking of school and careers, it's undeniably odd how, after we leave school having completed our education, we are suddenly catapulted into the 'real' world. In the final year, suddenly you've got careers officers talking to 15-year-olds to get them to decide what they want to do with the rest of their lives. For me, I felt it was just too early to absorb what these real-world adults had to offer. So the classic careers lecture went in one ear and immediately out of the other. I didn't pursue further education. What was I going to study in college? I was over the moon school was over. No more early mornings to study like a sheep getting fed the same info that I felt was going to be a waste of time. I never set foot inside a university, either. I didn't know what a university looked like inside until I passed the buildings on Oxford Road in Manchester whenever I made the ritual trips to Rusholme years later. And, of course, I had seen Oxford University in the *Inspector Morse* TV series. That was the closest I got to a university.

So, as I was growing up, education never really registered on my radar. I didn't see the significance of it and I felt it was mundane and an unnecessary obstacle to achieving my dreams.

Not everyone was on board with my plan, of course. Every parent wants their child to have a good education and to do well in school, which will prepare them for the outside world, and mine were no different. My brother, who is a year older, always had an edge over me in schooling and was one of the more intelligent kids. My IQ level and academic tendencies were nowhere near his standard. If I was to rate myself, I would say I was in the middle ranks – not near the top but not with the bottom bums, who didn't even try. My brother was in the top pack. Still, I don't want to sound derogatory, but he ended up doing a non-technical/professional job. However, he was also schooled in Islamic studies and prevailed therein. Yes, it may sound ironic that I never really embraced education seriously, considering the profession I eventually excelled in. But what I lacked in educational qualifications, I made up for in abundance in the form of motivation and an ambitious nature. This gave me a certain edge that I felt was absent in most others.

Sleeping in maths lessons became the norm; it became a haven for recuperation, as I was more often than not fatigued with the early mornings and occasional energy-level deficiencies. Yes, that's how boring it got. I didn't really perceive the positive benefits of counting numbers. Yet, I did have a keen interest in business studies. Actually, this was my favourite subject. Before I even hit my teenage years I had my first taste of enterprise. I used to buy stationary pens, writing pads, key rings and even baked cakes, and sold them to fellow colleagues and friends when I was still studying. I developed a passion for business early on in life – I found it exciting and challenging.

Regarding schooling and education, now that I am more mature, I by no means stand by my original philosophy, a philosophy that basically assumed that education is not important. If anything, I am an advocate of kids getting a good education and investing in their future. Yet, I can say with great conviction that if they lack the academic side, it's not the end of the world because you may have a talent in sport or an artistic endeavour. The key is to nurture what you're good at and interested in, and unleash your potential so that there is an alternative should you fail in your academic studies. Furthermore, I'm a firm believer that if you have determination and are very persistent, you can make it in this world without that piece of paper that they call a 'degree', that seemingly confirms your credibility. Besides, employers nowadays are looking for experience. It's no secret that a lot of graduates end up working in a call centre or supermarkets. There is nothing wrong with that. I'm just putting everything into perspective.

So, subconsciously, my mind was gravitating towards the literary world as a teenager. The writing course had instilled a sense of confidence that it was the golden ticket to living a future dream. But I had to look at the future through a practical lens.

* * *

After leaving school I enrolled on a Youth in Business course. It was a government-backed course funded by the Prince's Trust. What business was I going to pursue? Well, it would be martial arts-related, of course! I believe you should do what you love in life, and this is true not only relating to a hobby but a career. One study found that 75 per cent of people are in jobs that make them unhappy, and that's no way to spend a third of your time on this planet. Anyway, there were more than half a dozen youngsters who were on this course, including a David Bowie lookalike, each one specialising in a certain type of business. Music was often blaring – Gerry Rafferty's *Baker Street* would pump you up and motivate you – as we cracked on with our work. Well, I wouldn't exactly call it 'work'.

Personally, I set out to learn about setting up a martial arts mail-order business. Inspired by the mail-order adverts in the magazines, I decided that selling martial arts goods via mail order would be fun and the right career move. If I remember correctly, we received about £30 a week for being on this course. This would be paid in cash at the end of each week in a brown pay packet. You never really got paid into your account back then, it was the good old brown envelopes that everyone looked forward to every Friday. Getting your hands on that pay packet was what it was all about for most of us. While on this course I remember I was allowed to go out for research purposes, so I would often take a bus to Manchester and, instead of doing research, I would go into the Van Dang Martial Arts shop, which was on Portland Street back then. I would also visit a bookstore, which had a set of martial arts books in the sports section. It was fun and a treat, like being a little child given the keys to a toy shop.

With the business course coming to an abrupt halt – after a year the funding ceased so the course itself became bankrupt – it was time to be supported by the government for sitting on my arse. In 1993, freshly on benefits and signing on with the green logbook they gave you and with no real direction and career prospects, I eventually got a job and started to work in a lamp factory nearby. This job lasted only a few months, and then I worked at a socks factory. Again, I was out of there after a couple of months. It was slave labour that tortured you like the Roman's did to their captives rowing the ships. *Is this what life it's all about?* I thought to myself. It soon dawned on me that it's bloody hard to eke out a living. Things were looking bleak.

Then there were family associates poking their noses in. I remember there was an older 'uncle' who had his son literally slaving it out for long shifts in a hanger manufacturing factory. The son had to hand over the pay packet at the end of the week to his master dad. This 'uncle' brought the factory to my dad's attention to get me slaving away, too, but I never pursued it. I may have had certain harsh restrictions put on me as I was growing up and hard rules to abide by – because I had strict parents – otherwise I got clobbered at home, but my parents never in my life asked me for money nor forced me to work. I was cognisant that some youths my age were made to work and had to give their wages to their parents. I was lucky in that sense. I was never used in that manner. There's no right or wrong, and by no means am I saying that handing your pay packet to your parents is wrong. All I'm saying is it never happened to me. So, although some other kids had certain privileges in life in general, on the other hand there was some leniency on me at home.

After having walked through a couple of labour jobs after leaving school, and run like hell from others, a bizarre idea popped into my ever-crazy head. This may stun people who know me, but at 18 I seriously considered joining the army. Yes, can you believe it, the British Army! Looking back now I can laugh at the thought of pursuing such a career. It was more to do with going through a macho phase and being able to say I was in the army, which was an absurd idea to start with. I soon got hold of a prospectus. This was a special version that targeted and encouraged ethnic minorities, a category I fitted into. Sifting through this I found it was littered with Asian Muslims, including a brigadier, endorsing this profession. Judging from the material I had at my fingertips, the British Armed Forces were seemingly promoting diversity – racial equality. So I suppose an extra ounce of confidence shot up inside me that said, *You will be accepted*. With this in mind it wasn't long before I found myself visiting my local Army Careers office in town. As I walked in I received a warm welcome. The guy sat me down and had a chat before giving me a prospectus. I was in the mind set that the army gave you a sense of power and an inflated ego. And it was about doing something different, not to mention the adrenaline-booster syndrome kicking in. Playing Rambo!

So, here I was seriously intending to be part of the armed forces for a country I wasn't even born in. One of the first things I looked at was the pay structure. After all, it was a job. They had apprenticeship levels and the money increased as you progressed up the ladder and rank. The money compared to normal jobs was crap. I often think, *Is it worth it?* What do I think now? Not something for me. I suppose if it was the SAS then I could be persuaded. Everyone has a choice and if they want to embark on a career in the armed forces, then they can do. But I wasn't thinking rationally. I saw the so-called glam side, not that there was anything glam about it. I was merely going through a teenage-transformation phase.

Above all I thought about racism and acceptance in such an environment. I'd always heard about the racism surrounding the police, abusing their powers and position. It's something I abhorred. But the armed forces, they do instil discipline in people – there's no doubt about it. But if you're looking for discipline, you can go join a martial arts club. It's less terrifying compared to being potentially bomb or shot at by someone you don't know or have no personal beef with. Anyway, that idea went out of the window.

***

Disillusioned with life, I was looking for an avenue that would let me make a living and achieve peace and harmony – or at least not hate my work. As I mentioned earlier, I always had an interest in running a mail-order business, specifically anything related to the martial arts. Almost three years after leaving school, I finally ventured into the mail-order business in 1995 and placed a small advert in a boxing magazine offering *Tao of Jeet Kune Do*, the bestselling martial arts publication, which was compiled after the untimely death of Bruce Lee. This tome is a compilation of Bruce's notes and thoughts on his personal expression of combat, philosophy and life. One-third of it is

FEELING DESPONDENT

is about boxing concepts and theories. So I thought I'd introduce this product to a new market. I was so excited that I had sent a copy of the book, along with a photo of me and a punching pad, to Lennox Lewis' management, and also to Prince Naseem Hamed. Lennox signed my photo and pad and sent them back to me. I was over the moon. But I heard nothing from Prince Naseem. Suddenly I took a dislike to this flashy, big-mouth boxer whose attitude I detested anyway. I got the impression that this guy thought he was too big for us mere mortals. Maybe I was being too harsh, because maybe the package never got to him. But that wasn't the way I thought at the time.

If I remember correctly, I paid £35 plus VAT to place a small advert in the periodical. I ordered copies of the book from a wholesale martial arts supplier in London and fulfilled orders, which I received at a post box I rented. So, this was the start of my first martial arts venture. Further adverts followed in a couple of martial arts magazines. It suddenly dawned on me that the iron-pumpers worshipped Bruce Lee, too. The legend didn't just appeal to martial arts enthusiasts. Looking to branch out and tap into an additional market, I placed an advert in two bodybuilding publications. The King of Kung Fu had a crossover appeal and a healthy fan base in the bodybuilding fraternity and didn't hesitate to experiment. You couldn't miss the gimmick adverts in the martial arts periodicals selling courses, such as **HOW TO BECOME A BLACK BELT IN A YEAR** or other gimmicks promising all sorts of rubbish and nonsensical material such as, **BECOME A DEADLY FIGHTER IN THREE MONTHS**. Needles to say, these types of deadly courses weren't everything they were hyped up to be. The American marketing concept had arrived on our shores, unfortunately. These adverts influenced me as I thought running a business selling products relating to your hobby was fun. Moreover, working from home or office, fulfilling orders, cashing the cheques and despatching packages was a simple, straightforward process. I thought you could laugh your way to the bank eventually. I wasn't laughing but I was smirking, which was a start.

TO THE TOP

So, after random small adverts, it was time to expand somewhat. I'd seen a double-page spread advert in a magazine for a new martial arts book club. There were lots of book clubs around, of course, but this was the only club for martial arts enthusiasts. Now, an opportunity had presented itself and I was looking to find a more solid avenue in which to eke out a living. So I upped my game and placed a double-page full colour advert for attracting readers to a book club aimed at combat sports enthusiasts. Looking to expand further, I decided to add a mail-order video club, as part of the same set-up.

When I'd scoured martial arts magazines five years earlier, when I was 14 in 1990, I had come across the fascinating Gracie family of fighters, who possessed an invincible aura. I'd seen two graphically violent videos, from the *Gracies In Action* series, which had raw street-fight footage and was shocking to me as a young man. It featured members of the legendary Gracie family taking on all-comers, fighting them with almost no rules, often on floors with no mats or pads. The Gracies would take their foes down and pummel them on the ground, typically choking them until they tapped. It was amazing. I imported these videos directly from UFC creator Rorion Gracie and advertised them in magazines. I had spoken to Rorion directly and he'd offered me a wholesale discount. Again, this time I placed double-page spread adverts in two magazines to attract martial arts enthusiasts to join. Members received heavily discounted instructional videos and had to commit to purchasing at least one video every three months as a member. The American martial arts magazines were littered with adverts for instructional videos. Panther Productions was the leading producer based in Southern California. Unique Videos was the other company that was making strides. I dealt with them and several others. I was still a teenager and was now doing business with America, a country I had my eyes set on ever since I was a young boy.

Suddenly there was a problem. Red lights flashing. Yes, this would be my first run-in with the Americans. There was a mail-order company based in Birmingham that imported videos from Panther.

FEELING DESPONDENT

Because of the huge discounted prices my company was offering, the owner had complained to Panther and other suppliers that there was alleged piracy going on. He thought, *How can these be sold for such low prices?* Next thing you know I received a letter from the production company. You either communicated via post, fax or phone before the invention of emails. Then the producers stopped supplying me, which left me stunned. I protested and proceeded to explain that this was an introductory offer and the idea was to make money on future orders when members were committed to purchasing further videos. First they informed me I had to go through their already-established United Kingdom distributor, but then the matter was resolved and they continued to supply me.

So, I had purchased a writing course, went on a government-backed business course, even was on the brink of joining the British Army, worked as a labourer in several jobs, culminating in running a national martial arts mail-order business for a year. The situation, though, remained precarious. Money was scarce and times were hard. Financial difficulties would be something that would plague me for a long time throughout the years. But you always revert back to your passion, which for me was martial arts, to get you through life, consoling yourself that there is light at the end of the tunnel as you forge ahead with life.

* * *

No matter how much you forged ahead, you have your critics and people who drag you down and literally stomp on you till you bleed like hell. Growing up in the community didn't help matters. Hell, no! You have expectations and a standard to adhere to otherwise people would have disdain for you. Also, social pressures that impinge upon your daily life. Once, when I was with a group of friends and we were having a meal at a restaurant, somehow the subject of judging others came up. One friend said that people judge others based on how they dress. I have to say, that although that is true, I feel people first and foremost judge you based on what job you do – what profession you are in. This indisputably makes it onto the number-one spot on the charts I feel. I'm sure most people will agree. Secondly, it's a combination of what kind of vehicle you drive, friends and people you associate with, followed by what hobbies you take part in that determine what kind of a person you are to others. And in third place, how you dress. All this particularly resonates with most people.

When I left school I had become a victim of prejudice. It wasn't unusual when we had visitors at our house that, more often than not, I would get the standard, 'What do you do?' from these 'uncles'. A lot of the times I would be stuck for words. On the other hand, these men were not going to comprehend and appreciate my martial arts venture – it was beyond their basic IQ level. People got a sense of satisfaction demeaning others. They were expecting you to say that you were a solicitor, an accountant or a doctor – these were the three kings – or a taxi driver or takeaway worker. Arrogance was prevalent and people had memorised these professions like fuck. This is all that registered on their radar. They were in need of fresh radar in good working order and in need of edification on life in general. There was more to life than being a taxi driver or a solicitor. Oh, engineer was another popular word these people had a tendency to use. It just sounded too damn sophisticated, that's all. I bet most of them had no bloody clue what a fucking engineer is.

The elder generation from the South Indian continent came to the West in the 1960s and were relegated to the mill. They had no choice but to endure hard labour in a factory. Most weren't educated and the lack of language and technical skills was an obstacle for them. This was understandable. They encouraged us, the new generation, to endeavour to get a good education and pursue the better future that had eluded them. They always stressed that we had the opportunities and the language to develop skills, which would land us good jobs and career prospects and not get sucked up into dead-end jobs. This is something I came to comprehend later on in life. Furthermore,

FEELING DESPONDENT

failing to fulfil the hopes and expectations of your parents was, by some, frowned upon.

But at the same time, the attitude of looking down on and judging someone based on their profession is something I have always vehemently opposed. Back home in Asia the caste system reflected primarily on what you were 'worth' in terms of what you did as a living, and your status dating all the way back to your family linage. Profession reflects your social status in our society. So, in Pakistan, there is a caste system where people are judged on their profession. You've got a barber, shoemaker, etc., who will be looked down on. Then you have landlords and higher echelons of society. Unfortunately, where I'm from – and generally speaking – respect was earned this way. I am, of course, an advocate of equal opportunity, meaning if someone who has the skill to do a job then they shouldn't be ticked off because of their caste. I respect people regardless of whether they're a labourer or a doctor. Someone's character is much more important than their position and materialistic wealth. So I couldn't accommodate myself to others' way of thinking, even though I came from a good family background.

Despite this, I often became a victim of pompous people who, more or less, looked down on me because of my unimposing or introvert character. They themselves were never affluent or particularly of a high status. And this, I feel, gives me or anyone who is a victim of those who are showering you with disrespect, who themselves are lacking qualities, the justification to break the rule in one's own defence. But I never used my family status to my advantage and I had no one to hold my hand, be it a family member or friend, and get me to where I eventually got to. Furthermore, if you think being a university graduate makes you somewhat better and gives you a licence to look down on others, then again, this is something that I totally abhor. For some of these so-called self-proclaimed 'elite' higher echelons of society, you were useless, uneducated and deemed a failure – you were on the undercard. Ignorance reigned in the community and it wasn't going to be obliterated. You'd need an atomic bomb to cleanse these conditioned minds. Now, I'm all for people being achievers and making something of themselves, and it's something that I've aspired to do and have been doing all my life. But parallel to this I believe in a humble attitude, in treating everyone, like I said, with essentially the same dignity that any human deserves, regardless of their status, is a principle I abide by. As Muhammad Ali once said, 'I don't trust anyone who's nice to me but rude to the waiter. Because they would treat me the same way if I were in that position.'

Ironically, it didn't stop there. It is unbelievable how many people were so ignorant in our communities. If you gravitated towards a hardcore religious life style, some perceived you as a somewhat inferior person – a person of a lower social status or an individual lacking street cred. Some who harboured these feelings would often contradict themselves. Well, many from the religious fraternity in the communities had thriving businesses, drove top-class Mercedes and had five-figure sums in their bank accounts. So, this breed had the world in their hands than some ignorant people who were lost in their own hype. Most of the latter certainly didn't live up to their self-proclaimed status. Personally, having been brought up with strict religious principles, I would never allow anyone to mock those who ardently implemented religious principles into their lifestyles. So, everyone was striving to make it in society and life, most playing the judging game. Life for me was just about to get even more interesting. Yes, it was time to earnestly pursue the American Dream.

CHAPTER FOUR

THE AMERICAN DREAM

AMERICA IS a country that has captured my interest for as long I can remember. Like most other people in the United Kingdom, and around the world for that matter, my early exposure to the land of opportunity was, to a large degree, via the screen – Hollywood movies and TV. As a young boy I used to religiously watch *The A-Team*, and the image of the downtown skyscrapers in Los Angeles from the opening credits were forever embedded in my head. It wasn't long before I realised that Los Angeles was the Mecca of martial arts and bodybuilding. It was also where Bruce Lee had resided. Naturally, this further piqued my interest in the sunny state of California.

The second largest city in America, Los Angeles is a sprawling Southern Californian city famed as the global centre of the film and entertainment industry. Every neighbourhood in this vibrant, multicultural metropolis sets a different scene. It has 75 miles of coastline, and is the home to people from 140 counties speaking 224 different languages. That's a hell of a lot of languages being spoken in one city, more than half the population is Latinos.

I had heard, too, about the notorious Los Angeles gang culture, which includes gangs of almost every ethnicity and has led to Los Angeles' nickname, 'The Gang Capital of America'. According to the Los Angeles Police Department (LAPD), there are 450 gangs with an estimated 45,000 members in Los Angeles, and 1,300 gangs and an estimated 120,000 gang members in the whole of Los Angeles County. I learned that people were reluctant to pursue a career in the police force there because it's just too damn dangerous. The whole of Los Angeles has fewer than 10,000 police officers serving a population of under four million, while gang membership has continued to rise over the years even in times when crime has decreased. Whenever I think about gangs, it always brings back memories of the Hollywood action films in which they frequently make an appearance as fodder for the heroes to defeat.

Growing up, I had always fantasised about visiting the City of Angels one day. Being an ardent follower of Bruce Lee, back then my ultimate dream was to have direct lineage to the master. And this ambition motivated me more and more as I got closer to fulfilling it. Crucially, I wanted to be able to say that I had trained with one of Bruce Lee's original students, trained with the best and not settled for anything less. I had been inspired by a couple of prominent British martial artists who had made trips to Los Angeles in the early 1980s, training under well-known Bruce Lee disciples such as Dan Inosanto, so I got in touch with two people who had experienced training across the pond. One revealed to me that he had worked as a bricklayer, which meant six months of hard graft to save the money to finance the trip. The other was one of the first ever students to make the over-the-pond journey in the early 1980s. He, also, had done meagre labour jobs to save up the money. We had a chat and he was more than happy to give me his advice.

I felt a bubble of excitement rising in my stomach as I conversed with him over the phone. It felt, at the time, as if he was a famous person who had performed the pilgrimage, a pilgrimage that I had wanted to embark on myself. I truly believed that this could be the best thing that could happen to me in my life, as my desire to pursue California was fuelled by these men who had walked the same path. To say I was feeling elated just to have the opportunity to talk with this man, who I felt had a direct lineage to Bruce Lee, is an understatement.

So, in June 1996, just as I exited my teenage years, I packed my bag and jetted off to Los Angeles in search of the American Dream. At last I would be meeting and training with a disciple of Bruce Lee. A fantasy that had been beyond my grasp was now actually manifesting into reality. Not in a million years did I envisage this coming true. I thought to myself, *How an earth am I going to be allowed to jet off to America?* It was a daunting prospect, but I plucked up the courage to ask my parents and the trip was sanctioned to my great surprise.

With nothing but a small bag, a couple of credit cards, cash and an obsessive drive on my side, I arrived at LAX airport on my new American adventure. From the first moment I stepped onto the tarmac, everything seemed bigger. The cops were taller and well built, the cars were longer, the roads were wider and the sun was brighter. *This is what I'm talking about,* I thought to myself as I started to get goose pumps despite the bright sunshine.

Now, we all have a perception of things and certain expectations when we see things from afar, when things are out of our reach. I was no different in this regard. I had watched the movies like everyone else, read about the famous martial artists and bodybuilders and studied Bruce Lee's life diligently. This was where it all happened. This was the place where Hollywood actors, fighters, bodybuilders and music stars all lived in one magical splot. This was the place to be, the place to venture to if you want to make it big time. Indeed, this was where thousands of people came to pursue their dreams, even if many came only to find themselves unemployed and disillusioned. There is so much competition. Everyone wants a piece of the action and a slice of the cash cake. As I know now, it's where dreams come true, but equally where dreams are shattered.

I hailed a cab to drive me to south Los Angeles, and it dropped me off outside the famous academy. I had read about my to-be instructor and Bruce's protégé and the academy that perpetuated the teachings of its late master, after the untimely death that had sent shockwaves around the world. A couple of months prior to my departure, I had phoned the instructor to inform him that I was coming and to ask if I could become a member of his prestigious class. To my delight, he said I was welcome. To further galvanise me, I had recently seen this instructor being interviewed in a Bruce Lee documentary in 1993. All in all, I felt this trip would bring me closer to the late master in association and spirit. Yes, I longed to be accepted as a pupil of one of Bruce Lee's students.

As I stepped into the premises with my battered black handbag in my hand I was greeted by the instructor. When he saw me with a black Bruce Lee T-shirt, I immediately sensed alarm bells going off. My psychological human behaviour radar instantly kicked in as my intuition took the front seat. The expression on his face said, *Oh, not another Bruce Lee fanatic*!

* * *

During Bruce's lifetime he had a closed-door policy at his small but prestigious private gym in Los Angeles' Chinatown district. I had the pleasure of visiting this old school, located on 626 College Street, a couple of times when I visited Los Angeles again. This is where he had taught his devoted, carefully and screened hand-selected students, and my instructor had been one of them. The closed-door training sessions would become much talked about after Bruce's demise. Those who were part of the select, close-knit group were fortunate enough to train with Bruce at his house, too. Visiting this rather obscure-looking place in Chinatown was like a pilgrimage. The one part of the traditional Bruce Lee pilgrimage I never took part in was visiting the late master's grave, for the sole reason that to do so would have gone against my religious beliefs.

Bruce told his students that to keep something prestigious, you have to refrain from making it available to the masses. As a result his gym was far from a commercial school. Moreover, Bruce broke tradition – no uniforms, ranks and traditional rituals. He was an innovator and borrowed from everyone and integrated training concepts intended to elevate and unleash his students' potential far beyond what other schools thought possible at the time. His coaching method, which I found appealing, more or less resembled that of a boxing coach – today an approach typical among MMA coaches. He was an advocate of one-on-one and small group tuition, with none of the endless punching drills conducted in lines that characterised many traditional martial arts academies. This was another thing that attracted me to his art. I had never been a sheep and I wasn't planning on becoming one.

Still, division seems almost inevitable in any group, and sure enough there were two groups in the jeet kune do world. One was stuck in the past, latching on to the founder of the art's every word and technique as gospel truth and refusing to evolve. The other group, which seemed to be the majority, by and large, because Bruce's protégé Dan Inosanto had promoted this, used what was referred to as the 'concepts' method. This group evolved, integrating elements from different arts into Bruce's original. Dan firmly believed that Bruce would have evolved to incorporate new techniques into his art if he had lived longer. Plus he had made a promise to his master not to teach his art commercially, giving him less incentive to push a 'pure' form of jeet kune do. The classes at the academy I was training at primarily focused on this 'concepts' method, embracing a philosophy that emphasised finding your own path.

Now, of course, politics filter into everything, from religion to martial arts. And politics pertaining to Bruce's art have been present since the day he died, the regular debates being around who was right in their approach, who was allowed to teach, who was not. For all the argument, I think years later most people realised that evolution is inevitable and indeed almost an absolute necessity in order to survive in a modern combat environment, even if a few refused to embrace new concepts.

Either way, if you were one of the very fortunate foreign or out-of-town students to make it into one of the academies, your hopes were shattered if you were expecting to learn the complete original framework art that Bruce taught. Another foreign student, who had also religiously made the trip from Europe to Southern California in search of Bruce Lee enlightenment, agreed that the tuition we received when we walked into the academy wasn't exactly what we were expecting. It dawned on us that the art being taught was far removed from what Bruce was doing in his lifetime – although at times certain original material would be shared by the instructor.

I remember having a conversation with an older man who was checking out the academy because he wanted to enrol his son. He was telling me how he was impressed with Bruce's philosophy, and was of the impression that this subject would be touched on in classes. Well, I thought, he's going to be disappointed because this isn't the place you're going to find philosophy classes, far from it.

That said, several of Bruce's original students did continue their teacher's tradition by teaching privately and in small groups at their homes or in a private setting. Today, the commercial route is taken by most instructors as they fit into the modern-day commercially-driven world. That's not to say it's wrong.

I trained at the academy for three months, taking the jeet kune do classes. On some weekends, a couple of academy friends and I would go to a park and train there. Afterwards, Phil and I, a friend and fellow student, would go into Jack in the Box drive – through where I used to order a burger without the burger. Because I couldn't eat non-halal meat, I had to settle for the bun and salad. Phil found this hilarious.

Still, I was very happy to be in Los Angeles. The day I discovered that Bruce had developed his own brand of martial art, I had developed tunnel vision. Why would I want to train in Thai-boxing or karate when the man I admired the most trained in and developed his own personal brand of martial art? Like many other crazy enthusiasts that idolised the great master, I would try to follow his concepts and train at home and with other like-minded martial arts enthusiasts in what was more of a private setting. I was a fervent follower of the originator's method, and thought it was the gospel truth. But many years later, as I matured, I would learn the truth of what Bruce himself had said: a kick was a kick, a punch was a punch, and a lock was a lock, no matter who taught you or where it came from. OK, it was great to have a famous and well-known instructor, or at least one who knew what he was doing, but I realised you could learn and achieve a level of excellence in your own country, in a gym nobody had heard of, from an instructor nobody cared for, if learning an art and how to fight was your goal. If you train in the martial arts long enough, and seriously enough, the mystique starts to fade, and is replaced by practicality.

So, when I realised that to survive in today's environment, adaptability was paramount, my mentality changed. I eventually embraced grappling – the term MMA hadn't been coined yet. I arrived at a conclusion: as long as you can box and wrestle, and are prepared to use a few sneaky kung fu street tactics such as strikes to vital spots (which would be a groin kick, eye gouging, or biting), and had the mentality to do it all under pressure, then you can laugh your way to survival. That's all you need if you are genuinely looking for self-defence and a realistic fighting art.

Further, the texture of the art that I had been attracted to and so desperately sought had been somewhat eroded with the advent of the UFC. Many philosophies and principles of Bruce's art are still valid and I still believe are embedded in me. But you can't fool yourself, or at least you should try to break away from bullshit, even if there are those who are ardent followers who continue to be lost. At the end of the day, all arts have something to offer and all have weaknesses. You have to ask yourself, *What is it that you're looking to achieve?* Some people pursue the arts for self-defence, fitness, to compete, while others merely want to learn an art. The choice is yours.

So, I eradicated my closed-minded mentality as my goal gravitated towards studying for the right reasons. Training at the American academy opened my eyes.

Over the years I have always trained on and off. Bruce believed tournament fighting isn't an all-out fight so he was against competing. But as the sport of MMA – and my exposure to grappling – spread, my attitude towards this changed. One should even pursue at some point grappling tournaments to see what it feels like to dip your feet in the waters of competition, and to use your skills against a fully resisting opponent. Setting challenges and goals should be a never-ending process.

Anyway, as a 20-year-old I was training and soaking up the sun in my favourite city. One afternoon there was a meeting with a number of Bruce's original students and Bruce's widow, Linda Lee, at the academy. These were members of a prestigious board. Somehow, the news of this meeting reached my ears. At the time, I was residing in the apartment round the corner. Now that this rare opportunity had presented itself, I had to drop by to get a glimpse of which famous martial arts personalities were in attendance in the vain hope that I might meet Bruce's wife and the rest. I walked into the reception area acting innocent, but then left after a quick chat with the academy desk staff. Later that evening, when I came to the academy to train, I told my instructor I had come in earlier when the meeting was going on. 'You should've come inside,' he said to me. 'I would've introduced you to Linda.' I told him I didn't want to intrude. I couldn't believe it, Bruce's wife was there and I was in the same building. I had been on the brink of meeting his wife, but my courage had failed me.

* * *

My stay wasn't going to be complete without a visit to the Inosanto Academy, which was in Marina Del Rey and was headed by Dan Inosanto, famed for being Bruce Lee's training partner and number-one student. The Inosanto Academy had been connected in the past with the academy I was training at. Both were the most prestigious places in the world, offering instruction in Bruce's art. In fact, when I landed in Los Angeles I first dropped by at this academy. I asked Dan's wife, 'Do you have a weight training room at the gym?' She said, 'No, you can lift students up in the air instead.' I burst out laughing. The fact that they didn't have a weight training facility was the initial reason I decided not to train there. I was that obsessed with building muscle in my youth. However, I ended up training in Dan's class on several occasions on future visits to Los Angeles.

When I walked into the Inosanto Academy, my attention was captured by the signed, framed photos of famous martial artists, fighters and personalities from the action movie industry which adorned the walls. The Inosanto Academy is frequented by many Hollywood actors and stuntmen who come to train there. Bruce's original wooden dummy and heavy bag (which weighed 300 pounds) were displayed at this academy. A couple of years earlier the gigantic red bag had been at the academy I was training at, but then Dan took it. It was amazing to actually touch the training devices that Bruce had trained with. It was like being in a museum checking out these artefacts which were a part of history. The academy I trained at also had one of Bruce's original grip-exerciser machines. I would often use this to strengthen my forearm and grip when I trained with the weights. Bruce had used this same device to strengthen his arms.

I had met Dan before, in London in 1993 when I was 17. It was like meeting a celebrity. This talented master was not only Bruce's protégé, but appeared in Bruce's final film, *Game of Death*, in which he fights Bruce in a classic duel which includes an epic battle of nunchaku against nunchaku. After meeting him, I met Ted Wong the same year. Wong was one of Bruce's closest friends and personal students and workout partners. What really amazed me was how Ted had never disclosed to his work colleagues for 20 years that he was one of Bruce's best friends. I found that extraordinary.

TO THE TOP

Thousands of like-minded enthusiasts around the globe are exposed to Bruce's art, and some could only fantasise about making the pilgrimage to train with the original source. But it is out of their reach. Others find gyms with second-generation lineage to the master. But the crazy obsessed ones, a category I certainly fitted into back then, make the trip abroad in the hope of getting closer to the late master.

* * *

I found the people in Los Angeles very friendly. I realised there were more Hispanic Mexicans in this exotic city than there were Caucasians. That was something of a surprise. In fact, I blended in with the Hispanics well because being an Asian it wasn't difficult for people to mistake me for one of their own. To further illustrate this point, a kid on a bike stopped by one day and started speaking Spanish to me. I told him I wasn't Hispanic. It was the dark hair.

It slowly dawned on me that in American culture they worship money. Money, money and more money is the mantra; it's all about the dollar. Where I come from, although money is important, we don't religiously worship this paper in comparison to our 'cousins' across the Atlantic, and so the American mentality has always been somewhat disconcerting to me. I have done business in the past and worked just like anyone else, but my mentality has always been slightly off track, so to speak. We all want more money and to be in a position to be able to afford things, but having money at all costs is just something that doesn't resonate with me. As a matter of fact, I somewhat loathe this attitude.

Other than the fact that Los Angeles is the Mecca of martial arts and bodybuilding, I was inevitably attracted to all things Hollywood. We humans are programmed in a way that attracts us to fame and fortune, and I was no different. The palm trees that I had seen on TV and the skyscrapers of downtown Los Angeles brought back memories of my childhood. I remember seeing the Hollywood sign for the first time when a group of us were being driven to Hollywood and Beverly Hills. It was an exhilarating experience. We passed pop sensation Janet Jackson's house in Beverly Hills, where there was a party going on. Outside was a black limousine, and a chauffeur and burly bodyguard waited as the music blared inside the mansion. Madonna's pink mansion lay above a hill in West Hollywood on Sunset Boulevard, the famous road that I'd read about countless times and which stretches from Figueroa Street downtown Los Angeles to the Pacific Coast Highway at the Pacific Ocean. The road Sunset Strip portion of this 22-mile road in West Hollywood is famous for its nightlife. As the sunset, it was awe-inspiring.

It's surprising, but Hollywood really is often the way it's portrayed in films, which you think must be exaggerated. You've got a young woman with headphones jogging; a movie executive pulling up in a Mercedes on the phone making a multi-million-dollar deal; a soft-top Jeep stopping at the red lights with a guy in a tank-top with music blasting away; and a posh middle-aged woman in an expensive designer hat walking her cute little designer dog against a Beverly Hills backdrop.

Not everyone was golden, however. The sunny weather is one of California's attractions, but the heat always drained my energy. Los Angeles compared to New York is very serene and laid back. And as you take a stroll in Hollywood, you often get a rather pessimistic vibe of this movie-making capital of the world. Some areas of Hollywood were rundown and infested with tramps and homeless people in the streets, something which is invisible to many outsiders who have never visited the place. Ironically, hardly any prominent actors live in Hollywood itself. Instead they live in the classy Beverly Hills area and more to the north, in neighbourhoods such as Bel-Air and Brentwood – except for Quentin Tarantino, who lives in Hollywood Hills last time I heard. He's probably one of the only top Tinseltown personalities living there.

I knew Americans were crazy and that big cities were crime infested, and becoming a potential crime victim was often in the back of my head whenever I was on my walks. The probability of getting shot never quite left my mind. As I was walking one night, not far from my apartment block, these two African-American guys got into a fight on the court of a gas station, the first street fight I witnessed there. I didn't intervene, not sure who was right or wrong, or whether one might be carrying a weapon. Another situation I witnessed was in Hollywood when I was having a meal on Hollywood Boulevard, which I used to frequent on a daily basis when I stayed there and talking to a Moroccan guy who worked there and the two elderly Chinese owners. This Caucasian guy and his partner got into an argument with the Moroccan worker. I was having my burger and my instincts told me that it was going to kick off. The Caucasian guy launched a verbal tirade aimed at the staff member, coming across as being very aggressive. I felt he was being a bully and a loudmouth, but I don't know what it was all about, and so again I didn't intervene. Finally the guy and his partner walked out and the situation was defused. I never really became a victim of crime or felt vulnerable to any incident despite floating around in a city that was the gang capital of the world and gun crime was rife. I actually found almost everyone friendly.

Meanwhile, I did end up seeing stars. One appeared as I was talking a stroll in Santa Monica. *There's a familiar face*, I thought to myself. This blonde guy was being interviewed by a TV crew. It was none other than Hollywood actor Gary Busey! I had seen him in *Point Break*, which I watched at a gym I used to frequent as a young teenager, and I could never forget him fighting Mel Gibson in *Lethal Weapon*, where Mel employs Gracie Jiu-Jitsu skills that Rorion and Royce Gracie had taught him for the movie. For a moment I thought of going over but felt reluctant. Gary, I was unaware at the time, was a friend of the Gracies. Rorion and Royce were responsible for choreographing the fight scene in *Lethal Weapon*. They would be on set and would drop the mats and roll around with Mel, and later I would notice Gary in the first UFC video tapes, when they hit the market a year later after the first UFC debuted. If I'd known about the connection at the time, I might have talked to him; mores the pity.

CHAPTER FIVE

ENTER THE GRACIES

THOUGH I typically trained at the jeet kune do academy in Los Angeles, I was aware that the famous Gracie Academy was located only five minutes away. I decided to enrol there, too. This was purely because of UFC champion Royce Gracie, the skinny, lanky jiu-jitsu master, who won three of the first four UFCs. Students had flocked to the academy soon after Royce was catapulted to fame, after being crowned the first UFC champion a couple of years earlier, revolutionising the way we perceived fighting. The Gracie approach to combat accentuated the need for ground fighting, with most of the family's techniques revolving around ground grappling. Their realistic approach and extremely effective method struck a chord with the martial arts community, much of which saw, for the first time, just how likely it was that a no-holds-barred fight would go to the ground. And, yes, they had made me a believer, which was an accomplishment in itself, since I was an ardent jeet kune do lover, who at one time refused to even entertain the thought of practising any other style.

I had heard of Royce in 1990 and also later, in 1993, when I had come across an article in a new magazine, *Today Martial Arts*, which in was a report on the first ever UFC event, the winner of which was a Brazilian Gracie Jiu-Jitsu exponent by the name of Royce Gracie. By the way, this new magazine was the worst magazine of its kind to ever hit the newsstands. How they thought it would survive is beyond me. I wouldn't have read it for free, never mind parting with my hard-earned cash – or dole money – at the time.

The reason the Gracie family invoked my interest was because they were different and real. They had started what was known as the Gracie Challenge, an open bare-knuckle invitation to all challengers who wanted to take them on, which became the precursor to the UFC. Rorion, the elder brother, had first visited America in the 1970s, but by then, back in Brazil, the Gracie name was already huge. Their father, the diminutive Helio Gracie, had a reputation for taking on all-comers, and had fought in two high-profile grappling matches against a pair of Japan's best judoka. Now the elder son had bigger plans beyond the confines of his homeland.

Royce once explained to me what the Gracie Challenge was all about and cleared up a misconception. People misunderstand the idea of the Gracie Challenge. The major objective of this controversial challenge has always been to find out how effective the style of Gracie Jiu-Jitsu is – it's a practical way to prove the effectiveness of ground fighting. The Gracies wanted to propagate a message relating to the superiority of their art and open peoples' eyes and let them discern for themselves. 'Then they can say, "Hey, this jiu-jitsu is a great style and can compliment any other style",' Royce explained to me. 'So, when we were challenging people, a lot of people thought we were challenging other martial artists to put them down. No!' According to Royce, the Gracies had no intention of showing a lack of respect to other styles and martial artists. Rather, the objective was to address the importance and effectiveness of this once-unknown martial arts system, and to use it as a platform to ascertain whether they could make it work in a more reality-based fight.

'When we taught our students, we would tell them that Gracie Jiu-Jitsu was the best, as it addresses ground fighting and grappling,' the three-time UFC champion told me. Sometimes, he said, a martial arts student would walk in and argue with the Gracies, the classic being along the lines of, 'I have an instructor who teaches karate and he says Gracie Jiu-Jitsu grappling is nothing!' The valiant Gracies would encourage the individual to bring his instructor or friend over to the garage and they'd send the challenger home 'baptised'. 'That's a challenge right there! It's about putting your money where your mouth is,' Royce told me. Soon, the challenger would concede to the superiority of this technique-based style, typically after he was grappled to the ground, which would neutralise his striking tools and leave him floundering and with no idea what to do. The Gracies weren't all that concerned if you weighed 300 pounds, looked like the Hulk, were built like a truck, had world-title belts, or if you were a raw street fighter with a notorious reputation. If you wanted to test yourself in a real street-fight environment, you were more than welcome to step on to the mat, or at times hard wooden floor or the street, with these crazy men.

As I said, the Gracies had become notorious in Brazil and were treated with great reverence long before they made it in the States. Rorion once said that they didn't have to wait in queues as they were a household name, but when he moved to America he had to start all over again. In the beginning, he did menial jobs to survive while teaching his beloved art, cleaning houses, flipping burgers, and teaching the Gracie brand of jiu-jitsu in a garage at home. But as the word spread, it got to a stage where the garage would no longer accommodate the number of students who wanted to train. There was a waiting list of 150 students according to Royce. He and Rorion were conducting private classes three days a week – Tuesday, Thursday and Saturday – and Rorion would work on movies as an extra on Fridays. In the garage days the Gracies attracted some well-known martial arts personalities who had taken an interest in learning from them. Some of the more prominent personalities who sought out private tuition were John Saxon, Jim Kelly and Bob Wall, better known as co-stars of the epic Bruce Lee smash hit *Enter the Dragon*, and Chuck Norris, world champion martial artist, film star and co-star of Bruce Lee's

Way of the Dragon. The Brazilian brothers had something unique to offer the American martial arts fraternity, who slowly came to understand that they were missing an element, a part of the jigsaw, that would complement their own art. It wasn't uncommon to see well-known elite martial artists, professional baseball and NFL players on the mat, all being manhandled by the Brazilian beasts.

Rorion was eventually influenced by American marketing strategies and Gracie Jiu-Jitsu became a commodity, something that would appeal to people who weren't just interested in becoming better no-holds-barred fighters. One of the factors in the sales pitch of his 'product' was the effectiveness of his brand of fighting. The Gracies were astute enough to know that once America was introduced to Gracie Jiu-Jitsu, the entire world would recognise it. American culture, music and movies had all been embraced by the world. Once something hits big in the land of opportunity and has the American seal of approval, then it gets accepted by the world. It's that simple.

* * *

Rorion was a man on a mission. His goal was to spread his father's teachings and ultimately have Gracie Jiu-Jitsu embraced by not only the combat sports fraternity, but a wider audience as well. In an effort to achieve this, Rorion joined forces with an advertising executive by the name of Art Davie, who had a beer client he was trying to get to sponsor kickboxing shows. Art had read about this fantastic family of fighters in the 1989 September issue of *Playboy* magazine, and the bespectacled, frail-looking-yet-enthusiastic businessman wasted no time calling them up to arrange a meeting. Subsequently, Art became a student of Rorion's and witnessed several of the challenge matches that took place in the garage and later at the Gracie Academy. So he knew what these men were all about. Meanwhile, film director John Millius was taking lessons from Rorion. He also had been exposed to the exploits of these notorious men and witnessed their brutal and bloody challenge matches. The three men – Rorion, Art and

ENTER THE GRACIES

John – joined forces to develop the idea of having a no-holds-barred tournament, which would give martial arts fighters from different styles the opportunity to showcase their skills. The ultimate concept was to ascertain what the best and most effective fighting style was. Finally, after hundreds of challenge matches in the garage and academy in front of dozens of students who loved the exciting action of a real fight, they were ready to take the idea to another level. And the UFC was born.

The creation of the UFC was to be a turning point in the history of martial arts, giving the Gracies a major platform from which to communicate their message to a wider audience. 'When Rorion explained to the guys the concept, a lot of people were like, "Hold on, we are not allowed to fight on the street because we get arrested, and you're planning on putting this on national TV?"' says Royce. "Are you out of your mind?! It's going to be like human cockfighting! You can't fight on the street." Sure enough, when Royce started working on getting the brutal fights televised, plenty of obstacles lay ahead, from getting the money, to finding the fighters, to finding broadcasters willing to put the show on. Not surprisingly, one of the main hurdles was to find a place that could host this type of a tournament legally. Colorado, it emerged, was the only place without a boxing commission. And so that was the only place to legally hold the tournament.

Originally, the first UFC was intended to be a 16-man tournament, but it was changed to an eight-man, single-elimination tournament after some deliberation. The title 'Ultimate Fighting Championship' stuck after several other names were considered. Rorion at one time suggested 'War of the Worlds', but that soon went out of the window.

Art Davie, who came in as a partner, became the matchmaker responsible for putting together the fights and hiring the fighters. He was kind of the 'legs' of the show, Royce told me. But who would represent the Gracies in the Octagon? Those who were around Rorion advised him to pick Rickson, the third-oldest son of the family, because he was much more menacing, heavier, muscular and stronger. He was the family champion and had fought countless times back in Brazil, at one time claiming to have amassed 400 fights with no losses.

However, Rorion had his own ideas, and he said, 'If I pick Rickson and he wins, it's no big deal.' It would be a like a tank running everybody over. Rorion believed his younger sibling Royce, an unimposing figure, was the perfect warrior in disguise who would do the family proud.

Art was stunned. To Art, Royce was the young brother who lived above Rorion's garage with a fishtank, didn't have a bank account, didn't have a credit card, and was just a big kid. 'He's the one who babysits your kids,' Art protested, failing to grasp the younger brother's significance. 'Royce is a really good kid, but Royce!?' Art was far from impressed with his business partner's choice. 'He would show up at the academy on Saturday afternoon and Rorion would open the safe and take out three or four $20 bills and he'd give Royce the money.' He recounted in an interview more than two decades later. 'And Royce would go down to Redondo Beach pier and hang out, surf a little bit and flirt with the girls.' He wasn't many people's idea of a fighter.

The reason behind Royce representing the Gracie family, though, was that he was a perfect example of what Gracie Jiu-Jitsu exemplifies – a smaller, not very strong person capable of overcoming much bigger, stronger adversaries. 'I believe my brothers and cousins were capable, but I was chosen to take the mantle,' Royce once told me. His younger brother, Royler, was too light – at the time he weighed 155 pounds. On the other hand, his older brother Rickson was too heavy – he was 195 or 200 pounds, too heavy and strong to drive home the lesson. If you witness a 200-pound muscular guy beat up someone with the stature of Ken Shamrock, a 220-pound guy, it doesn't look that impressive. On the other hand, Royce, weighing 175 pounds with a skinny build, beating up someone weighing 220 pounds such as Ken, who is full of muscle with an impressive body frame? Now, that is very compelling. The concept, beyond putting on a show, was to prove a point and impress people. Royce had been training and teaching with Rorion at the academy, so Rorion had total faith in his younger brother's ability, despite the naysayers who felt it was a potentially a suicide mission.

The first ever UFC event debuted on 12 November 1993 in Denver, Colorado. Much of the American public was outraged and found it excessively brutal, but for others it instantly struck a chord. I remember watching the first couple of UFCs and being knocked out, not just by the brutality, but the realities of real fighting, too. It was messy and scrappy, with fighters losing teeth and (illegally) gouging eyes, tumbling to the floor and engaging in grappling exchanges they barely understood. Meanwhile, fight fans around the world were drawn to the sight of Royce, this rather frail-looking grappler who proceeded to wipe the floor with everyone they had put in front of him. His performance was nothing short of superb. This man didn't need to punch his adversaries into oblivion. Instead, he would gently make them submit with his trademark techniques and walk off calmly. He beat a boxer with barely a punch thrown, choked out Ken Shamrock with a gi technique, then put a clinic on the brutal, savate expert Gerard Gordeau, who had earlier eye-gouged another competitor so excessively that the man lost his vision in one eye. A legend was born. Royce Gracie was my new hero.

* * *

It was only a year after watching Royce in the UFC via VHS tape that I was training at the Gracie Academy. To my delight, Royce would come in and teach the intermediate classes, greeting me with a 'good morning' when he walked in. I was just a young 135-pound guy, who had just exited his teenage years months earlier, in a foreign land. He was one of the most famous and feared fighters on the planet. But a man of his calibre and position made me feel special.

Back in those days Royce had a serious demeanour. I can't blame him, because at that time he had earned the Moniker of the 'Baddest

Man on the Planet' and had to have his guard up – he was the man to beat. Can you imagine having that weight on your shoulders? He couldn't have people taking liberties. If you laid eyes on him in the street and didn't know who he was, you'd think this man probably never stepped into a gym in his life. But believe me, you wouldn't want to make the mistake of messing with this man.

In class it was mesmerising witnessing an average-looking guy teaching students who were bigger, meaner and stronger-looking how to fight. Some were from law-enforcement agencies such as the LAPD and FBI, but he would handle them all.

I was a novice grappler at the time. For me, the academy was an experience, and it was all I could do to hang in there getting beat by a lot of experienced students. I was quite aggressive but it was time to get technical. To build up a base Royce even suggested I take some additional beginner classes, but I was there to train with him, so I wasn't going to deviate from my original plan, do anything that would put a dent in my ego. To me this was the best fighter, the guy who had the capacity to put you to sleep within seconds with his trademark chokehold. And I was in his presence not merely as a fan but as a student.

Even though he had a serious demeanour with regular people, Royce always cracked jokes and had a laugh with us in class, so the atmosphere was relaxed. Once in class I was having a problem choking one of the senior students named Corey. I was then shown the right way to do it. I proceeded to choke him and he had to go get some water as he continued coughing. From the corner of my eye, I could see Royce joking with another student, Lewis, and several other pupils. 'Now he has to go get some water, he's been choked,' he said as he laughed with a group of students. Not only did you learn discipline, technique and how to fight in a sparring situation, but you learned to get on with people from all walks of life. The academy had developed a reputation around America, and so it attracted students and visitors not only from California but other states, too

ENTER THE GRACIES

I always took the morning classes, usually at 10am, which by my standards was an achievement in itself because it was too early for me and my body to be awake after my evening lessons at the jeet kune do academy. The Gracie Academy was a modern training facility with rooms on the ground floor and a massive hall upstairs. And there were tonnes of offices, which gave you the impression it was a big professional company with people working in different departments, which it was in its own way. Rorion had mastered the American business strategy and made the most out of it. Some days I saw some prestige sports cars parked up, which I thought belonged to the Gracies.

After Royce emerged victorious in the first UFC, he exclaimed, 'It will open everybody's eyes – especially the weaker guys – that you don't have to be a monster to be a champ. You don't have to be the biggest guy or the one who hits the hardest.' Oh, boy, did he open everyone's eyes and become a catalyst for change. I'm glad he proved that a smaller, less physically imposing fighter could beat a much bigger, stronger and heavier giant. This man gave hope to the smaller guys, just as Bruce Lee had done. Never did I know that one day I'd be meeting the man himself – and training with him – and that years later a friendship would ensue.

I compared my stay in Los Angeles to the experience of a university student. I had left my country and embarked on a voyage to study martial arts at two world-famous academies, my own form of university. Back in the 1960s and 1970s, just before and after the kung fu boom, some Westerners had made trips to the Orient, notably Japan and China, to experience the arts from their birthplace, training with the great masters and then returning to their respective countries with newfound knowledge and wisdom. This, for me, was the same. After three months it was time to go home. I had overstayed by a week, which would have dire consequences when I returned two years later. But I had achieved what I longed for. I could tick this off because this was the one thing I really wanted to achieve in life. Little did I suspect that this was just the beginning.

CHAPTER SIX

RETURNING TO LOS ANGELES

BACK HOME several months after my trip I got a job in a gas station and, at almost the same time, set up a martial arts business – a publishing label, specialising in martial arts publications for a niche market, from my bedroom. I was only 21 years old, and as I further established the business venture I continued to hold my day job for a good while.

It was a life of constant grind. Waking up at 5am on freezing mornings to drive to my job, I would reassure myself it was only a matter of time before I made a success of myself in the martial arts business world in one capacity or another, that the early morning torture would fade away into oblivion, that the harsh morning wake-up calls were merely temporary.

I quickly attracted some prominent martial arts authorities from the USA and eventually moved into an office. Fortunately, I had made several connections and a couple of friends in America – all of them consummate professionals involved with martial arts and MMA, and a few connected to the motion picture industry in Hollywood. I recall having a meeting in New York with a company I was doing business with. When Gail, one of the directors, first laid eyes on me as I walked into her office, she was surprised. 'I thought you'd be a lot older,' she said, letting out a smile. Being in the trade I was, she suspected I would be in my 50s. I was merely 24 at the time. I laughed and told her that I started early.

When I returned to Los Angeles, on what would be my third or fourth trip, I received a call from my friend Ron Balicki. He had fought professionally in shoot fighting – a style similar to MMA that incorporates wrestling and striking but very limited groundwork, as practised by the UFC's Ken Shamrock. Ron and his wife, Diana Lee Inosanto, picked me up from my apartment in Santa Monica for an evening meal. Diana, a very amicable person, is part of Bruce Lee history. Her father is, of course, Dan Inosanto, who named his daughter Lee in honour of his friend. Ever since I've known Diana and Ron they have treated me like a family member, a real honour.

On this occasion, they said there was a nice restaurant not far from where I was staying, but first we drove down to their house, in Hermosa Beach. Sometimes, Ron's phone wouldn't receive when I called from abroad because the signal is very bad near the coast, but it was worth it for them to live in a beautiful place right on the beach. By the time we arrived it was late evening and was getting somewhat dark. Ron ushered me upstairs and showed me his extensive library. I was impressed with his vast collection, which included videos, all relating to the martial arts. We talked and relaxed while Diana got ready. Then we drove to the restaurant to start our evening out. Other than Ron and Diana, there was Joey, a teenager back then, now an MMA fighter – who was like an adopted son to Ron – a martial artist and actor who appeared in a Hulk Hogan movie, and Diana's first son, Sebastian, from her previous marriage.

When it comes to food I wasn't the most clued-up person. Furthermore, because of my Muslim heritage I have to restrict myself to eating halal food only. Some years later when Ron, Diana and I were at an Indian restaurant in Thousand Oaks, which is where they later moved to and further north of Los Angeles, I had another food dilemma. The place was a typical Indian restaurant. It did feel somewhat weird, though, an Indian restaurant in Los Angeles. I just couldn't imagine it. Anyway, we ordered food and these big dishes were brought to us. The service was impeccable. For a moment I thought to myself, *These can't be Pakistanis, they do look a little darker* – I'm referring to the staff. Wait! Let me put this into perspective before the racism card comes out. Like Chinese, Japanese and Indonesians, although they're all from the Orient, there is a difference in skin tone and look. Indonesians have a darker, tanned skin, Chinese and Japanese have a lighter skin. It's similar for the Indian subcontinent where my family hail from – I'm generalising here. I had assumed all along that the place we were dinning at was serving halal food. After giving it a great deal of thought, I got the attention of one of the waiters. 'Is this halal?' I asked politely. He said it wasn't, which caught me by surprise I froze for a second. So I spent the whole evening pretending to eat my food. I told my friends that I wasn't hungry as I watched them tuck into their delicious dishes as we conversed about martial arts, movies and Bruce Lee. Luckily there were some halal dishes at this Thai place that we were at. I think this was the first time I had actually been to this type of a restaurant. I learned that there were certain similarities to the Asian food that I was familiar with. So it wasn't a complete shocker.

Diana had been the best friend of Bruce Lee's son Brandon when they were kids. Bruce's daughter Shannon was also friends with Diana, but Brandon was closer to her in age and so they shared more of a bond. She would be playing with Brandon and their dads would be training and discussing martial arts. 'As a child I used to play with Brandon,' I remember Diana telling me. 'We used to have arguments and disputes about playing with toys. It was kind of funny to see Uncle Bruce intervene. He would kind of have to sort things out between Brandon and me.' It was fascinating to listen to her reminisce about growing up with Bruce Lee and his kids. Had Brandon lived, I can say with great conviction that I would have got to meet him, since he was very close to Diana. Unfortunately he died in 1993 on the set of a movie at the tender age of 28. It was tragic. It became apparent to me that, whenever Diana would talk about Brandon or his dad, more often than not there was this sad emotion that radiated. Losing not one but two of the closest people to her family left an indelible mark on her. In fact, she admitted that she still cries a little bit when someone mentions Brandon's name. The bond was so strong with the Lee's and Inosantos that you'd think they were blood relations.

Having grown up in a normal family, I always wondered what it was like to grow up with famous parents, and so I asked Diana how other kids treated her when they found out that she was close to the famous Bruce Lee. 'I actually didn't want to tell people because I thought they might think I was lying,' she told me, laughing. 'Or, sometimes I'd get challenged. The school bully would want to challenge me and say, "Hey, what can you do?"' It got easier, she said, but as a kid it was a huge amount of pressure.

Bruce had promised Diana's dad that no matter what, for the rest of her life she could take lessons with him, that he'd be her teacher. Surprisingly, though, Diana didn't seriously pursue the arts until much later in life. Her father started teaching her some martial arts after Bruce had passed away, to help her defend herself against bullies, but she didn't embarked on the martial arts journey in earnest until much later. A talented individual, she wanted to make her own choices and pursue her passion in ways that went beyond the confines of being known for being the goddaughter of one of the most iconic figures of the century. She eventually went to Hollywood – first with stunt work and acting, and later taking the leap into directing. Her brother Lance, a musician, kept a low profile, but Diana was working on movies and TV shows, doubling on *Buffy* the *Vampire Slayer*, and in *Face Off, Hulk, Blade* and *Barb Wire*. Ron was working as a stuntman, with a schedule consisting of teaching martial arts seminars around the world as well as performing stunt work. He told me that, in addition to working on major Hollywood movies, he had done extra work and low-budget films, with credits including *Escape from LA, The Rock, Glimmer Man* and *Barbwire*. The Inosanto's talking about their backgrounds really opened up a whole new world for me, a world that I would eventually dip into myself.

Diana and Ron are very much family oriented, which is something I have great admiration for. Ron grew up in the windy city of Chicago, a place infamous for its gangsters and a high crime rate. He had been a police officer, a career Diana had considered when she was younger, but he had talked her out of it. I was also shocked to learn that Ron's best friend back in Chicago was Pakistani. This took me by surprise because I didn't know there were enough Pakistani's there for him to have met one! Where I come from there is a huge Asian Muslim community, the Asians emigrated much later. By now the community has grown, of course, and a new generation has sprung up. Having known and been friends since 2001 – so 20 years – it's always great to see Ron and Diana. It was a great evening.

* * *

Not long after that meeting, I got to work with another close friend of Bruce Lee. My focus now was to work with, in one capacity or another, as many of the prominent individuals who were associated with the late martial arts master as I could, but it was never easy. Bruce had taught very few students and had only done so in a private setting. Among the gentlemen who were fortunate enough to be part of an elite group was the late Larry Hartsell, a leading authority on Bruce Lee's art of jeet kune do. He trained with Bruce at the Los Angeles Chinatown closed-door gym from 1967 to 1969, after serving in Vietnam. A personal student of the great master, Larry would later gravitate towards the grappling aspects of combat, and in the jeet kune do world he was referred to as the 'JKD Street Fighter'. In the 1980s the grappling supremo also worked as a bouncer in the kind of bars that would have made *Roadhouse* look tame. And Larry even offered his services as a bodyguard to Mr T and the notorious magazine publisher Larry Flint.

Although I had heard of Larry in 1990, the first time I met him was in 1995, when I was still a teenager. I had heard him say that his students could say they trained with an original student of Bruce Lee, gain a certification and be a member of his Association – something that really inspired me, because of my interest in lineage. His hybrid street-fighting style, encompassing boxing and grappling, which leaned towards practical techniques, was also right up my street. If you can learn to strike and grapple full contact, I thought, what more do you need? Six years later I was in business with Larry.

Occasionally, whenever I was in Los Angeles, I went to his house to train privately with him in his garage. I became a private student for a little while, training one-on-one. Larry lived in the affluent seaside community of Marina Del Rey, a part of west Los Angeles, the world's largest man-made small-craft harbour with 19 marinas and capacity for over 5,000 boats. When Ron first moved to Los Angeles, he stayed with Larry and told me that Larry kept a gun at home. Apparently, he enjoyed his beer and would often get out of control and start shooting at the ceiling in the house. He was a wild man, but he was always very polite and embodied the humble approach. You couldn't find anyone nicer than this guy who, by the way, had the capacity to break your limbs in a split-second.

Larry's home-garage gym was spacious enough to house a standing punch bag, striking pads, weights bench, rowing machine, free weights and various hitting devices, and also mats to work on grappling, his speciality. Once when we were training together, he whacked me on my chin, catching me with an uppercut by mistake. Boy, I felt it. For a second I thought I had been stung by a bee really hard. Then he got me with a Thai-style round kick outside my left thigh and gave me a dead leg, which left me literally unable to walk for a while. Take into account that this wasn't even sparring but a controlled demo, and that this was a 60-year-old man. The man was hard. He could give men half his age a rough experience.

One day I asked him if I could grapple with one of his other students, who was also there having a lesson. Larry said that this guy was an instructor under him and that he'd crush me because the guy was bigger than me, but when we got down to business I managed to give the guy a hard time. Renowned for being an experienced grappling authority, I thought Larry might have been more optimistic about my chances, since grappling's not always about size, something which earlier UFC's proved. I found it out of character for a man of his calibre and understanding, but maybe he simply wasn't thinking straight.

Although later we parted ways, purely due to a business misunderstanding, Larry was a great guy. All blame, without a shadow of doubt, should be directed at his business manager. She was constantly vying for control and wasn't as smart as she thought she was, which often led to tension between Larry and some of his other associates. If I had known the grim realities of this individual's manner of conducting business before signing on the dotted line, I would've refrained from getting involved in any business with them. Our falling out was over an overpayment. Simply, Larry had been sent some boxes of his martial arts-related product by my company that had produced it. And he wasn't invoiced but was told in advance that the fee would be deducted from his next payment. Ironically his manager couldn't understand a simple thing like that when the money was deducted. It should have been a simple matter, but spiralled out of control, and I never grasped the opportunity to have my say despite being slandered.

I was very saddened by the deterioration of our relationship. I later learned that back in the day Larry had had a business relationship with a video producer that also went down the drain because of another misunderstanding. So, several others had experienced the same wrath that I was subjected to, but it didn't help my cause. I was the fresh meat – the new victim.

* * *

Sadly, Larry was not the only revered martial arts personality I fell out with in the early years of my business. The company I owned had signed up a prominent, but retired fighting legend we will refer to as 'Mr Z', who was set to pen his autobiography. This particular individual had worked with another American martial arts specialist publisher previously, and unbeknownst to me there had been some issues. Eventually, I'd have to contend with unnecessary problems, ego, misunderstanding, control and hard-to-work-with individuals.

What was all the fuss about? Well, 'Mr Z' and I fell out over concerns surrounding creative and production issues. Well, there was a disagreement over what image to use on the cover. My company had already brought to this notorious fighting legend's attention the image we'd sourced, which he had actually cordially OK'd. And after the proofreading process his rep had sent the manuscript to my company as the deadline was approaching. The production process went ahead but then 'Mr Z' and his rep had a problem with the image and also claimed they were still in the process of finalising the proofreading – which was absurd.

Not wanting to get into a legal battle, my company presented the man with another opportunity. The image in question was changed immediately and the original manuscript replaced with the newly delivered version from 'Mr Z', after the first print run arrived. But after a new print run he still wasn't happy. He'd confirmed that the image was OK and one he'd provided for the inside too, but he then went back on his word, coming up with endless petty and feeble complaints. My company had incurred significant costs to please this individual, but he was now pursuing legal action. To aggravate matters further, I was dumbfounded when he had the nerve to say, 'Well, it's done now. I'll take the money.' This is the same guy who was suing my company and had earlier told me that it wasn't about money to him at all, but about getting things done his way or no way. Here was a man who had been sucked into the money machine. It wasn't surprising, because his background said it all – the breed who worship money more than most. As a matter of fact, when I later offered him what amounted to $8,000 based on what he was entitled to at that point, he refused to accept this. He said this would mean I could say I'd paid him. In retrospect, I'm glad he didn't accept because he would've continued to make defamatory remarks. Moreover, I actually ended up giving away that money to someone else – it was a small investment but because the other person was struggling, I just wrote it off completely with no hesitation.

Interestingly, I spoke to several other professionals who had worked with this long-time retired fighter, and they all revealed that he was very hard to work with. By then, though, it was too late. One of his close friends, a famous martial artist who appeared in a couple of high-profile martial arts movies, had even disclosed to me in front of a witness that he would never do business with 'Mr Z'. This put the whole thing into perspective in terms of his track record. If God had sent an angel to warn me what was in store for me, not in a million years would my company have worked with this man. We didn't need him.

'Mr Z' had also accused his own brother of stealing from him for many years – something he himself divulged to me. According to him, his brother, who was a fight promoter, stole and cashed his cheques for many years. But it gets better. Supposedly, one of the biggest action movie stars to have graced the screen owed this man money, too, according to 'Mr Z'. Why would a multi-million-dollar action star, one of the biggest stars in Hollywood, hold back several thousand dollars and rip off some fighter? Furthermore, one of his friends had produced a documentary about him but when it was completed, he was totally against releasing it because he wasn't happy with it. It seemed like everyone was either stealing from him or producing material that he'd never sanctioned. You couldn't reason with the guy.

Many years later another company produced a documentary on 'Mr Z'. When questioned about it in an interview on a prominent MMA radio show, he told the famous radio host, 'I don't know the first thing about it. My business partner doesn't tell me anything. She just says, "Sign here." She said this is the way it's going to be done.

I've been in business with so many people. I got the short end of the stick. So she doesn't let me know too much.' When I heard him say this, I thought to myself, *Is this guy for real?*

After we parted ways it dawned on me that this personality was an ambiguous character, but it was too late now to do a U-turn. In a sense, facing this notorious martial arts champion was quite a daunting prospect. He was, after all, known for inducing pain in people and was often referred to as one of the most dangerous fighters in the world. There have been plenty of hard fighters and grapplers in Pakistan and other countries who could match him, and if they had a platform in the West it's plausible some could even triumph against someone like him. The Gracies would have beaten him. As a matter of fact, they did challenge him. In the period when the UFC was still a spectacle and later when it started to gain traction, some prominent and noteworthy UFC and MMA fighters sought out 'Mr Z' for instruction and advice. He was well-respected in the fight world.

Something else pissed me off too: a collaborator who was assigned to work with 'Mr Z', who was a nasty, wannabe who couldn't tie his own shoe laces, was looking for his five minutes of fame. After the mishap with 'Mr Z' this overgrown lump of a man at one point got quite personal. Enraged, I told him what I thought of him in no uncertain terms. This collaborator and the personalities of two so-called reps were the bigger culprits than the man himself. This third-party tampering had caused chaos and commotion putting a dent in what could've been a prosperous relationship.

I must admit that initially I found 'Mr Z' to be a nice guy. He had an affable side to him. However, I had to find out the hard way the dark side of his character. He had an extremely unreasonable and somewhat bullying side. Nevertheless, he was quite an extraordinary character at the same time.

In any event, after our unfortunate and stained relationship, although I was apprehensive, I did arrange a meeting at his house in

California. I was in Los Angeles, and 'Mr Z', barking over the phone, said he wasn't going to break my neck and wanted me to visit him at home. There would be times when this man would be on the phone to me after the ghastly experience, and I couldn't help but resort to being facetious and laughing out loud as this gentle-looking teddy bear screamed down the phone. Then he'd go into 'normality mode'. In one of the conversations he even threatened to shoot me. I'm dubious about how serious he was – I think it was a figure of speech. Having said this, later it surfaced that this individual had been involved in a shooting decades earlier, and as an accomplice to murder had been convicted of being an accessory to the crime.

Anyway, that night at the house a hanger-on threatened to run me down with his car. This guy would often be found hanging about like a desperate individual who had nothing better to do. It was me and the man himself and the hanger-on left in the house. I sat there with my enemy 'Mr Z' and he called me a cab. He had the capacity to decapitate me instantly. He said that if I was dropping dead he wouldn't give me a drop of water – or was it a grape? There was a world-famous martial arts action movie personality there, who I mentioned earlier who said he wouldn't do business with his own friend. After our meeting he left but not before leaving me perplexed and stunned when he suggested a plan that would create the perfect storm for publicity of our product. I was confused; I didn't know what to make of this whole situation anymore.

This was all interesting and at the same time daunting, but no matter who it is, especially when you know you're not in the wrong and have not gone out of your way to cheat or hurt a person intentionally, you have the right to defend yourself by whatever means possible. If I had to do anything possible to someone to defend myself and my family, then I wouldn't hesitate to do so. I don't care how tough the guy threatening me is, or how many black belts and trophies he's got.

Eventually, I came to the realisation that what I had experienced was nothing out of the ordinary. If you are in the entertainment or sports business, it's inevitable that you will sooner or later fall out with a few people. Look at the rapacious boxing promoters, music and film agents and stars: they're involved in a plethora of legal battles. It's a dirty business – sometimes creative differences are the cause, but more often it's about money. I didn't need to be so hard on myself, which I was in the beginning and for a long time. There's a saying, 'Never judge someone by the opinions of others', but unfortunately people will. It's amazing how someone's influence has an immediate and blinding impact on others. They start seeing the accused person through a tinted lens. His word seemed to have more weight than mine. And my company's name and reputation was tarnished and my character defamed, leading to pressure that took a toll on me. He had tarnished several people's names and most people seem to 'buy' his story based on supposition, because of his notorious position and fame. The version in circulation was that my company had stolen from him, that he hadn't been paid a dime. His representative spread defamatory lies that would rankle for a long time. I should have sued for libel but let it go. In any event, what I did learn is to exercise prudence in the future, and the grim realities of working in the sports and entertainment business.

'Mr Z' even threatened to ruin the name and career of my friend Diana Lee Inosanto, accusing her of siding with me. It was a deliberate attempt to isolate her. She had done nothing wrong whatsoever. He even had demeaned Bruce Lee, openly, several times in interviews, and God knows how many times in private in front of others. That's one thing I abhorred. No one demeans Bruce. Not me, not you, not anyone! He claimed the late martial arts star was not a real fighter and that some of the other fighting champions would have given Bruce a run for his money. He also told me that Bruce had used steroids and claimed to have taught Bruce, when in actual fact they exchanged ideas during about a dozen sessions. Claiming they worked out for the better part of a year gives the impression this individual trained for almost a year with the famous star. There's little evidence to substantiate this claim.

TO THE TOP

So in America I had made some good friends. Equally, I had made a couple of enemies, which left a somewhat bitter taste. Sometime later a more affable UFC champion, Randy Couture, would have his *New York Times* bestselling autobiography published in the United Kingdom, through the company I owned – and would follow up with a second book, inking both a North American and United Kingdom deals. Nevertheless, another door through it already opened amid all the disarray. And I was going to get my foot through it.

CHAPTER SEVEN

ENTER THE JOURNALIST

BEFORE THE widespread use of the internet, magazines and newspapers were, of course, your best source of information for news and sport. And in the martial arts press the now-defunct *Martial Arts Illustrated*, which was published for three decades, was, in the United Kingdom, the bestselling and number-one martial arts magazine despite sometimes ferocious competition. Directly in competition was the now-defunct *Combat*, which had been going since 1974. The latter was printed on paper that felt like toilet paper, and for me – well, that was more or less what much of the content was suited to. *Martial Arts Illustrated*, I felt, was the more serious magazine, focused on giving coverage to more freestyle, semi-contact-style fighting – and later adding MMA coverage – as well as staying true to, and promoting, the traditional arts, and martial arts cinema.

I had met the editor, Bob Sykes, back in early 1997 when I visited him at his offices, in my first unsuccessful attempt to carve out a writing career following my first trip to America. When I tried to visit the magazine offices in Huddersfield, West Yorkshire, I had a rather difficult time finding the premises, which were located in a rather obscure building in the town centre. To get to the offices you had to go upstairs and through some corridors and doors. They were hidden away as if it was a CIA or MI5 building that no one could figure out or penetrate. There wasn't even a sign on the door to identify the business, it seemed, but eventually I found it, and there inside was a different story.

As I walked into the offices, one thing that immediately caught my attention was all the magazine covers adorning the walls. Bruce Lee, Jean Claude Van Damme, Chuck Norris, Steven Seagal and Jackie Chan graced the covers of my favourite monthly magazine, large as life. It was quite something to know that this was a magazine I was about to work with.

I met Moira Spencer, the advertising director, first. Moira and I had spoken several times a couple of years earlier when I was advertising, and she was very friendly. Bob also made me very welcome. I found him to be a really down to earth and humble individual. These days, Bob looks like a prisoner of war, as dramatic weight and muscle losses, grey hair and a couple of hip surgeries have had a profound impact on his deteriorating body. But in those days he looked healthy and physically fit and solid.

Five years later, I reconnected with Bob and he offered me a regular slot in the magazine, kick-starting my writing career. Several years earlier, in 1998, I had submitted two articles on Bruce Lee to *Black Belt* magazine in America, for which I received cheques in dollars through the post, which had been amazing to me as a 22-year-old. But this was my first big break, when my journey as a journalist began. I had become an official member of the combat sports press and felt a sense of validation. I would finally be writing about the subject I felt the most passion for. I thought it couldn't get any better.

I was wrong.

This was merely the beginning, a platform and a stepping stone that would lead to even bigger and better things. I started out by conducting interviews, which eventually became my forte. Fans are interested in finding out what famous fighters and athletes have to say. I know this because I was a fan and enthusiast myself. So, in the beginning my primary focus was on conducting interviews with prominent fighters and figures in the world of martial arts, and I did my best to get as much out of them as I could. Working with the monthly magazine gave me an opportunity to hone my craft, meeting and interviewing dozens of people, including many who trained with and were close friends and associates of Bruce Lee. My official position, as a columnist, afforded me a platform to connect with these individuals who were part of the legend's history, first-hand witnesses to the Bruce Lee phenomenon.

Most editors have substantial experience as journalists and a good grasp of the magazine and their industry. To be an editor of a specialist publication, you need a huge amount of knowledge and experience in that subject area. And on more than one occasion, I told Bob that he was the best martial arts magazine editor in the world – and I meant it.

Editors can be difficult people to work with. They have their own vision and a lot of the times a writer receives rejections. Bob, however, would always accommodate me and my ideas. It was as if he felt he had a moral duty towards his writers and the people featured in his magazine. Yes, Bob was sometimes too affable, and allowed many martial arts experts and businessmen to promote their own products, but everyone who met him developed an affinity with him. He knew everyone in the martial arts fraternity, and inspired reverence from these authorities on the deadliest arts known to man. Part of his appeal was his non-political approach. He refused to get involved in the petty squabbles that often become a hindrance in martial arts circles. Despite his position – a position that most individuals in the trade could only aspire to – Bob was gifted with a quality that most lacked: he seemed to genuinely help people. And the role he played gave him enormous power and pride.

In the literary world, making it is not easy. People are always happy to call themselves 'writers', but being a 'published writer' is a whole new ball game. It's the same with a fighter – people who merely train aren't true fighters unless they actually competes or fights. I have always, without a shadow of doubt, acknowledged Bob and his magazine for giving me that big break. All I wanted was to prove myself worthy of the opportunity.

***

Bob and I had an amicable working relationship from the moment I joined the magazine. In fact, he became one of my best friends from the world of combat sports, a friendship which to this day has endured. Sure, he pisses me off sometimes – all editors do from time to time – but I'm sure I piss him off more than he does me.

I always felt Bob had the best job in the world as a matter of fact. Popping into the office about three times a week, spending about 30 minutes there on each visit, picking up his papers, shoving them in a bag – often a black bin bag – and spending the rest of his time working from home was his weekly routine. Bob is an old-fashioned guy. He didn't believe in briefcases, or even own one.

Sometimes I'd visit Bob at his house, which was about 15 minutes from Huddersfield on the outskirts of a small village called Linthwaite. Huddersfield gave me a taste of West Yorkshire, countryside living, a region full of amiable people. I would always look forward to the drive down, which took 35 minutes and then another ten minutes of off-motorway driving to get into the sleepy countryside town. More often than not I would spend more time at Bob's house than in the office. The place Bob lived in looked like a bungalow from the outside, but it was a good place, and very comfortable. As we sipped tea in his living room – Bob, unfortunately, did not make good tea – we would converse and he'd start taking the piss out of somebody he'd just had dealings with. That was his style, but whether it was me, fellow columnist Andy Staton or some other martial arts personality, it was all done in good humour.

Actually, sometimes Bob took things too lightly. Sometimes you'd be faced with a dilemma, and be unable to gauge whether he was serious or pulling your leg. And when he pulled your leg, he had the capacity to tear it off if you drifted into believing what he spewed out.

'I should marry Shannon Lee, Bruce Lee's daughter, and carry on the family tree,' he used to joke with me. I feel he would've made a good comedian. In his less humorous moments, he eventually started to complain to me about martial artists using him, trying to squeeze favours out of him. Although he was always willing to accommodate, he got to a stage where he was stressed out and felt used. At one point he told me he'd simply had enough of doing his job – after all, he'd been at it for 25 years. I joked with him, saying I was going to steal his job, a job I'd have loved to have at the time despite having reservations.

When I wasn't making my memorable visits to see Bob, I spent an inordinate amount of time talking with him on the phone. It wasn't long before I fell into the habit of ringing him at 10pm, which he didn't mind. I always worked anti-social hours. The only time he would find me infuriating was when I rang him when he was in the middle of watching his favourite TV show, *Deal No Deal*, in the evening. He would rant and rave saying I was disturbing him. I don't know why he was hooked on this show; it was mundane as hell.

At that time, besides the martial arts specialist press, no other media was seriously offering coverage to the UFC. Those who were astute enough to see the benefits of cross-training continued to appreciate the rise of MMA, but, in sharp contrast to these more open-minded exponents, the ardent traditionalists often felt it was a bad look for the martial arts to promote such a bloody spectacle. Take into account, too, that the advent of the UFC exposed some traditionalists, as far as the effectiveness of their own approaches went. Many of the traditional arts became the target of derision as the more practical styles prevailed, with fans wondering why they were so unsuccessful inside the cage. Bob, for his part, didn't quite warm up to MMA as much as he, I feel, should have done. And he actually made this known to me. Maybe he felt it was too violent, or he felt it lacked traditional arts within its framework. I think it was this combination. Still, his own distaste didn't stop him from promoting MMA in the magazine and giving the public what they wanted. It was a natural evolution.

Aside from his prestigious position in one of the most well-known magazines, what set Bob apart from other martial arts and sports magazine editors is that he was an active competitor, meaning that he had a broader outlook and understanding of the arts than most of the armchair authorities in his field. In fact, he had given world champion, Bill Wallace, a good go in an exhibition fight in 1987 – two years before the magazine first hit the shelves. Wallace, who would be a co-commentator on the first ever UFC and who had trained Elvis Presley's daughter and even battled Jackie Chan in *The Protector*, was no joke. He was among the best world champion fighters, and could really fight. Bob didn't rest on his laurels after his retirement from competition, either. He would often invite top martial arts exponents to train with him before a photo shoot and interview. Not many magazine editors do that.

* * *

As time went by, I started working for other magazines published by the *Martial Arts Illustrated* stable. They had several magazines, including *Impact: The Global Action Entertainment Magazine, Horse Riding, Combat & Survival, Equestrian*, and later *MMA Uncaged*. *Impact* ran for 15 years, and I was a regular contributor for three. *MMA Uncaged* used me as a columnist/contributing writer for five years.

The martial arts press really surfaced back in the early 1970s. During the kung fu boom of the decade, publisher and entrepreneur, Felix Dennis, launched a poster magazine aptly named *Kung Fu Monthly*. Although I wasn't around at the time of the boom, later I got my hands on some of these classic out-of-print magazines. Back then Bruce Lee had exploded on to our screens and people in the West were going kung fu crazy. Felix jumped on the bandwagon and in addition to the magazine produced some booklets on the kung fu star. Felix and his business partner were small-time publishers who had become bankrupt, but as Bruce Lee emerged he reignited a flame, saving them from debt.

'Our salvation came in the form of a Chinese martial arts athlete called Bruce Lee,' Felix recounted in his autobiography. '*Kung Fu Monthly* was born in 1974, and within six months there was £60,000 in the bank. We were rich beyond our wildest dreams. Every day sacks full of postal orders from Bruce Lee fans would arrive in locked Post Office bags, deposited in our Goodge Street hallway by a postman who refused to lug them up the rickety stairs.' The enormous success of the eight-page poster publication lead to the licensing of foreign editions. At its height *Kung Fu Monthly* was being published in 14 countries and in 11 languages.

I tried tracking down Felix at one point for an interview, to get him to re-live the Bruce Lee boom with me. Instead I got to speak to a member of staff, Bruce Sawford, who had been the editor of *Kung Fu Monthly*. He told me that Felix had made a lot of his money from computer magazines. This is the same publisher who publishes *Men's Fitness* and the defunct *MAXIM* magazine. But *Kung Fu Monthly* was one of the first martial arts magazines it had nothing but King of Kung Fu plastered all over it. What really struck me was the history of it all.

There was a photo-frame shop near where I lived and I often popped in. While talking to the owner one day, I came to learn that he was a martial arts enthusiast and had collected the *Kung Fu Monthly* copies back in the days. He had a photocopier in the shop and was kind enough to photocopy his precious collection for me. No way in hell was he going to give me his original collection. It was his treasure trove and he refused to let his 'babies' go. He was a smart man, because nowadays a single copy can fetch hundreds of dollars.

* * *

TO THE TOP

Although my main love was Bruce Lee, like many people growing up in the 80s I had spent part of my childhood watching Jean Claude Van Damme, the Muscles from Brussels, perform helicopter kicks on the screen. I'd even attempted them myself a couple of times, but one of my friends could replicate Van Damme's kick perfectly. So, in 2005, when I heard that Bob was going to be hanging out with the Hollywood martial arts star, I wasted no time calling him up.

Known for his mood swings and out-of-character attitude, Van Damme has had more than his fair share of drama off screen. At least once, the actor's grandiose attitude got him into a physical altercation. A known martial artist and bodyguard to the stars, Chuck Zito, knocked out the action movie star in a New York nightclub with just one punch. He had lived the celebrity lifestyle, which goes with drinks and drugs and everything else that often comes with it. Once, when I attended an exclusive event, on stage he kept on sniffing as he talked to the interviewer. On another occasion he walked out of a TV interview in Australia after complaining that the questions he was being asked were boring. 'It's difficult for me to answer those questions,' he complained, 'so I start to sweat and I don't feel good because they are boring.'

Bob's friend Jon Jepson, a martial arts instructor and businessman, managed to secure a tour with his childhood idol. It was quite the trip. Jon, Bob, me, the editor of a rival martial arts magazine – who was a friend of Jon's – and several others, jumped in a fleet of BMWs with Van Damme and his then partner, and some bodyguard for the drive from Derby, Burton-On-Trent and then London. Bob spent the bulk of the time in back of the X5 telling me what a twat Van Damme was, and the rest of the time on his phone texting a lady friend and making derogatory comments about the fallen star. Bob had, in his previous encounters with the star, fallen victim to the karate champ's attitude. To say that JCVD had an ego the size of an elephant would be keeping it light. Bob was always a cheerleader for the underdog and detested show-offs, which meant that he had no time for Van Damme. Now, I'd be able to witness his behaviour myself.

ENTER THE JOURNALIST

Sure enough, Van Damme was a demanding diva from the start. When we were all at the hotel relaxing in the reception area, Bob realised the actor was treating Jepson like shit. There had been a problem with transportation somewhere beforehand, and Van Damme was kicking off. Van Damme was no longer in the top ranks of Hollywood by this point; he was a fallen star but seemed to still act like he was the dog's bollocks. Treating people with dignity should be part of every true martial artist's character, but apparently Van Damme never got the memo.

In this world, if you want to be liked by others, it's good practice to actually treat them well. It doesn't cost money. Bob embodied this behaviour, and tried his best to keep our spirits up, but it was an effort from the off.

When I told Bob that we should pose for a photo with Van Damme, he told me not to bother. Like I said, he had dealt with him several times in the past and knew exactly what he was all about when it came to treating others. Besides, Bob was never star-struck. As a loyal friend, I gave up on my quest to pose with Van Damme. However, Bob had brought along a young man, Nikol Gojka, who he had adopted from Eastern Europe who was a big Van Damme fan. So he wanted to make sure the kid got to meet his hero. He did and was over the moon. Mission accomplished!

On the tour, the Muscles from Brussels was embraced by screaming fans who were treated to inspirational speeches and a little demo, which I found rather mundane. In London it was a black-tie dinner with a karate tournament attached. For a couple of days' work the actor bagged a substantial sum of money. From what I know, he was in need of it.

* * *

The martial arts action star was lucky enough not to get a pasting by someone while on the tour. He had come close years earlier when one of Bob's friends attacked Van Damme. The first time Bob encountered the Belgium-born star was back in the early 1990s when the star did a photo shoot to coincide with the release of one of his movies. So Bob had already dealt with him when he was part of a wave of martial arts-turned-movie stars and at the height of his fame. One of the most bizarre incidents took place in London when Bob, his brother Tony, martial arts journalist Bey Logan, and friend Nirman Sahota Singh, went down to London to meet Van Damme, who was doing a press junket. The meeting and a photo shoot had been prearranged.

When Van Damme walked into the room with his entourage, Bob and his crew proceeded to greet him and exchanged a few friendly words. But Nirman had devious plans up his sleeve. This, he felt, was a rare opportunity to make a name for himself. As Nirman moved towards Van Damme to greet him, he kicked off and went for him, charging like a lunatic and making a high-pitched noise. This maniac couldn't speak properly because he was dumb and deaf, but he was certainly quite aggressive in his attack. Van Damme, dressed smartly in a nice suit, despite being mystified, reacted spontaneously, throwing a side kick out to intercept the oncoming assault. He flicked the kick out real fast and held it out, stopping his attacker in his tracks while barely touching him. He was quite vulnerable to attack because he didn't have bodyguards, but he certainly held his own.

'Everyone was shocked,' Bob recounted. 'Nirman didn't think Van Damme was that good, but on the day he showed how good he was with that lightning-fast kick, and he held it out.' Nirman's temperature dropped on the spot and everybody else just clapped. 'We were all shocked at what Van Damme actually was – the real deal,' Bob told me. 'You thought he was just a movie star, but you could tell he could move.' Truth be told, Bob admits he hadn't been convinced about the martial arts actor's credentials prior to this incident. Bob and his brother, who was also a martial arts champion, weren't into the action showbiz razzmatazz, and martial arts movies were never really their cup of tea. When one of Bob's closest friends and martial arts champion, Buster Reeves, originally from Huddersfield, invited him to his wedding in America, Bob declined. Among the guests there would be some heavyweights from the Hollywood crowd, but it didn't mean anything to Bob. Buster was a big Hollywood stuntman and rubbing shoulders with the likes of Brad Pitt and Tom Cruise, but Bob couldn't have cared less.

Anyway, Van Damme shook off the incident. But unbeknownst to him, he was in for a second surprise – round two. Nirman wasn't quite satisfied and yearned for his two minutes of fame. After the professional photo shoot was over, Van Damme agreed to have a picture taken with his attacker. To aggravate matters further, the Huddersfield madman flicked out a sneaky spinning back kick, which just missed the star's head. Again, Van Damme laughed it off. Nirman's foot had just skimmed pass his head. 'I think what Nirman tried to do was he was trying to hit Van Damme in the head,' Bob recalled, 'but he just moved out of the way with good reflexes.' Well, he'd had his two chances now. It's an experience Nirman could take away with him and cherish for the rest of his life and boast about over a pint in his local drinking establishment, even though he couldn't land a blow on the action star.

Nirman was a street fighter who used to sometimes get into three fights a night, apparently. That's a hell of a number of fights in a day. Making it into the local paper was a regular occurrence. Only a few years before his death he made it into the newspaper for running around in the street with a samurai sword like a lunatic. The story made front-page news. I guess he got what he craved – fame and attention. I was falling over laughing when Bob was telling me this story. *This man is a lunatic*, I thought. 'He was mental and a dangerous man,' Bob said. 'Van Damme sorted him out. Nirman was lucky to survive. If Van Damme had hit him with that kick, well, he's got super control.'

On the way back home there were further tensions as Bob and the crew were quite mean to their fame-seeking friend. 'We ripped up his train ticket on the way home,' Bob told me. 'He was fighting all of us.

So we did that. And then he started banging on the side of the train so they had to stop the train. The staff told us off.' I could listen to Bob's adventures in the martial arts all day long. Having experienced so much and dealt with so many people, he could really tell a story. There was never a dull moment with Bob the Ninja.

CHAPTER EIGHT

UFC ASSIGNMENT

NOW THAT I had settled into my role with the magazine after the better part of two years, it was finally time to experience a little of the jet-set life style some journalists hope for. In 2004 I flew over to Los Angeles – my fifth trip to the City of Angels, but my first in the capacity as a columnist. This time, I was to meet up with Royce Gracie again, and interview him. The last time I had seen him was in 1996 when I was training with him at the world-famous Gracie Academy. This time I was staying in Santa Monica, the beachfront area in western Los Angeles. After settling in, I phoned Royce's office from my apartment and left a message and my phone number. Royce's admin was done by an assistant his now ex-wife Marianne's office. Marianne was a podiatrist and she said we could arrange a time for the three of us to have lunch.

Later that evening I received a call from the man himself, in great spirits, and the next afternoon I made my way to Marianne's office in the Hermosa Beach area. There, a tall, bald man wearing dark blue jeans and a blue T-shirt walked up armed with a radiating smile and shook my hand. I got the impression that Royce was half-asleep. Given the non-stop nature of his travel schedule, I assumed he was jetlagged. After all, he spent six months of the year flying around the world on seminar tours spreading Gracie Jiu-Jitsu. Still, jetlagged or not, it was great to see him again. As we settled in for a chat what immediately caught my attention was the fact that he was much friendlier and more relaxed compared to the Royce Gracie I had known eight years earlier. He had been living life to the full and exuded confidence and positive energy. I never sensed the ego that some famous personalities possess – to be honest, you rarely see it from real fighters – but now, with the pressure of his fighting career gone, Royce was happy and in great humour.

We sat down for a long chat. I had endless questions to throw at him. Perhaps the one I was most curious about what went through his mind when he faced a 250-pound muscular guy who was ready to tear him apart?

'The mind is blank,' he told me, after thinking a little. 'I think he's more concerned about it than I am. He's the one looking across the ring and seeing someone much stronger, much faster than him. He's the one who sees a monster.'

Wow, I thought, *he is super confident*. Royce is far from intimidating. His fluid, non-aggressive style and calm demeanour is something that always put a smile on my face, and it all came from a guy who could walk the walk. I think this is one of the reasons why so many found him intriguing – he was a normal-looking guy who could rip a monster's head off with ease. In the Octagon, he always looked at home, calm, even amid the storm. If you look at the earlier UFCs, he's utterly focused, and completely determined.

Still, now that grappling was more widely understood, did he believe that a weight advantage played a pivotal role in the art of grappling? 'My next opponent is 490 pounds,' he laughed, 'That's a lot of stones.' If both fighters know the same technique, and have the same level of technical skill, he explained, then whoever is faster and heavier will win. It had been almost nine years since he had exited the UFC, and now he was fighting in Japan, set to face the giant sumo fighter Akebono. Much as I revered his technique, I just couldn't get my head around how he was going to submit this giant. It just wasn't plausible. From our conversation, it seemed that I feared for Royce's safety more than he did.

Another thing I had always been curious about was whether Royce had ever encountered any real-life incidents in the street outside the professional arena or at the academy. 'Have you ever come close to a fight because someone recognised you from the UFC or wanted to make a name?' I asked him. Again, he responded with brimming confidence, 'No, never! People read on my forehead "Don't fuck with me",' he said, laughing. Royce's siblings and cousins have been part of countless street fights – Rickson, Relson and Renzo are the tough nuts of the Gracie clan – but Royce is more of a gentleman. Not that I doubted that this professional fighter, who has dedicated himself to years of study and training, would accept defeat at the hands of an average man on the street. The Gracie family embody the warrior spirit of being willing to fight anyone, and their philosophy of life has inspired me profoundly.

Why did Royce exit the UFC? This was simple. He left the world's most prodigious battleground in 1995, after they started to implement rules. He also admitted that MMA had evolved and everybody was cross-training, wrestlers were knocking people out and kickboxers choking people out. 'I think the competition has got much better,' said Royce. 'The guys are better prepared and more versatile now, even if I cannot say they've got bigger.'

Royce was in the middle of a training camp so I was keen to ask him about his typical training schedule and was impressed when he shared it. His day started at five in the morning. He left the house at 5.30 and did his first training from six until 7:30. Fight strategies would be drilled with three training partners, grappling for five-minute rounds with a two-minute rest between each round. After this gruelling session he would go home, have breakfast, sleep and rest for an hour. Then, at around 11, he hit the weights for an hour or hour and a half under the watchful eye of his conditioning coach James Strom – former strength coach for the tennis superstar Serena

Williams and the American football team the Los Angeles Rams. Then it was lunch, rest and at six in the evening stand-up training, again for an hour or hour and a half. A couple of times a week he'd run and ride the bicycle. 'I take a lot of ice baths to put the body together, too,' he laughed.

Despite all the fame and fortune Royce had garnered, he didn't really seem to have a chip on his shoulder. He certainly didn't act like a tough guy throwing his weight around. Whether he was engaging with a famous fighter or a celebrity, sharing a platform professionally or on a social level, or meeting fans, I never witnessed anything that gave me the impression that he felt he was above people. Being able to mix with people, devoid of ego, is something which really elevates the respect I have for Royce, and any other champion for that matter. In fact, he actually once said to me, 'I know where I come from. I don't let it get to my head.' Take into account that he came from a badass family that was famed in Brazil, where their father was treated like a sports hero and his siblings were revered also. Some people perceive Royce and the Gracies as being arrogant, but outside the fight environment they are great human beings. It was a great feeling reconnecting with the legend and was the initiation of what would be a fruitful friendship.

* * *

Being an enthusiastic student, whenever I flew over to Los Angeles I would arrange to train one-on-one with Royce, if it was possible. Back then he taught out of a friend's modest martial arts gym called Nando's Hapkido, which was in Redondo Beach. Eventually, he moved his base and was teaching private lessons at Evaldo's Brazilian Jiu-Jitsu Academy in Long Beach. From my first experience at the Gracie Academy onwards I've learned that not only is Royce a great fighter, and extremely confident warrior, but also a great teacher. He has the ability to disseminate information that is easy to absorb and follow, and he always emphasises the importance of rudimentary techniques.

UFC ASSIGNMENT

He really exemplifies a teaching of Bruce Lee's: you should fear the basic technique a man has practised 10,000 times.

The next year, in 2005, I met up with him again. Royce often picked me up from my hotel or apartment as I didn't drive in Los Angeles, and would drop me off after the training sessions. *How many world-famous fighters and champions would do that?* I thought at the time. Once when I was taking a private lesson, a skinny, 22-year-old named Xavier, who was his brother Robin's neighbour in Spain, had come over to train. This lanky guy was far from being physically imposing. Furthermore, he was not physically strong in the pure sense of the word, and as Royce said, 'He can't do two push ups.' I was on the mat, and this guy gave me a real hard time on the ground. His skill and technique had been honed to perfection. He'd been diligently mastering the art and training for years. I had already learned not to judge anyone when I had trained at the original Gracie Academy, let alone in the fight game, but this guy was good! He knew how to distribute his weight and use leverage. Royce always taught that smaller and weaker students can build a strategy and a game around the assets they have, and this young man epitomised the beauty of Gracie Jiu-Jitsu. It was inspiring and humbling.

With Royce, I always had fun rolling around and a good laugh. I would refrain from going hard, although even if I did I'd be destroyed by the champ. Men of his calibre had the capacity to control you like a little baby and literally wipe the floor with you. He could obviously submit me within seconds if he chose to, but never did he take advantage or go in hard to impress me. Back at the Academy, when I first trained with him, he was assertive, almost aggressive, when you didn't perform the technique the correct way after he had repeatedly explained and demonstrated it. But that was good because in order to instil discipline in the students, that assertive approach was almost imperative. At times, I remember, to me it felt like being told off by my parents.

On another occasion when I was training with Royce there were about half a dozen fire fighters in attendance, on an official training programme financed by a government department. Almost all of them were bigger and heavier than the Brazilian master. Again, just as I had experienced when I first trained with him at the academy years earlier, it was quite surreal whenever I saw people like that and a rather diminutive-looking Royce teaching these monsters. Royce's brother Relson – a veteran of 60 street fights – couldn't have put it better when he once said, 'The big strong guy goes to class. And he keeps getting tapped by the skinny, technical guy. It begins to change him. It makes him humble. That's what jiu-jitsu does to you. It makes you humble.'

On this day, Xavier, Royce and I finished our training session, walked over to the beach and did a short run. We also did a photo shoot on the beach for the magazine where I assisted. The Californian sunshine was in full glow, and the next stop was at Royce's physician. We jumped into his Jeep and drove down to his physician's office. 'Man, your body is like Bruce Lee's,' he commented as we made our way to the upper level floor in the lift. That was a compliment I almost blushed at, particularly coming from the legend.

Although I was brought up in the United Kingdom, I've always had a mixed accent – a British-Pakistani one. When I was a young kid, I couldn't say the number 'three'. I had a problem pronouncing it so I would avoid saying it out loud in school so as not to embarrass myself. I was always and still am very conscious about my accent. I can filter in and out of it consciously or subconsciously, and more often than not I have to consciously make that transition mid-conversation. I've often encountered people with an Asian background who didn't know me, and whenever I opened my mouth they got the impression that I was an immigrant. When I say that, I mean from Pakistan. A few even went as far as accusing me of looking for a British passport. Oh, yeah, I was off a banana boat according to one person. Anyway, on this day, Royce told me that he had a similar problem as far as

UFC ASSIGNMENT

not losing his accent. 'Look at mine, man,' he said. Royce never lost his accent even though he had been in America since 1984, just like Arnold Schwarzenegger never lost his. Watching *Sesame Street* on TV to get a better grasp of English was an avenue Royce took in his early years in America. He also picked up English from his nephews – Rorion's kids. Again, this humble man was ready to learn from anyone who had something to teach him.

* * *

I've never really believed in first impressions. You can't always judge a person from your first impression – that's my belief. I think it is preposterous to believe that first impressions will 'always' give you an empirical background. We more often than not perceive ourselves differently to how most people may see us, because of a picture that we allow to build up in our own head. Life is limited only by how we really perceive ourselves and feel everything about our being, and with each new experience in life you learn something new about yourself. And I was on this journey learning about life, ultimately through the martial arts and its most revered exponents and fighters.

If you contemplate for a minute, you will come to the realisation that you are the best source of information about your attitudes, beliefs and tendencies. In one sense no one is more qualified to know who you are, even if you are not cognisant about the mysterious, unconscious motives underlying what you gravitate towards – even though some do get it wrong sometimes. In fact, this statement is often contradictory because sometimes one has a false perception of oneself which can mean lacking the ability to value others. My education in the martial arts helped me embrace the 'never judge a person based on their outer personality' philosophy, because it's the easiest way to set yourself up for a shock. Big muscles or a skinny guy, the way he talks and carries himself won't allow you to discern a fighter's true ability. From my participation on a physical level as well as a writer, I've been around some of the most dangerous men in the fight world who you wouldn't even think were fighters. One of Bruce Lee's personal students, one of the most amiable people but a tough street fighter, the late Larry Hartsell, was often underrated. He's a perfect example. He was an affable figure and epitomised the gentlemanly, softly spoken individual. If there is anyone who seem to be unimposing it was Bruce Lee's original students – they hardly looked like fighters. But most of them, I believe, had the capacity to decapitate you with their lethal techniques as far as street fight encounters were concerned.

Having studied the lives of some of the toughest men and fighters in the world, I came to the realisation they, by and large, are very nice people. I had learned a lot in life from so many of these physical specimens whose vocation involved blood, brutality and violence. I remember way back when I was training at the Gracie Academy in Los Angeles, as a youngster with Royce, and also at another prominent world-renowned academy that was headed by one of Bruce Lee's personal students, I learned something salient – a lesson that would be embedded in my head for the rest of my life. At the Gracie Academy there was a bespectacled older-looking gentleman, a pleasant person who hardly looked like a fighter – he was far from formidable. But, boy, he could wipe the floor with you with his ground-grappling skills. His striking wasn't of a high standard, far from it, but he was an extremely efficient grappler who could eat you for breakfast. Then he'd have you for lunch and even dinner if you weren't careful. That's how dangerous and vicious he was. But he was always very polite.

What amazes me is that, despite the fact Royce is a top professional fighter, he has this nonchalant demeanour. However, the confidence he possesses in his fighting and technical ability is on another level. His bearing and look doesn't give the impression of him being a fighter, let alone the best fighter, but this slender-built man is as savage as they come. Don't let his friendly approach fool you. This man is one of the deadliest men you'll ever lay your eyes on. Your big mouth and muscles aren't going to get you anywhere, nor intimidate him. Royce's physical capability and mental strength is matched by very few. I soon learned that he is one of those people who refuses to be beaten; to beat him you have to kill him.

He once told me something that I found extremely thought-provoking, based on a conversation that he had had with his older brother, Rorion. He said to me, 'One time, my brother said to me, "In a perfect world, you wouldn't be a fighter." And I looked at him thinking, *After all I've done in the fight world!*' Royce went home contemplating and after a week phoned his sibling back. 'You're right, in a perfect world I wouldn't be a fighter,' Royce admitted to Rorion. 'I never had a fight in the street. I'm not a mean person. All my fights are won in kind of a nice way where I'm not pounding my opponent's face inside out. I don't have to. So, yes, in a perfect world I wouldn't be a fighter, but the world isn't perfect. However, if I want to be a fighter, I might as well be the best.'

There's a saying, coins always make sounds, but paper money is mostly silent. Royce Gracie is the living embodiment of this philosophy. This man doesn't need to act tough or talk trash. Been there, got the T-shirt, don't need to prove anything. As I often say, he's the most unlikely looking fighter to have come to prominence on the world stage in the fight world. In the street, the average person who doesn't know Royce, he is more likely to perceive the fighter as some below-average guy who's never had a fight in his life.

I believe there are two types of fighters. Firstly there's the big, rough-looking, mean, 250-pound fighter who looks like a ferocious beast. In contrast to this, there's the Royce Gracie type – calm demeanour, smaller, unimposing, an appearance that can easily be misleading to the eye and a person who's hard to antagonise. Even fighters of repute such as Randy Couture would fit into this latter category, though you'd certainly never mistake Randy for weak if you saw him in shorts!

Some of the greatest fighters don't look tough or give you the impression that they are tough. But deep down they are hard as an ox.

Moreover, I learned that some of these men were of a shy disposition, lacking certain social skills and confidence. But confidence comes in different shapes and forms. When you're in their arena you could bet your bottom dollar that these men could play with you like a baby. Being a combat sports journalist afforded me the opportunity to meet, interview, observe, interact with – and even train to a certain extent with – a multitude of elite exponents and champions, giving me the inside track on their behaviour and tendencies. I soon learned that professional athletes revered on the world, national, regional or even local stage, have a common denominator – respect and humbleness is ingrained in them by the training they undergo. I learned that when your value increases, you keep yourself silent and humble. These great champions do just that. They have the capacity to really incapacitate a mere mortal, but are good role models, because martial arts teach you ethics and respect.

On the other end of the scale, one also encounters those who are not even at amateur level, but are lost in their own self-hype and feel the need to prove themselves and put others down. This resonates mostly with the average wanna-be tough guy who is devoid of real martial arts skills and ethics. It's strange how the world works, or should I say how people's delusional minds work.

I learned that the worst fear in the world is of the opinion of others. The moment you are unafraid of the crowd, you are no longer a sheep. You become a lion. A lion never loses sleep over the opinions of sheep. The idea is not to let the behaviours of others destroy your inner peace. Still, I have had to contend with certain situations and didn't always embrace this philosophy, unfortunately. Remember, becoming dependent on validation from others means you are letting other people control how you feel, which in turn will create a rollercoaster of emotion in your everyday life. So it often becomes an inner battle. Craving validation from others is something which we have a tendency for. We want to feel smart, pretty, successful, cool, popular and good at things, and so on. Although sometimes validation will make you feel content for a while, soon you need a new fix.

UFC ASSIGNMENT

Showing off and proving yourself, why do we do that? Again, it's about craving validation from others and feeling content. However, this need for validation often shines through and that is why a thing like bragging seldom works. Instead of seeing the cool and successful person you are trying to project, people just see the insecure and needy person looking for validation, and your bragging falls flat. When athletes or fighters reach a professional level or are content and of a high calibre at an amateur level, they don't need validation. That's perhaps the greatest lesson I learned from Royce Gracie.

CHAPTER NINE

REALER THAN THE UFC

JUST BEFORE the UFC exploded on to the global stage, martial arts in Britain were going through a transitional phase – a revolution was taking place. The individual responsible for this was a Coventry-born-and-bred doorman and martial arts exponent named Geoff Thompson. Coming from a traditional martial arts background, the once-bullied teenager went on to study an array of fighting disciplines – Greco wrestling, freestyle wrestling, Thai-boxing, judo, boxing, traditional karate and several other martial arts systems. Eventually, he came to advocate what he referred to as the 'real approach'. He wasn't the biggest guy, and didn't even really come across as intimidating – until, of course, he switched on the red destruction button of his and you saw a whole new Geoff, ready to pulverise. In a quest to vanquish his own fears, he worked on the roughest doors in the country for ten long years – an odd approach to most, but one that certainly worked for him.

'I had a debilitating fear of violent confrontation,' Geoff said, 'so I became a doorman to confront my fears.' Thrown into the frontline of street violence, he soon realised that what worked in the confines of the dojo environment didn't necessarily work outside on the street. Consequently, he started to address real street-scenario drills in his dojo. The purpose of everything he taught was to survive a real encounter, eradicate the bullshit and embrace the raw street approach and mentality. To many traditionalists' horror, Geoff advocated shouting and swearing in his epic training sessions as he proceeded to add an element of realism that was all too absent in the confines of the dojo. He played out realistic scenarios with his students to get them to acclimatise to the street environment, so they wouldn't be overcome by adrenaline the first time someone got in their face. Only by stepping out of the comfort zone could one really get a 'feel' for what real fighting encompassed, Geoff would explain. After all, even the UFC had rules.

Everyone feels fear. Geoff, in particular, embraced it. He became known for broaching the subject of fear as much as for his brutal fighting tactics. Indeed, fear was at the forefront of his teachings, unlike most instructors, who spent time in merely the physical component or spiritual aspects of the arts. I found it compelling that the psychological aspects of violence, which play an integral role in confrontations, were the focus of this doorman, who had experienced the harsh realities of confrontations in what he referred to as the 'pavement arena'.

A big part of Geoff's teaching is that we can eliminate, or at least minimise, the fear within us when we know ourselves better. As the great Sun Tzu said, 'When you know yourself and your opponent, you will win every time. When you know yourself but not your opponent, you will win one and lose one. However, when you do not know yourself or your opponent, you will be imperilled every time.' You cannot elude fear altogether. For an athlete and exponent of combat arts, fear is infectious. Thus, the key is to understand, master and control it. Embracing and understanding psychology pertaining to savage, raw street encounters is essential. I soon came to the realisation that when it comes to fight psychology, I don't think you can get more of an expert than Geoff. He is a fight professor. Moreover, for me, he was one of the first people to really admit it was OK to have fear. And when I say this, I mean in all situations in life. 'It is easier to deny fear than admit it,' Geoff once said. 'One of our greatest fears is to admit when we're afraid.' When he documented his own life experiences and fights, instead of just talking about how he beat people up, he took a more honest avenue, confessing the fear he frequently experienced. On studying his work, not only did it dawn on me that it was perfectly fine to embrace fear, but also that it was OK to divulge to others that you had fear, that you were scared at one time or another, that you sometimes wanted to run from whatever situation was presented to you, not just in a combat environment but in life in general. This was an eye opener to say the least. I had grown up with people around me who, by and large, concealed their fears. The bravado and 'I am perfect' attitude was all too common. Fearing to fight, fear of losing, fear of embarrassment, fear of being subjected to verbal attacks, or any situation for that matter, was perceived as a huge dent in one's ego and pride.

Of course, Geoff also had plenty to teach about fighting. Violence was at the centre of Geoff's life as he fought his way through hundreds of street encounters, not losing once. Domestically, if you were seriously involved in the martial arts field and hadn't heard of Geoff Thompson, you were living on another planet. What I found equally gripping was his life story. How do you relate a doorman and street fighter with over 300 fights on his resume to the literary world? Firstly, as I mentioned earlier, never judge anyone from their look because appearances can be deceptive. I discovered that behind Geoff's brawn was an amazing intellect. Here was a martial artist and doorman who ultimately had wanted to become a writer ever since he was young. Yes, this may be hard to comprehend for some, and indeed he was surrounded by naysayers who screamed, 'People like us don't write!' Eventually, though, Geoff found his way, writing about his own tragic and painful experiences. Having started his journey working with specialist martial arts press and authoring books (writing more than 26 martial arts books) the doorman-turned-author transitioned into writing for more mainstream outlets culminating in articles being published in *The Times* newspaper. His transition into mainstream territory further resulted in churning out self-help tomes. As of today, he has written over 40 books. His crowning achievement was his autobiography, *Watch My Back,* which became a *Sunday Times* bestseller and really made him a household name. This fight psychologist even churned out scripts for short films, grabbing a BAFTA along the way. Now, you were talking my language. I could resonate with this man in more than one way. Geoff spent many years writing columns for martial arts magazines, and we both had several mutual friends including my editor friend Bob Sykes and the co-founder of Geoff's combat association Peter Consterdine.

But it was never a smooth ride. It was not all plain sailing. When Geoff attracted the attention of the martial arts fraternity, and not surprisingly the media as well, they made him out to be a controversial character because he provoked widespread outrage. Like anything else, you will always have the critics. Some people voiced their opinions, griping that he was advocating brutal violence. These people were missing the point though. Geoff never enjoyed violence for the sake of it. The concept behind his teachings was to address the realities of street survival and the fear factor.

In spite of his harsh critics, he garnered a big following in the martial arts circles. *Black Belt* magazine in America voted him the 'Number-One Self-defence Expert in the World', which is no small accolade. His influence was being felt across the pond as the UFC was being sold as a blood sport. In due course he got invited to America to teach alongside some top masters. It was interesting to see a man of his calibre praising and being in awe of some of these American martial arts legends, such as the Machado Brothers, who are cousins of the Gracie clan. It put everything into perspective for me in terms of the talent coming out of America.

Anyone looking for street fighting self-defence has to look no further than Geoff Thompson. He is part of those higher echelons of the martial arts world who defied the odds and triumphed.

TO THE TOP

Occasionally I would talk to him and update him on some of my work and he'd encourage me and appreciated it. Whenever I rang him or left a message, he unfailingly returned my calls and gave me his time. Geoff's philosophy of fighting and life and literary works heavily impacted my own life and how certain things unfolded for me. Just like him I left school with no qualifications. I, too, wanted to become a professional writer and author. I read voraciously, just as he did on subjects of diverse taste. Geoff's story is an inspirational one of a boy who had a crap job and scribbled on pieces of paper in the factory toilet because he was desperate to write. *Watch My Back* became one of the books which influenced me and so many other people.

As I was making waves behind the scenes in combat sport, I would encounter a man who is a giant amongst men. Residing not far from Geoff, he was involved in another sport, which more often than not was tarred with controversy, but also with martial arts and MMA.

CHAPTER TEN

THE GIANTS

FOR AS long as I can remember there has been a kinship between the martial arts and bodybuilding. Some alpha males take up a fighting art to prove their manliness, others are inclined towards pursuing the iron-pumping game, and more than a few do both in their quest to become the deadliest fighters they possibly can be. In the early days of the UFC, and even before, many martial artists trained only with their own bodyweight, or didn't do supplementary resistance training at all. But now, you'd be hard pressed to find a professional or amateur MMA fighter who doesn't incorporate some sort of weight training into his regime – it is part and parcel of a fighter's routine.

Two Canadian brothers, the late Joe and Ben Weider, are perhaps the most responsible for the current popularity of the once-mocked sport of bodybuilding. Joe, in particular, is widely acknowledged as being the founding father of this once-misunderstood sport. After coming across the name Weider when I was 13, I came to admire the brothers and what they stood for. Scouring the muscle magazines, I came to realise that a whole industry was built around the Weider name.

The Weider Brothers were born in a tough part of Montreal to Jewish parents who had emigrated from Poland. They had an impoverished childhood, and growing up in the 1930s these 90-pound Jewish weaklings were regularly picked on by neighbourhood hooligans. The slightly built Weider boys could hardly make it home from school without being beaten up or having insults thrown at them. Consequently, Joe tried to join a wrestling team, but was rejected by the coach, who feared he was so small that he'd get hurt grappling. Joe, however, wasn't going to give up, or even slow down. After picking up a copy of *Strength* magazine at a local newsstand, which would have only set him back a penny at the time, he started lifting weights to build his body up and feel strong. Being so poor that he couldn't afford real weights, he made a barbell out of an axel and a set of car wheels, and trained with them in his garage relentlessly.

This young, ambitious teenager merely managed a grade-school education because his parents didn't have the money to send him to high school, but it didn't matter to Joe. He had bigger dreams, and a vision that involved conquering the world and spreading the joy of physical strength to the corners of the globe. He became a magazine publisher at the age of 17, starting his empire from his kitchen in 1940 with a periodical called *Your Physique,* and continued his love affair with the sport as he religiously lifted weights, built his body, and entered early physique competitions. By the age of 18 this teenager, who had been the victim of local bullies for most of his childhood, became the strongest kid in the neighbourhood, a feat that led to his victory in Quebec's best-known weightlifting competition. The road to success wasn't without struggle and adversity for Joe, but this only inspired me more as I read about him. Joe's journey resonated with me – here was a man who developed an obsession for a physical pursuit and excelled at promoting something he loved.

One thing I can't quite believe about the brothers' business, however, is their apparent disdain for making a profit. 'Two things never entered my mind: that I was going to make money; it was never Joe's goal or my goal,' Ben said, in an interview before his death. 'What we did was because we loved what we were doing and we wanted to do it the best way. The other thing that never entered my mind was it wouldn't work – it has to work.'

For me, that's somewhat hard to digest. You're a businessman, and considering your background your goal does not include making money? Come on! I have dealt with many business people and believe me, the majority cite money as their number-one priority, no matter how much they love their work. I'm not saying every single one, but a large percentage fall into that category. Dana White loves what he does. He's been obsessed with the UFC, but as much as he enjoys it, I'm sure the billions it brings in are very important to him. On the flipside, Rorion Gracie, who, like the Weiders, had a vision to bring his sport to America, once said to me money was just a consequence of his work. He always maintains that his main objective is to promote his art and message. As for the Weiders, I believe there's an element of truth in Ben's words, but I think money was just as important as their passion.

Regardless, the bodybuilding brothers made their mark. Inspired by the chiselled physiques of actors on the screen, the public grew to embrace bodybuilding, just as Hollywood stars did the same. Action stars such as Sylvester Stallone graced the cover of *Muscle & Fitness*, and Arnold Schwarzenegger's best friend and Mr Olympia winner, Franco Columbu, was assigned to train the star for his second outing as John Rambo. Judging by Rambo's physique, Franco did a commendable job. Stallone looked ripped and huge, but I was still most envious of Bruce Lee, who had embraced the benefits of bodybuilding and working out with weights, leading the way for future action-actors to follow. Bruce not only looked great, but had a physique that was functional enough to make it completely believable when he dispatched a whole herd of men with his fists and feet on the big screen. A resident of Los Angeles, Bruce himself made trips to Joe's muscle store in Santa Monica to purchase protein powders. As pumping iron became a cool thing to do, music rap stars pumping iron and displaying their chiselled frames in the music videos inspired the younger generation.

These role models were associated with bodybuilding, as were athletes from a wide spectrum of sports.

Building muscles and fitness can be closely associated with almost all sports that require the body to perform when exhausted. As I mentioned earlier, the modern-day gladiators, MMA athletes, implement weight training, as do fighters competing in any combat sport. Building that quality muscle mass, which will increase your power in striking and grappling techniques, aids overall precision and technique, improves stamina and endurance, makes the body fitter and boosts performance. There had long been the negative belief that big muscles impede a fighter's movement and speed. This myth has to be put into perspective. Athletes have their goals in mind when working out with weights, which they do not to build massive muscles but to achieve specific aims.

Pop your head into any well-equipped MMA gym and you will see state-of-the-art equipment, including kettle bells, medicine balls, all sorts of benches and weights and weight resistance machines, heavy ropes, even a gigantic tyre that MMA fighters flip, and a big hammer to develop your body power. Experts agree that athletes around the globe benefit from using weights. And although there will always be controversy surrounding bodybuilding, there is no doubt that the benefits that can be derived from training with weights are huge.

* * *

Although my primary focus was covering fight sports, bodybuilding was another area I felt I could venture into. Because there has long been a kinship between the two endeavours, I could relate to it quite easily. Whatever area I moved into, I set my bar high. I started to branch out and to contribute to *Muscle & Fitness* occasionally, while maintaining my position at the martial arts periodical. I had heard of the bodybuilder Dorian Yates way back in 1990. What made this champion different to the other elite, iron-pumping physique champions? Well, essentially, the sport of bodybuilding was American. If someone told you they were going to rule the bodybuilding contests but lived outside America, then you'd laugh at the thought. Dorian was British. He lived in a city called Birmingham, which most Americans had never heard of. Mr Olympia had always been won by the Americans; this was where the champions trained or came from and the rest were relegated to 'also ran' category.

But 'The British Bulldog', as he came to be known as, broke the mould, proving what one can achieve if one puts one's mind to it. This giant became a pioneer, a leader, the best bodybuilder in the world, and achieved the coveted title of 'one of the all-time greats'. I knew Dorian was a martial arts and Bruce Lee fan. So that's one thing we had in common. He had trained in karate as a young teenager before making the conscious decision to pursue the iron-pumping sport. Back in 1995 I had actually tried to contact him. I somehow got hold of a number for his gym and phoned up. Being an ecstatic teenager, I wanted his input on Bruce Lee after I had read a piece on the late martial arts master in which Dorian was quoted. At the time I was just a crazy fanatic. I guess the guy on the other end of the phone didn't pass on my message because I never heard from the man himself. Or if he did, the champion may have dismissed it as some fan looking for attention. He was at the peak of his career. I'm sure he had many ardent fans trying to contact him.

More importantly, I had always been curious about which professional bodybuilders Bruce actually meet and interacted with. Bear in mind that Bruce wasn't globally famous in the 1960s. One ironing-pumping legend he did meet was Bill Pearl, who gave him his training booklets. They met at Venice Beach and shared a mutual respect. 'He was very muscular, he was extremely agile and a tremendous athlete and I admire him,' Bill told me when I had an opportunity to interview him in 2009. I pressed Bill further after he answered a few more questions I chucked at him relating to Bruce. Sensing I was stuck in a time frame, he suddenly said in a somewhat sarcastic tone, 'He was God!' Needles to say the Bruce questions came to halt as I steered myself back to the bodybuilding questions.

Fast forward ten years from that first phone call to Dorian's gym, in 2004 or 2005 to when I officially arranged to meet and interview the six-time Mr Olympia winner in Birmingham at his world-famous Temple Gym, which was located in the heart of the city. I found the place without much trouble, although it was tucked away in a backstreet alley, the kind of bricked alleys with garbage bins you see in films set in New York City. When I arrived at this obscure location, I found that you had to go down the stairs into a basement cellar. It was far from a visually pleasing, modernised, well-equipped gym that people frequent. Instead, it looked more like a dark dungeon. As a matter of fact, it was nicknamed 'The Dungeon'. A year or so later, when I was at IFBB star Shawn Ray's house in California to interview him, I asked him if he had been to Dorian's gym. 'Is that what you call a gym?' he mocked. Well, Dorian may have trained in a 'shithole', as Shawn referred to it, but he proved you didn't need a fancy place and equipment to excel and become a champion. Sometimes training in such a gritty environment is actually beneficial. Training is rough, tough and torturous, and the environment you train in should reflect this.

The reception area was actually in the gym training space – it wasn't partitioned off. It wasn't the biggest gym. Anyway, I waited for the man to arrive. Adorning the gritty walls were the signed photos of famous bodybuilders and fitness competitors, which captivated my attention, and magazine covers adorned with Dorian's image. Dorian walked in some time later. He was holding a gym bag in one hand and shook my hand with the other as we greeted each other. He was shorter than I thought he would be, but he was very wide. I could tell, despite being retired about nine years before, that he still had good size on him. The beast looked the every bit the bodybuilder I'd imagined. I asked him if I could have a peek at his physique. He rolled his top up so I could see his abs and part of his pecs. His physique had diminished quite considerably, he said, but I told him he still looked good. Having met and worked with so many famous professional athletes and fighters, I had the ability to gauge their inner and outer personalities. Dorian is a very humble person. He's more on the diffident side and reserved end of the Richter scale. Some people, fuelled by their own ignorance and stubborn machismo, may have had a totally different effect. But he was welcoming. What he achieved in his sport is matched by very few.

We sat down and talked. The conversation leaned towards bodybuilding, his love for the martial arts and Bruce Lee and, of course, his involvement with a new sport that had changed peoples' perception of fighting – MMA. The piece that followed showed that martial arts had a crossover appeal. Being a fan of MMA, he trained in the sport for fitness purposes, he told me but he made it clear to me that he was no expert. 'I've always been interested in martial arts,' Dorian explained. 'I really couldn't pursue any other sport when I was bodybuilding because it's going to interfere with what I'm doing. If you want to be the best in any sport, you have to focus totally on that.' He was cognisant of the fact that if you dedicated too much time to activities and training that were not the core part of your main sport, your growth and performance could be hindered – getting side-tracked was inevitable. So, the interest in martial arts was always there for him. However, he had to walk only one path when he was a teenager. For him bodybuilding was the road he took.

His involvement in MMA training further invoked my interest, so I probed him with relevant questions curious about his answers. He told me how he had met the UFC legend, Ken Shamrock, in California, when he was out there in the mid-1990s. 'I had a friend who was a bodybuilder,' Dorian said. 'I trained him. He did very well in competition then went into the US Military and started doing MMA. He was training with Ken Shamrock at the Lion's Den. The UFC was starting in the mid-1990s. It just appealed to me.' Ken had told Dorian that he had participated in some small bodybuilding shows when he was younger, but he couldn't handle the dieting side of it. Ken had a great physique for a fighter, a physique that resembled a bodybuilder's. Dorian appreciated the physical torture these MMA athletes went through to excel in a bloody and brutal endeavour that not even the most muscular men could handle. 'The training and the dedication the guys put in; bodybuilding training is tough and the diet and everything makes it even harder, but this is a totally different type of training and I have a lot of respect for the guys because it's very tough,' he admitted.

After we finished discussing Ken, I was very curious to find out what his thoughts were on a skinny-looking fighter who had beaten the hell out of muscular and stronger giants. The man in question, of course, was Ken's nemesis and former three-time UFC champion, the one and only Royce Gracie. If I'm honest, I had no clue about what answer to expect from one of the best-built men the sport of bodybuilding had ever seen. But I was dying to get this question out and adamant I'd get an answer. Dorian said he was impressed by Royce very much. He said Royce showed that with technique you could beat someone bigger. 'Royce Gracie was one of the first guys in the original UFCs that I watched when I spent time in the States,' Dorian said. 'So I watched it when nobody over here really knew it. It was amazing to watch him beat guys double his size.'

Talking of MMA fighters and bodybuilders, the biggest bodybuilder in the world, Rich Piana, once told a prankster who was trying to pick a fight with him on the street, 'I'm not a fighter but someone who works out. A fighter is always going to be tougher than a bodybuilder.' Piana, a gentle giant and a huge fan of the UFC and the slender-looking Royce Gracie, once told Royce, 'I believe that the technique that you have, knowing the technique a certain way, I don't think it matters how strong I am. That if you have the right technique then you're going to be able to get me in an arm-bar regardless.' Royce explained that it was all about his opponent making a mistake, which he would capitalise. Furthermore, it was about using strategy in a fight, he'd explained to the humble bodybuilder. I've been on the end of a Dorian's choke and it only takes a second to tap out. I'm sure that had he pursued fighting he would have made a decent fighter. Mariusz Pudzianowski, five-time World's Strongest Man, has won 13 and lost seven of his MMA fights with one no contest.

Dorian's love for the martial arts has never faded. 'I do martial arts no-holds-barred because I like a challenge,' the six-times Mr Olympia told me. 'And I'm still doing the weights, but I've kind of changed that now from bodybuilding training to more functional stuff.' Cardiovascular training was boring to Dorian, but he found MMA training interesting because you're learning something and at the same time pushing yourself and elevating your fitness levels. He advocated that training with weights was a great way to accelerate one's potential in whatever sport you participated in. If you were a fighter, for example, if you could put 25 pounds of muscle, you would progress better, feel stronger and in turn improve your martial arts discipline. He said he could take me and put an extra 25 pounds or so and really enhance my martial arts progress.

'Now it's pretty much accepted that weight training can improve your performance in a whole variety of sports,' the intelligent former Olympia winner continued. 'I think people have seen what Evander Holyfield did, moving from cruiserweight to heavyweight, and he was trained by Lee Haney who was Mr Olympia. So the guy put on bodyweight in terms of muscle. He should have been much slower and less effective, but obviously he wasn't because he was knocking heavyweights out. Everybody is doing weights from tennis players, distance runners to athletes.'

At the time Dorian was working with some UFC fighters, advising them on the diet and weight training. Dorian was the first professional champion bodybuilder I interviewed and I eventually started contributing to fitness-related media not long after. I ended up doing some business with Dorian for a while.

CHAPTER ELEVEN

HOLLYWOOD, HERE WE COME!

FELLOW MAGAZINE columnist, friend and Bruce Lee historian, Andy Staton, and I would occasionally have long telephone conversations about Bruce Lee. One day when I rang him, somehow the conversation leaned towards the documentary film he had worked on in 1993, which was aptly titled *Bruce Lee: Martial Arts Master.* Andy was the technical advisor and credited as an associate producer on the project, and in this call I revealed to him that I'd like to produce another documentary on Bruce. To my great surprise he said he wanted to also. Now he had my undivided attention. Documentary production was foreign territory for me. I had no real idea of what exactly it entailed, but I was always keen to expand my skills and learn about an area that that would present potential opportunities for me to work on bigger projects.

Andy is one of those rare Bruce Lee authorities who never really put his financial interests on top of his list of priorities. If anything he is more likely to ignore monetary considerations altogether, willing to get involved for purely promoting Bruce's legacy for the greater good. That's what I love about 'Uncle' Andy, as I call him – he's doing it for the pure passion of it. For decades this man has promoted the legend and his legacy. He's been there for years, and is still going strong when most so-called authorities have lost interest. He ran a fan club, the

HOLLYWOOD, HERE WE COME!

Bruce and Brandon Lee Association, for more than 20 years before its membership waned to the point where he shut it down, and Bruce Lee fanatics apparently often inundated him with phone calls as if he was a celebrity. If only we had more Andy's in the world.

Andy has been a devoted follower of the renowned martial artist ever since he first encountered the majestic presence of the kung fu star in *Enter the Dragon*. I think, like myself, Andy was possessed by the spirit of the Little Dragon. The cultish fandom surrounding the late master has never wholly diminished over the decades and inspires an almost cult-like zeal among its most ardent fans. For a few years, my obsession led to an irrational fear that I would die at the age of 32 – the age Bruce had died – and as soon as I hit age 33, I was relieved. Nobody encouraged the same intensity of emotion as this charismatic fighter whose action sequences rendered the sometimes laughable dialogue in his Hong Kong-produced movies redundant. Andy, who felt the same way as I did, was the perfect collaborator, and now that we were both running on the same track, we agreed on potentially collaborating on a new film venture.

If there's one strength I have, it's my persistent approach. Once an idea makes its way into my head, no one's going to stop me from reaching my objective. It also doesn't require much for me to get motivated. I think I was born like this. I knew I was stepping into unusual territory with documentary production, but I wasn't afraid of, creating new challenges and embracing them; it's something I've done all my life. If there were none coming my way, I'd create new ones and grab them with both hands. Now, with this new project to focus on, I felt the first twinges of the high I always got from stepping into the unknown.

Producing a documentary is much more complex than it appears to many outsiders. It means getting the right technical people involved and securing financial backing, requiring endless phone calls and patience. Most documentary producers come up with a proposal and approach TV channels in the vain hope of getting their project commissioned. That's the norm. But that route never appealed to me. I never even entertained the idea of pitching the idea in the faint hope of receiving financial backing. I was accustomed to being in control of everything I did, doing things my way, and I wasn't going to change for anyone. This was my 'baby'. I wanted to make this a reality and wasn't prepared to play the waiting game and hear from a TV channel only to be left disenchanted when the project stalled in someone's inbox. The waiting game was never my thing, and anyway, 97 per cent of pitches are rejected. That's an awful lot of disappointed people. I wasn't going to join that queue, or invite defeat in the form of a potential rejection. I'd go it alone.

Besides, producing a documentary would put me on a whole new platform. Propagating Bruce Lee's philosophy and life story to the masses via the medium of film, I must admit, was something that hadn't entered my mind up to that point, as I'd always regarded it as somehow beyond me. But in life you evolve, explore and reach new heights. And it was time to do exactly that.

Going back to the film that Andy had been involved with for a moment, it was probably the best documentary film ever produced on Bruce Lee. I had been really impressed by it, and I thought it would be difficult to improve on as a straight documentary. For my newly conceived project, then, I envisaged a theme that would be slightly different. Author John Little's writings had inspired me ever since I picked up a copy of *Muscle & Fitness* magazine in 1993, in which there was a special pullout booklet written by Little, which focused on Bruce's bodybuilding secrets. In the piece he explained how bodybuilding luminaries, boxing champions and athletes from different sports all admired Bruce Lee. The message the author was trying to convey was that Bruce was not merely the greatest martial artist of the century, but was also a king among athletes and an influential figure to the stars of the action movie genre and beyond. I was enamoured with that concept. To me, this is what really set the martial arts exponent apart from his peers, and I wanted to explore the idea further.

HOLLYWOOD, HERE WE COME!

So, this was my plan: in addition to presenting the life story of the legend, legendary figures from other sports, including MMA, and the action entertainment industry would pay homage to the King of Kung Fu. It would be a first, I thought. Although several well-known personalities had expressed their appreciation for the late martial artist openly, I had never really seen major sporting figures paying homage to the great man on camera. So, with this added element as a hook, I had a strong conviction that this film would do the great master justice, and catapult his legacy to another level. I'd been inspired by his story, and now I'd found an opportunity to inspire others in the same way. This was my opportunity to take up the mantle.

While I would usually be inclined to go solo, this was intended to be a joint venture with Andy. But I was still planning to take control. However, if you know Andy you'll know that he has a weakness, which is that more often than not it takes him umpteen years before he takes the first step on a project. Constantly pushing him to get things done can get taxing. Sometimes I was surprised that he met his deadlines as a journalist. Having said this, he did have another full-time job at an education institute, which took up a lot of his time. Still, I knew I could not let the project drag on and rely on someone, especially when I was on a high and had such a strong concept, which I was concerned about being stolen. Having the idea transform itself into reality meant, I had to walk the path alone before it turned to dust. So, when he dallied on the project, Andy was out of the picture as fast as he had slipped into it.

* * *

Even when it's based on interviews, a project of this size requires a script. Why? Because using a script is a logical way to make a film. One of its chief aims is to communicate the concept of the film to everyone concerned, and the way it will flow. If the story wasn't strong enough, the project could be doomed even before setting sail.

TO THE TOP

So, scouting for someone to write the script was on the agenda, and I had just the right man for the job – or so I thought. The man I had in mind was one of Andy's former associates, a Bruce Lee historian. I was even willing to give this guy a further co-producer credit. I tried to get hold of him but it backfired in a surreal way. This individual's partner ended up complaining to Andy about me, saying I was trying to get hold of her partner. I'm glad I never brought this guy on board otherwise the ship would have sunk before leaving port. It would have led to total disaster. It suddenly dawned on me that this guy was one to avoid. The Bruce Lee world was infested with egos, backbiting and politics, something I was just starting to really understand. Anyway, it was his loss.

Enter Hong Kong! At my wit's end, I rang up Bey Logan. He has been a big Bruce Lee appreciator for most of his life. After beginning his career as a writer for *Combat* magazine, he moved to *Martial Arts Illustrated* and then became the editor at *Impact: The Global Action Movie Magazine*. He got involved with bigger things when he moved to the Orient, working at the Weinstein Company where he held the position of Vice President of Asian Acquisitions and Co-Productions, then moving into screenwriting and producing, and writing the screenplay for *The Medallion*, starring Jackie Chan. He was an ideal candidate to bring on board, and told me he'd do whatever he could to help. I also got *Impact* magazine's Far Eastern editor, Mike Leeder, involved. He is based in Hong Kong too, and served as Asian Casting Director for Brett Ratner's Jackie Chan flick, *Rush Hour III*.

I started to jot down notes on pieces of A4 paper, listing prominent personalities who I hoped to interview. First, I dipped into my ever-expanding contact list with all the direct and agency contacts I'd acquired in America. It always pays to reach out and expand your circle. One lady, who was a friend of a friend, and a close friend of Mike Tyson and Sugar Ray Leonard, sorted out an interview for me with the latter. She also threw a few more A-list names into the mix, including Tyson – who I would learn had a capricious personality –

HOLLYWOOD, HERE WE COME!

Jamie Foxx, and Snoop Dogg. Meanwhile, I found myself reaching out to some A-list celebrities across the Atlantic who had never been on camera praising the late martial arts master, which proved more difficult than I expected. I got in touch with Sylvester Stallone's PR team, Rogers & Cowan, the heavyweight PR talent agency in Beverly Hills, only to be rejected. Muhammad Ali was also on my list. I had someone promise me they would arrange a chat, only to find out later there was no substance to it. Even the governor of California, Arnold Schwarzenegger, was approached via his representative who I contacted personally.

After doing some leg work, slotting in interviews with various people in Los Angeles for September 2006, we were ready to fly out to Hollywood. But a fresh knot of anxiety gripped me as I was hit by another major problem requiring my immediate attention. Even though I had a standard visa, I learned that a media visa was required for the kind of work I planned to do in the States. Also, I had hired a cinematographer who would be flying out with us on our American adventure, but it was brought to my attention that his professional camera equipment would be liable for heavy tax and duty in America. I'm talking thousands of dollars. Running around like a headless chicken in the hope of solving this issue, I was hit by the realities of the intricacies involved in being a producer, as further frustration set in.

First, applying for a media visa was imperative, so I wouldn't risk being immediately ejected from America before I could even get out of the airport. I wasted no time in applying for one and went to the American Embassy with the cinematographer accompanying me. After sitting around for most of the day bored senseless, he walked out with his stamped visa, but I was told my visa would come through the post, pending further investigation. I waited, waited and waited more, but no visa. This was a problem. Flights had already been booked. Interviews were already arranged. We were ready to rock and roll. And now I couldn't get into the country.

Meanwhile, to get the ball rolling in the United Kingdom at least, I made a trip along with the cinematographer to Dorian Yates' gym in Birmingham to interview the bodybuilding star. Numerous IFBB champions are ardent admirers of the late master, who cultivated a phenomenal physique despite never entering a physique competition in his life. After the interview I offered an advance payment in the form of a cheque to the cinematographer. After he left he phoned me to ask if it was OK to pay him in cash instead. I had no problem doing that, I told him. I said to him to rip the cheque up and I sent him cash via registered post the next day. Big mistake!

Perhaps predictably, this guy went astray and ran off with the money. From that point, he would not answer the phone, or answer his emails. We've all been there. He had signed a legally binding contract, but now he was breaking this legally binding contract. After I inundated him with text messages I got a call from the police. The officer said that this man claimed I had been threatening him. I couldn't deny this because the officer had apparently seen the messages on the culprit's phone. Since the police were now involved, I decided to leave the matter there and walk away, although I was considering other courses of action that would have landed me in trouble. This guy took the piss – he was a professional cinematographer and had a good resume, but he thought he could default on the contract and make a dash with the cash leaving me in dire straits. His excuse was he'd spent a hefty chunk of time on research and making calls, and had already earned his cash. I thought, *£1,500 advance for all that?* I had figured there was something fishy about this bald, overweight guy from the off. When I meet someone or deal with someone, sometimes I get a feeling about them; I should trust my intuition. Well, this time I learned the hard way and paid a hefty price for it. It was an expensive lesson.

Fortunately, there was another lesson I'd learned much earlier in my career: always have a plan B in the bag, otherwise you're fucked. If you're a fighter, invariably there's a plan B strategy if plan A goes

HOLLYWOOD, HERE WE COME!

down the drain, and it's no different with business. So, for me, it was time to find a camera crew in Los Angeles. I was back to square one and it was driving me crazy. After checking out professional cinematographers, eventually I found a guy I thought I could trust. We agreed on the price for his services and stipulated the terms so there would be no misunderstanding or loopholes. I was ready to go as I no longer required a media visa because no camera equipment would be going with me. I wasn't going to take my chances and be burnt again, I thought. How wrong I was. Three crew members and I jetted off to Los Angeles on a rollercoaster journey that would end in despair.

* * *

By this point, I had been to Hollywood many times, so I was quite familiar with the place. We stayed there for two weeks in an apartment block on Sunset Boulevard in the heart of Tinseltown.

Problems started early. Robert Lee, Bruce Lee's brother, as well as Bruce's protégé, Dan Inosanto, were both scheduled to be interviewed at the Inosanto Academy. But becaue of unforeseeable circumstances, including third-party tampering, this didn't materialise. Still, it wasn't all doom and gloom, as I had managed to secure an interview with the great basketball legend, Kareem-Abdul-Jabbar, who also appeared in Bruce's half-finished martial arts epic *Game of Death*. This wasn't usually easy. Kareem is one of the greatest NBA players in history – some believe the greatest basketball player of all time – and was also NBA's all-time leading scorer, but didn't give many interviews. Excited, our team drove down to a Long Beach studio, which had professional lighting and backdrops, and waited for Kareem to arrive. His manager, Debra, worked out of an office there, but after so many setbacks I started to think that he'd had second thoughts about doing the interview. A sense of panic started to set in as I sat there with all kinds of emotions running through me, even as one of my crew guys consoled me, assuring me that Kareem would turn up. His words calmed me and I tried extremely hard to convince myself, even though at the back of my mind the ever-present 'enemy' kept telling me to prepare for the worst. I already had to contend with a plethora of problems and had no desire to add another one to the ever-growing list.

After a long wait, Debra walked over with a *Game of Death* laminated poster personally signed by the man himself. 'This is for you. Kareem apologises for coming late,' she said apologetically. It wasn't long before a serious-looking 7ft 3in giant in dark blue jeans and a light blue shirt sauntered towards us. We greeted each other and shook hands, then sat down and I proceeded with the interview. Interviewing Kareem Abdul-Jabbar is one of the highlights of my career – an experience I'll never forget. I had always seen him as the man who was Bruce Lee's celebrity friend and co-star, rather than a basketball player. Their shared screen time in the movie's climatic fight resulted in one of the greatest fight scenes ever to be captured on camera, a little man against a giant. But Kareem is more than that, and much more than any of his other minor roles. Kareem is one of America's sporting legends, and was a fascinating interview subject.

To my great surprise, he revealed that Bruce had a copy of the Quran in his personal home library. Although I knew that Bruce had amassed an extensive library, I was oblivious to the fact that he had a copy of this holy book. 'I gave Bruce books to read on Islam and Bruce knew Chinese Muslims,' Kareem told me. 'They have a lot of Wushu techniques that are unique to them and from the martial arts in Indonesia and Malaysia. He was aware of Islam, and he investigated different techniques from the Islamic part of China.'

For his part, the African-American athlete had converted to Islam in 1971 at the age of 24, just like his famous friend Muhammad Ali had seven years earlier. Kareem had been introduced to Islam in the 1960s when he was still a freshman at UCLA, by which time the basketball legend had already achieved a certain degree of national exposure and fame as an athlete. By the time I interviewed him, despite his elevated profile, he endeavoured to keep his private life private. Apparently, his celebrity made him disconcerted and nervous and this gentle giant felt timid in the public eye. During the course of his illustrious career he developed a reputation of being introvert and sullen, and despite becoming the NBA's all-time leading scorer he chose to shut out the world, including the fans, and focus on the sport he loved. He mostly refrained from speaking to the press, and I later learned that he froze out reporters who gave him a too-enthusiastic handshake or even physically embraced him. Moreover, during many interviews he refused to stop reading the newspaper, according to a source.

I was oblivious to much of this when our interview started, but it wasn't long before I couldn't ignore my interviewee's unique worldview. I can say with great conviction that he is one of the strangest celebrities I have ever met and interviewed. Long Beach has an airport, which is under one of the strictest ordinances in America on airport noise and the number of fights. Commercial flights are restricted, but there are many charters, private aviation flight schools and law and enforcement flights and helicopters operating from it, making it one of the busiest aviation airports in the world. So, we regularly had planes flying over the building, which meant the noise of the aircraft would inevitably intrude into the interview, and every time we heard a plane we had to stop the interview for a short period. This episode repeated itself several times and my interviewee would give us an upsetting frown each time. I was embarrassed, but also a little shocked at his attitude. I had heard Robert Lee saying in a documentary about his brother's co-star and celebrity student that he was really a very nice gentleman. Now I was thinking, *Was Robert seeing the same man that I'm talking to?* I couldn't understand the guy. It was embarrassing for me and I was beginning to feel a little uneasy.

As the interview resumed after one of these stoppages, I brought up the subject of modern-day icons such as Arnold Schwarzenegger and Sylvester Stallone, and asked Kareem if we will ever see another

Bruce Lee. 'I don't think Arnold Schwarzenegger and Sylvester Stallone really distinguished themselves in the same way as Bruc; they've only distinguished themselves as actors,' he replied. 'Arnold was a bodybuilder and he said he did it using steroids, and it's a thing which really doesn't get that much respect.' I got the impression Kareem had something against Arnold, but I didn't want to jump to conclusions. It was simply the tone he used and the expression on his face when answering this question that made me think something was amiss.

Another interesting fact that I learned while conversing with Kareem is that he really looked up to the Gracies. 'I think Bruce and the senior Mr Gracie [Helio Gracie] in Brazil were way ahead of everybody in understanding that the martial arts have to be pragmatic and useful – you just can't stick to one style above everything else,' he said. He went on to say that Bruce and Royce were unique and way ahead of their time, and did it by forming their arts around the concept of MMA. 'Bruce was very pragmatic. It's funny that Bruce was more of a boxer or striker, and Gracie was a grappler – you have to combine those two things to be a successful martial artist today,' Kareem said. The basketball star had been exposed to the martial arts way back in the 1960s and became a private student of Bruce's. When the Gracie's were making a name for themselves in the 1980s teaching out of their garage, they attracted the attention of quite a few professional sportsmen, including NFL and NBA stars, and so Kareem kept a close eye on their activities, I assume.

Interviewing Kareem Abdul-Jabbar was an interesting experience. I learned a lot. Off camera, he told me his daughter had studied at university in Ireland, and after we wrapped up the interview, I witnessed more of his bizarre behaviour. The manager asked her client if he could stay behind and sign some of the photos and memorabilia that fans had sent in. By this point, his manager knew that he was likely to get stuck in traffic as it was peak rush hour time, which is horrendous in Los Angeles, and suddenly that frown on his face was back. I watched the manager literally shake in her boots as if she wanted to ask her dad if she could stay out till late but couldn't spit the words out of her mouth. She was a nice, professional woman – she even told me that if I wanted a distribution deal in Japan for my documentary, she had contacts there and she'd help – but Kareem inspired respect in everyone.

***

I couldn't wait to tell my friend Diana Lee Inosanto that I had interviewed Bruce's one-time collaborator. I went to her house and when I told her, she said it had been so long since she'd seen him, back in the days when he was training with her Uncle Bruce and her dad. She decided to reconnect with the former LA Lakers star.

As always, it was good to see Diana. I would endeavour to make time for her and her husband Ron whenever I visited Los Angeles and we would go to dinner. I had been to their previous residence, but they were now living in another part of Los Angeles, Thousand Oaks. They had a nice home, but recently moved again.

Speaking of the house, one memory I'll cherish forever is when Ron slid in a *Game of Death* DVD, the scene where Bruce is fighting Diana's dad, Dan Inosanto, which of course turns out to be an epic battle. Alongside the Bruce–Kareem fight, this is one of the classic fight scenes in cinematic history, climaxing in a nunchaku-against-nunchaku battle between two of the greatest martial artists on earth. Suddenly I had goose bumps sitting there – it was pure exhilaration to watch this scene alongside the daughter of the man appearing in it. Dan was somewhat responsible for teaching Bruce some nunchaku techniques (although Fumio Demura, who was the stunt double for Mr Miyagi in *The Karate Kid* and who I once interviewed, also shared his skills with Bruce), and here I was at my friend's house watching her dad fighting Bruce Lee on the screen. It's something that you never really think about happening when you're younger. I could see that Diana was emotional watching the action unfold, and she eventually went into the other room. I could see how much she missed Uncle Bruce.

While there, we had to discuss a film project she was working on. Diana had made a transition into directing and producing, influenced by directors such as Guy Ritchie and Ang Lee. She had already written, directed, co-produced and co-starred in a new martial arts drama movie, so I was at the house to discuss both my documentary and her film, an indie film. Being her directorial debut it was a very important project for her. Diana's friend Louis Mandylor, known for *My Fat Greek Wedding* and the TV show *Martial Law* was to star in film alongside Keith David, who played the father in *Something About Mary*. Although it was an action film, it was also a thought-provoking drama, and, despite the fact the film was a low-budget deal, Diana was really passionate about doing it.

At the time they were scouting for investors to come aboard. Diana had clearly put all her effort and every ounce of her being into this project, as did Ron, who had lost weight with all the accumulated stress of making calls trying to get potential investors on board. We talked about potential investors as we sat at the house. One or two people came to my mind, and I later asked a millionaire I'd met who was a big fan of Bruce Lee, martial arts and MMA, but he flatly declined. As we talked, I started to think about my own aspirations of making more documentary films, and later, it dawned on me that I could possibly pursue further projects of this nature, perhaps by making documentaries about MMA.

Not everything, however, was going according to plan. To my regret I had introduced Diana to someone I had known for only a year. This guy, who was present at the meeting along with several others, said that he wanted to invest but was simply tantalising us with his bullshit. He also clandestinely persuaded me to get him and a couple of others involved in my own documentary project, and this was one of the biggest mistakes I made in my life. The guy turned out to be a user – all talk, a Walter Mitty character who dripped with deceit.

HOLLYWOOD, HERE WE COME!

I had been naive to fall for this person's talk and I felt used when the truth emerged. I even gave him some of my contacts, which I usually clung on to for dear life.

I felt betrayed, embarrassed and conned. I had been played. I had been had. This guy was interested in rubbing shoulders with prominent personalities that I was connected with, and was a compulsive liar. He had the ability to get you under his spell and then leave you to fall flat on your arse. After this mishap I made a pledge to myself that I'd keep my guard up and never fall victim to such a huckster again, or expose anyone else to one. I felt protective of Diana and my other well-known friends, and a little dispirited. But you have to pick yourself up, dust yourself off, learn from your mistakes and forge on.

So, undeterred, I continued with filming further interviews. Among the interviews in the can included Lenda Murray, the greatest female bodybuilder of all time, who I interviewed at the world-famous World Gym in Venice Beach. I also talked with another IFBB star, Shawn Ray, who was the epitome of a bodybuilding star – the cool, young, professional bodybuilder with shades and a Ferrari sports car to go with it – at his home – and Franco Columbu, Arnold Schwarzenegger's best friend and an amazing bodybuilder in his own right. I also managed to interview Royce and Rorion Gracie, and several original students and friends of Bruce. The footage was in the can. But there was a lot of work left to do. I wasn't going to rest until I'd pulled it off.

CHAPTER TWELVE

HOME SWEET HOME

AFTER TWO weeks in Hollywood, I arrived back home in the United Kingdom with a bump. To be completely honest, for the next three weeks I couldn't get out of bed. I plunged into depression, feeling completely despondent as my life hit rock bottom. The hurdles and obstacles I'd already encountered, the charlatans I'd dealt with and the politics affecting the project had drained my energy until my morale was at an all-time low.

Adding to the complications was my cell phone bill. Being the often careless person that I am when it comes to making international calls, I continued to use my cell phone in America, and to my horror I was hit with a bill of almost £2,500. I couldn't believe it. All I had to do was change the sim card – but, no, not me. I had to learn the hard way. Again, there's a lesson from martial arts: sometimes a single, simple mistake can cost you an arm and a leg. Always keep your guard up.

Still, I was determined to push on. Documentaries on famous figures are something that I've always enjoyed watching. I think it's a wonderful medium to showcase someone's life. And so, I felt I had to put my heart and soul into this project. I was on the brink of reaching new heights in my career. I really believed this film was going to elevate my career to a new level. Another lesson from martial arts: sometimes, it's when you're just about to find success that things feel hardest.

So, without any further delays I jumped back on the project with new vigour, calling up more fighting champions and forging ahead.

The next stop was Ricky Hatton's gym in Hyde, Manchester. Ricky was the pride of Britain, and was one of the many famous world boxing champions who had been inspired by Bruce Lee. I had interviewed him once before, thanks to Paul Speak, who acted as his manager and who was good enough to arrange it for me. Considering Ricky was a big name and resonated with the American public as well as the British, I felt he would be a great addition to the film.

What I never set out to do with the documentary was to throw in random interviews just because a face was instantly familiar to the public. I had set myself stringent criteria and vowed to conform to them. Ricky had cultivated the aura of a peoples' champion, and sure, he was OK, but I know countless combat sports stars who qualify for that title more so than him – especially UFC champions. So I wasn't impressed by him in that regard. Maybe it was because I was used to MMA fighters, who at that time didn't expect to be treated like celebrities but were regarded as celebrities in the combat sports field. Maybe I just hadn't warmed up to him, or perhaps he hadn't warmed up to me.

I was heavily invested in this project, financially but also emotionally. Andy Staton had let slip how *Bruce Lee: Martial Arts Master* had done financially around the world. I can't be specific, but we're talking several millions of pounds including TV rights and DVD sales worldwide. As I worked on the project, I realised that this could be the big one, but also my biggest reward as far as the monetary side is concerned. What other opportunity in my life could potentially make me millions of pounds? I never did the lottery, and I wasn't going to find a briefcase in the bushes with that sort of money inside, even if I daydreamed about that scenario sometimes. I have always put my passion at the forefront of any project, with financial gain following, but now I was balancing these two out in my head like a seesaw. Andy said he'd be happy with a million, not that his primary intention was to benefit financially. Hey, if I could make several million then Andy was welcome to his one million. When he told me he had received £54.75 pence for his services for the documentary he had worked on, I was shocked and almost fell over laughing. But he explained to me that he wasn't on the payroll and that amount was part of the expenses he was reimbursed.

The company that had produced *Bruce Lee: Martial Arts Master* had sold the South East Asian rights to Golden Harvest, a company that had produced Bruce's movies in the 1970s. Andy told me he had to resort to unorthodox tactics, including getting an executive at Golden Harvest, Russell Cawthorne, drunk to seal the deal. I actually knew of Russell. He was on my list to interview several years later for a different project, but his wife got back to me declining the offer. Since Golden Harvest owned the film footage I needed, however, I would need to come to an arrangement with them to avoid inflating budget costs. Obtaining film footage would be costly, eating into a large chunk of my budget, and so I was prepared to sign over South East Asian rights to save me a huge licensing bill. Eventually, I made contact with Golden Harvest, and did everything I could to make the deal happen. After the initial communication, though, things took a turn for the worse. I wasn't receiving any replies. I thought there could be political reasons why the company wouldn't respond, but it didn't matter. I simply couldn't force them to respond. I called back as often as I could, but in the end things just didn't pan out. I was pouring my own money into this grand project without any financial backing. With the film going nowhere in terms of progressing to the next level, the project had to be shelved.

What happened? I think it must have been politics. At the time, I was suspicious – back then, being paranoid was one of my worst weaknesses – and eventually, I was at least partly vindicated. Three years later I came across a production company that was, in conjunction with a production company owned by Bruce Lee's daughter, Shannon Lee, producing a documentary with a core theme similar to what I had conceived. To this day, I often wonder if my idea was borrowed, leaked out by someone I spoke to. I have my suspicions, but I will never really know unless the producers one day make a surprise revelation to me. I guess I'll have to live with it

After learning about the Shannon Lee project I called the company in charge and spoke to the managing director, hoping to console myself with the fact I could at least make a contribution. I wasted no time in revealing to the producer that I had some great interview footage and was prepared to hand it over on a platter. The producer was excited and said he'd be sharing the good news with Shannon, especially after I dropped the names of some elite athletes and A-listers into the mix. The producer also contemplated interviewing me for the film.

After that, I was full on board with Waddell Media and supplied some great footage for their project. But when I watched the completed *How Bruce Lee Changed the World*, I was ambivalent towards it. I'd had my own vision all mapped out to perfection, and wanted to contribute to the lore of Bruce Lee in my own way. I was happy to have contributed to the official documentary, though.

※ ※ ※

I had learned another lesson. You can give something your all, whether it's a sport, a martial art, or a project dear to your heart, and still find yourself prone to politics stopping you in your tracks. I was a little disheartened, but was determined to learn from the master how to do better. And so, many years later when I finally interviewed Shannon myself, I asked her about the hurdles her father encountered, including racism, and how he ultimately defied the odds to prevail. 'Well, racism is an obstacle that continues even to this day … there's still a long way to go. I mean, Hollywood in general has not embraced diversity very strongly. There are lot of conversations being had, but here we are, 47 years later, and not much has changed. When he first came to the

United States, and watched movies like *Breakfast at Tiffany's*, he was very dismayed by the portrayal of the Asian characters in Hollywood. A lot of the times they were portrayed by Caucasian actors. And when there were Asian actors portraying them, a lot of the times it was as a caricature – either a villain, or servants. He just didn't see himself like that, and how he felt he was represented in Hollywood. He wanted to edify the public. He felt these weren't authentic portrayals, so he made it a mission of his to have a reflection of at least who he was – an authentic Asian male – in Hollywood. He worked hard at that. Of course, that would require teaching somebody something that wasn't going to be embraced easily by others.'

I also asked her opinion of Quentin Tarantino's derogatory depiction of her father in *Once Upon A Time in Hollywood*. 'Quite frankly, you know, my position nowadays with certain things is that I'm happy to have a conversation with Quentin Tarantino anytime if he would like to have one,' she said. 'I really don't feel the need to scold him or set him straight or any of that kind of stuff. First of all, what's done is done. Second of all, he had his reasons for doing it. I don't know what they are. I don't know why he felt the need to go in the direction he did.' She further added that, quite frankly, it doesn't matter and she feels very confident in who her father is, who he was, and know he wasn't a perfect human being. 'It's unfortunate that Tarantino wanted to take a chip out of my father's legacy, but I really see no reason to convince him of anything if he feels he needs to be convinced,' she said. 'It's not my job to convince people that Bruce Lee is awesome. My job is just to present a man – his message is his words of who he was – and let people make up their own mind. So, it's not one of these things, *If I were to get into a room with Quentin Tarantino, I'd set him straight!* If I were to get into a room with Quentin Tarantino for any reason, if that ever happens, I would just have a conversation you usually have. I'm not here to scold him. If he had asked my opinion before he made the movie then I certainly would've shared it, but he didn't. If I could ask him a question, the question would be, "Why?" Why did he choose to do what he did?' I wouldn't say, "How dare you!" Or, "You need to be taught a lesson." I think there's too much of that in society right now. If he would have shared with me the reasons why, that would have been great, but I imagine he has zero desire to speak to me.'

Though I found this inspiring to hear all those years later, my failure had a very unhealthy impact on me mentally. I had become so emotionally attached to the original project that losing it caused me what felt like actual pain. But life goes on and you've got to take it on the chin and forge on. It took me several years to come to terms with the project's failure, but I resolved to push ahead.

Still, life wasn't getting any easier. I was plagued with further problems at this most inopportune time. Adding to my misery, the cinematographer in America decided to put the boot in. This guy had uploaded a couple of the interviews on You Tube, and when I came across them I was absolutely furious. Despite my phoning and messaging him, demanding he take the footage down with immediate effect, he ignored me.

My concern, of course, was that having these fabulous interviews on You Tube would undermine them, and make them less valuable. The rights were owned by me and I wasn't going to let anyone steal my material and dilute it – it had been exclusively produced for a single purpose. After countless messages and repeated calls, which weren't too nice, it was time to contact Sugar Ray Leonard's PR agent and Kareem Abdul-Jabbar's manager to inform them of what was happening. After threats of legal action against him, including getting the sport stars' managements involved, he finally threw in the towel. But it was a battle I shouldn't have had to fight.

I think the power of You Tube has changed how we perceive the world. Nowadays, many people, including me, often don't bother watching or renting a DVD; we can just watch clips and scenes on You Tube for free. How many times have you watched Bruce Lee fights, or a UFC fight, on the You Tube platform instead of sticking the whole film or event into a DVD player? It's much easier to bypass the storyline and get right into the action. Without a shadow of doubt modern-day technology has really changed how we can view media, but that isn't always positive.

One thing I learned on the documentary, a lesson repeated since, is that if you try to help certain people, or get them involved in your pursuits, it will backfire. They will take advantage. It's happened to me not once, but several times, and I will never walk that path again.

Nevertheless, it was time to move on and it wasn't the end of the world. The world had not erupted, everyone seemed to be alive. God had granted me good health and I was continuing with what I loved the most – working in combat sports with some fabulous personalities. On the financial side, I never really wanted to become a millionaire anyway, so I wasn't complaining, even though I wouldn't have said no to finding that briefcase in a bush.

CHAPTER THIRTEEN

MMA HITS THE MAINSTREAM

THE UFC and the sport of MMA were on the verge of mushrooming into the mainstream when the first *The Ultimate Fighter* series drew millions of viewers in January 2005. Produced by Fox Sports and the UFC, the series played a pivotal role in exposing the UFC to a much wider audience and educating those viewers. Its broadcast on Spike TV was constantly ranking number one on that channel. At last the martial arts were on the brink of commanding the reverence and wider exposure that some of the other sports had enjoyed for decades. Now that the sport was attracting attention from fans from across the board, although the media had publicised it as 'human cockfighting' journalists couldn't ignore it any longer. Indeed, the surge in popularity can no doubt be attributed to the power of mainstream media after much adversity in the past. In the early years Senator John McCain was one of the biggest detractors of the sport, yet he knew nothing about it. Finally the press had to accept the increasingly shuddering impact of UFC as a spectacle and a sport. So, a new burst of interest and support for MMA was developing. Arenas were selling out UFC shows. UFC fighters were now stars in their own right and were being taken seriously.

I would often hear MMA being referred to 'the world's fastest growing sport', a phrase which would constantly float around.

And, boy, it felt good to hear that over and over again. One night I remember sitting in a friend's house and watching UFC on TV. I quickly learned that friends, who were casual enthusiasts, were now familiar with the fighters' names. They had grown up watching boxing, but now enjoyed and gravitated towards UFC more than the sweet science. Inside I felt a sense of joy at the fact the UFC was being embraced by not only the martial arts' fraternity, but beyond the confines of the martial arts' public. Indeed, it was making its way into the consciousnesses of people who otherwise wouldn't have tuned in.

Back in the days, martial arts' champions were famous within their own world, but with the UFC breaking barriers, this gave the arts and its combatants the exposure they had longed for since the kung fu boom of the 1970s. Suddenly there was a kung fu craze in the West, which would fade as the decade came to an end.

The UFC was making waves in North America for sure. UFC coverage in America was way ahead in contrast to anywhere else. In America the sport had exploded. I would say Japan went on to embrace the MMA movement more than any other country outside of North America. Japan seems to embrace a lot of things. American sports such as baseball is big in Japan, too. Judo and martial arts are popular. UFC stars were now bona fide celebrities in North America. Major TV network deals were being inked. Pay-per-view records were being broken. By now the UFC in North America was being broadcast on major channels and making stars out of Chuck Liddell, Randy Couture, GSP and other champions. The marketing became a well-oiled machine, and the UFC publicity department ensured its fighters were seen. There were MMA TV chat shows and fighters were appearing on shows. The *Jay Leno Show* had fighters on promoting themselves and the UFC. If you got on the *Jay Leno* or *David Letterman* shows, you knew you had 'arrived'.

Anderson Silva once said to me, 'Obviously MMA in the USA is more in the media spotlight right now, and even though we've been doing it for a long time in Brazil, where it's got its heritage and is a traditional sport, it's not so much in the headlines compared to America.' He further added. 'It can get even bigger and that's what they're working hard at and there are chances it will.'

Yet, there were still hurdles to overcome. On one Fox TV show UFC welterweight champion, Matt Serra, was promoting the UFC with Dana White when a presenter argued that MMA was not good for kids. I asked Matt, 'What are your views on this rather controversial subject?' He said, 'Do I think little kids should fight in a cage? No! Do I think they should be studying martial arts or mixed martial arts? Yes!' He further added that it taught the kids self-defence. Matt said he disagreed with the now-defunct promotion Elite XC which was trying to make a spectacle of the street fighter Kimbo Slice. He made it clear that he wasn't knocking him and understood that the bare-knuckle fighter wanted to make money and that was fine. But the promoters hyping up this internet sensation. 'Now, as a result, you are going to get a bunch of moron kids with camcorders trying to be in the UFC by fighting each other in the backyard. That's not the proper way to do it. Anybody can fight anybody in the street; you should come up the right way get involved in the sport, get involved in wrestling, jiu-jitsu, boxing, Thai-boxing – get involved in those kind of matches.' This is the approach the UFC fighter was advocating, a medium which allows you to hone your skills and you will be ready to fight competitors, and in his own words 'not on the street looking to make a name that way'. He further added that when no-holds-barred first emerged, it wasn't a sport but 'a freak show'. Now the UFC was doing the right thing and it was legal. However, it wouldn't have been right if it didn't start off in the beginning like it did. So, there was progression.

Plus, when stars from showbiz start turning up ringside you know you've made it. I recall former UFC heavyweight champion Tim Sylvia, who had made his UFC debut at UFC 39, proudly saying to me, 'If you look at all these celebrities and pro athletes, such as NFL football players, soccer players, they're all coming to watch us. They know we are the next generation and the next big thing.' Tim was right. Press conferences were very professional, like boxing conferences. In some cases weigh-ins would attract several thousand fans – up to 8,000. It was crazy. The phenomenon had gripped the nation.

* * *

So, evidently, MMA was being embraced by the wider press in North America, but what was happening across the pond? The UFC had produced champions in America, but Britain had now produced a bona fide star. The first time I saw and heard of Mike Bisping was when he fought in the UFC in April 2007 at the MEN Arena at UFC 70. I had been given tickets by Paul Alderson – an associate who was running some exclusive events for martial arts and MMA fans – and a friend accompanied me. My friend pointed out 'The Count', the fighter who had come to prominence in *The Ultimate Fighter: Season 3* TV show earlier the same year. Prior to his fame from the reality TV show, the Lancashire fighter had held a national kickboxing title and won virtually all his MMA fights. And any belt on offer domestically, he'd won. Eventually he contemplated fighting overseas for larger promotions. He pursued the UFC. When I fist interviewed Mike, he told me that the UFC had had its eyes on him and told him that it would offer him a fight in the UFC. 'But they said I'd be great for *The Ultimate Fighter*,' Mike said to me. 'In the meantime I spoke to the executives at Spike TV who were creating the show. I was pretty much chosen before I went to the auditions.' Mike snagged a decent contract with the promotion. After his triumph in the Octagon in the TV show, he collapsed on the floor and the ring doctor rushed to his rescue. Mike assured him he was fine and that there was nothing wrong with him. 'I'm just lying on the floor; it's a sheer relief,' he told the concerned doctor.

When he made his United Kingdom debut for the promotion, no matter how much the MMA experts endeavoured to educate the public, there were always the naysayers sticking out like sore bell ends. During the same interview I conducted with Mike, I asked him how he perceived his relationship with the mainstream media. 'On the whole, now, compared to a couple of years ago, the media have taken more interest in covering the sport and more people are interested in the sport,' he responded. 'They ask intelligent questions about the sport, as opposed to the start when they asked stupid questions like, "Is it dangerous?" or "Has anyone died yet?" Now the reporters know what they're talking about.' Yet, there were the exceptions, who were still not convinced.

Leading up to the UFC 70 Mike had a radio interview with BBC Manchester. A lady presenter who sometimes presented the weather was going to be grilling the so-called 'barbarian'. Mike arrived at the studio oblivious to what trap lay ahead. He sat there calmly as she talked on air to her audience before introducing the UFC fighter. 'Up next, if you've seen the film *Fight Club*, our next guest is Michael Bisping.' Mike related this story to me, which didn't surprise me. 'So then she turns to me and she says, "Right, Michael, so you fight in the UFC?" And I said, "Yes." She says, "Look at the size of you, how big are you? You must be at least 18 stones."' Mike told me he was around 14 stones and that he wasn't a small guy but not overly big, either. So, she got his weight wrong for starters. He continued, 'And she says, "You're 18 stone and covered in scars." I said, "I'm not covered in scars. I've got a few scars on my head. I banged my head as a kid but I'm not covered in scars."'

The conversation leaned towards all things controversial in what seemed like a partial debate, as the BBC host continued her assault on the fighter. The constant onslaught of negativity poured out of the host's mouth. Mike continued, 'She says, "This sport is for barbarians, isn't it?" I said, "No, it's not for thugs." She says, "It's barbarians!" I said, "It's not a sport for barbarians." She says, "Well, you look like a barbarian."' Mike had heard enough by now and counter-attacked with his own verbal artillery, which he had so far held back. It was time to bring out the canons. 'I said, "Really?"' he continued. '"I'll keep my thoughts on what you look like to myself, shall I?"' She looked like mutton dressed as a lamb Mike told me. 'Then she started criticising the sport saying people can die.' The UFC fighter asked the host if she had ever watched the sport. Ironically, she hadn't, she conceded. He asked her how the hell could she sit there passing judgement and talking about the sport when she'd never seen it, and what was she basing her facts on? 'We got into an argument on air. Basically she didn't have a leg to stand on. She wrapped up the interview and ushered me out.'

After the scathing response from the presenter, the UFC poster boy had to focus on his bout. He went on to dominate his Australian opponent Elvis Sinosic that day. Mike's combination strikes in the second round really offset Sinosic. I could see his opponent dripping with blood, which was visible all the way up to the upper tier seats. The ferocity of the fight was just hardcore, and brutality was being demonstrated at its best. Mike, without a doubt, dominated the fight in true fashion. He looked dangerous and an aggressive fighter with a heart. I remember thinking just how tough the sport is and the dangerous position these warriors put themselves in. When it comes to watching fights at an arena, I'm the type who observes quietly, while most people are raving and ranting, and some overzealous fans acting like hooligans. What rattles my cage the most is when you get idiots in the audience making crude comments as the fighters engage. In Japan the fans are so quiet you can hear a pin drop. But in the Western world it's a different atmosphere as far as the armchair audience is concerned.

Something that really stood out that day was the reaction of the packed crowd of over 15,000 screaming fans. Undeniably this fighter had huge support and love from the fans. Marking his first UFC bout in his home country, this was a pivotal moment. The crowd had embraced him as if he was an Olympic athlete representing their country. Not only was Mike fighting for his own glory and survival, but he was fighting for the whole nation is the vibe I got. The crowd would erupt every time the British poster boy, the hometown favourite, landed a strike, or took his opponent down as he proceeded to brutally punish his foe. The atmosphere became increasingly raucous and raw in the packed arena. At the same time I realised he was humble whenever he was interviewed. He always thanked his fans for their support. I felt he believed he had a moral duty to express this. I can sense his feelings were genuine and he wasn't merely putting up a fake front.

Among the UFC stars fighting on this card were Andrei Arlovski, Mirko Filipovick and Lyoto Machida. Among the personalities in attendance at ringside were Randy Couture, Dana White and Jean Claude Van Damme. I looked down to where Van Damme was sat ringside. His shock reaction was priceless as 'his' fighter, Mirko Filipovick, got knocked out with a kick to the head by the Brazilian Gabriel Gonzaga. Van Damme had his both hands on his head in disbelief, as if he had just lost all his fortune or something in the biggest gambling deal of his life. I could sense he was in a world of his own, a fallen star, nobody was paying attention to this 'has been'. Clearly he wanted some attention, wanted to say a few words in front of the camera, but I saw no media going up to him. This was my personal observation. And I'm seldom wrong.

According to a source, the UFC had shelled out a collective $843,000 to its warriors but Mike only received $24,000. He was a new and rising star. The lowest earning for a fighter was $3,000, the highest $350,000. Mirko was the highest-paid fighter that day. To give you an idea of how Mike's earnings changed, nine years later, when he fought Anderson Silva in February 2016 at UFC Fight Night 84, attendances still strong with over 16,000 at the O2, and he reportedly banked almost half a million dollars. This was broken down as follows: sponsor Reebok paying him $20,000; $275,000 to show; $150,000 to win; $50,000 Fight of the Night bonus. So nine years later he was making 20 times more money. Not bad for a small-town boy who had slaved away in numerous labour jobs that he utterly abhorred.

This event was broadcast live on pay-per-view on Setanta Sports and in America on Spike TV, which reportedly drew 3.5 million viewers for the main event. According to the UFC organisation was targeting this event for its debut on America's giant HBO. Dana White, who has done a tremendous job in really pushing the sport forward, has a drive and passion and is committed to breaking records and boundaries. This visionary man's desire to constantly expand and dream to make UFC massive has no doubt been realised. Unquestionably he has worked tirelessly to bring the sport into the mainstream – what critics had long derided as 'human cockfighting'.

* * *

With the UFC landing on British shores, the media was making strides, too, as it was a propitious moment to jump on board. Those members of the media with open minds were now persuaded of the more positive sides of the sport. Suddenly, magazines and websites that were exclusive to the sport started to spring up out of nowhere, together with overnight 'experts'. The MMA industry just took another turn. More and more major magazines – *FHM*, *Men's Fitness* and *Men's Health* – featured articles and interviews with the star athletes. Not surprisingly this included *Sunday Sport*, which printed ludicrous stories. Its controversial content contained a high quotient of nudity. Eventually stars graced the covers of *Sports Illustrated*. I had managed to get my foot in, too. In addition to my regular slot in the combat sports press, I started liaising with newspapers and major periodicals, even if it was as a source in the beginning.

Still, to my disappointment, the major TV channels in the United Kingdom refused to embrace the UFC, and the major newspapers, although most were on board, refrained from giving the sport much attention when it came to print press coverage. In the beginning it was an arduous task for the MMA promoters to persuade the higher echelon sportswriters to come on board. Relegating the sport to online coverage seemed to make these editors content. Some major papers were still reluctant to publicise a sport of brutality that raised the ire of many. Editors knew they would be inundated with complaints from the 'civilised' public, who thought there was no room for promoting extreme and brutal violence. Oh, boy, the public was in need of edification. Basically, kids have had role models who were bad guys, in particular gangster rappers. For years kids have been told you have to be bad to get ahead and be on top. I think with the UFC, it showed you can be a good guy and tough and learn discipline. Having said this, now it's pretty much every other fighter has to portray the bad-boy image pre-fight hype, something that I'm no fan of.

As I started connecting with newspaper sportswriters, I realised they had the power and the capacity to publicise anything. One of the first to jump on the bandwagon in galvanising support for the UFC was the *Daily Telegraph*. Gareth Davies is a big sports fan himself and started his own MMA blog. He was one of the sports journalists from red-tops and broadsheets who had developed a hardcore interest in the bone-crushing sport of MMA. His enthusiasm radiated as he eagerly set out on a mission to help break misconceptions, despite the fact he needed to increase his knowledge of the sport. All in all we were seeing some sense.

Kevin Francis was the sports and boxing correspondent for the *Daily Star*. This tabloid was now offering coverage to the UFC and Kevin became the correspondent. He was a nice, older gentleman and reminded me of Paul Heller, the producer of *Enter the Dragon*. I would often phone Kevin to ask if he could do something for me in the newspaper. The *Daily Star* was one of the few to wave the white flag and start to give print coverage to UFC. Its readership was 18 to 35-year-olds, the perfect market for the UFC. Kevin was always nice to me and tried to accommodate me whenever he possibly could. The first time I met him was at the David Haye press conference that took place in Manchester at the MEN Arena. As a resident of Cheshire, he was in the vicinity of the soccer stars and wrote about soccer and other sports, too.

Another prominent sportswriter at the time, Mark Gilbert at *The Sun*, was instrumental in us winning positive coverage. He was my contact there. It wasn't long before *The Sun* also became known for its UFC coverage, which I must state was relegated to its website. It too refused to cover the sport in the print version of the paper in the early years. The reason for this was obvious: it would have been inundated with complaints, some people inevitably taking to twitter in their droves to remark openly. In fact, Mark told me himself that that fear was holding them the paper back. But now it does promote the UFC in its sports pages just as do others. After all, the public wasn't quite ready for this brutal pastime, which carried the labels 'cage fighting' as I mentioned earlier. There would have been further outrage. Nevertheless, heavyweight tabloids were taking note of the UFC and coverage it on their websites was a landmark victory for the UFC.

I would often find myself on the phone to Mark in deep conversation about the UFC. The young writer told me he would always tell his boss positive things and educate him about the sport. I, myself, contributed to *The Sun's* UFC coverage at a minimal level at the time. I could have done more if I'd wanted to, but having my fingers in a lot of pies was good enough for me. Besides, I never was an 'online' journalist; I preferred the medium of print, which I was enjoying. One of the things I learned about the media was that the mainstream outlets had huge platforms with which to reach the masses.

We, the specialist martial arts and MMA magazines journalists at the time, had more knowledge as some of us had had 'mat time' and had a genuine interest in the fighting arts. We were able to appreciate MMA and fighters and had the technical background and experience in the arts. Most of the sports columnist and writers in the mainstream press had never been on the mat, nor had they experienced the sport on a physical level. Despite this they played an integral role in bringing the sport into the forefront and having embraced by a wider audience. Without their attention and action, MMA may have fizzled out at some point, or at least been relegated to the hardcore niche market. So, yes, these men and women are as important as anyone and must be credited and appreciated. Mainstream magic had arrived in North America, and the United Kingdom had got a taste of it even though it was still behind its cousins across the Atlantic. Yes, I still felt the United Kingdom was not doing enough in terms of coverage.

CHAPTER FOURTEEN

RINGSIDE & BROCK 'THE BEAST' LESNAR

PERSONALLY I was disappointed and quite frankly disgusted that the two major channels in the United Kingdom, the BBC and ITV, were reticent in covering the UFC. In the spring of 2008 the BBC did broadcast a news story when Dave O' Donnell's Cage Rage promotion garnered publicity. I'm sure it was only because two women were fighting in a brutal bloody cage despite ours being a modern civilised society, so it naturally added to the outrage and attention. And when there's public outrage in the country, the media wastes no time in sniffing and adding fuel to it. One of the female fighters was from Ireland and fought under the banner of SBG Ireland, Conor McGregor's gym – my friend Karl Tanswell's SBG gym being the country's head office and his world head office being in Portland, Oregon in the USA.

Talking of women in MMA, Rosi Sexton, one of Karl's former top fighters, has a PhD in Theoretical Computer Science, a BSc in Osteopathy and an MSc in Mathematical Logic from University of Manchester. She was the first female from Britain to fight in the UFC. She pioneered women's MMA, especially in Europe. This was before Ronda Rousey emerged. I often bumped into Rosi and had interviewed her because she used to frequent the same gym. She was a very down-to-earth and quiet person, but if you got on the mat with her this innocent-looking girl would eat you up and chew you out before you could utter a word. She had the capacity to bruise your face up and ground-and-pound you to oblivion.

Meanwhile, I wasted no time in getting in touch with BBC correspondent David Willis, who was covering the story. He told me to give him a call if I had anything that might be of interest pertaining to MMA. Willis was very approachable. Unfortunately, before I could squeeze anything out of him he left the BBC. *Never mind, it wasn't the end of the world,* I thought to myself.

Cage Rage was one of the more prominent MMA promotions in the country. Promoter Dave O'Donnell is a colourful character. He looks and sounds like your typical London gangster, with a shaved shiny head, gold jewellery and a cockney accent to go with it. He was always dressed in a smart suit. As a matter of fact he could stunt-double the infamous London gangster Dave Courtney. I've known Dave O' Donnell for many years now. The Cage Rage promotion was built up by the cockney martial artist who worked hard to get to where he is today. Whenever I phoned him, he was always polite and we had a laugh. Whenever I could help him out with articles promoting his events I would try my best. He would throw in complimentary tickets for me. Then again, I would always try to squeeze something out of him. Sometimes, though, I had to squeeze hard.

I, along with three friends, went to his show in Wembley when UFC pioneer Ken Shamrock was headlining. When news reached Royce Gracie about Ken fighting at Cage Rage, he asked me how much his former adversary was getting paid. I said that I'd do my investigations and find out for him. Allegedly it was only £20,000. Royce was quite shocked. Here was a UFC legend that had made a name in the history books and now he was accepting £20,000 to fight. It was quite sad.

Now, they talk about this north and south divide. I would never live down south. I have some good friends in London and they are affable people but the north is where home is. Most would agree that people are much friendlier up in the north. Believe me, I've even had some southerners agree with me on this one, so there must be some substance to it. Driving down south was always mundane and a trek. As we got into Wembley we stopped to ask for directions from some people standing at the bus stop, only to be met by strange looks – they ignored us. These zombies thought we were aliens. The last time I checked in the mirror I resembled a human, even though I have slightly big ears, which seem to have grown out of place the older I've got. We found the 'bus-waiters' attitude rude. No, they weren't racists because half of them were of ethnic ethnicity and we were all Asians. (Then again, believe it or not, there is racism that goes on within the ethnic minority communities, too). But I guess that's the norm there. I compare this to the East Coast (New York) and West Coast (Los Angeles) of America. On the West Coast people are much friendlier and approachable, but on the East Coast it's quite the opposite. In different parts of the world you're going to get different attitudes. Even in different parts of the same country there's likely to be a contrast between the general attitudes. I think I need to grow a thicker shell and not take minor situations such as this to heart.

Anyway, we finally made it to the arena, no thanks to the bus-stop idiots. I think there must have been 10,000 screaming MMA fans in the arena that day. I felt elated watching the crazy crowd. You could see Ken still possessed a good physique, but his best days were behind him. I was mingling ringside and bumped into some people I knew. I was right by the cage when Ken got knocked out by Robert Berry and went down on the canvas. His opponent then proceeded to pummel him on the ground before the referee intervened, stopping the fight in the first round. A left jab followed by a glancing right hand to Ken's cheekbone dropped the former UFC champion. Ken's opponent kept busy and looked much more relaxed than Ken. The latter, I remember, looked weak; his nerves were getting the better of him. He was being cautious, avoiding rushing in, but every time he'd get hit he'd flinch. He actually looked a miniature of his original self. Not what I had anticipated.

Now, many of us have experienced, at some point in our lives, be it in a combat sport context or a street situation, the feeling of being bombarded with blows to the head. We know how overwhelming this can be – it can be a shock to the system. You feel the adrenaline shoot up and often a person feels helpless. Witnessing someone getting brutally beaten up in front of you, although you're not the one on the receiving end of the beating, triggers your adrenaline and an element of fear starts to invade your territory. That's how strong emotions can be.

As Ken went down, oddly enough it felt like I was next on the receiving end. Furthermore I could honestly feel the friends that were in the upper-tier seats being treated to the same experience. It was a sixth sense that I can't explain. So imagine what it feels like being in the cage environment, when you're facing another man who is ready to knock your head off. Being on the receiving end of violence, the brutality that comes with entering the cage, is something these fighters have to endure day in, day out in a training environment and in competition. A lot of preparation, skill and mental toughness and guts are prerequisites for survival.

My immediate thoughts, when I reflect back on this, are that I kind of felt sorry for Ken. I felt bad that another human, a few feet away from me, was being brutally savaged. Not that I was ever a friend of Ken's, if anything I had some reservations because of his long rivalry with my friend Royce. I had interviewed him once. He seemed like a nice guy. But it was just spontaneous empathy.

MMA fighters came from a diverse background: you had college and university graduates, even school teachers such as Rich 'Ace' Franklin – the former UFC middleweight champion – who was the spitting image of Jim Carey. And on the other end of the spectrum, you had those who had a rough upbringing. Ken was one of those: had a hard childhood and had to move from home to home. He was adopted by Bob Shamrock. 'I got into trouble when I was about ten years old and I got shipped off to different group and juvenile homes,' Ken told me in an interview. 'I ended up in a place called the Shamrock Boys Home with Bob Shamrock after I had stayed at several different places. I was 13-and-a-half years old. This was a time when I started learning how to change my ways.'

'When you were growing up did you get into trouble a lot?' I asked. 'Well, I grew up in group homes so you were always fighting – all the time,' he replied. 'And I would fight for my territory and my space.' The adopted young boy had to fight for respect. The MMA legend continued, 'So it's something I did at a really young age when I was ten years old. I was fighting all the time. Fighting to me was just kind of who I was and what I was all about and where I grew up. I had to fight in order to keep anything I had and any respect I had. Then, when I got into mixed martial arts and started fighting professionally, that was fun.'

For weeks I had been communicating with a Cage Rage official to set up a camera interview with Ken for the documentary that I had been working on a year and a half earlier. He had assured me that he'd sort it out. I had confidence because more often than not Dave would comply with my requests and his staff, I thought, would accommodate me. But when I got to the arena, this guy who was sitting with Malcolm Martin – the co-presenter – acted like he didn't know what I was talking about. I thought to myself, *Is this guy for real?* He said Ken was unlikely to do an interview now before his bout. This was understandable because the focus is on the fight and in no way should other distractions affect you mentally. But, after the fight, still no interview. If I thought I was going to grab the interview I was gravely mistaken. Nevertheless it was a good night and my friend had his small, mobile sheesha with him, which he had taken into the arena to smoke as he watched the entertainment. This was no UFC, but it was apparent that people from all backgrounds were flocking to these events. So the sport had hit the mark and was winning legions of fans.

RINGSIDE & BROCK 'THE BEAST' LESNAR

* * *

I had plenty of top UFC fighters and champions whom I ended up speaking to and really learning about their backgrounds and how their minds worked. One in particular was Brock Lesnar, who I spoke to about four months later in July. About a month earlier, he had tasted defeated at the hands of Frank Mir in what was Brock's UFC debut – it was his second MMA fight. His transition from professional wrestling into a whole new world, inevitably, garnered attention. The UFC felt that having this very popular WWE wrestler, boasting a global fan base, fight in the organisation would definitely have crossover appeal – WWE fans into the UFC. And their instinct was proven right. I wonder how the Russian Olympic wrestler Aleksander Karelin would have fared in UFC. A beast weighing 290 pounds, the most feared wrestler of all time, acknowledged as the greatest wrestler of the 20th century, he was virtually unbeatable. He did fight once in shoot wrestling in the Japanese RINGS promotion against Akira Maeda, and won.

Growing up on a farm in South Dakota, Brock had a lot of work to do but not enough money to pay the bills. He wanted to wrestle in the Olympics when he was young, but he never had any specific career goal when he grew up. He was certain he didn't want to be a farmer, though. Boxing had sparked the young man's interest, but the boxing gym was 50 miles from his house. He could never get there. Friends of his actually went to boxing but he could never afford to and never had the time to get there because of his work commitments and the distance factor. 'I had interest to get into MMA many years ago, back in 1997, but I didn't really know how to', he told me. At the time, 1997, he was living in California training for a summer of wrestling. 'Probably that was the only place I knew that had a gym that specifically trained for MMA fighting near me.' He wanted to fulfil his college and pro wrestling dream which prevented him from pursuing MMA. When he got out of amateur wrestling MMA wasn't very huge, and Brock had a guaranteed contract with pro wrestling sitting on the table, so it was easy enough for him to make the decision.

I asked him how he felt when he first fought in MMA. 'It was an excellent feeling; it was very surreal,' he said. 'To me it was a great feeling to get in the ring and be competing.' Before fighting in MMA he checked out Pat Miletich's gym and numerous facilities in Arizona and Indianapolis. Since he had been on the road for a long time when he was wrestling professionally, it was really important for him to be at home and train and do what he always wanted to do, and that was to fight. For him, he told me, to be able to come home every night and sleep in his own bed and train was a major factor in choosing a gym.

'What is the difference between the pro-wrestling training you were accustomed to and the MMA training you do now?' I asked. 'It's not even the same,' Brock said. 'It's like amateur wrestling training is different to pro wrestling. Pro wrestling is entertainment.' He's right, there's a sharp distinction between the two. You have to be an athlete to be in the wrestling ring, no doubt about that, but MMA athletes train in an array of disciplines every day – striking, kicking, jui-jitsu, elbows, Muay Thai. At the time he was training one or two times a day, five or six days a week. The whole key to training is that you are then able to recover and get the maximum out of it, and be ready for the next day's work out. 'We train pretty hard. I have to listen to my body. I'm not a spring chicken either and day by day, week by week, the more we do the more I can absorb and try to prepare myself when a fight's coming up.'

In his first fight in the UFC, Brock fought Frank Mir, an expert in Brazilian jiu-jitsu and former UFC heavyweight champion with experience and submission skills on his side. It took Brock less than five seconds to take Frank down, countering his right low kick and land multiple right punches from the half-guard position. He overpowered his opponent completely, only to have the referee break up the action. A point was taken off Brock as he had hit his downed opponent in the back of the head. Given another chance on the feet,

Frank repeated the same leg kick, and Brock countered with a good right hand, knocking him down again. Again, the giant exploded with multiple hammer fists to the face, but this time Frank almost got him in the arm-lock, forcing Brock to pull away and giving Frank space to grab his right foot and secure a deep-knee-bar foot lock on the giant, who was forced to tap out in the very first round.

'I knew he would attempt to go for my legs and I got over excited,' Brock told me, in our interview. 'I spent time learning how to defend and learning every discipline, so only lack of experience is the key word there for my loss. Someday I may have a rematch with Frank.' This was prescient. At the time we talked, Brock was preparing for his next bout with Heath Herring, who would suffer a punishing defeat at the hands of the former WWE star. Next, knocking out Randy Couture, a fighter who'd also been champion at light-heavyweight at UFC 91 on 15 November 2008, made Brock the UFC heavyweight champion. As for Frank, Brock would avenge his loss by beating his opponent via a TKO at UFC 100, which would leave him on a three-fight winning streak. Eventually, Brock lost his title and returned to the WWE, then briefly returned to the UFC before apparently giving up the game for good. Still, he was one of the big pay-per-view draws in the UFC – and one I felt privileged to interview.

CHAPTER FIFTEEN

UFC 105 ENCOUNTERS

AFTER HIS devastating loss to Brock Lesnar, Randy Couture suffered a beating at the hands of Antonio Nogueira less than ten months later. Randy would go on to fight Brandon Vera at the MEN Arena – officially the busiest arena venue in the world for many years – in Manchester at UFC 105 on 14 November 2009. When the news of this fight reached me, my brain went into overdrive. It immediately dawned on me that this would be a perfect opportunity to schedule a meet-and-greet autograph signing with the five-time UFC champion. Randy and I already had a business relationship established. I quickly got in touch with the sports presenter, Mike Hall, at ITV's Granada Studios. I had met Mike at Ricky Hatton's old gym some years earlier when the boxer was going to Las Vegas to fight. He was a very approachable and nice guy and I kept in touch with him because I knew potential TV coverage was the future. Mike told me to give him a nudge nearer the time of the event, and start setting things up.

Things were off to an auspicious start. Now that the wheel of publicity had started to turn, I got my pals from Fighters Inc. involved. We secured a venue, the Hard Rock Cafe in Manchester's Printworks, which was a stone's throw from the arena. Fighters Inc. were great to work with and had experience in combat sports event management. They had previously worked with the likes of Chuck Liddell and other major names, so I was quite content that they would do a good job and not undermine Randy, an imperative when you're dealing with A-listers in the game.

A day before the big bout, I and two friends, Andy Farrell and Azmat Ali, arranged to meet Randy at the Crown Plaza Hotel where he, the UFC fighters and staff were staying at, just down the road from Hard Rock Cafe. Not long after we arrived, Randy's opponent Brandon walked up to us. I introduced myself and we had a quick chat. I asked him what he thought of his adversary.

'Randy's my hero,' he said. I was expecting him to be negative because he was going to fight Randy the next day, but Brandon had the utmost respect for his foe. This was one thing most UFC fighters had in common – a deep admiration and reverence for Randy, who'd proved to be a class act and a great role model when the sport was still growing into the behemoth it is today. I sometimes felt he was like their elder brother or a father figure, someone they wouldn't even dream about insulting. It was easy to see the appeal, as Randy was, by nature, the most affable and humble fighter and individual anyone could ever meet. He was never the type of athlete who would talk trash about anyone, and yet he still managed to sell out arenas. He was revered by his peers. I just prayed Randy would be choking Brandon out on the day of the fight, or I'd be choking up myself.

Anyway, we soon spotted Randy in the hotel lobby with a young blonde woman on his arm. She must have been in her mid-twenties. She looked petrified, as if she was on the planet Mars and surrounded by aliens. We walked towards them and I introduced myself, then all got into the lift. The woman was stuck to Randy's body like a magnet, as if she was scared of the rest of us. We made our way up to his hotel room, leaving a few boxes of goodies there because Randy was going to sign some in advance. 'I love your red shoes,' Randy joked with Azmat. He was always personable.

TO THE TOP

After some back-and-forth banter we left Randy and his girlfriend in peace to relax. After all, he had an important fight the next day and I was counting on him to win.

As we walked out of the room and made our way to the lobby, we hit the hat-trick of headliners, including Mike Bisping, who was going to be fighting Denis Kang on the same card. As soon as Mike saw us he smiled, and he shouted, 'This guy kicked my arse!' He was referring to Andy, who Mike had fought before he became a UFC fighter and star. Apparently unconcerned about his fight the next day, Mike stood there telling us proudly how Andy had slammed him again and again in their encounter, which Andy had won. That was a very humbling conversation. Mike didn't have to do that, but in front of us and his own team members he did. Andy, I must add, had already told me of his encounter with 'The Count', so I was already aware. But when Mike confirmed the beating he received at the hands of my friend, I thought to myself, *I have a friend with great potential who could be a star in the UFC.*

Andy, a former professional rugby player and natural bodybuilding champion, a Brazilian jiu-jitsu and MMA champion and a contestant on *Gladiators*, is one of the nicest people you can ever meet. He's a cool guy, the type of a guy you can have a good laugh with, but is also blessed with a great bodybuilder's physique, a strong grip and a handshake that could crush your hand. He is one solid guy. On the day of the signing meet-and-greet event Andy's job was supposed to be protecting Randy. I gave him the responsibility to bodyguard the UFC champion. Believe me, you get some fans who react strangely when they meet a professional fighter. Some have unusual requests – they want to get choked, leg-kicked or even punched in the face by the star. I sometimes wondered if, one day, a lunatic would take it further, either verbally or physically.

While in Manchester, Randy worked out at my friend Karl Tanswell's SBG gym, which was the number-one MMA facility in Manchester – and had been the number-one MMA gym in the country several years earlier – at the time. On the Saturday, the day of the fight, MEN Arena had a packed-out crowd of almost 17,000 fans. Astonishingly, this event broke the merchandise records previously been set by Britain's number-one boy band, Take That. I remember some Amir Khan fights were apparently only attracting 8,000 people, with one of his fights reportedly only selling 4,000 tickets, and he was the biggest name in British boxing. *This is insane,* I thought. *The UFC is not only outselling world champion boxers, but setting merchandise records.* This further bolstered my confidence in Randy's appeal, the future of the sport and my MMA business endeavours.

In the end, I decided not to go to the fight, leaving Andy to go without me. I was wracked by nerves – had Randy lost the fight, I would have likely plunged back into depression, and besides, Andy Farrell would be updating me on Randy's performance and the outcome. Randy was 46 years old and still fighting in the toughest sport at the highest level, against a much younger man who many thought could be the future of the division. In the event, Randy tried to execute his normal game plan. After closing the distance he would resort to dirty boxing in the clinch position followed up by a takedown, then ground and pound. Against Brandon he failed. His opponent defended much of Randy's takedown attempts, forcing them to battle on the feet for much of the bout.

In the end, Randy had a very tough fight with Brandon but managed to secure a win via decision. I was constantly on the phone to Andy for updates, and he assured me that Randy never seemed to be in trouble. Still, this fight caused quite a controversy; some thought Brandon had been robbed, and at least one member of the media called the decision 'daylight robbery'. It didn't matter to me. I was joyful because Randy was the one to have his hand raised. That was good enough for me; the opinions of others didn't register as long as the judges made the right call. After the fight, I couldn't give a damn about the performance. I was interested in the end result.

'I wouldn't have been terribly disappointed had the decision gone the other way,' Randy told presenter Joe Rogan in the post-fight interview, in front of the packed crowd. 'I was very impressed with Brandon.' He went on to say that you just never know what the judges will decide and this had been seen in the past. You just don't know what the judges are looking at and how they perceive the fight. 'And that's what ultimately, in a close fight like this, determines the judge's decision,' he told Joe.

Now, not many fighters would have said this – perhaps only Randy. To be honest, I'd rather he hadn't said it, because it felt like admitting defeat and giving others artillery to use against him. But that was Randy – he spoke his mind.

Brandon, for his part, made it known that he was really pissed off. Wouldn't you be if you thought you were robbed? No one could blame him for vocalising his concerns. He expressed his views saying that the sport of MMA is, as he put it, 'a bitch' because if you let it go to the judge's hands, then you're no longer in control of the outcome. He felt that he should have finished his opponent when he was presented with the opportunity, but let the chance slip away. And yet, regardless of the controversial decision, he was still in awe after the loss. 'I'm super happy I got to fight Randy Couture, my hero, my legend,' the defeated fighter told the crowd. It was a great night.

* * *

The next morning, I and my team – really, a group of friends – Seyfi, Abdul, Tash, Andy, Ahsan, Andy, Azmat, Daz, and our Fighters Inc friends (Paul Alderson and Joe Long) arrived at the Hard Rock Cafe. Several of us were in Azmat's Range Rover with Randy, when suddenly a police car appeared out of nowhere and followed us, signalling for the driver to stop. As the two officers got out and made their way to the driver, to their astonishment they realised Randy Couture was sat in the passenger seat. The officers had stopped us because Azmat didn't have his seatbelt on. Azmat tried turning things around by taking a humorous approach, saying to Randy, 'Randy, please save me the fine and have a picture taken with them.' Well, that day the officers were of an understanding nature and let my friend off, and Randy got out of the Range Rover to pose with the officers for pictures. As it happens they were fans of MMA, and Randy had made their day.

During the post-fight event, Neal Pickup, a multiple European and world arm-wrestling champion and a presenter, was the MC for the day. We had a packed house, with eager fans waiting to meet their idol. Neal conducted an interview onstage with the UFC champion and took questions from various members of the audience. During the Q&A session one young guy from the audience shouted out something to Randy. I think he was saying Randy needed to speak up because he couldn't hear him, because the mic had suddenly gone off, but his tone was a little on the sarcastic side. Randy, a soft-spoken gentleman, countered by saying that maybe the young man should come forward. As much of a dangerous fighter as he is, you can't picture 'The Natural' getting mad or angry, screaming or even raising his voice. A rather quiet gentleman, he is blessed with a mellow personality, which some may find ironic considering his brutal profession. Besides, he always did his talking in the Octagon. That's where it really counts.

After Randy answered questions about his life and fight career, he signed and paused for photos for over 250 ecstatic fans. The atmosphere was electric. The looks and smiles on the fans' faces was something that I will cherish forever. The event was an advance-reservation event only, so although we let a few extra fans in, we had to turn back others, leaving them disappointed. Obviously the city was flooded with UFC fans from the fight night the night before, and so it was inevitable fans found out where Randy was. I'd have liked to give more people the chance to meet their idol, but there simply wasn't time.

For my part, I was relieved that the ITV Granada News team had made the effort to show up. I wasn't sure if they were going to follow through, if I'm honest. As the autograph signing and meet-and-greet came to an end, we were ready to leave the venue because we had to be out by 1pm, but the TV crew stopped us in our tracks. I could see a sense of uncertainty in Randy's eyes. He was like a little boy lost, being whisked here, there and everywhere. It dawned on me how some of these stars are shuffled all over the place like ragdolls, without much say or certainty about their next engagements. I saw the human side of Randy, the side the public seem to overlook when it comes to meeting their favourite celebrity. Now that we have celebrity reality TV shows, we are able to discern a lot about celebrities' true personalities, which we otherwise would never have been exposed to. We come to the realisation that they have feelings and vulnerabilities just like mere mortals. But back then, even those glimpses were rare.

My conclusion? We all want to be appreciated, and often crave attention, but when you get there and you're famous, sometimes you become vulnerable. People expect you to do certain things, behave in a certain manner, and they want a piece of you. People expect you to give them a piece of yourself. If you don't, you're suddenly the bad guy and labelled 'arrogant'. What they forget, however, is that you're a human, too. In fact, one of my friends, John Dawson, who had a martial arts gym and used to write for the martial arts press back in the days, was in attendance that day in the capacity of a fan. Like all the other UFC fans there, he and some of his students were looking forward to meeting Randy. When the signing was in full force, I had my team control the queue because personalising autographs and posing for selfies can be time consuming if it's not regulated. The event ran from 11am to 1pm, so we had two hours to get through everything on the schedule. After the 30-minute interview we had to get every single person in the room to meet Randy, get their autograph and give them the opportunity to snap a photo. I had someone move the guys along as soon as Randy had scribbled his name and they'd snapped a photo with the star.

John, even though he was there as a fan, politely complained to me about this process. He said he wanted to talk to the UFC champion for only a few minutes, but was left disappointed because it didn't happen. Suddenly Randy was a bad guy! Let me tell you the truth, Randy is anything but bad. Randy had the tendency to scold me and his handlers if we set restrictions on the fans when he did fan meets. He was a fans' favourite and always endeavoured to please them. He cared immensely about the image he projected, but also about his fans. Be that as it may, you had to look at it through a more practical lens. If every fan had three minutes with Randy that day, we'd have been there for 12 hours or more. Randy might have done it – he's that much of a nice guy.

Anyway, after a quick on-the-spot interview with the TV crew, we rushed Randy out. Azmat had arranged a black Hummer as part of the logistics and transportation. We jumped in there and made our way to Zooks restaurant, a fairly classy place on the outskirts of the city centre opposite the old BBC building. Azmat had recommended this place as he knew the owners, who, sure enough, really took care of us. Another friend who was supposed to come to the event suddenly rang me when we were on our way to the restaurant. I just told him to join us at the restaurant. He had a lady friend with him, but that was no surprise because he was always surrounded by nice women.

At the restaurant, Randy revealed that he was on a special diet. He had got heavily into food and nutrition, and fish and vegetables were a major part of his eating, with red meat almost off the menu entirely. We all listened attentively. Despite being one of the older UFC fighters, he was known for a level of physical fitness and supreme conditioning that the younger fighters could only envy in a sport that's a test of almost every aspect of human fitness. I once asked him what kept him going in his 40s, and he told me: 'What keeps me going is, I'm very passionate about the sport; it's what I love to do, and as long as I'm still capable of doing it, I don't see why I should do anything else. And I'm getting paid for it … I'll keep training.'

Randy was a scholar when it came to training. He told me: 'I like to peak ten weeks before a fight. I study tapes of my opponent and decide what his strengths and weaknesses are and try to watch out for them. We get a game plan together; a lot of striking, sprint work, conditioning and also lots of plyometrics. This topped with a couple of days a week real hard sparring where my partners try to wear me down – this is done with multiple partners. Other times, sparring and striking in different situations, and worst-case-scenario training, putting myself in the worst position an opponent can potentially put me in, so that I have to find a way to survive and neutralise it and try to win the fight. All in all, a well-rounded approach.'

As the afternoon progressed, we talked about fighting and Randy's movie career, which was progressing nicely. We all listened to the two-weight-class UFC champion as he shared his wisdom with us mere mortals. 'I ask myself, what is the worst thing that the opponent can do to me?' Randy said to us – which seems sensible, until you realise he's in a sport where people lose teeth and break arms. It takes a lot for someone to summon the courage to even step into the UFC arena. The worst thing that could happen is that the opponent could maybe knock him out in a fight, he explained. The impression he gave us was that it was no big deal and that it wasn't going to be the end of the world for him if he lost a fight, or got knocked out cold in the Octagon. He went into his fights armed with this mentality, which helped him control fear and keep relaxed instead of being too anxious. As he once put it, 'A lot of the guys who don't have a strong set of striking skills can take advantage of other gifts they have, such as mental attributes and approach.'

* * *

Business was good. After a few months, I decided to purchase a sports X5 BMW with cash – In my mind I often credited Randy Couture for that car. It was nice to be rewarded and I felt I had earned it, but I never ever let my success go to my head. My philosophy had always been: there's always someone better than you. So I would never look down on anyone nor let status and materialistic things go to my head. I can say with great conviction that almost everyone who knows me personally can vouch for this.

Talking of cars, I ran into an idiot one afternoon, no pun intended. I and a family member picked up this family friend, who I have known almost all my life. I can't exactly remember where we were going, whether it was a wedding or a funeral. I think it was a wedding. If it had been a funeral, there would've been two now. As 'Mr Idiot' jumped in the car, he quipped, 'You've not had a police raid yet, have you?' implying that I had sold drugs and was reaping the benefits now – why else would I be driving a car of this calibre?

Although it was meant in jest, it got to me. If I'm honest, I was expecting 'Mr Idiot' to spew out something of a derogatory nature. I had encountered many like him during my lifetime so it wasn't a shock to my system at all – far from it. He was the epitome of jealousy.

You know what the funny thing is? His son was an active drug dealer. Wait! It gets better! He allegedly bought him a car with the drug money. Talk about fucking double standards. Yes, there were plenty of double standards where I grew up. I had seen his son at least twice selling drugs in the street. He was on it like a car bonnet.

Drugs are something I never touched or used. Selling them was out of the question. Near where I grew up, some young lads were doing drugs, some driving sports cars, and they had just left college. Wanting to make fast and easy money and live the life was apparently their only ambition. I had no real urge to criticise, yet some of the parents of these young men had a real propensity to talk negatively about other innocent people, a bad habit that I utterly abhorred. I always say, 'Look at yourself before you point the finger.' If we all embraced this philosophy then maybe the world would be a better place. I couldn't believe these idiots would never miss an opportunity to disparage others, especially the innocent, when they were guilty as hell themselves.

I think dealing in drugs is a huge risk and if you get caught your life, in essence, is over. It's better to live modestly and have less money than get plunged into the drugs game. And those who take drugs, well, everyone gets a kick out of one thing or another. I have been in the company of friends who have taken drugs, even hardcore ones such as cocaine, but I was never tempted for one minute. 'You've been around celebrities, you must have taken some cocaine?' a friend once said to me. I told him I never. I've never really been interested in drugs, certainly not because some famous people take them. Considering my background as a journalist in the fight-sport game, I know a lot of the top professional fighters have never touched drugs. I'm not referring to steroids here – we know that steroids are used by some athletes and this is a whole different and controversial subject. On the other hand, some fighters use both – capitalising on both the performance enhancement of steroids and the buzz of class-As.

Not all of them, though. I remember sitting in the home of one of the toughest and most notorious fighters on one trip to Los Angeles, and I've never forget what he told me. He said he'd never taken drugs and he didn't drink, but instead got the biggest buzz out of training and competing. There's a lesson there: in life, getting a buzz can come from many different things. For some it can be their hobby, whether it's a simple thing such as playing chess or a more adrenaline-pumping activity such as racing cars or having a bone-crushing wrestling session. Some find that going out at the weekend, having a laugh and impressing friends by trying ever so hard to look and act cool – trying to be something they're not – gives them a buzz. For others, it's alcohol or drugs. People often think that getting in the cage is dangerous – but for those abusing drink or drugs, maybe they'd be better off finding their buzz elsewhere.

CHAPTER SIXTEEN

BOXING VS UFC: THE TYSON-GRACIE CHALLENGE

BY THE late 2000s, the UFC's enormous success had prompted a slew of rival MMA organisations to jump on the bandwagon. But its biggest competitor was, and still is, the sport of boxing. For years the UFC had played second fiddle to the sweet science, and for our fledgling sport to surpass the global popularity of this ancient sport seemed almost impossible. Well into the explosion of the UFC, boxing superstars such as Mike Tyson, Sugar Ray Leonard and Floyd Mayweather were still more recognisable names outside their sport than any UFC athlete. And most casual fans still regarded the boxing heavyweight champion as the Baddest Man on the Planet.

Could the UFC make the leap ahead? *What are the chances of a 70-year-old grandma knowing who Randy Couture is?* I thought to myself at one point. You have to remember, the promoters had initially sold UFC as a blood-and-guts spectacle before the new owners instituted more rules in the transition to making MMA a true sport. Not even a decade before, the sport had provoked widespread outrage, but now, with personable champions and a growing audience, things were changing. Boxing had a serious challenger to its crown and the old-school promoters had no choice but to play down their foe.

The arguments they put forward will be familiar to any UFC fan. Boxing pundits and promoters argued that the brutal and minimally skilled fighters of MMA could not compare with the warriors of the sweet science – that boxing was simply a more sophisticated sport. What they failed to comprehend, or neglected to mention, was the fact that UFC athletes, even then, were highly skilled in multiple disciplines. Some of this was simply wilful ignorance – afraid of being overpowered by this exciting new sport they were vocal and disparaging of everything MMA. To this end, a lot of them made sure their fighters did not promote, directly or indirectly, anything that related to the new sport.

Whenever hardcore and casual boxing fans dismissed UFC fighters as being unskilled, knocking each other out for beer-drinking fans, stereotypical thugs only interested in violence, it made my skin crawl. Some of these diehard boxing lovers had no clue whatsoever as to the calibre of skill that UFC athletes possessed. Just like boxing, MMA demands years of study and dedication, but unlike the sweet science, the MMA fighter has far more to worry about than his opponent's fists. Some of the jeers at MMA, of course, come from a lack of understanding. The complexity of arts such as Brazilian jiu-jitsu – the technical brilliance and strategic elements – mirrors that of playing a game of chess, at top speed, when the other competitor isn't waiting for you to move. While even a novice spectator can quite easily follow what's going on in a boxing match, most have no real concept of what's going on when they watch two men rolling around on the ground. The fight for small positional advantages can be invisible, just as much as the more nuanced footwork in a high-level boxing bout is incomprehensible to the average fan. As commentary improved and knowledge grew, things changed, but it took a while.

Boxers, too, were quick to disparage this sport that allowed kicks, joint locks and throws as well as punches. Floyd Mayweather, always outspoken, was happy to throw some low blows. 'It takes true skills to be in the sport of boxing,' he remarked to an interviewer on CBS

BOXING VS UFC: THE TYSON-GRACIE CHALLENGE

Sports, 'and MMA is for beer drinkers, boxing is for everybody. There are no white fighters in boxing that are dominating, so they had to go to something else and start something new.' As a long-time UFC fan and writer, I found this hard to take. I felt this guy needed to do his homework, like so many other boxing fans. And while, yes, things have changed, many hardcore boxing fans still utterly abhor MMA today. Part of the boxing fraternity has been living in denial and is delusional.

On the other end of the spectrum, it wasn't long before you had boxing champions pictured at ringside at UFC events in America and the United Kingdom, fully appreciating the Octagon gladiators. Despite the fact that part of the boxing fraternity had strong reservations about UFC being a threat to their financial interests and fan base, there was no getting away from the fact that this new phenomenon had landed and created a new type of fighter. The smartest pugilists now, by and large, recognised the hard work, fitness and skill that went into making of an MMA champion. These men trained harder than Olympic athletes, aiming to master not just one skill – that of wrestling, say, an Olympic sport in itself – but three or four. And in this spirit the more open-minded ones started to not merely acknowledge but applaud the new breed of athlete, who they perceived as elite-tier sportspeople. These modern-day gladiators might be a potential threat to their pay packet, but anyone who understood the game had to respect them.

As the boxing versus MMA feud reached epic proportions, it was time to ask the king of boxing promoters to share his thoughts. I'm always prepared to ask anyone for an interview, but to say that I was surprised when the most famous boxing promoter, Don King, personally shared his views with me relating to the UFC may be an understatement. It had taken me literally 18 phone calls to arrange to speak to Don. He was always up to something, meeting presidents, world leaders and the higher echelons of society, and globetrotting all over the world. King is certainly the king of the promoters, although

Bob Arum might give him a run for his money. Moreover, Don had been the subject of controversy ever since his early years in the sport. He was an intriguing character who I couldn't wait to talk to.

Sure enough, the conversation was an epic one. During a lengthy and thought-provoking conversation, we talked about Muhammad Ali, some of the current boxing champions and this new threat to the sport of boxing – the UFC. I asked Don whether he thought UFC was a genuine competitor to boxing game – a sport that had made this flamboyant promoter millions of dollars and afforded him a lifestyle that mere mortals can only dream of. 'I like ultimate fighting, it's a raw thing like street fighting,' he told me, his voice hitting the half-yell familiar from his other interviews. 'Ultimate fighting is raw, that's why it's got a huge number of fans. I intend to be able to promote that, too.' He had his own take on the evolution of the sport. 'It was a raw type of barbarism, now it's become a sophisticated type of barbarism that the public loves. I think it's sensational and I have nothing but praise for those who have been successful and carved a niche out.'

I was astonished at what Don was saying. I wasn't expecting it, far from it. In fact, ahead of the interview I feared he might even decline to answer any UFC-related questions. After all, the promoters of boxing often evaded questions about their competition, if they weren't already bashing the new sport openly.

After a little thought, though, it was easy to see why he was full of such elation. Being an astute businessman, he was more than willing to jump on the MMA bandwagon himself and probably saw it as a way to reach a younger fan base that didn't care for boxing. How could I have missed this? I was, frankly, disappointed in myself. He told me with great conviction that both sports could survive and bring people together, and that he was all about bringing people together. This is how to understand Don King or any true promoter: where there's money to be made, they'll show up. 'I think now, with the ultimate fighting, there are new kinds of fans,' he continued, exuding the charm he's famous for. 'Not as per se boxing fans, but as fans of

BOXING VS UFC: THE TYSON-GRACIE CHALLENGE

a brutal combat sport with elbows, kicking, biting. I have no quarrel with ultimate fighting because it's a peoples' sport, and a lot of people and youngsters are coming to see it – it's exciting!' Like I said, many other boxing promoters were, and still are, vehemently against this new craze. But Don was seeing another golden opportunity, which apparently had the potential to fatten his bank account.

Some people at the time were opining that boxing was dying and the future looked bleak. The new generation, and some of the old generation who had grown up watching the sweet science, are now flocking to UFC events, which often offer more action – and more fighters to root for than the headliners on each card. I have always said that the popularity of boxing is, to a large degree, due to the mainstream TV coverage it's received for many decades. I once put the question to UFC legend Randy Couture to get his personal opinion – was boxing dying and the new generation turning to a new combat sport? Or could it be that MMA had caught up with the sweet science and both sports could co-exist? 'I don't think boxing is dying,' the five-time UFC champion told me. 'I think the attitude is that it's more one-dimensional compared to MMA. And the UFC has done a great job pioneering that and it's something the younger generation are into – extreme sports – they like it.'

* * *

How did boxers feel about the skill levels in the two sports? Once, I asked Sugar Ray Leonard for his opinions on the Gracies – the fighting family responsible for creating this new craze in the fight world. After all, this was Sugar Ray Leonard, one of the all-time boxing greats, whose opinions mattered more than any promoter's. I expected his opinions to be interesting, but still I was surprised when he told me that he was friends with Rickson Gracie, something I was oblivious to. Both fighters had visited Japan where they did joint autograph signings. In the 1990s, Rickson had been fighting in Japan where he endeared himself to fight fans and became a living legend. The former boxing champion's path had also crossed with Royce Gracie on a flight to Los Angeles. 'Royce's presence is so unassuming,' the former five-weight-division champion exclaimed. 'He's so approachable. Because he's a tall skinny guy, he doesn't look ferocious. And that's what I like, because he could really take your head off.' He let out a laugh as he remembered the UFC fighter.

As I've mentioned, before the first UFC took place on 12 November 1993, when Royce beat three opponents in the same night to become the first ever UFC champion, a lot of people had a misconception about fighting. The general vibe was that the heavyweight boxing champion was the toughest guy in the world. However, when the world witnessed a rather frail-looking man prevail with technically superior submission skills as he tapped out a field of brutes, that myth would find its way out of the window – a window that has been firmly shut since. But before that, the Gracies tried to show the superiority of their style in a rather more direct way.

'Iron' Mike Tyson became the youngest ever heavyweight champion at the age of 20, and was widely considered an unstoppable force – at least to those who considered boxing the only true form of fighting. Envied, revered and feared, Tyson is one of the most ferocious fighters the heavyweight division has ever seen. When he faced opponents in the ring, they were often beaten before the bout actually got under way because of his intimidatory tactics. His savage, aggressive and violent style and aura of invincibility made him fearless. Furthermore, he had tested himself countless times in savage street encounters that often made the front page of newspapers. Driven by an intense will, he was equipped with psychological armour, which is as important as your raw skill when you are caught up in a street scenario. He was the perfect physical specimen you'd like to watch fight, but you would most definitely want to avoid being on the receiving end of his brutal blows. And you definitely would want to avoid encountering him in a dark alley – or at least, that was basically the public's perception of him.

BOXING VS UFC: THE TYSON-GRACIE CHALLENGE

The Gracie family, of course, didn't think this way. In fact, the notorious boxer was challenged by the Gracie Brothers, in particular Royce, back in the early 1990s. The UFC champion's perception was that Tyson was the best boxer in the world, but he refused to accept that Tyson was the best 'fighter'. The Gracies had a point. They had been beating all-comers from various styles long before the Octagon was first engineered. And Royce wasn't going to rest until he did everything within his means to provoke the heavyweight champion into accepting a real fight in a no-holds-barred setting. To settle the matter once and for all, Royce formally challenged the most feared boxer of our time to a fight to the finish, and so did his elder brother Rickson, who was widely regarded as the most technically proficient Brazilian jiu-jitsu fighter in the world. 'Will Mike Tyson have more courage than Joe Louis, who was content to rest on his laurels and declined to step into the no-holds-barred arena?' they asked, referring to the fact that their father Helio Gracie had challenged the 'Brown Bomber' back in his prime.

As news of the Gracie challenge spread like wildfire in the combat sports world, I often came across absurd comments in Readers' Letters sections in the martial arts press, most notably in America's *Black Belt* and *Inside Kung Fu* and the United Kingdom's *Martial Arts Illustrated* and *Combat*. The readers, who, in those days, had very little experience of grappling, especially the ground grappling that was the speciality of the Gracies, would happily voice their opinions on this hypothetical matchup, most believing that the blistering power and brute force the heavyweight was capable of producing was enough to demoralise just about anyone you put in front of him. *If Tyson caught Gracie with one punch, Gracie would be knocked out*, was the most common trope. Fair enough. But you have to put it into perspective. Royce's challenge to Tyson was a no-holds-barred fight; not a boxing or grappling match. As a matter of fact, during one of my many conversations with Royce he actually told me that if Tyson hit him once in the face, he'd wake up in hospital a week later.

Royce has never claimed to be punch-proof. But For Royce, any fight was a matter of who could implement their own strategy, and much of the Gracie style was developed to avoid even the chance of their opponent landing a lucky punch. What Royce lacked in brute force, he clearly made up for in technical skill, as his opponents – including a professional boxer – quickly discovered. 'There's only one way to find out,' he told me, as a smirk crept across his face followed by loud laughter. Sadly for posterity, Tyson declined.

Still, while Tyson was at least respectful, the armchair tough guys were much less so. Again, their argument was that Tyson was so lethal that the Brazilian grappling master was doomed in the stand-up. He would, they opined, have no chance to use his skills. Being an ardent admirer of the Gracie clan, I always beg to differ. These so-called critics obviously hadn't experienced Gracie Jiu-Jitsu first-hand, this amazing art that had sent shockwaves around the globe and changed many peoples' perceptions of fighting. Jiu-jitsu can seem simple to counter until you experience it – feeling the crushing top pressure of a master grappler, and having your options removed inch by inch.

As much as the Gracies were revered by many, they were equally abhorred by others. Part of the reason was their love of challenge matches. As well as inviting other martial arts instructors and fighters to their Los Angeles academy to fight them bare-knuckle with no rules, they had a penchant for turning up, announced or unannounced, at martial arts schools to challenge top masters.

In 'Iron Mike's' case, one rejection wasn't enough for Royce. In 1997 the Gracie's challenge made the headlines again, after the publication of a one-page advert in *Men's Health* in America, in which the UFC champion once again challenged the former heavyweight boxer 'officially'. Anywhere, anytime, no rules! Years later I asked Royce about the famous challenge, and discovered that the heavyweight had been, at least in theory, willing to put up. 'I heard that my brother tried to bring him in (to the UFC),' Royce explained. 'He had accepted but people around him – the lawyers, managers, and the Commission – said no way, because boxing had too much to lose. But he had accepted and he wanted to do it. I talked to him before and he's like, 'I'd love to try this stuff out, man.' But people around him did not allow him to do it. If he lost a fight, if it happened, well, boxing was already in the decline in America so it wouldn't be good for boxing.'

What would have happened if the bout had materialised is one of the great 'What if ...' stories in MMA history. Perhaps Tyson would have landed a lucky punch and derailed the Gracie hype train, or perhaps Royce would have choked the Baddest Man on the Planet unconscious, and sent Brazilian jiu-jitsu into the stratosphere. It would have never happened, though. Tyson wasn't going to put his hard-earned reputation on the line, nor were the money men in the boxing game, in their infinite wisdom, going to allow this fight to take place. The notorious boxer was making millions of dollars, so it wouldn't make sense for him from a financial perspective, bearing in mind that the UFC pay packets were meagre in comparison to what top boxers were raking in.

* * *

So what does the notorious boxer think of all this? Was he 'bad' enough to beat Royce Gracie, the man who had never beaten anyone with his fists, in a no-holds-barred bloody fight to the finish? Tyson was asked by a UFC host on *UFC Tonight* to transport himself back and consider how he would have fared in a fight against the then-UFC champion. 'Well, in 1993 I was in prison, so there wouldn't have been a fight,' was his response, before the champ gave his interviewer a surprise. 'There is no way I would have won.'

One thing that surprises modern interviewers most about Tyson is his humbleness. This is a man who dismantled the heavyweight division of his era and made history. But he has great reverence for the greats of boxing before him and now UFC athletes, too. 'Iron' Mike has since gone on record admitting his appreciation for the

Gracies and just how mesmerised he was watching the UFC when it first debuted and his challenger ruled the Octagon. Ever since being introduced to the UFC, Tyson became completely hooked, and continues to be captivated by the sport even now. The first time he watched the UFC, he says, was at his home with friends of his. His guests would normally be inebriated and Tyson would put on the UFC tapes, which back then were available in VHS format. They'd watch the warriors of the Octagon every time they'd got the chance. The former heavyweight champion has followed the careers of the great fighters ever since that early era of Ken Shamrock, Royce Gracie and Dan Severn. He follows the sport to this day, and he recently paid homage to the Gracies and his former challenger. 'The Gracies are not as big as they should be, and they showed that size didn't matter,' he said. 'The fighting world has the utmost respect for the Gracie clan, there's no doubt about that.'

These words had a knockout effect on me. I mean, here is the guy who was the most feared fighter in the world, as well as the most famous sportsman of the 1980s and 1990s, praising his old nemesis who back then was virtually an unknown beyond the confines of the martial arts world. It was a momentous victory for the martial arts, which had always taken a backseat in the minds of the majority of the public, as far as combat sports are concerned. The reason why the Gracies are less known compared to today's modern MMA superstars who have captivated the attention of the fans is simply because when Royce was fighting in the Octagon, the sport had not yet filtered into the mainstream. However, few would argue that the Gracie name undoubtedly is the most prominent in the history of the MMA movement. The fact remains: the most unlikely looking fighter you'll ever lay your eyes on had changed the way the world perceived fighting when he tore through his opponents in the earlier UFCs, steamrolling much bigger adversaries. He proved that he, and the grappling style of Gracie Jiu-Jitsu had prevailed, solidifying his legacy in the history books. Today, every single MMA competitor has

BOXING VS UFC: THE TYSON-GRACIE CHALLENGE

to implement Brazilian jiu-jitsu training as part of their core training, in order to survive in the Octagon.

Now that the UFC has gone mainstream and he lives in Las Vegas, Tyson can often be seen ringside enjoying the fights. Royce and Tyson were both VIP ringside guests at UFC 160 in Las Vegas in May 2013. It seemed like they were having a wonderful time laughing and joking around with each other. I obviously had great insight into the tension between the two when the famous challenge was made. So, once again, when I spoke to Royce I asked him how he perceived Tyson now, the man he had challenged back in the days to a no-holds-barred literally fight to the death. 'I like Tyson. I'm a big fan of Mike Tyson,' he told me in his usual calm manner. 'We met a couple of times and he's a very nice guy.' Royce is a man of few words. And despite the fact that some people may perceive him as cocky or even with an ego, he's respectful of other fighters, even though he is never hesitant to speak his mind, and respectful of those he encounters. In fact, he is one of the most laid-back fighters you'll ever come across. Both men have mutual respect for each other, that's for sure. Both epitomise true sportsmanship and many fans could learn a lesson from them.

CHAPTER SEVENTEEN

UFC, ROYALS & RICH ARABS

ONE THING that had caught my attention about the UFC was that its star athletes often did autograph signings – something you didn't see happening in the boxing game much. For the UFC stars, allowing access to fans for meet-and-greets at expos and pre-UFC shows was common, and these sessions would attract thousands of fans. To further strengthen the British fan base and ensure UFC's continued popularity, in October 2010 the organisation announced its first expo in the United Kingdom. This coincided with UFC 120, which was to take place at the O2 Arena, and which would go on to set a European attendance record of 17,133. The previous record was 16,693, set by UFC 105 when Randy Couture fought at the MEN Arena in November the year before. I thought this would be another golden opportunity for Randy to do some promotion, as I knew there would be thousands of hardcore fans attending the expo at Earls Court.

Expos in the USA had been very successful. The support the UFC received from all the fringe industries connected to the sport of MMA was impressive. This time, the UFC promised to have the largest assemblage of fighters to hit Europe as they ventured into the lucrative European market. The world's premier MMA organisation always made a noise about setting records and bringing their loyal fans the best fighters to meet, and so this time Randy was going to be flown over by the UFC to be one of the star athletes in attendance. With over 100 MMA-related vendors exhibiting, I contacted *Fighters Only* magazine, the world's leading MMA publication, and they agreed to have Randy at their stand on the first day of the expo. Randy would meet fans and sign autographs for two hours – 10am to 12 noon. I would have loved it if we could have done signings throughout the day, but Randy had been allocated a limited amount of time because of his obligations and commitments to the organisation that had flown him over.

Seyfi, Ahsan and I drove down in the morning to Earl's Court to meet Randy. He arrived a little later outside the venue, where we were waiting for him. I was somewhat disappointed and surprised when Randy told us that he had taken the tube from his hotel. I felt the UFC officials should have been assigned to him and escorted the champion from the hotel to the venue. But I believe the organisation and Randy were on shaky terms by that point, which would explain it, even though I'm sure a few fans were probably surprised to see him riding the tube. As I've mentioned, Randy is one of the most humble stars you will ever meet, never the one looking for star treatment. Whenever we picked him up from the airport he wouldn't let us carry his bags; he insisted on carrying his own luggage. This down-to-earth attitude made him a fans' favourite, and despite his high-profile, Randy never had a high opinion of himself. He was never condescending, to anyone, no matter who they were.

Outside the venue you could see a whole herd of UFC fans making for the gates. It's not rocket science to spot UFC fans. They are young and old folk alike with MMA branded Tapout T-shirts, caps and hoodies, all eager to meet their favourite fighters. If there is one single thing that I have learned about fans of UFC, it's the fact that they come in all shapes and from diverse backgrounds. Even though the UFC core fan base is the 18–34 demographic – predominately male – which is the most coveted target audience in the world, the sport has been embraced by people from all walks of life: from young kids to the youth, housewives to older men, male and female. Sure, there was once an image of tattooed tough guys flocking to fights, but these days the majority of its followers are armchair fans, with only an extremely small fraction going to the gym to train and experience the sport.

Speaking of fan statistics, it's interesting to note that in a 2010 survey (Simmons Research Database) the size of the UFC fan base in America was estimated at 31 million. The 'avid' fan base was estimated at 35 per cent of that overall number, or 11 million. In Canada the sport had exploded. With a population of 34 million, it was estimated that a whopping six million were fans, or roughly 18 per cent of the population, almost one in five people. The UFC's interest levels in Canada far exceed those of the USA in every demographic – perhaps partly thanks to the dominance of Canadian hero GSP in the sport's welterweight division. Closer to home in Britain, it was estimated that eight per cent of the population were fans, which equates to five million people. For the rest of the world, estimated fans numbers were near the 20-million mark. So the overall global size of the fan base was estimated at 65 million a decade ago. Considering the sport of MMA hadn't been around for long compared to other sports – and Conor McGregor hadn't emerged – and major positive mainstream media coverage eluded the sport for a long time, this was huge. Today, over 300 million people are fans of the UFC.

Interestingly, according to Dana White, the split between male and female fans of UFC is 56/44. But I feel that although there is a fairly large female following, this figure is disputable. This is my personal opinion and I'm sure I'm right because that split just doesn't make sense at all. The sport is still considered by many to be a violent and brutal pastime, and plenty of people I know still think of its bouts as unskilled slugfests. But the growth rate has been tremendous nevertheless.

These statistics, by the way, relate to UFC – the number-one brand – not MMA as a whole. Why do you wear Nike trainers or a Hugo Boss suit or a T-shirt with Mike Tyson's mug on the front? A brand represents your product and quality. Your brand is derived from who you are, who you want to be and who people perceive you to be. The added value intrinsic to brand equity frequently comes in the form of perceived quality or emotional attachment. A good example is Nike, which associates its products with star athletes, hoping customers will transfer their emotional attachment from the athlete to the product. It's no surprise that the UFC is so protective of its imagine – it doesn't want to become tarnished by associations with less-regulated organisations. The UFC went on to ink a $70 million six-year sponsorship deal with Reebok four years later. It was a mega brand affiliated with the UFC.

Anyway, on this particular day, the UFC was going gangbusters. In two hours Randy must have met 400-plus fans. I'm sure half of them didn't purchase what was being sold, although we had a strict rule that only those making a purchase were allowed to meet Randy. I did get into an argument with one fan who thought he could ignore the rules, but there were other fans and a professional film crew snapping pictures as they walked past so I resisted my initial urge to escalate things. In any case, Randy looked like a major sports celebrity being flocked by fans.

Suddenly, a smartly dressed man in a dark navy suit approached me. 'I work for the PA of the Prince of Dubai, DJ,' he said politely as he introduced himself. 'Can DJ meet Randy, please?' This guy was the driver for the Prince of Dubai's personal assistant. He looked like an accountant, or maybe the bespectacled guy who did the Halifax TV adverts (we all remember that one, don't we?). After a couple of seconds of thought – because the queue was long – I said to him, 'Yes, five minutes!' DJ sauntered forward and introduced himself to me and Randy. 'How long are you in the United Kingdom?' he enquired. 'We would like to show you around London.' Randy said that he wasn't going to be around long, but that DJ should give his number to me. Sure enough, the PA wrote his number down on a piece of paper and handed it over to me, emphasising to me not once but twice that I should call him. I assured him that I would call him later in the evening.

After a short chat and having snapped a photo with Randy, DJ grabbed my right hand, and, as he was leaving, placed a bunch of rolled-up crisp £50 notes into my hand and closed my fist. 'No, it's OK,' I half-heartedly protested, in a vain attempt to hide my embarrassment – though to be honest, I appreciated the tip. *I was certainly going to make the call, even if it meant I had to crawl to a telephone*, I joked to myself. This type of tipping, I came to learn, is common in the parts of the world where these royals came from. They weren't short of cash and often threw it away like tissue paper – well, some of them did. Later that day when I checked, I realised I had been tipped several hundred pounds. I've never been tipped before in my life as far as I can remember.

As soon as it hit noon, a female UFC rep came to our stand and told us that she had to whisk Randy away. He had to fulfil other UFC promotional obligations. We thought we were about to face an angry mob, as there were still around 150 people waiting in the queue to meet Randy, but what happened next caught me and members of my team by complete surprise. Simply put, Randy burst into the queue, randomly signing whatever the fans shoved in his face, without any worries about public order. Now we had fans flocking around trying to get a piece of 'The Natural,' with some resorting to desperate measures because he had to leave. It was total chaos. One silly kid repeatedly threw his head next to Randy's in an annoying manner several times as his friend desperately snapped a quick photo. Other fighters present at the expo were Wanderlei Silva and Junior Dos Santos, both champs, but nobody was as popular as Randy.

As we waited outside for our car to pick us up, we spotted a bespectacled young man struggling with about 20 UFC Expo bags full of goodies. He was a member of DJ's entourage. Suddenly, DJ and his driver emerged from the venue and walked towards us. Once again he greeted us and once again, I promised I would call him later. I joked about the bags, and DJ told me there were another 20 on the way, which made me laugh. Seyfi had barrowed DJ's pen earlier, DJ remembered, and Seyfi had to hand it back. I don't think Seyfi was happy about getting caught. He thought he'd banked a golden souvenir pen from a member of the Dubai royal staff.

Later that evening I made that all-important call to DJ. I told him that next time Randy was visiting our shores we would be in touch, because Randy was on a tight schedule and was soon leaving the country. Although the event was attended by a huge number of fans who were all willing to part with their cash, some industry insiders felt it was much smaller compared to the American UFC expos, and long-term opportunities for the business networking weren't particularly good. Still, we had a great time and I felt that the event had been attended by thousands of fans. And, perhaps most importantly for me, I had got one foot in the door with Middle Eastern royalty.

* * *

I found it intriguing that the royal families of Dubai and Abu Dhabi had become ardent UFC fans. In fact, they are big fans of combat sports in general, alongside many other adrenaline-fuelled sports – motorsport, soccer, diving, horse riding, you name it. This high echelon of society is an adventurous breed with a passion for living life to the max and beyond. I guess if you've got billions of dollars stacked up in the banks, then all you want to do is live life to the extreme and enjoy and explore the world.

Enter Sheikh Thanoon Bin Zayed of Abu Dhabi. While studying at the university in San Diego, California, he fell in love with Brazilian jiu-jitsu, an art which, at the time, was spreading across the USA, inspired by the Gracie craze. After watching the first UFC he became driven by the Gracie family, and Royce in particular. He went on to train with Renzo Gracie in New York, eventually earning the coveted black belt. One story I've heard is that, when the prince was taking a private lesson with Renzo, he had told his instructor that he had a flight to catch, but continued to chat for a prolonged period. 'Don't you have a flight to catch?' Renzo asked his private student. It was then that the Brazilian jiu-jitsu instructor learned that this student had his own jet, as the sheikh revealed his true identity.

Renzo has personally told me since that the sheikh is blessed with one of the most creative minds he's ever known and that while he was teaching him Gracie Jiu-Jitsu, Renzo was learning about life from his student. Renzo, who has taught many UFC champions, told me he was very lucky to have been chosen to be the prince's teacher, and that several other members of the royal family also privately study Brazilian jiu-jitsu. The prince, his love affair with the great grappling art was far from over and he went on to purchase ten per cent of available shares in the UFC, now probably worth more than a billion dollars.

As for Abu Dhabi itself, the royals have transformed the city from a dessert town to a thriving business centre. It has become a hub for sports, cricket, motor racing, combat sports, and even bodybuilding to an extent. Because of their profound passion and financial strength, the royals have had the opportunity to promote and accommodate MMA in their region to a greater extent than almost everywhere except for Las Vegas and Brazil. There is a training centre, the Abu Dhabi Combat Club, which is a facility for MMA and grappling training that Sheikh Tahnoon has built into perhaps the best place to learn MMA and Brazilian jiu-jitsu in the Arab world. It has given its name to the world's most prestigious grappling competition. Sheikh Tahnoon has been at the fore of promoting the art in the region, and it always seemed inevitable that the UFC would sooner or later make its debut in Abdu Dubai. On 10 April 2010, UFC finally landed in this magical city, with none other than Renzo Gracie headlining.

Renzo, who hadn't fought for almost three years at the time, was set to fight one of the all-time greats, Matt Hughes, at UFC 112. I had seen Matt fight two years earlier when he was knocked out by a flying knee to the face, but he was still a dangerous fighter.

Matt had dominated the UFC welterweight division for a long time. He wasn't much of a striker, but he was a savage wrestler and solid ground-and-pounder who'd developed a dangerous submission game. Still, I was looking forward to watching Renzo obliterate Matt. Ever since Matt fought Royce, I had started to dislike him because he had beaten my friend. He also seemed a little conceited, but maybe I was being judgemental – maybe he was a nice guy. But even if he was, he wasn't getting my vote. No way was I going to idolise a fighter who had beaten my idol. I was banking on Renzo to avenge his cousin.

Perhaps not surprisingly, given its two legendary participants, the bout was huge. It broke pay-per-view records with over 620,000 buys, and was the first event to break the $20-million mark in gross pay-per-view sales. UFC 112 was the first UFC to be held in an open-air arena, and it was attended by over 11,000 fans. Sadly, the fight didn't go the way I would have liked. After a striking contest that many felt was more like a sparring session, Matt prevailed, winning the bout via TKO.

Needless to say, I wasn't thrilled with the result, but when it comes to combat sports, often you have to accept a loss and come to terms with it and motivate yourself to come back stronger. Renzo, a veteran of countless street fights, is still one of the best Gracies in my opinion, aggressive, with the heart of a lion. He's the type of a fighter who could beat anyone on any given day.

Having a passion for sports and enterprise, the Middle Eastern royals have invested in America and Europe over the years, from acquiring soccer clubs to purchasing shares in Planet Hollywood. Money is like paper from a writing pad to these royals. Having said that, I've always firmly believed that money can't buy you everything in life, and I stand by this. Yes, money can, of course, present you with rare opportunities that you never otherwise would have had. But there will always be something that money can't buy you. If you have a billion dollars, for example, you won't be able to transform yourself into a great professional sportsman nor a Tom Cruise, nor will you be able to become a Conor McGregor or Mike Tyson – the kind of character who inspires the devotion of millions. There are billionaires who would give an arm and a leg to be in the position of some of the most revered athletes or movie stars. In fact, the nephew of the richest man in the world is in a professional soccer team, yet is still to make a full appearance or a name for himself. He is worth $20 billion, making him the richest soccer player in the world – but no one has really heard of him. Money can certainly buy you great training, good food and a well-equipped gym, but if money was the one-and-only secret antidote then the toughest guys in the world, or the most admired and loved personalities, would be the ones with a billion dollars. Money can elevate your status to a degree but can never give you that natural talent and achievement that is a result of unleashing your true natural potential. Fame and fortune is extremely inciting to the human animal. Fame exceeds fortune in many ways.

I know of people who have so-called friends because they have money. If these particular people had no money, they wouldn't have these folk around them. Yes, it's a sad state of affairs. People who think that money is everything, frankly, are delusional. I've always admired talented people who have worked hard and achieved something – with money that has come as a consequence of their work. But it won't get you everything. Besides, personally having millions would make me sick because the thrill of the struggle would be gone from my life. Having everything in life would kill my motivation completely.

It's beyond my comprehension why some, or should I say most, people kiss ass if someone has a fairly large amount of money. And when I say this, I'm not even talking about a millionaire; I'm talking about average people who happen to have a fairly decent office job and career, drive a fairly luxurious car, and have 50 grand in the bank for good measure. Why would you respect and adulate such an individual more than a person with a less attractive job and car. Unless that person is going to hand over some of their cash, or pay your bills, then why hold that person in higher regard than the rest of us mere mortals? How are they worthy of it?

Remember: the way people treat you is a statement about who they are as a human being; it's not a statement about you. We've heard of the saying 'treat others as you would want others to treat you', and if only people would embrace this. No matter how educated you are, talented, rich or cool, how you treat people ultimately says everything about your integrity. As a journalist and student, whenever I travelled to America and met or spoke to some of the world-renowned martial arts instructors and MMA champions, for instance, I learned that almost all of them would treat me well. Although I was thrust into a fighting environment, there were ethics and respect shown no matter who you were or what level you were at. If you look carefully at the professional fighters who eventually made a name for themselves and made a fortune, they've often been through bleak periods. While dedicating themselves to the sport of MMA in the hope of one day making it, they either had to have a day job or made meagre money to support themselves – often dipping into their own pockets to pay for travel and accommodation. In the case of Ronda Rousey, she slept in her car for months to save rent.

The key, I believe, is financial security. Indeed, for some, that's not enough. I had struggles like many other people during my early years, and continued to have ups and downs financially, even when I was doing fairly well. I've often had times in my life where I couldn't pay bills, and I can say with deep sincerity I have experienced my fair share of struggles. Obstacles I struggled to surmount, the mental draining of the self, are all too familiar to me – there were several periods when I felt almost helpless. Still, I understood it's something most of us go through, whether you're an average individual or someone who eventually goes on to become famous in some shape or form. But now, experiencing those lows in life has enabled me to put things into perspective. And so, although developing a working relationship with my royal contact and doing something MMA-related was enticing, I went into the relationship knowing that I'd do just fine whether it worked out or not.

CHAPTER EIGHTEEN

MIKE, MANAGERS & ME

BY THE end of the 2000s, Mike Bisping had firmly established himself as the United Kingdom's number-one UFC fighter, blazing a trail for other fighters from his country by first winning *The Ultimate Fighter* reality show and then taking on a legion of top-tier competitors. He was a recognisable face in North America, and a star there. He was also a divisive figure, and, although many Americans warmed up to him, others despised him in equal measure. You either loved or hated Mike – there was no middle ground. My personal opinion is that I can't see a valid reason for loathing him. He puts on a persona to hype up his fights, but he's a hard worker, a great representative of the sport who's always been appreciative to fans. But you know what, that's life – you will get your haters even if you're Mother Teresa.

Mike has certainly enjoyed the success he gets from his exposure more than any UFC fighter from his country. As soon as he was catapulted to the top, he was at the forefront of the business, promoting the UFC as much as he could. His enduring popularity is a testament not just to the UFC's astute marketing skills, but also to his own. He's a great interviewee who speaks his mind and is always ready to talk to fans. This would, I felt, make it easier to 'sell' him to the public because he had an established fan base, and so I wasn't going to let a lucrative potential opportunity to elude me. A collaboration on an MMA project would, I thought, result in great success. Mike had given me his mobile and home number when I first made contact, so one day I got in touch and we had our first meeting to discuss potentially working together. I drove down to his home town of Clitheroe, a small town next to Blackburn, Lancashire to meet the man. We met at his local.

I hit it off with Mike right from the word go. Before he came to prominence in the UFC, he had fought in kickboxing, making a then-respectable £300 a fight. He'd been a DJ prior to his professional fighting career. 'When I was younger I used to go to a lot of amateur tournaments and the kickboxing,' he told me. 'I used to get paid for fights, but it wasn't much.' You couldn't really eke out a living and make it as a profession, even fighting once or twice a month. The young man had toyed around with the idea of going back to university in a quest to get a degree, which would increase his career prospects and provide a better income for his family. '[I wanted to] just generally better myself because I wasn't happy with the way I turned out,' he explained.

Although Mike enjoyed school and did quite well in classes, the lacklustre effort he put into his schooling was all too apparent when he got his grades. He could have, according to him, done a lot better had he focused and tried harder. Instead, he ended up doing factory jobs, and working inside a slaughterhouse, until his career took off. 'The UFC has changed my life utterly and completely,' Mike said. 'I was never happy doing the other jobs I did. I used to hate them, to be honest.' I'm sure a lot of us can relate to this as we've all, at some point in our lives, been in dead-end jobs. I certainly went through a few unpleasant jobs after I left school before my dream manifested into a sports writing career, and that feeling of dejection and gloom was all too familiar as I listened to this UFC athlete reliving his days in hell. 'Now I'm earning more money,' he told me across the pub table, 'but the main thing is I'm doing what I love. I'm very lucky.'

TO THE TOP

It was no surprise that he was such an approachable guy. This professional fighter had walked the path that many of us had, lacking direction in life after leaving school and being unhappy in his job. He could relate to the fans and the average man on the street. Back when he signed up with the organisation, the real money was in boxing, but by the time he retired, the money was better and he was able to save enough to live very comfortably; now he's a multi-millionaire. Mike's tale is inspirational. He is the epitome of the rags-to-riches story.

If I'm honest, there was a part of me that was a little reluctant to working with him on a project. The USA had always been a major focus, and many fans there seemed to dislike him intensely, but Mike assured me that he was more popular in America than he was at home.

As we sat there conferring, Mike told me he had a lot of interesting stories that he had never revealed in interviews. I would later learn that Mike was the ideal athlete to interview because he would always have something compelling to say. He would elaborate instead of giving you one-liners. He would put every fibre of his being into telling his anecdotes. Some fighters were so damn hard to interview, you would be hard pressed to squeeze out of them much other than one-sentence answers. Others, who have been around for decades and lived a fascinating life, often tell the same old stories, even when they have experienced so much that they should never run short of material. But Mike always had something new to say, which always resulted in a riveting interview. As we sat there sipping our coffees in the pub, he insisted that I didn't take a photo. He said to me, 'It's my local, they'll think, "Look at him, he was in here taking photos."' This made me laugh. Mike is a humble guy and never let fame get to his head. I often phoned him late in the evenings – it's a bad habit of mine – and, by and large, he was OK with that.

On this occasion, the name of another sportswriter came up, someone who was apparently going to collaborate with Dan Hardy on a MMA-related project. Dan was another UFC star, making a name for himself behind Mike. Dan had just earned a title shot with

MIKE, MANAGERS & ME

GSP, making him the first ever British fighter to fight for a UFC title. In that one-sided fight, GSP dominated his opponent, though Dan toughed his way through two very painful-looking submission attempts. By that time I'd sensed that Mike and this sports journalist, who I will refer to as 'Mr BA', had drifted apart to an extent. Whether that was in the open or not, I don't know. Mike made a lewd joke and told me what he thought of 'Mr B' in no uncertain terms. I couldn't help but laugh. I was bewildered for a while about his apparent resentment for this guy, as ever since 'Mr BA' had jumped on the MMA bandwagon, he had always promoted Mike quite extensively. But 'Mr BA' was not liked by many. Plenty of members of the sporting press seemed to detest him, and one newspaper sports correspondent called him all the names in the book. Even fans of MMA often would rip into him – they found him ill-informed, over-opinionated and biassed. 'Clearly he has no background in MMA,' one commented, 'which I appreciate isn't a requirement in sports writing. But if you aren't an experienced fighter, you'd better either be highly amusing or unusually insightful, and he's neither.'

For my part, I would get in touch with 'Mr BA' whenever I had something to offer or ask for in return. He was always, I may add, a pain to get hold of. No matter how many times you rang or emailed this guy, he gave you the impression he was one arrogant person. If you told him you had an exclusive for him, he invariably ignored you. He was too busy apparently covering some other, more mundane sport, or running around like a headless chicken. One thing that annoys me more than anything is when you can't get hold of someone when you need to.

The first time I met 'Mr BA', or should I say bumped into him, was when UFC 105 was taking place in Manchester. 'Mr BA' was coming out of the hotel turnstile entrance. I said a quick 'Hi' and nodded. But inside I was burning to call him all the names in the book and rain curses down on him. Still, I reminded myself that that wouldn't be very professional. In spite of what many people thought of 'Mr BA', his enthusiasm, dedication and commitment to pushing MMA was making inroads into a broader market, and that is something that I feel he should be recognised for without a shadow of a doubt, even though I may, along with some others, have no affinity for him.

I always dealt with Mike directly, not through any management. At the time, he was managed by the Wolfslair team, located in Merseyside, which was then the most famous MMA gym in the country. Eventually he relocated to sunny California, joining the same management as Conor McGregor. I think Mike made the right decision to move and be managed in America as his career blossomed, even if it was bad news for me. After several meetings and countless phone calls, the talks just drifted apart and nothing came to fruition. He said he'd just changed management and we concluded that maybe down the line we could talk again. It's like they say in martial arts: fall down seven times, get up eight.

Eventually, Mike went on to bigger and better things. He had seen title shots elude him for a decade, but some years later he finally got his, knocking out Luke Rockhold in the first round at UFC 199 in Los Angeles' The Forum arena to become the UFC middleweight champion and the first UFC champion from the United Kingdom. After he was crowned champion I rang him in California to ask whether we could reopen the negotiations. He said he did want to do something, but had his plate full and said that we could talk when things calmed down.

*　*　*

Being the multitasking individual that I am, I was writing for magazines, researching and exploring the lives of some of the most iconic figures and more – and taking care of the combat sports company I was a director of – as I attempted to explore these endless opportunities within MMA, and now I had a new idea. I wanted to manage a UFC fighter on the side.

MIKE, MANAGERS & ME

MMA management companies were springing up all over America. Some lawyers started to manage UFC fighters as they oversaw their contracts, and it was a good sideline for these big cats, while others made it their sole profession. Suddenly, you had American sports agents who represented athletes in the NBA and NFL adding UFC athletes to their client list. Furthermore, some big-name UFC stars were being represented by some of the most prestigious talent agencies in Beverly Hills, who were helping these fighters break into Hollywood. Mike Bisping, Rampage Jackson, GSP, Ronda Rousey and, of course, Randy Couture made inroads into the movie business, starring in films ranging from *The Expendables* franchise to *The A-Team*. It was the next step towards global domination for a sport whose champions have true crossover appeal.

Since I had been part of the world of MMA for a good number of years, adding this new tier to my resume felt like a good idea, but most importantly from my point of view, it would be an intriguing venture, possibly resulting in another stream of income. Managers typically get 10–15 per cent of a fighter's purse and other earnings, which can amount to a nice figure if you're able to land a client with the power to do well in the business.

Since I had been dealing with professional fighters from the combat sports world in the media for years, I could plausibly venture into another arena quite easily – or at least that was my thinking. Unfortunately, the top UFC star from the country, Mike Bisping, was already taken, and stealing someone's fighter would not be a good idea, especially when you have the sort of management he had to deal with. Still, there was another potential window that I could open. Andy Farrell, who I mentioned earlier and who had encountered Mike before he had pursued a UFC career, was eager to fight a prominent name in the MMA world and asked me to arrange a fight for him.

The idea was that I would manage Andy through my company as a side venture as I was busy with other commitments in the literary world. In an attempt to get the ball rolling, I phoned a major MMA promoter, who I often had a good laugh with when I tried to squeeze free tickets out of him, which worked most of the time. Andy had an MMA fighter in mind who he wanted to lock horns with. I won't mention names, but this fighter had married a glamour girl celebrity which made him a household name. 'Everyone wants to fight that guy!' the larger-than-life promoter laughed. Nevertheless, we agreed that I'd send over the info about my fighter and we'd take it from there. I told Andy to get a show reel ready, so I could send it to the promoter and, more importantly, to the UFC, and hopefully sign him up with the most prestigious MMA organisation in the wake of what I was sure would be an emphatic win.

Always in the habit of pushing anything I touched to the extreme, I kept on pushing Andy to focus on the UFC. That was my only goal. I never had any interest in the sort of domestic shows where you'd get a couple of thousand people attending and the fighter walks away with a few thousand pounds. That didn't interest me, and I wasn't going to invest my time in managing someone who would fight at that level. It would be a waste of time. I always wanted to pursue things on a bigger scale and set the bar high. If you don't, you might as well never get out of bed in the morning. I feel every budding professional MMA competitor should make it one of their primary goals to sign up with the world's number-one MMA promotion – the UFC. If that's not your aim, what are you even doing in the sport?

Besides, I had complete confidence in my friend as far as talent was concerned. The fact that he'd triumphed over the best UFC fighter from Britain, was a big confidence booster for me. I thought I could use it to attract the attention of the UFC matchmaker, who at the time was John Perretti. Andy was in his early 40s then, but had a great physique and was in phenomenal shape. If there was any obstacle for the UFC matchmakers, it would be Andy's age, but I felt we could overcome this hurdle because of his almost-clean record. And he could prove he had what it took, just like the other fighters on the UFC's roster.

Unfortunately, our partnership never did bear fruit. If you were to ask me, 'What is the biggest thing that puts you off when it comes to dealing with people?' I'd tell you I abhor people who don't follow through with commitments. Being a persistent and highly motivated individual who has a tendency to be on the ball, I constantly pushed my friend. But despite my repeated attempts to guide him, he never did what I told him in spite of showing great enthusiasm and promising me the world in our conversations. Eventually, that idea made its way down the drain, which meant I was never going to produce a UFC champion. I was convinced I could have made it happen with more commitment on Andy's side.

Anyway, sometimes things don't work out and you have to live with it. This was one of those things. Often we get carried away when excitement takes over, when more often than not it's a good idea to look at things through the lens of reality. In this case, I was oblivious to Andy's commitment. I felt my friend would do well in the UFC and probably become a household name and a star if he put in the work. I could visualise him being interviewed by the mainstream press and signing autographs at UFC events.

I think being a professional fighter – be it in boxing or UFC – is, arguably, one of the best jobs in the world for some. The acclaim, fame, fortune, power and glory that go with it, are just part of the appeal. You're also giving your all to something you're truly passionate about. That said, I truly believe that world champions are blessed individuals. Genetics play a pivotal role, and not everyone can make it to the top, however dedicated they may be. For those who have a profound fascination with professional fight sports, but lack what it takes to make it to the top, there are always behind-the-scenes roles in a professional capacity, be it coaching, managing, promoting or journalism. The latter is what I, of course, pursued. Having been an enthusiastic student of the game who never quite possessed the genetics and skill that are required to excel in the arena – not that I ever had the inclination to pursue the arena on a professional or even amateur level in the first place – I was able to excel in another role of course.

Back when I was considering management, UFC fighters were not making really big money compared to now, but for some it was a lot considering where they came from – their background. The bigger names and the bigger paydays came later. Revenues from sponsors also poured in as the sport was being recognised in wider circles. I still wanted to get involved. Back then, $150,000 was a decent payday for a headliner, with a few making $500,000 or more – not a bad amount to get 15 per cent of. It was such a shame: I had complete confidence that Andy would be crowned a champion and hit the big money. If only I could have pulled it off.

Fighting in the UFC is an even bigger thing now than it was then. I found it quite amusing when I once called up one of the fighter's coaches to request an interview for the magazine. He said everyone was jumping on the bandwagon to get to his fighter because he was fighting in the UFC. I found this hilarious, absolutely hilarious! This fighter wasn't even a major name; he was a domestic name fighting on the undercard in the UFC, but his manager was acting like he was some big star who was in high demand. Talk about getting lost in your own hype. This guy was certainly the living embodiment of it. I had access to most of the big names and champions in the UFC, so what would I gain from an interview with this domestic fighter? If anything, he was lucky I was asking to interview him and promoting him. I usually gravitated toward the top fighters. I could sense that a small taste of success had gone to this coach's head. In fact, I readily welcomed his remarks as he did me a favour because it saved me my valuable time. I had more prominent fighters to invest my time in who were more humble – the type of fighters I had great reverence towards.

Anyway, although Andy had left me disenchanted it wasn't the end of the world. I was having a damn good time revelling in the media spotlight, keeping busy working on other projects. I was able to use my MMA coverage as a springboard to get more involved in the sport of boxing as a sportswriter, and eventually it paid off in a huge way. The greatest sportsman in history, the man who I would eventually come to idolise, would let me into his life via those who were close to him.

CHAPTER NINETEEN

MUHAMMAD ALI ENCOUNTERS

BOXING AS a sport and art was something I never really explored on a serious level until much later in life than most other people. I was intrigued by the martial arts, and when the UFC surfaced I immediately became an avid follower and advocate of that, too. But it wasn't until the time when the UFC was making waves that I found myself interviewing world boxing champions. I did this partly to tap into another area within the realm of sports – from martial arts to pugilism, which I considered a 'promotion' as a writer, the moment when I stepped into the higher echelons of the sports world. If you were to ask an average guy on the street, 'Who is the world kickboxing champion?' no one will have a clue. In contrast to this, the chances that the same individual would be able to name the world heavyweight boxing champion are pretty damn high. Boxing back then was on another level – on all levels, from the money and fame it offered, to sponsorships and major broadcasting deals. Certainly, MMA has now an equal footing, but back then, it was different.

Anyway, after exploring and piecing together the life and legacy of the late, great Bruce Lee, I contemplated researching the life of another iconic sporting figure. Above all others, Muhammad Ali's image floated into my head. A biography on Ali would be the perfect next project. Ali has long been recognised as the world's most famous man – no one was bigger. One of the 20th century's towering figures, he transcended sport and had a huge impact on pop culture. To be honest, Ali didn't captivate me as a young boy growing up, and he wasn't an idol of mine even when I transitioned into my adult years, but I still was aware of him. It wasn't till many years later when boxing fever hit me that I was able to discern what I had been missing.

Another reason to investigate Ali was his huge appeal – my days of trying to appeal to a niche audience were long gone. 'The Greatest' has sustained his celebrity status as he achieved more outside of the sport than inside the ring, becoming a political activist and a symbol of hope to billions. The media's wrath towards him during his career turned to adulation long after he retired from fighting as journalists came to appreciate his humanitarian work, and his status as a symbol of reconciliation.

The one thing that set the three-time heavyweight champion apart from all other public figures was how he evoked a feeling of shared belief and emotion with people from all walks of life. He came to prominence at a time when the USA was in a state of political and racial upheaval and stood, as I would come to learn, at the intersection of the athletic and political. His association with Malcolm X and the Black Muslims, alongside his refusal to fight in the Vietnam War show his faith in his beliefs – one never repudiates one's deepest values.

Speaking of Malcolm X, about a year ago I managed to get hold of John Ali's cell phone number. John, a Nation of Islam secretary back in the day, was allegedly responsible for orchestrating Malcolm X's murder. He went into hiding after the death of Nation of Islam leader Elijah Muhammad in 1975. He was allegedly an FBI agent – the FBI's top informant in the Nation of Islam in the 1960s – or operative of US intelligence agencies. This reclusive figure emerged after more than four decades, and I wasn't going to let this opportunity elude me so I called him on his cell phone. I wasn't sure he'd answer – but he did. I told him who I was and that I'd like to interview him. He told me to call him Tuesday. When I did he didn't answer. I followed up another day and this time I managed to get hold of him, but again he asked me to call on Tuesday. This exact scenario repeated several times, until about the fourth attempt when I got hold of him and we got talking casually – not about Malcolm X though. The man – now in his mid-90s – was initially reluctant, but then said he'd want paying if I wanted to interview him. Sadly, nothing came to fruition.

* * *

My burgeoning interest in researching Ali led me to some very interesting people indeed. But where do you start with such a well-known figure? Well, in my opinion, family members are always the best to start with. I was surprised to learn that most people don't even know Ali has a son (in fact, he has an adopted son, too). But it is near impossible to come across any interview with or media coverage of Muhammad Ali Jnr – his biological son – although in recent years he's made headlines for all the wrong reasons. Well, that seemed like a good starting point. And though my position has given me opportunities to talk to an array of diverse people – from boxing legends, UFC champions and bodybuilding champions to Hollywood actors – whenever I get asked, 'Who was the best person that you've interviewed?' Without hesitation I say Muhammad Ali Jnr is close to the top of the list.

What impressed me most about Ali Jnr was his humble nature. For almost all his life he was rarely one to seek publicity, despite being the son of the most famous human in the world. Furthermore, I was really shocked to hear that he was unemployed and looking for employment. *What?* I thought. That's another story in itself. As my research unfolded I came to learn that he had a job at a fairground. Years later, after the passing of his father, he reportedly inherited some money, which he rightly deserved, but for much of his life he was forced to work like any average person. Despite his father's status, he hasn't had an easy ride at all, unlike many children of A-list celebrities. The disparity between Muhammad Ali Jnr and the son of Michael

Jackson, for example, who is often in the spotlight, is profound. So, I was quite astonished that Ali's son had maintained an extremely low profile and that he was living in obscurity.

Still, sometimes all you have to do is reach out. When I phoned him to discuss his father, he kindly obliged. He was living in Chicago, the city where his mother, Belinda, is from and where Ali spent many years. Early in our conversation, he told me about the political stand his dad took – not going to war and standing up for his rights. He revealed that he was sheltered while growing up for fear of kidnap attempts because of who his father was. He also hadn't spent as much time around his father as most sons spend around their dads; his grandparents had brought up Ali's four children. 'My father let me be my own man,' this soft-spoken, mild-mannered man told me. 'But I was actually sheltered my whole my life because of who my father was. We had family threats on our lives. It really hindered me instead of helping me because I wasn't able to put myself out there.' Compared to the rest of Ali's other children he had a different upbringing, out of the public spotlight. 'It really put a dent on my whole life. But everything is OK, it's not a total loss,' he assured me.

He stunned me, however, when he revealed that Bruce Lee had taught his mother. For a split-second I froze mid-interview. This was news to me. I didn't know what to make of it, to be honest. As far as I knew, there had been virtually no direct contact between Bruce Lee and Muhammad Ali, but had I missed something? For a second my mind wandered towards picking up a lie detector machine, but I did find out subsequently that his mother had learned karate, something cleared up many years later when I queried this with Ali Jnr's sister, Rasheda. She told me that it was actually Jim Kelly, the co-star of Bruce Lee's *Enter the Dragon*, who taught their mother.

Ali, of course, has more often than not been compared to Lee. A question that countless drunks have argued in bars is who would win a fight between Ali and Lee? Well, Ali's son had his own opinion. He said Bruce Lee was the Muhammad Ali of karate (martial arts), and let out a timid laugh. 'I think it would've been a good fight between my father and Bruce Lee.'

That said, he seemed to have strong reservations regarding Mike Tyson's status as a boxer. 'Now, my father and Mike Tyson? My father would've kicked his butt,' he told me. 'Everybody says "Oh, Mike Tyson would've kicked your father's butt."' I say no way. Mike Tyson can't go the distance, he couldn't go 15 rounds. He's not a boxer; he's a street fighter.' I was eagerly listening to him now, hanging on to his every word. 'Bruce Lee, on the other hand, that would've been a good fight. They were both young, they were both agile and both took it to the limit with their training. They were both the best at what they did.' Now, this man was talking sense. He had my full attention.

I switched the conversation to religion, something that Ali held close to his heart after he converted to Islam, especially when he became a Sunni Muslim in 1975. 'Your father went to hajj in Mecca and later became zealously committed to his religion,' I said. 'Did he relate any stories to you about how he felt about the experience?'

'Oh yeah, yeah,' Ali Jnr replied. 'He felt actually sorry for a lot of things he had said like, "the white man's a devil". He really felt bad about that, because the fact is that when he went to hajj he saw black Muslims, white Muslims, yellow Muslims – all different types of races, all Muslims.'

'Did your father give you advice as you were growing up?' I asked him. 'Oh, yeah,' he said. 'One thing he said to me, which I remember, is: don't care what people call you. Don't care what people think of you. Everybody is equal under the eyes of God.'

It was becoming apparent that, however distant his upbringing, Ali taught his son humility and principles as any good father would. In the early days of Ali's conversion, he had very different views, as he was brainwashed into thinking the white man is a devil. But by the time he was old enough to talk to his son, he'd mellowed.

'He said, "I care about people as human beings and not what colour they are,"' Ali Jnr told me. 'He said that you should look at people and respect them as human beings. Don't judge people, period. He said what you need to look for is the content of their character. If they've got a good character and they're not stuck up, if they're not racists, then they're good people. If they are, then just leave them alone. He said watch what you say and watch what you do and respect your elders.' It was a delightful experience to have the son of 'The Greatest' share these insights with me. We continued talking off the record for quite some time.

* * *

One of my more controversial interviewees from the same period was Joe Lewis, a karate champion who trained with Bruce Lee. Joe has had his fair share of critics for criticising his friend and training partner, but you can't deny that Joe walks the walk. 'Bruce Lee wasn't a fighter,' he explained to me in a two-hour conversation, the first time I interviewed him. This was far from the first time he'd made questionable statements. 'People say, "Oh, yes, he was. He was a fighter."' But we're not talking about street fighters. Street fighters have records down at the police departments. A real fighter has a record. He has wins, loses, knockouts and draws. If you don't have a record, you're not a fighter. That's it – it's a simple definition.'

Joe himself had experienced boxing training at the famous Main Street gym in Los Angeles. In fact, he had Bruce accompany him on numerous occasions there, when Joe had the great fortune to train with Sugar Ray Robinson, a fighter Ali had once admired.

Joe also had a run-in with Ali in 1975. The editor of a prominent martial arts magazine phoned Joe to inform him that Ali was planning a media tour in Los Angeles to promote his upcoming fight with wrestler Antonio Inoki, which would be the first major boxer versus wrestler bout in the USA. Joe showed up to see Ali, who was wearing a longed-sleeved black shirt and black pants. There were about 20 journalists from the press and the major TV networks present, who peppered the heavyweight champion with questions.

Joe found his way to the ring apron alongside Bob Wall, the world karate champion, who played a villain in *Enter the Dragon*, and the editor who'd invited them.

'I turn to Bob Wall and say, "You know what? Ali is talking about how he can beat any martial artist, boxer or wrestler." I'm thinking, *You can beat any wrestler? What the hell are you talking about!*' I was laughing imagining it. If there was one person who could tell a compelling story, it was Joe Lewis. He would shock you, entertain you and have you laughing. Joe explained that wrestlers (and grapplers for the matter) are the best fighters on the planet, and that with the advent of the UFC this fact had finally been proven on the world stage. I had been oblivious to the fact that he had a wrestling background before he pursued the martial arts to become the greatest karate fighter of all time, but he had, first and foremost, been a wrestler, he revealed.

'So I'm watching Ali thinking, *You can't beat no damn wrestler,*' he told me. Joe had been in the ring with boxers, of course. They were like babies, he told me, if you shoot to the legs and take them down, they last maybe 30 seconds. So Joe wasn't exactly impressed by Ali's claim to be 'The Greatest'.

At the event he attended, the famous professional wrestler, 'Classy' Freddie Blassie, was in the ring with Ali as part of the pantomime. Bob and the editor encouraged Joe to needle Ali about his grappling ability and see what would bounce back. One of the photographers in the ring walked over to where the three were standing to get a shot. Turning to the photographer, Joe said, 'Ask Ali what he would do if a wrestler faked a jab at the head and ducked down underneath, took the legs and took him down.' The photographer shouted out, 'Here, you ask him!' Ali! Ali! Come here! Come here!' Joe, he told me, was thinking to himself, *Oh, my God, I don't want to ask him. I'm embarrassed.*

Ali walked over until he was a few feet from Joe. 'What do you do if a guy fakes a jab to the head and then dives at your legs?' Joe put the golden question directly to 'The Greatest'.

'Come on in here, boy, and show me,' Ali responded. 'Nah, I don't want to,' Joe conceded. But he wasn't going to slip out of it that easily – after all, he had Ali's attention now. Three people shoved Joe into the ring.

Joe was down to 180 pounds because he was getting in shape for a film – he was pursuing acting at the time. He was still pretty strong, though, and could deadlift 400 pounds. His PB at one time was 550 pounds, he told me. So lifting somebody Ali's size was pretty much a walk in the park for him, if he could get his hands on him.

Ali got ready in a boxing stance with his hands up, shuffling from side to side, always the showman and never reluctant to spar with anyone at any given opportunity. 'I could feel the energy of everyone in the room,' Joe explained to me as I hung on every word. '"Come on, come on, show us!" the raucous crowd was shouting.'

Joe, maintaining his distance, proceeded with a shoulder fake to Ali's head in an attempt to draw a reaction. Ali responded by trying to catch the jab with both hands. Joe, in a flash, ducked down and shot for the legs for a double-leg tackle. As soon as Joe wrapped his arms around Ali's legs, he paused because he was hesitant to actually follow through by taking the champ down to the ground. However, a burst of laughter from the ecstatic crowd followed. There were 100 people in attendance besides the photographers and the press.

'I'll tell you what he did,' Joe said to me. 'He lay on my back as I was underneath holding his legs and he made that face where he opened his mouth real wide. As soon as he laughed it pissed me off. So I picked him up, spun him upside down and dumped him.' Joe refrained from applying a submission, instead just pinning Ali. Freddie, with the help of two other people, grabbed Joe and took him off Ali. 'Whoa, whoa, just playing,' Joe assured everyone as he stood up. 'I figured he thought I was trying to kill him or something. Which I could have because from what I remember was his body felt like a woman. He was real soft, like jelly, and that shocked me because I'm used to wrestling and doing weightlifting where the body is hard as a brick.' According to Joe, Ali felt really, really weak. He felt no strength in the champ – not wrestler strength, anyway. Ali stood up and he stood next to Joe. And a whole herd of photographers were now snapping pictures, and Ali put his arm around Joe's shoulder. 'You were lifting weights when you were younger, weren't you?' Ali joked. Joe claims Ali could tell he was a lot stronger than anyone he'd been in the ring with before.

The action wasn't over.

'Come on, do that again,' Ali insisted.

'You're shitting me,' Joe responded in amazement 'What do you mean, do it again?' So they squared off and Joe repeated the fake hand and dropped down for a double-leg tackle, taking Ali down again. Ali was lying on the floor pinned and, again, took the whole thing humorously. Ali's entourage came to the rescue again. Joe quickly assured everyone that they were just playing. 'I did it quite hard and it looked kind of mean,' he said. The greatest karate champion of all time dubbed as the Muhammad Ali of karate was now the centre of focus, as the press wasted no time in snapping more pictures.

After all the commotion and chaos Ali sent his representative to approach Joe. 'I represent Muhammad Ali and he would like to invite you to dinner tonight,' the representative told him. Joe turned down the invitation, just as three years earlier he'd turned down a part in *Way of the Dragon* which his friend Bruce Lee had offered him. If he'd accepted, I believe that literally nobody would know the name Chuck Norris, who got the part. Instead, Joe would have been a star. Joe admitted to me that, perhaps, he shouldn't have turned down Ali's invitation, just like he shouldn't have turned down his friend's.

* * *

Ali, although never formally trained in the martial arts of the Orient, did dabble a little as he had a couple of friends – I would say they were more like associates – who were revered martial artists. On one occasion, one of his associates at Deer Lake training camp, who sometimes worked out with him, wanted Ali to attend a karate tournament he was hosting. This was, by the way, two or three years before the Ali–Lewis incident took place.

'Would you come to my karate tournament?' he asked Ali. 'There's going to be several thousand people and a lot of them want to meet you.' Perhaps surprisingly, Ali immediately said, 'Yes!' Now a lot of times, Ali would say yes to projects and not mean it or forget about it. So this associate approached Ali's corner man, Bundini Brown, and followed up. 'Look, I've talked to Muhammad. He said he'll come. Can you do me a favour and see that he gets there?'

'What time you want him there and where at?' asked Bundini. The associate told him, and Bundini said, 'I'll give you my word he'll be there.'

On the day, sure enough, Ali's corner man made sure he attended this event. Both men showed up and Ali signed autographs and even sparred with some people. One thing Ali stipulated was that his opponents would not be allowed to kick below the belt, but you could do basically anything else. Ali, I was told by this associate, did learn how to evade and counter kicks so that he couldn't get kicked. So, the heavyweight champion sparred with karate competitors that day in front of the crowd, and yet it still went the way of the champ. The martial artists could basically do what they wanted and Ali still beat most of them, according to this associate of Ali's. Ali said to his associate, 'I wish karate people earned a lot more money. I could get good at this.' I mean, honestly, how many world champion boxers would do that now?

Late in the day, Ali sparred with a well-known martial arts exponent from that era called Danny Pai, who was winning the sparring fight on points when he kicked Ali above the belt, which was fair enough, according to the rules. However, the associate stopped the fight there because he didn't want them fighting for real; he sensed that things could spiral out of control. Ali also sparred with two other champions and actually beat both of them. Ali was fast, the fastest thing this associate had ever seen, he told me. Whether the brash boxing champion would've made an all-round great fighter or not is, like most things, debatable. One thing that is thought-provoking is that if Joe Lewis was able to take Ali down repeatedly, would Ali have beaten Bruce Lee in a real fight? Take into account that many are of the sentiment that Ali would've killed Bruce. In the ring, in a boxing match, no doubt, but in the street things would've been reversed, I believe. Antonio Inoki would certainly have been too much for Ali in a no-holds-barred real fight.

CHAPTER TWENTY

FROM MARTIAL ARTS TO MOVIE MAGIC

BEFORE I parlayed my sports writing career into action movie journalism, I already had a platform to connect with those who were involved in the martial arts action movie industry. My work on *Martial Arts Illustrated* meant I could talk with many martial artists who worked in the action genre.

Martial artist Dave Lea, who had pursued Hollywood in the late 1980s and successfully made it as a stuntman, was one such individual. Dave had performed stunts on the 1989 *Batman* film, doubling for Michael Keaton (in the same film, a Thai-boxing maestro from the United Kingdom named Master Sken also displayed his versatile fighting skills, fighting Batman in the finale). Dave went on to work on numerous major Hollywood flicks starring A-list stars. It's hard to miss the ponytailed stuntman fighting Sylvester Stallone in *Tango and Cash*, where there's some eye-catching stick work on display, which I'm sure Dave picked up from Dan Inosanto at the Inosanto Academy in Los Angeles, where he frequently honed his skills. Dave epitomised the rags-to-riches story, growing up with little but a passion for martial arts, which allowed him to pursue the path of a professional stuntman.

I got in touch with Dave after getting his phone number from Moira at the *Martial Arts Illustrated* magazine office, and did a lengthy interview with him – resulting in a major feature and one thing leading to another. Back then, most stuntmen were based in Los Angeles. I knew a few, and had several friends in the Hollywood stunt business. Ron Balicki and Diana Lee Inosanto both performed stunts in movies, while maintaining their martial arts teaching duties, and I found this combination very appealing. Working on Hollywood movies in whatever capacity possible was something that really caught my interest. I thought it would be great to pop on set when the opportunity presented itself, and perhaps experience the thrills of working on big-budget movies myself one day. I mean, come on, that's a dream no one would say no to.

There were a few things in my favour. My involvement in the martial arts media had given me a plethora of contacts and friends, and, in fact, it got to a stage where I provided contacts of American talent and famous fighters to a few key managers in America. When it came to contacts, I seem to be able to dig anyone's up, and that's vital in my game. And, of course, now there's more demand than ever for skilled martial artists in Hollywood. Back in the 1950s and 1960s, John Wayne-style fisticuffs ruled the screen, but after Bruce Lee exploded on to the scene in the 1970s, he influenced a whole new generation. Then, later, films such as *The Matrix* and *Kill Bill* reintroduced audiences to the Chinese style of ultra-fast fight choreography that's so appealing to watch. Nowadays, in any action movie with fights, you can bet your bottom dollar that martial arts will play a part.

Back in the 1990s, Saturday evening TV was defined by a programme called *Gladiators*. Action, pomp, laughter, gurning for the camera and pugil stick fights – it had it all. In 1995, my friend Andy Farrell graced our screens as a contender on the popular ITV show. I remember watching a clip many years later with a smirk on my face, as I saw Andy don the spandex before challenging the Gladiators. Well, competing against Andy was a young man from Huddersfield called Buster Reeves, a British martial artist who rose to prominence in Hollywood from the mid-1990s onwards. Buster is my age, and back in the mid-1990s he and fellow show winner Eunice Huthart were catapulted to fame when they appeared as contestants on this primetime show. Eunice and Buster went on to become very successful Hollywood stunt coordinators and have worked on top action movies. Buster doubled Christian Bale in *Batman* and Brad Pitt in *Troy*.

* * *

Impact, an action movie magazine with offices in the United Kingdom, USA and Hong Kong, which was published for 20 years from 1992 to 2012, was the premier magazine for lovers of martial arts in movies and action movies in general for as long as it was published. My colleague, Andy Staton, wrote for *Impact* in addition to penning his column in the martial arts magazine, but it wasn't until I'd been at *Martial Arts Illustrated* for six years that I followed in Andy's footsteps, jumping aboard with the *Impact* team. Both publications, of course, were owned by the same company and ran from the same offices. Prior to this, it hadn't even crossed my mind that I had a life-changing career opportunity waiting for me right on my doorstep.

Joining the *Impact* team was one of the best moves I ever made in my career. It afforded me a prestigious platform to talk to A-list names outside martial arts and MMA and have a behind-the-scenes glimpse into Hollywood. It also gave me a sense of achievement and a way to further cement my own credibility as a journalist. I felt on top of the world. This was major league, not the first or second division. It was the ultimate way to elevate my profile, diving into a new world while staying true to my love of combat sports.

It wasn't long before I found myself interviewing the Hollywood fraternity, touching on their fitness, training and everyday lives as well as their glittering careers. Long gone were the days of being merely part of the combat sports press, but with all the excitement I still composed myself. The former editor of *Impact*, Bey Logan, who had written for martial arts publications, had now transcended the martial arts and now was doing bigger things. If I played my cards right, I thought, I could follow his lead.

When I joined the magazine, John Mosby was the editor. John was OK but not as accommodating as *Martial Arts Illustrated* editor Bob Sykes. Then again, no one was like Bob, and no one will ever be like him. He was just too damn accommodating. I was like a son to him and could ask him to do anything for me, whereas with John, it was strictly a professional relationship with no special treatment thrown in.

So, while martial arts had been my platform and passion, now I was ready to use them as a springboard to bigger, broader endeavours. I got my start with the country's bestselling martial arts periodical, progressed by contributing to bodybuilding-related publications and eventually contributing to mainstream life style publications, and of course MMA publications. And now I'm working with the biggest newspapers and A-listers. The sports that I had an affinity with were somewhat interlinked. It was a natural progression, and I wasn't finished yet.

Soon, I started to focus on movie personalities, but I also further extended myself as far as boxing and UFC stars were concerned, going after bigger and better interviewees. Conducting an interview with a martial arts world champion was no longer something I much cared about. I had done that, been there, worn the T-shirt – whatever cliche you like. The last thing I wanted was to abandon my roots. I couldn't and wouldn't forget about my background or the arts that had given me the foot in the door in the first place, but I was ready to move up. Journalists such as Bey had walked the same path I was walking, and now they were writing scripts for major films, but their passion for the martial arts was still intact.

Anyway, now I felt I had arrived. A whole new world of showbiz opened up at my feet. I was being offered advance movie previews, but didn't bother attending. Occasionally I'd apply for a press pass to a big movie premiere. I would secure interviews with some of the stars and directors in Hollywood.

FROM MARTIAL ARTS TO MOVIE MAGIC

It was a rush, and it wasn't always stress-free. American PR agents and talent managers and agents can be a nightmare to deal with. You often had to chase them up with repeated calls and emails, for days, weeks, or sometimes months on end. That was no problem because it was something I was accustomed to – being obsessively persistent – and as my contact book grew I found it easier and easier to work around these agents. I already had direct numbers for dozens of fighters and managers, but now I was dealing with huge talent agencies like CAA, WME and ICM, who have hundreds of employees and different agents. This is where the multi-million-dollar deals are being made, and the agents are hard at work as they look after their A-list clients, dealing with producers, casting agents, promotions, brand sponsorships and the media.

Whenever I contacted these talent agents I was reminded of the movie, *Jerry Maguire*, with Tom Cruise and Cuba Gooding Jnr. The film portrays Cruise as a high-powered professional sports agent, and the amount of yelling and high-pressure tactics in that movie – well, if anything, it's not as aggressive as the real thing.

Managers and publicists have great powers. They are there to make sure not only that their client receives the best possible deals, but equally avoids being undermined in the media or in any deal they secure. When they're canny and protective, it is quite understandable, but it can be frustrating. Fortunately, by this point in my career, I was pretty thick-skinned. Whenever an interview was refused, the usual, 'Thank you for reaching out to us but,' would make its way over the Atlantic electronically. It was never a good feeling, but it was better than the silent treatment, which would annoy me and occasionally send me into a state of paranoia.

Rejection is part of life. When you're rejected for a job, a deal, a literary manuscript, representation, or by a person, you sometimes feel you're doing something wrong or start to question your validity. You might wonder what influenced the decision, and it's easy to start questioning yourself. I'm sure that sometimes the publicists didn't even bring a request to the attention of their superstar clients, which was understandable but frustrating. I had built up a resume which included interviewing some of the biggest names in boxing, UFC, martial arts, and bodybuilding, as well as countless actors and personalities from Hollywood, so felt I had served my apprenticeship.

* * *

Once, I arranged an interview with the late David Carradine, who played the title role in Tarantino's *Kill Bill* movies. He was best known for his leading role as peace-loving Shaolin monk Kwai Chang Caine in the TV series *Kung Fu*, a role that Bruce Lee had developed for himself. On the day of the interview I rang David on his cell phone at the scheduled time. 'I can't talk right now!' he barked at me. 'I'm in the elevator, call me back in 30 minutes!' *He sounds rude,* I thought to myself. Well, rude isn't even the word I would use here. The word that best suited him was 'twat', and what a twat he was, as I was soon to find out. I called him back half an hour later and had a chat with him. I came to the conclusion that he was one of the worst idiots I have interviewed in my life.

What I found most ironic was that, despite having released and promoted a series of tai chi fitness DVDs, David, seemingly, wasn't into fitness at all. I asked him how he kept fit and if he could describe his regime. To my great surprise he revealed he didn't enjoy working out and wasn't really into exercise. He conceded that he was lazy. I thought to myself, *Why produce a series of DVDs promoting fitness when you yourself are not an advocate of fitness through training for a healthy lifestyle?* Well, there's an obvious answer to that, of course. I could also sense there was a cat running around in his house and that David was multitasking while talking to me. I could hear him shouting at the cat, which seemed to be running amok. The interview was getting stranger and stranger.

This was the man who not only took Bruce's part from him in the *Kung Fu* series, but also played the role in the film that Bruce had developed and written, titled *Silent Flute* after Bruce's death – a movie that, in case you haven't seen it, was a complete mess. When I asked him about this, though, he flipped.

'Why do people assume the part was originally for Bruce?' he screamed at me, as if I'd just sworn at his mother. 'It was never intended for him!' That was a blatant lie, because from several notable and reliable sources, including a letter that Ted Ashley, the Warner Brothers executive, wrote to Bruce, it was quite clear that Bruce was originally being considered to play the character David ended up playing. In the letter, the executive informed Bruce that he had been rejected because the studio thought it was too big a risk to invest in an unknown Asian actor – that the American public would not embrace a Chinese actor. Racism had prevented Bruce penetrating Hollywood, so they invested in David, who was a Caucasian and looked just oriental enough for the part. David, at the time, had no real martial arts experience and had someone train him for the part from scratch. Nevertheless, the show was a big hit.

Tragically, David died a little over a year after our interview. He was a strange guy, and hard to get on with, and didn't make it into my good books.

* * *

Any top actor who even had an ounce of interest in the UFC, combat sports or bodybuilding always caught my attention. When *The Wrestler* was released in cinemas, I thought it would be the perfect opportunity to talk to the star Mickey Rourke, and find out what makes him tick. What I found appealing in Mickey was the fact that his father had been an amateur competitive bodybuilder, while Mickey himself pumped iron and had boxed professionally. He was a fan of combat sports, including the UFC, and Dorian Yates had told me once that he'd had breakfast in New York with Mickey and that the actor was a big bodybuilding enthusiast. I got in touch with Mickey's manager and sent some goodies to pass on to his client to try to capture his interest.

TO THE TOP

After several failed attempts to secure an interview with the actor through his Beverly Hills agent and manager in New York, I finally got in touch via a lady called Maria at Optimum Releasing, the theatrical distributor for the film. I phoned her first before putting the request in via email. 'Mickey is currently busy with the Oscars,' she wrote back. 'I think it would be best if we touch base again in March/April, when things will have calmed down with him. Please let me know if this is OK.' Always a step ahead, I had done my homework. I told her that her client was going to be shooting the new *Expendables* movie in Brazil next month, so the chances of an interview materialising would be slight since he was going to be away on location. Maria assured me that he had set aside some time for press to coincide with the DVD release.

The *Wrestler* was released in January 2009, putting Mickey back on the big screen with a bravura performance that won him a BAFTA, Golden Globe and an Academy Award nomination for his portrayal of the pro wrestler Randy 'The Ram' Robinson. I felt he was the perfect actor to play the role, and I wasn't the only one. The movie was a success and his performance was rapturously received by the critics. Still, I had to get my interview.

To me, Mickey was a fascinating figure. He'd boxed professionally between 1991 and 1995, seriously pursuing the sweet science. A much loved pin-up in the 1980s and 1990s, Mickey lost his good looks after years of boozing and boxing, and required reconstructive surgery, which further damaged his face. Mickey, undeniably, was an interesting character, who often made the headlines for the wrong reasons. But I wasn't looking to delve into his troubled life. I was interested in his physical preparation as well as his love for fight sports and career. Preparing for his role for the film, he reportedly trained with the intensity of a professional bodybuilder at Gold's Gym in Venice, a facility that's produced some of the world's best physiques. He also used to train at Freddie Roach's gym, the Wild Card, in Hollywood. I had stayed in Hollywood several times, only a couple of blocks away from this famed destination for fighters.

Anyway, it was time for round two so I got in touch with Maria again to set up the interview as March approached. This time, a phone interview was lined up and I would receive a call late at night United Kingdom time. I sat alone in the dark looking forward to interviewing this legend of cinema. Looking at my watch in the vain hope that the phone would ring, I consoled myself with the hope that he was going over the allocated time with other interviews. After an hour of waiting, I eventually realised that this call wasn't going to happen that night. On the one hand I suspected the worst – that I'd been cast aside – but on the other my brain was telling me that there must have been some schedule shift, so a rearrangement might be possible. I wanted to believe the latter, but my thoughts gravitated towards the former. Well, I could only wait.

The next morning I got in touch with the publicist, who apologised and explained that four interviews were lined up, but her client did two and decided not to fulfil his other media commitments. I was somewhat disappointed. Mickey was one of those stars who was unpredictable, and was famously known to be hot-headed and unreliable, so this wasn't surprising, if I'm honest. It wasn't the end of the world. I wasn't upset with the actor, so he didn't make it on to what you might call the 'twat list'.

However, an individual who did make it on to the 'most pathetic people I have ever interviewed' list' was the Hollywood film director Ivan Reitman. When his new movie, *No Strings Attached*, starring Emily Blunt and Ashton Kutcher, was being released, I got in touch with the publicists. This Hollywood bigwig has directed some top-grossing Hollywood flicks, with a resume including *Ghostbusters*, *Twins*, *Kindergarten Cop*, and the not-so-successful Arnie flop, *Junior*. This was another phone interview, and I proceeded by asking the director questions relating to his new movie, I then decided to switch gear in the hope of swaying him to talk about his previous works with Arnold Schwarzenegger. The director half-heartedly answered the first Arnie question or two before mumbling something to his publicist. Then it happened again. This time, the publicist startled me by telling me that there would be no more questions and that the interview was being wrapped up.

In the morning, my editor had a word with me. Apparently, Ivan's people had logged a complaint saying that the interview was supposed to be the focus of the new movie but that I had digressed. I explained that I wanted to talk to him about his new film, but also the success he had had with Arnold, though to be honest, I wanted to talk about Arnold and couldn't give a damn about his new movie. I thought that if I was ever presented with an opportunity to speak to him again, I would make it known what I thought of this miserable man. But I never did get that opportunity nor would I want to.

* * *

One movie star that I personally wanted to connect with and tried to lock down several times to no avail was Nicolas Cage. Not only is he a phenomenal actor, he's also the nephew of film director Francis Ford Coppolla, the director of the classic *The Godfather* movies. As I moved into A-list interviews, Nicolas had recently released a whole herd of movies after a bleak period when he had declared himself bankrupt, and many were the kinds of movies I was raring to cover because of the actor.

Nicolas is a man of taste, and has diverse interests. A big fan of Elvis Presley – he married Presley's daughter – he's also into Bruce Lee, martial arts and UFC. He has made a name for himself as the man who has used his wealth to indulge in his unbridled passions. His plethora of 'interesting' purchases include a comic book collection worth $1.6 million, a 67-million-year-old Tarbosaurus skull, a shark and a crocodile, a private island, and the Shah of Iran's Lamborghini. He is known for living life to the max and isn't afraid of overextending himself.

FROM MARTIAL ARTS TO MOVIE MAGIC

One subject that I was primed to talk to him about was his involvement with jiu-jitsu with his former instructor Royce Gracie, who had taught him privately at his home. Among the Hollywood celebrities who had embraced the UFC, Nicolas was one of the most prominent. After he had been mesmerised by the lithe skills of Royce in the first ever UFCs, he sought out and became a private student of the three-time UFC champion, alongside several other celebrities, notably Guy Ritchie and Jim Carey.

Although not known as a martial arts actor, Nicolas utilised his martial arts skills in some of his movies, including showcasing the wing chun system – a style Bruce Lee originally studied before embarking on his mission of self discovery to devise jeet kune do – in *Bangkok Dangerous*. In fact, I was pleasantly surprised to learn that Nicolas had originally been inspired by Bruce to get into acting.

'When I was eight, in the early 70s, my dad decided to take me to the theatre and I saw a movie that changed my life, my world really, because this force was in a movie called *Enter the Dragon*,' Nicolas had told an interviewer while promoting one of his new action films. And it wasn't just because the way the kung fu star moved, although Nicolas had been blown away when he witnessed the famous back flip that Bruce did, which was actually one of the few times Bruce used a stuntman. Instead he said it was the star's presence and charisma that called out to him; the way he could pose. 'I was like, you know, I wanna do that!' said Nicolas. 'I wanna be a film actor.'

Later, Nicolas discovered James Dean and Marlon Brando, which was a whole other level of emotional acting, but the first idea of wanting to be in movies came from the late martial arts master. Royce told me that Nicolas would ring him up and he'd go over to his house, they'd lay the mats out and train. The actor was a very coordinated and intelligent student and easy to teach, as well as being strong. I thought it would be nice to maybe join Royce one day when he was scheduled to teach his Hollywood student. I'm sure Royce wouldn't have minded me accompanying him, as I would be more than willing to play the dummy. The thought of Nicolas putting excruciating pain, arm locks and chokes on me was actually kind of interesting. Still, it never quite materialised.

It was reported at one point that Nicolas' troubled son Weston wanted to fight in the UFC. UFC head honcho, Dana White, told the press, 'I would never allow Weston Cage to set foot in the ring after two domestic violence arrests.' Weston had been taken to hospital allegedly for a mental evaluation, after an altercation in Hollywood with his trainer, apparently caught up in a downward spiral of mental instability. Some time later, I communicated with Weston directly and he seemed like a very nice and intelligent individual. He told me that he had 23 years of martial arts experience, though if that's the case, he started training at the age of two. He told me that he had fallen in love with sambo, a Russian art he has been studying for the last five years. Royce had taught Weston innumerable times from the age of eight to 16.

Because of my friendship with Royce, I asked him if I should go through Nicolas' publicist or if he could sort out an interview. He said going through the publicist was the best plan. In 2009, then, I embarked on a quest to track down the actor. I contacted the WKT PR agency in Beverly Hills to request an interview with Nicholas. 'Thank you so much for reaching out with this request, however, we need to pass on Mr Cage's behalf,' was the response I received, not the kind I was hoping for. From the tone, I knew the agent hadn't even brought the suggestion to her client's attention. Well, it did say 'on behalf of our client', so, yes, the agent was making the decision herself. This didn't exactly leave me despondent because I was the most persistent human being you'll ever come across. It wasn't going to be the last time Nicolas' people would hear from me. Hell, no! I was going to try every plausible avenues and angle. Being an actor in the public domain it was inevitable that sooner or later he would be releasing a movie and taking part in a press junket, and then I'd get him.

FROM MARTIAL ARTS TO MOVIE MAGIC

So in January 2010, not long after the Beverly Hills publicist had fobbed me off, I got in touch with NBC Universal as *Kick Ass*, Nicolas' new movie, was hitting the theatres. Unfortunately, it led to another dead end. 'Universal passed on your email as we're looking after the United Kingdom publicity for the film,' Vicky from the United Kingdom PR agency wrote. I tried again for the film *Season of the Witch*, but again, no luck. To my great relief, Lionsgate Films' publicity director for the United Kingdom secured me an interview with *Trespass* director Joel Schumacher to promote a film starring Nicholas. Finally, one foot was in the door, but getting the other foot in was going to prove difficult, as I was to find out. *Trespass* starred Nicolas so I thought the rep would be instrumental in locking down an interview with the star. 'Sadly we are unable to facilitate access to Nicolas until we have a release date. Nicolas is filming at the moment and isn't completing any interviews,' the rep, Lorna, informed me. It looked as if Nicolas Cage wasn't going to happen. Like I said, I'd always had a persistent approach, which was conducive to my success, but on this occasion it wasn't going to materialise no matter what I did. More recently, in 2020, when his film *Jiu Jitsu* was releasing I got in touch with his agent Mike Nilon, who kindly told me his client was busy shooting. One day!

Writing for a leading action movie magazine really allowed me to experience the many highs and lows. I was enjoying being part of the entertainment press, but I didn't merely want to write for a monthly action movie magazine; I had a bigger vision. It was time to explore and research the life of one of the biggest names in Hollywood.

CHAPTER TWENTY-ONE

I'LL BE BACK

NOW THAT I had been revelling in life as a member of the entertainment press for a while, it was inevitable that I would gravitate towards all things Hollywood. And the iconic figure whose life I most wanted to dive deep into was the star of countless high-octane action thrillers and family films, Arnold Schwarzenegger. He's the rare celebrity who's succeeded in several spheres: not only has he achieved legendary status as the greatest bodybuilder of all time and then as the biggest action movie star in the world, but he's continued to use that status for good, moving into politics and championing the environment.

Arnold's story is fascinating and inspiring in equal measure. As a young boy, growing up in a small village in Austria during the 1950s and early 60s, he daydreamed about a land to which where people from all corners of the globe emigrated in search of riches and fame. After coming to America in 1968, with $25 and a gym bag and almost no understanding of the English language, he quickly became a famous face in what was then considered by many a mocked sport, popularising the sport of bodybuilding like never before. To many, he's the epitome of the American Dream – an immigrant who succeeded through sheer hard work.

Then there's his status as the greatest bodybuilder in the history of the sport – just as Bruce Lee is widely acknowledged as the greatest martial arts exponent of the century and Muhammad Ali the greatest boxer of all time. For me, researching the life story of the greatest iron-pumper ever would complete the set. Having occasionally contributed to bodybuilding magazines, I was familiar with the sport and its participants, and since I was writing for an action movie magazine, it seemed like the perfect marriage – a merging of my interests.

For my part, I first came to know of Arnold when I went to my next door neighbour's relative's house in 1985 and watched the testosterone-fuelled action epic *Commando*. I was ten years old – too young for that film in hindsight – and I remember one of the neighbours saying to me that Arnold was Mr Universe. I didn't know what that meant; I thought he was someone like Flash Gordon who literally had something to do with the universe. Eventually I came to learn it had something to do with bodybuilding (it's actually a smaller competition, often considered a stepping stone to the Mr Olympia). *Commando* was a good action movie, I thought at the time, little knowing that I would later get to interview the director, Mark Lester, as well as Arnold's co-star Bill Duke. So, Arnold took up residence in my subconscious early. Despite this I hadn't followed his career in great detail, nor did this giant stand out from the rest of the musclemen I admired growing up – I was too engrossed in the martial arts – but I did find his movies quite interesting.

Later, as I immersed myself into his incredible life, I learned that fame and fortune wasn't handed to the Austrian on a plate – far from it. Early in his career, doors were slammed back in his face faster than they opened. His thick accent, a body that was too big, a name that no one could pronounce, and lacklustre acting skills were all hurdles he would have to overcome. The 'Austrian Oak's' appeal may have been his coveted bodybuilding titles and box-office success, but what I found equally appealing was his mind and motivation to succeed – how he pursued business ventures and career goals relentlessly and made a success out of anything he touched. When you study him, no matter what profession you're in, you can take away inspiration and use it as a blueprint to become successful.

From the perspective of a biographer, there are two imperative prerequisites I have in mind when it comes to producing work. Firstly, I want the audience and critics to go away with a sense of satisfaction. Pleasing the reader is of the utmost importance. Secondly, the calibre and quality of the interviewee is crucial. It's important to do your homework. I decided to get to work.

* * *

I started with Arnold the actor as I nailed down the seven-time Mr Olympia's bodybuilding friends and buddies. Arnold's acting hasn't got him an Oscar, but his determination to succeed in Hollywood was present in his head the day he set foot on American soil. To begin my quest, I spoke to his acting coach Eric Morris, who is one of the most controversial and famous acting coaches in America. If there was anyone who could enlighten me on the work ethic the sportsman-turned-actor demonstrated to make it in such a cut-throat industry, it was this man. Arnold told his coach that he loved his work in the gym but that the kind of work he was most passionate about was movies. Eric apparently had great faith in him from the beginning, and told me he had great conviction his pupil would succeed.

Another little-known fact: when Arnold was taking acting lessons, karate master Joe Lewis was a member of the same class, honing his own acting skills under the watchful eye of Arnold's coach. I had always been intrigued by Joe's stories – he'd treated me to some amazing tales of encounters with Bruce Lee and Muhammad Ali – and I wasn't going to pass on the chance of speaking to him again. Joe could breathe life into any story. Besides, I felt I could learn something different and new because he had hardly spoken about Arnold publicly. I asked Joe if he was surprised when his former colleague became a big movie star, mentioning that he wasn't exactly an obvious box-office draw.

'No, but John Wayne wasn't, either. Bruce Lee wasn't, either,' Joe told me. 'That's not what makes money on the big screen. It's your persona.' Joe proceeded to explain that it's ability on the screen, that presence and the unique energy that you project, which captures the public's imagination.

For his part, Arnold was able to endear himself to the audience because of that special energy and image he portrayed. 'I was shocked,' recalled Joe. 'Because, first of all, his accent was very strong. I'm thinking, *What kind of role can he get?* You can only get roles where you need that accent.' As we all know now, Arnold made Hollywood embrace him and refused to take no for an answer, first taking on roles like the robotic T-800, and then other roles in which his accent barely mattered.

Next, I asked Joe about his relationship with Arnold – if he socialised with him often – so I could get a glimpse of Arnold's personality through the lens of this martial arts champion. Joe said they'd had mutual friends who had brought them together. 'Arnold was kind of a unique figure, he was a man's man. But he wasn't necessarily somebody you could befriend easily because he was kind of a loner.' According to Joe, Arnold was always dedicated to his work. 'He didn't really hang out with the guys so to speak. He was kind of like me. I didn't like hanging out with the guys, either. People didn't think he was real friendly. Then again, it could've been the fact he needed to learn the language.'

One subject that I was keen to get Joe's take on was Arnold's link to the martial arts, if there was any. I asked the karate champion if he had trained the 'Terminator' in martial arts because I had seen Arnold featured in an article in *Black Belt* magazine, which claimed that Joe had trained him. 'In the very first paragraph he said he trained with me and Chuck Norris,' Joe said. 'Now, I don't know if he said that for real, or the magazine just says he said that.'

I was disconcerted by what I was hearing. At one point, Joe gave a copy of the magazine to Jim Lorimer – Arnold's close friend and the co-promoter of the annual Arnold Classic – and asked him if Arnold could sign it for him. Joe made it clear to me that he's not the type of person who you might call an autograph hunter, but thought it was kind of, as he put it, 'neat' that Arnold had used his name in there, so he made an exception.

'Jim threw the magazine in the bin,' Joe continued. 'If he wants to tell people he trained with me, let him say that.' I didn't know what to make of it all, and it left me scratching my head. But I found the whole episode quite interesting, if a little ambiguous.

Whether Arnold had any martial arts training or not outside of films continued to be unclear to me until some years later when I was at the Los Angeles office of Franco Columbu, Arnold's best friend. Franco told me that Arnold has never trained seriously in martial arts. Franco, who had been a competitive boxer in his native Italy, started training in Brazilian jiu-jitsu when the craze spread after the first UFC, but the 'Austrian Oak' had other things on his mind.

Arnold did prepare himself for some movies that required martial arts training, however. For instance, he took extensive training from the stunt coordinator, Mike Vendrell, when filming *Commando*, and mastered the sword under notable Japanese master Kiyoshi Yamazaki to prepare himself for *Conan*.

'I remember once we walked into a magazine office, for *Inside Kung Fu*, and he saw me on the cover of a magazine,' Joe, a fervent iron-pumper himself, told me. 'And he told the publishers, "Hey, this guy has a good body."'

Since Joe's friendship with the late Bruce Lee had been well documented, I asked Joe if he'd ever discussed Bruce with Arnold, or vice versa.

'I was with Bruce Lee from 1967,' Joe said. 'Arnold didn't get really well-known till he beat Sergio Oliva in the Mr Olympia contest in 1970, so my thing with Bruce Lee did not come up. I mean, Bruce Lee has a lot of fans who are famous people. Today, for example, Mike Tyson talks a lot about Bruce Lee. The Klitschko brothers, the famous world champion boxers, think a lot of Bruce Lee. The most famous basketball player in this country, probably the best basketball player in the world, Kobe Bryant, is a Bruce Lee fan. So it's kind of odd talking to Bruce Lee about other famous people when he was going to become probably more famous than they are.' This answer was good enough for me.

Speaking of Bruce Lee, as I was researching Arnold's life I interviewed Hollywood executive producer, Andrew Vajna, who worked on some of Arnold's most successful movies. Researching the interview, I realised that he was the same producer who had offered Bruce a two-film deal before the kung fu star passed away. I thought I'd hit the jackpot. I had been aware that a Hungarian film producer had made the offer to Bruce prior to Bruce's untimely death, and Andrew revealed that he had bought Bruce the house Bruce lived in in Hong Kong at the height of his fame, as part of the advance payment for a movie they were discussing.

Unfortunately, the producer would never get to work with Bruce. He went on to produce several action movies, including *Rambo* with Sylvester Stallone, a couple of the *Terminator* movies and *Total Recall*, which were all extremely successful at the box office, and many more. Andrew was an aspiring filmmaker and partnered up another enthusiastic filmmaker, Mario Kassar, who I have direct contact with. Both men dedicated themselves relentlessly to their craft and in due course made their mark in Hollywood.

I found Andrew's story inspiring. He had come from an Eastern European country and pursued his dream, eventually conquering Hollywood, but remained a very nice gentleman who made time for me. Mario, originally from Beirut, had brought the rights to Bruce's first movie – one of the first foreigners to do so – for parts of the Middle East. It was interesting to learn of the Bruce Lee connections of these big Hollywood executives had. Both went on to work with Arnold and Stallone. I have often contemplated which movies Bruce would have made and who he would have worked with. For film fans, a partnership with Stallone or Schwarzenegger could have been phenomenal.

How do Bruce and Arnold compare? Of course, both were excellent physical specimens but one was a fighter and the other a bodybuilder. One story that has stayed with me ever since I was a young teenager is from when I was walking to the weights gym one Saturday morning with my friend who used to accompany me. We were talking, as we often did, about the man we idolised – Bruce Lee. He chuckled saying that if Arnold got hold of Bruce in a fight, he would tear him up. I'm thinking, *What the heck?*

I could see it in his eyes as he made what I felt was demeaning comment. My friend was of the opinion that someone like Bruce could never defeat a man of Arnold's stature, a true behemoth. I was frankly disgusted at his comment, although I didn't show it. As much as I was an admirer of bodybuilding athletes, and Arnold was just one of them, no more, no less, I refused to embrace my friend's opinion. Frankly, my friend didn't know what he was talking about. His opinion reflected the classic 'bigger is always better' philosophy, one that seemed to be quite prevalent at the time before the tremendous explosion of Gracie Jiu-Jitsu.

Since the sport of MMA has enjoyed immense success it has become part of Arnold's annual expo, simply dubbed 'The Arnold' by many fans. Arnold approached Relson Gracie to start the Arnold–Gracie World Submission Championships at the event in the early 2000s. 'I just love to watch the fights,' Arnold, who has taken a real shine to the sport of MMA, once remarked. 'I think they're very entertaining and you get inspiration because they're in extraordinary shape.'

On other occasions, this champion bodybuilder admitted that MMA was his favourite sport to watch. Whether he meant it or not, I couldn't say, because Arnold had learned the American marketing strategy of saying outrageous things to get the public's attention. Arnold said that, despite the fact that MMA was a sport, in equal measure he perceived it as show business. He showed his appreciation for the athletes and personalities and was equally impressed by the fighters' intellectual skills and their technical brilliance. He remarked, 'They can all talk very well, they can explain what they've done, why they won, why they lost.'

Like Bruce, Arnold used his sport as a platform to pursue a film career. And just as the martial arts had been kicked into popularity by Bruce Lee movies, Arnold was hugely responsible for elevating the sport of bodybuilding, making it more acceptable and fashionable to have muscles and train with weights. Every action movie star now works out and strives to attain an aesthetic look. In the years after Arnold's success, it became the norm for a Hollywood action hero to strip off to show his physique on screen. Bruce, who had an invincible aura, paved the way and Arnold followed a decade later.

* * *

Arnold's career trajectory took another turn when he stepped into the political arena, eventually becoming the governor of California. But this immigrant wasn't content. In the back of his mind was the belief that he could reach great heights, and he contemplated running for president, a prospect that gave me goose pimples. Unfortunately, the US Constitution prevents foreign-born citizens from holding the nation's top job. But I'm sure if the opportunity had presented itself, he would have prevailed, landing the job of president of the most powerful country in the world.

When you are exploring the life of a public figure, be it a fighter, sportsperson or entertainer, you can't leave out their best friend. But when I interviewed Franco Columbu I had a rather bizarre experience. This time I interviewed him over the phone. We got talking and I asked him whether a competitive dynamic existed between them when training. Franco has a very strong Italian accent and apparently misunderstood me. Mid-conversation he suddenly told me to call him back later, giving me the impression that something urgent required his immediate attention. I rang him back several times but he didn't answer the phone.

When I finally did get through to him, he hung up on me, but I'm a persistent bastard, and he was going to see this first-hand. I got through to him again, and when he answered this time, he said I should call him back later. The sudden U-turn left me bemused. I thought to myself, *Have I said something wrong? Was he upset?* Then it dawned on me. He thought I was trying to talk about his best friend's controversial past.

At one time, Arnold had had a sudden and drastic fall from grace because of his personal life. A segment of the public abhorred him. Speculation ran rife about events in his personal life, but in no way was I pursing that route. That was never my intention, nor did I ask Franco anything to do with Arnold's personal life. Franco's lack of understanding brought the interview to an end before I could squeeze in everything I wanted to. It may sound bizarre, but I'm sure one of Arnold's closest friends simply thought I was an underhand tabloid journalist.

I have always endeavoured to refrain from embellishing my subjects for the sake of sensationalising them, which many journalists and biographers are only too happy to do. I never really had an interest in treading that path. A lot of writers would gravitate towards the controversial side and exploit it because controversy sells. No story gains traction quite so rapidly in today's media-frenzy environment as one that tears down an A-list celebrity, even if it's the death knell for a star's career. The pleasures and perils of the celebrity lifestyle became obvious to me as I investigated it. I learned that the media creates a buzz, hype and fuels interest, but can just as quickly tear you down. The stories regarding Arnold's father's Nazi connections and his own personal life, I had no real interest in putting in the spotlight. I was having none of that. Besides, I had been influenced by writer John Little – a Bruce Lee historian and biographer who actually wrote for the bible of bodybuilding, *FLEX* magazine – who glorified Bruce

Lee to the max, and wouldn't print a word against him. I think his influence rubbed off on me and shaped my own approach at the time.

Speaking of friends, Arnold was in a prime position to bring in some of his friends into the motion picture industry, and he did. However, most people will agree that he could have been a lot more instrumental. Franco, for instance, was in *Terminator*, a hit of epic proportions, for a few seconds. One of Arnold's best friends, Sven Ole-Thorsen, was given a few minor roles in movies, but nothing more than that. Arnold is a driven man and has an ego, no doubt, which is confirmed by many who know him well, and this propels him forward. It is my understanding he yearned to get to the top and wasn't prepared to carry his friends on his back. If everybody's doing it, then it's nothing special; you're not exclusive. That's the philosophy some successful people embrace and I must admit I've been guilty of this in the past when I was younger.

One of the deepest drives of human nature is the desire to be appreciated. To be held in esteem, to be a sought-after person is fundamental to us as human beings. The key is to control this and control the ego, develop a healthy mindset and aim for being content. Some people have the narcissistic personality disorder. These types have a tendency to be outrageously negative and are insecure creatures. Many of our habits are deeply ingrained and various core personality attributes may be immutable.

As Arnold once said, 'We all like to be liked, loved, appreciated, but some like it more than that. I'm one of them.' His words have been embedded in me ever since I heard him say them in an old documentary called *Total Rebuild*, which I had in cassette form back in the early 1990s. The former governor of California became a motivator and an advocate of self-help, and a beacon of hope for young men like me. Arnold had become an influence on me with regards to capturing your dreams, more so than his physical attributes and high-octane movies would suggest. Interestingly, I also learned that Arnold's father always favoured his elder son – this struck a chord with me. His father believed that his younger son was useless: Arnold's brother was not only a better athlete, but a better person overall. I believe this motivated Arnold to defy the odds and prove he was worthy and could succeed. And succeed he did, as he took the world by storm, achieving the ultimate not only in a physically demanding sport, but in the entertainment and political arenas.

CHAPTER TWENTY-TWO

FROM HOSPITALITY TO MMA CHAOS

BY THE end of the 2000s, there was a new breed of athlete making waves in Hollywood – UFC stars. Randy Couture's acting chops may have come as a surprise to many UFC and action fans, but among the UFC fighters who crossed over into Hollywood, he was the first prominent personality to have a big impact. In 2011, the UFC champion was working on *The Expendables II,* filming in Bulgaria with an all-star cast. On his way back to America after filming finished, Randy stopped by the United Kingdom for a few days to hang out and do some publicity and promotion, which I arranged. For my team, this would work out perfectly.

We stayed at the Jumeirah Hotel in Kensington, London, for several days before touring around the country. Kensington and Knightsbridge are full of affluent Arabs, many of whom come to the capital to escape the baking hot summer months in their own countries. On this occasion, we were guests of DJ, who I'd met before and who was the personal assistant to the Crown Prince of Dubai Sheikh Hamdan bin Mohammed Rashid Al Maktoum. The sheikh had a profound passion for adrenaline-fuelled sports. The prince was also involved in philanthropic work and had a penchant for poetry. Although I never got to meet him, he was aware of my work. DJ was kind enough to have us as his personal guests at the hotel owned by the royals. The Jumeirah is frequented by well-known personalities, and it was expensive as hell, but our host had made it explicit to us and his staff that everything was on the house. My team, who were all my personal friends, wasted no time tucking into the small sliced cheesecakes, which would normally cost £12 a slice, and anything else they could get their hands on.

In the late evening, we congregated into the restaurant on the ground floor of the hotel. The ambience was that of the a very expensive establishment that only well-off people frequent. As we sat there gazing at the sophisticated menu, DJ asked Randy what he would like, recommending Kobe steak. The UFC champion was unfamiliar with the dish, so our host proceeded to explain how they breed the cattle in Japan. They don't let the cattle run around in the field, which prevents them from developing big muscles, which can make the meat too tough. Instead the cattle are pampered from a young age and massaged with milk. My friend Seyfi, being curious, asked if it was halal. To his amusement DJ started sniggering and his Muslim friends from abroad joined in. They advised Seyfi to have the fish instead. Needless to say, no more was said on that subject.

At the dinner table we talked about the UFC and anything and everything besides. DJ was an interesting individual, very inquisitive, and it didn't take me long to learn of his profound passion for the martial arts and UFC. He was on the committee of some karate and tae kwon do organisations in the Middle East and had competed in karate tournaments as part of the UAE team. This man was on a mission to get karate into the Olympics. He was quite well versed in the subject and I was impressed by the enthusiasm he showed. The white uniforms he had competed in were all framed up, he told us. I came to learn that quite a few Middle Eastern royals have competed in martial arts, including a princess who competed in the Olympics in tae kwon do, and several other royals who have done well in Brazilian jiu-jitsu tournaments. It dawned on me that these royals took their hobby very seriously. As for DJ, he was a pleasant person to be around. I was rather surprised at his humility, considering his position.

The conversation continued as we sipped our soft drinks while others enjoyed forbidden (and expensive) wine. The service was impeccable and lavish to the extent that we almost found it too pampering. The waiters were on you before you could even open your mouth, and your glass would be filled before you even placed it on the table. DJ, injecting a touch of humour, told Randy to get rid of the clothes he was wearing because he was going to take him shopping in the morning. The Arabs love their shopping. It's one of their favourite pastimes. I'm sure a few of the group thought they could get used to this kind of treatment.

As the night progressed, DJ pulled out a small colour booklet – 16 pages or so – filled with images of him and the prince, including photos of them practising martial arts. 'Maybe we could work on a project in the future,' I said to DJ, trying to get a reaction – a feeler. I got a sneaky smirk back, indicating that a potential opportunity was certainly on the 'menu'. This felt like a huge opportunity to potentially collaborate with Middle Eastern royalty on a larger capacity pertaining to combat sports, and project ideas started to run through my head. Looking back, I think I was running before I could walk. That was my problem – I'd get too interested in new projects with little provocation – but I was enthused by the possibility of joining forces with these people. After all, we shared a mutual passion and I was in a position to bring something to the table their money couldn't always buy. These men weren't short of money; they lived a lifestyle most could only dream of. The realisation grew inside me that perhaps some of these men had a bit of an ego, but DJ was more or less devoid of that trait, and so I thought a project might be of interest to him and the prince. For my part, I had great conviction that I could come up with the goods and create a win-win situation for both parties. Sadly, I soon found myself disenfranchised of an opportunity to present and pitch any idea.

In Dubai, MMA stars are treated like kings. It's not uncommon for a royal to hand over the most lavish of gifts, such as a watch worth $200,000, like the one sheikh presented to former UFC welterweight champion GSP. DJ invited Randy to Dubai through me, and so I joked with Randy, telling him that he'd be receiving a $200,000 watch from the royal family. Randy, a gentleman, and not one to take advantage, just laughed it off and didn't seem to be bothered about receiving any sort of gifts. That said, he wasn't devoid of financial concerns: I had once asked Randy if the UFC should be paying fighters more and he'd said, 'Yes, not just in the UFC but mixed martial artists in general should be getting paid better across the board in other organisations. The top boxers are making $20 million to $40 million for a fight. On the other hand, the top mixed martial artist in the UFC makes $500,000 per fight. As one of the top fighters, I'm certainly not complaining; the money I've made in the sport has been a great way to make a living. But, at the same time, it's paying low level compared to other professional athletes.'

He added that wrestlers don't have a professional outlet for the sport once their amateur career is over. Professional wrestling, as everybody knows, is entertainment, not a real sport. 'Boxing, both at amateur and professional level is a sport, and MMA is a sport,' he said. 'Olympic and amateur wrestlers have no real outlet to make money. You can see more and more Olympic wrestlers making a transition into professional MMA.' Randy had wrestled for the USA team and it wasn't till the age of 37 that he started fighting in the UFC, but he expected to see more young wrestlers make the jump as they saw the rewards on offer.

Excited at the prospect of a potential Dubai visit, I told Randy to keep me posted of his availability so that we could grab some publicity and chill with the royals. Unfortunately, his hectic schedule and filming got in the way of making that trip materialise. It would have been a great experience.

FROM HOSPITALITY TO MMA CHAOS

One thing I learned about DJ and the royals is that it takes a long time to earn their trust. I don't blame them. Given the position they are in, worth billions of dollars, it wouldn't be uncommon for people to try to take advantage of them. I would be lying if I said it never crossed my own mind, but in my case I was less interested in money and more keen to be given an opportunity to work with these people. Then again, I also felt I had something to offer, and if I benefited I wanted to earn it and not be given it on the plate for free. Still, although I had struck up a certain level of rapport with DJ, I found him to be somewhat cautious later on as he started to avoid my calls. He obviously didn't appreciate the full significance of my offerings. I often had the urge to work with him and potentially his employer, and contacted him frequently. I genuinely felt that had DJ accommodated me, I would have opened doors – doors that he was oblivious to the existence of. Not only that, but we shared a mutual appreciation for martial arts and MMA, and it made perfect sense to work together. I knew this individual had met and dealt with many highly influential and eminent figures around the world, from presidents, kings and prime ministers to actors and athletes. He'd experienced life and people from all cultures, and I was merely another guy. His reticent attitude left me rather disappointed, but it was not the end of the world. At least he was an affable person and always showed us respect and hospitality.

* * *

The next morning, I wasted no time in phoning world heavyweight champion David Haye's representatives to notify them about Randy's visit. David's respect towards MMA had been publicised in the sporting press, hence he was the perfect boxer to join forces with. David agreed to assist in whatever way he could to help publicise Randy's appearance. I had arranged a press conference at the hotel on the first floor, in a nice, spacious room. ESPN and Sky Sports, among other media, were present. David arrived with his representative and a camera crew that was filming footage for a documentary on the boxer.

I had interviewed the boxing champion a couple of years earlier. At the time, he'd been in Cyprus, so I'd spoken to him over the phone and hadn't met him face to face. He seemed like a nice, down-to-earth guy – so I thought. But when I finally met the 'Haymaker', I didn't really find him to be a very approachable person, or even that friendly. I wouldn't say fame had got to his head. If anything I feel he has been quite humble. He certainly wasn't a diva with a big entourage, and was pretty much as normal as a person can be. It emerged that he had once met the UFC champion in Las Vegas when Randy's son Ryan was fighting. In addition, David's father had been a martial arts instructor and David himself had some interest in competing in the UFC one day.

As everyone congregated in the room, I sat with David and Randy onstage as journalists fired questions at them. Afterwards, we organised one-on-one interviews with both of the champions. David broached the subject of acting. He would love to get into acting, maybe joining Randy in *The Expendables* once he hung up his gloves, he told the Sky Sports reporter. Still, I didn't think he would succeed, nor take the required steps to seriously bring his ambitions to fruition.

When the press conference kicked into action, I spotted DJ standing in the corner, with a group of his friends who were visiting from the Middle East. One of them was an ardent student of the martial arts, and was wearing gym clothing as if he was there to attend a seminar and glean knowledge from the UFC champion. His enthusiasm was infectious, and he stood out like a sore thumb (my team and I actually ended up giving this fanatic the name 'super fan', as he was constantly peppering Randy with questions). After snapping some pictures and enjoying some off-camera chat we relaxed. The press conference had gone well and I profusely thanked David's representative for their time. In spite of David's attitude I have to give him and his team credit for their support.

FROM HOSPITALITY TO MMA CHAOS

The evening started with attending a high-end establishment in Mayfair for a product launch. DJ's hospitality continued and he took us to a very posh Japanese restaurant straight afterwards. The chauffeurs and bodyguards dropped us off. There must have been 12 or 14 of us. The staff at the restaurant seemed very familiar with the royal representative and his crew. After all, he was an elite client so they treated him like, well, royalty. After the meal, in which most of us had no clue as to what we had eaten, the bodyguards picked us up again. It was straight to another establishment, one of the most famous celebrity hangouts in London. There was a slight problem – there was not enough space in the cars. So, one of the bodyguards asked my friend Seyfi if he had any cash on him, because apparently they never carried cash. Seyfi had to make his way in a taxi arranged by the bodyguard, who assured him that he'd be reimbursed. Seyfi told him that it was fine because DJ had been looking after us. Later at the venue the bodyguard approached Seyfi and placed a note in the inside of his jacket. When my friend got home he realised it was a £50 note. He later joked to me that he'd made a profit of £30. I nearly fell over laughing.

Because of the high-end atmosphere and security presence, celebrities frequented this place. It was packed out. The management was familiar with DJ, so as usual he, and we, his guests, would be given VIP treatment at the highest level. We sat and relaxed in our VIP booth while two tall bodyguards stood on each corner, including the one we had named super fan. Randy sat taking in the sights and sounds, but I could tell that, like me, he wasn't a party animal, or one to strut his skills on the dance floor. Essentially it's not my scene and I'm not the type who frequents such places. He had good footwork, of course, but he saved it for the Octagon.

If you're talking of wild UFC fighters who love to party, you'd have to think about Chuck Liddell, who became as notorious for his partying as he did for his fighting. He was a star and living the life. In a sense, Chuck and Randy are two polar opposites, though they were very evenly matched in the Octagon.

TO THE TOP

Back in the nightspot, I could see in the corner of my eye that Seyfi was attracting what I would call the wrong sort of attention, getting chatted up by a young blonde. I watched as she wrote her number on a piece of paper, and slipped it into his hand. Apparently she thought Seyfi was a rich Arab. I don't blame her, because he looked the part. This was the right place to find rich men who had wads of money to throw away, the perfect joint to target the multi-millionaires. And we were seeing this in action as hungry vultures tried to work their magic and hypnotise the vulnerable rich and famous. Some of these creatures were so perfect in their approach that you'd think they deserved an Oscar for their acting skills. At about two in the morning, I insisted that we call it a night because I was responsible for Randy and we had an early start. Unfortunately, that didn't go down too well with DJ as he wanted the party to continue. His displeasure was only too clear, but I would not permit Randy to be out till four in the morning, as we had work to do the next day. Revelling all night is not conducive to a productive next day when you have work on the menu. So we called it a night and all of us went back to the hotel to hit the sack, much to our host's dismay.

* * *

Despite the fact we were having a great time, a major obstacle lay ahead of us, which would put a dent in my relationship with Randy's manager. We were scheduled to do a promotional event at the BAMMA fight at the Motorpoint Arena in Nottingham, promoting a product of Randy's. With thousands of MMA-mad fans attending the event, it was a perfect opportunity. I had discussed Randy's potential appearance at this venue with his PA, Valerie, back in Las Vegas. 'We do have a fighter fighting in Nottingham on 10 December that Randy would like to corner,' she had informed me. 'So he is going to push to be there for his fight.' Randy's management already had contemplated having him make an appearance at this MMA promotion, a direct competitor of the UFC, and now I proceeded to make a deal with the promoters that stipulated that Randy would come and promote his new product and nothing else. He wasn't going to be promoting the organisation, as he was still tied up in a contract with the rival UFC.

Perhaps inevitably, it wasn't long before the BAMMA PR department sent out a press release with the massive headline: RANDY COUTURE HEADING TO BAMMA! *What's going on?* was my immediate reaction. Valerie and Randy's manager back in America didn't waste any time in contacting me, warning me that Randy was still under contract with the UFC and that the press release was certain to put a further dent in his relationship with the UFC. Randy was not allowed to promote any MMA event while still in contract with the UFC, even though he wasn't actively fighting. BAMMA, meanwhile, had worded the headline so that it gave the impression the UFC star was heading to their promotion to fight or back it – both of which were nonsense.

Things escalated quickly. Randy's manager was now getting involved, and furious, apparently having emergency meetings with the UFC. It's no secret that the UFC's relationship with their biggest star was not exactly rosy by this point, something I mentioned earlier. They had had disputes concerning certain issues in the past, and were far from being best of buddies by this point. The contentious relationship fighters have with promoters and companies is nothing unusual at all, and in America lawyers have a tendency to sue here, there and everywhere. It's typically about money. Fighters want more money; promoters want to pay them less money. Really, it couldn't be simpler.

Now, though, my master plan was in peril. The thought of Randy not making an appearance at the BAMMA event, the event that was going to benefit us the most, was a daunting prospect. This was terrible news for me. This was another American mess, a mess that someone else got me into. And this time it wasn't someone across the pond who had instigated it, but someone in the United Kingdom.

Shortly afterwards, I received a message from Randy's manager. 'Randy's potential promotional involvement with any promoter outside of the UFC is probably a technical breach of his contract with the UFC,' he said in an email. 'We have very specific rules for what he can and can't do with other promotions. Until his contractual relationship with the UFC changes, which I am currently negotiating, he is bound by those existing obligations.' You could tell this guy was coming out with the standard technical jargon. He also made it clear to BAMMA that the appearance and marketing related to the appearance at the BAMMA 8 event would, most likely, put Randy in technical breach of his existing contract with the UFC. According to the manager he was in the middle of transitioning that relationship into a retirement status, making things even more delicate.

'I was shocked to have seen the press release hit the media yesterday morning – especially since I had just emailed Neys last week regarding the plan schedule for BAMMA 8,' the manager continued. Ney was a staff member at BAMMA who, I assume, dealt with invoices. 'I think I have made my frustrations pretty clear in the last 24 hours, even to random passers-by on the street.' By this point, I wasn't liking this guy at all. In fact, I was on the verge of losing my temper. Next the manager said that, in terms of going forward, he had not decided on the best plan and that it wasn't his style to do something without telling all involved first. It was hard for him to pull back the press release, since we had already mounted a marketing campaign based upon it, but the real contractual damage to Randy had the potential to occur at or around the event, he said, so a lot would depend upon a conversation he intended to have with the UFC. Coming up with a creative solution was something he was working on, he told me, promising he would keep everyone in the loop. 'By the way, now would be a good time for BAMMA to pay the remaining amounts due Trigg,' he wrote in the email. 'Neys has the invoice.' Allegedly, BAMMA were delaying payments and not paying some fighters on time. Still, that was between those two parties, and I had no interest in their previous business dealings.

FROM HOSPITALITY TO MMA CHAOS

Next, Ashley, the BAMMA promoter, frantically informed me that they couldn't get hold of Randy's manager. Apparently the manager wasn't responding to emails and phone calls, so Ashley had no further details on proceedings. He asked me if I could get hold of him so we all knew where we stood with regards to the scheduled appearance. The situation remained precarious. Brimming with frustration, I got on the phone to the manager. Painful minutes ticked away as I sat in my home office in my high-back black leather chair, dialling his cell phone number six times on the trot. It was 2am United Kingdom time. I was always working in the late hours of the night. Making calls to America, Canada, Australia and Malaysia and other parts of the world was nothing unusual for me. On that note, I must say that if the home office isn't effectively separated from the home environment, it can easily affect your home life. So promoting a healthy balance which allows you to switch off mentally when you're supposed to be relaxing is paramount. The loss of distinction between work life and home life is something which many self-employed working-from-home individuals experience. I've had more than my fair share of stress, but now I am able to achieve a harmonious balance. I have always been one of those individuals who has kept work and family separate, like some professionals do. I went a step further: I didn't mix work with social life.

Whenever I was researching and working on a major project I compared it to a fighter preparing for a professional fight – you blank out most things and any distractions. It's time for a complete focus. To illustrate this point further, I remember that whenever a champion UFC fighter friend of mine used to prepare for a fight, he would completely focus on the training camp, and you couldn't even phone him for ten weeks. Mental focus was as important, if not more important, than the physical preparation. Hearing that, I carried it into my own work. My typical routine working from home is that my day starts at 10am. I'm checking and sending emails and making phone calls, from newspaper editors to celebrity representatives, whether I'm securing an interview with a world champion fighter or someone from the Hollywood fraternity. If I'm in the middle of writing a book, I'll spend all day on the project and sometimes also spend late nights working.

Anyway, Randy's manager finally answered the call, and I succinctly made things clear to him. I was upset and expressed my anger with some venom. I could feel he was disconcerted with my onslaught, but he continued his own assault as I parried his verbal attacks. I was actually appalled by his behaviour. I thought, *No wonder UFC had a hard time with their superstar athlete – lawyers and agents like this guy want to work against you instead of with you.* Managers and lawyers often cause friction and I had experienced it from other Americans I'd dealt with in the past. I said to him that he was lucky I was being nice. This was met by mockery. He was one of those people you just couldn't get through to.

Sometime after that call, the BAMMA rep in the PR department, Liam Fisher, messaged me saying, 'To be honest, this sounds like a complete mess. In no way does either of these articles sounds like Randy promoting BAMMA. They are very clear on stating that Randy is signing his product at BAMMA. Any issues you have with Valerie and the manager need to be sorted out between you. We simply cannot issue any sort of retraction without causing major embarrassment to BAMMA.' This guy was concerned about his organisation being embarrassed, when in fact it was him who came up with the headline that set all this off. This further, not surprisingly, elevated my dislike for this new guy on the scene.

Finally, BAMMA and I agreed that no further announcements would be made and that it was still possible to have Randy make the scheduled appearance. Still, it was still uncertain whether he would appear. By now Randy's manager was not responding to any emails and there were only a couple of days left, before the event, prolonging my agony. He wouldn't say yes or no, or even that he would be getting back to us with a final solution. The guy had done a vanishing act.

FROM HOSPITALITY TO MMA CHAOS

Not knowing what action to take, I conferred with Randy to establish the best course of action. Randy said he was cool to go ahead, at any rate, so we plodded on. It was time to hit the arena.

When we got to the arena the fights had already started. We set up and we had people passing by and meeting Randy when they spotted him. It was open space, so we had security controlling the large crowd. Andy, being the head of my team's security, did a kind of side-to-side seesaw action simultaneously controlling the large crowd, which was funny and we had a good laugh afterwards. By the intermission a large crowd had clustered around Randy, and it got rather crazy. I asked Randy if he wanted to sit down, but he said he was OK. I had him work his arse off and sign autographs for more than two hours non-stop. I could tell after the two hours he wanted to call it a day, but I was insistent in carrying on for a little longer. I wanted to reach my target. I could sense Randy was somewhat tired, but boy, did I make him work that day.

Finally, I spotted Liam Fischer walking towards us. He had two people with him – one on each side like bodyguards. Smiling and relieved, he said everything was cool now. I acknowledged him and decided to let it slide, but in the back of my mind I had negative thoughts flooding in. Liam was one of those people who had 'problematic' written all over him, the kind that you're always sure to regret dealing with. It wasn't over yet, either. A couple of months later he would be the centre of another controversial hiccup that involved Randy, his manager and me. The trouble with the BAMMA guy, far from being over, had just started.

CHAPTER TWENTY-THREE

ADVENTURES IN NEW YORK

IN LATE 2011 I got in touch with Paul Paone, the promoter of the MMA World Expo in New York, which was going to take place on 17 and 18 December, with an idea. At the time, MMA fights were still illegal in New York, and so fans had to settle for attending non-fight events, or venturing to neighbouring states. It wasn't until late 2016 that the UFC finally ended its long journey to legalisation in one of the boxing centres of the world. The UFC held its first New York show on 12 November at Madison Square Garden, and came to the city in style, as none other than UFC's golden boy, Conor McGregor, headlined UFC 205. McGregor knocked out Eddie Alvarez in round two, making history as he became the first fighter to hold two belts simultaneously. UFC 205 reportedly broke the pay-per-view record with 1.65 million buys, and would cement McGregor's reputation as an all-time great.

That was all for the future, though. Back in 2011, I secured Randy's appearance at the MMA Expo. Considering the fact that Randy was the biggest name in the UFC at the time before the emergence of McGregor, and to a certain degree the clout I carried because of my position, I wasted no time in requesting certain privileges from the promoter. So, in addition to Randy's and my airfare and accommodation, I requested and was adamant about receiving an additional flight and accommodation for my friend Elbiz. It didn't take me long to convince the promoter. He complied with my request and booked in all three of us at the W Hotel. Paul was a gentleman and easy to get on with, the type I'd go the extra mile for.

Always endeavouring to help one of my close friends, Joe Egan, I had informed him that I could get him to be a special guest alongside Randy in the Big Apple. Joe had mentioned to me that he was going to be spending Christmas in New York visiting his sister, who is married to a New York policeman, making it a perfect opportunity to kill two birds with one stone. Neither of us was aware of the trauma Joe would suffer on his stateside trip; if I'd known I'd never have arranged his appearance.

Back in those days I was the proud owner of a very basic cell phone. I never really embraced modern technology, and certainly never wanted a posh new phone or the latest model. Back then, I didn't even know what the hell an app was, it was all just too damn sophisticated for my liking. By 2011, I'm fairly sure I was the only guy in my business with a phone so old that you could no longer purchase it in a shop. I'm sure at the time people couldn't fathom why I carried this phone around with me, when I could quite easily buy a more modern. In fact, some would say this to me to my face. But I'm not like everyone else. I've never followed like a sheep and most certainly never let peer pressure get the better of me.

Anyway, by the time I arrived in New York, my phone battery was completely dead and ready to be buried. Still, I wasn't ready to offer it to the grave just yet. Unfortunately, my charger had been left behind in the United Kingdom when we were touring with Randy, so now I was trying to get hold of a charger to connect with the world again. At first I tried the hotel reception, only to be told that they had any number of chargers but none were compatible with mine. Next I went to several phone shops, but they told me it was an old phone so they didn't stock these chargers and batteries anymore. I was completely cut off from the outside world.

Joe had the hotel address but he had no clue of what anyone's room numbers were. He had been trying to get hold of me, but obviously couldn't, and when he arrived at the hotel and asked for me, the reception staff wouldn't disclose our room numbers to him. Whether or not they thought he was a crazy fan trying to get to Randy, I can't say with any certitude. Unable to catch a break, Joe phoned one of my friends back in England to see if he could reach me, telling him that he had been trying to make contact with me, but was having no luck whatsoever. To his dismay, my friend couldn't help.

To say that Joe was furious would be an understatement. Eventually he ended up spending a fortune calling England from his mobile trying to find out if anyone had made contact with me. Meanwhile, I was curious as to why Joe hadn't linked up with us when he had the hotel information.

While all this was happening, Elbiz, Randy and I stepped out for lunch in a small Italian restaurant not far from our hotel. When it comes to eating out, as I mentioned, I'm one of those people who are never venture out of their comfort zone. I stick to what I know. It's either pizza or chips (well, I've made some progress now and might throw in a steak occasionally). Sophisticated long menus fluster me, and I've never been one to venture into unknown territory. Needless to say, I stuck to the good old pizza, as it was an Italian place, and I told the waiter to throw in the chips for good measure.

As we settled in the Big Apple we had ample time to relax, but it was business that we were there for so we weren't going to deviate too far from our main objective. In the reception area of the hotel, people would often recognise Randy, walk up to him and take pictures with him. The doormen had recognised him, too, and we made sure they got a few photos. After some time hanging out in the lobby, we stepped outside ready to be picked up and taken to the venue. Suddenly an unmarked police car pulled up with a brash, fairly well-built guy who knew the doorman. Talk about being loud, this guy was a fucking rocket. He was yelling at Randy like a lunatic. Well, it sounded more like he was offering Randy out for a scrap as he sat on the comfort of his warm cosy seat in his car, if you ask me – but he was actually just being sarcastic. To the passers-by I'm certain it looked like something nasty was brewing. This cop looked and sounded like the actor Mike Starr, who was the big bully in a Steven Seagal movie and led a team of bodyguards in Kevin Costner's *Bodyguard*. For some reason this guy always played a big fat bully and got nailed by the star.

Anyway, this cop came across as a typical Italian-American. Sure enough, he pretty soon said something to Randy which sounded derogatory, but was apparently meant in jest. The doorman, coming to the rescue, said something to his cop friend along the lines that he couldn't speak to Randy in such a disrespectful manner. Not listening to his friend's words, the cop said he could do what he wanted as he flashed his badge. *What an idiot*, I thought. *If only Randy could administer a bit of pain on this big mouth to teach him a lesson*. Randy, not one to trade verbal barbs, laughed it off. He never took these types seriously. In fact he had told me once, 'I don't like confrontation.' The fat cop sped off in his car like a rally driver. We stood outside in the freezing cold until Paul's brother picked us up and we made our way to the venue.

* * *

The MMA World Expo was far from the calibre of the expos that the UFC promoted. It was sparsely attended in comparison to the UFC organised expos, and didn't attract the same quality of talent. There were the usual booths promoting their brands, clothing lines and Brazilian jiu-jitsu, and MMA seminars and tournaments taking place, but the highlight of the day was Randy's appearance – he had top billing. The New Yorkers were thrilled and looking forward to meeting their idol, and it was reflected in their expressions when they eventually came face to face with the champion in the cage where he was meeting the public. Randy was unsurprised, as he always believed that there was a wider audience beyond the confines of the UFC brand. 'It's not just about the UFC, but the sport of MMA,' he told me once. 'The UFC is only part of it.'

No MMA expo is complete without having prominent names and fighters of repute in attendance. At this one, I spotted Phil Nurse, a Thai-boxing instructor who had left Europe to set up a gym and promote Thai-boxing in New York in the mid-1990s. When Phil spotted Randy in the cage he ran up to us sporting a little kid's smirk, and shook Randy's and my hands like an excited teenage fan. Phil has done a great job of promoting the art of eight limbs in America, and trained several UFC champions, including one of his prize pupils, GSP. I think he made a good move, because it was perfect timing to go over the pond to spread the sport, a sport that had exploded in Britain with the help of five Thai masters who had emigrated to Britain in the late-1970s. The American market, beyond doubt, had always been there to be penetrated. Phil, a student of the famed Master Sken, had seen the opportunity to tap into a huge market and grabbed it with both hands.

After Randy finished meeting people, Randy, Elbiz and I stepped outside the cage and spotted Matt Serra signing autographs. There was a long line of fans waiting to meet him. As soon as 'The Terror' spotted Randy, I recall him jumping out of his seat like a pin had hit his arse. 'Hey, it's Randy Couture!' he yelled. We had a short chat with the former UFC welterweight champion, who seemed to be in a jovial mood and was in awe of Randy. It was good to meet Matt, who had fought some elite champions in the welterweight division, including Matt Hughes and BJ Penn, and had shocked the world by knocking out GSP to take the crown. A native of New York, he walked and talked like the typical Italian New Yorker. His instructor, Renzo Gracie, was giving a seminar nearby and we said a quick hello to him, too.

Next, I was introduced by Randy to another gentleman, Mark Garrow, a Jewish Canadian who had a MMA TV media company. Clued up when it came to business, he was the spitting image of Billy

Crystal, and even sounded a little like him. Mark and I got on right from the start, but having encountered many ambiguous characters, and been duped many times before, I was being cautious with this one. Anyway, we talked about working together in Canada in the near future. He had worked with Randy, so we had a great starting point to build a rapport.

The promoter had assigned his younger brother to take care of us for the duration of our stay in New York. He would drive us around, escort us to where we needed to be, and give us a tour of the city. Strangely, this man was the spitting image of Royce Gracie's cousin, Rodrigo Gracie. Apparently I was seeing many famous doppelgangers at this event. An extroverted guy, he was always joking around, and eventually decided to take us to a nightclub. Elbiz, Randy, Mark and several others and I packed into two cars. He was actually a FBI undercover agent. He was apparently quite high up in the ranks. He was carrying two guns and was drinking in the car. On our way to the club we pulled up next to a police car and he knew the officers. He was openly drinking and driving but the officers said nothing.

It was surreal, hanging out with the UFC legend in New York. As we approached the entrance to this nightspot, the bouncers immediately recognised Randy. 'The Natural' was in a joking mood, he even went for a half-speed double-leg tackle on the big giant Afro-American bouncer, who must have weighed at least 20 stones. It was hilarious, as this giant tried to sprawl on the wrestling legend. The champion was in a mellow mood, and I knew that Randy wasn't someone who took substances to get high. He had a clean-cut image. Fighters like him didn't need to slip down the substance abuse road to get a kick out of life. Competing in an adrenaline-fuelled combat sport is their high.

The club was an old red-brick building, but inside, it was packed out with night owls. It was heaving with bodies of all colours and creeds, so packed that you had to really squeeze through to get anywhere. Fortunately, Paul's brother had secured a VIP area for us, and to my great surprise there were quite a few Asian Indians already in the joint. Clubbing isn't my scene, as I've already mentioned, but Elbiz was in his element partying, as he has always been a crazy party animal not shy to strut his stuff on the floor. Randy had more of a laid-back approach, as most of us did who were there with him. He enjoyed a sit down and just having a good time watching others revel.

When it was time to leave, at around 2.30am, we made our way outside and some of us got separated. Although this club wasn't huge, it was like a maze – if you weren't familiar with the layout you could very easily get lost. I had no form of communication with the group because my phone was out of commission the day we landed in New York City. Suddenly I found myself, in the early hours of the morning, in, from what I could tell, what was a not-so-good New York City neighbourhood. In a situation like that all sorts of things start going through your head. Being robbed or attacked with a knife or at gunpoint felt like it wasn't far away that night. A trick I often used to employ was to put almost all my money in my sock and maybe keep $20 in the wallet in case I did become a victim, but finally I got a taxi to take me to the hotel.

All in all New York was great. We had fun. I had always been a lover of the West Coast – Los Angeles in particular – but now had a newfound respect for the Big Apple, even if I had previously visited this bustling city several times before. There aren't many better ways to see it than alongside a UFC star.

CHAPTER TWENTY-FOUR

LAS VEGAS

NEW YORK was fun, but Las Vegas wasn't far off. Famed for being the boxing capital of the world, Las Vegas is also the spiritual home of the UFC. The original creator of the UFC, Rorion Gracie, had sold the UFC for $2 million to SEG in 1995. SEG later sold it to Zuffa in 2001 for the same amount. Zuffa built it up to a $1-billion-dollar business. The Ferreita brothers, who owned the UFC at the time, happened to have business interests in Vegas, and, after taking Rorion's revolutionary concept from its small beginnings to a global phenomenon, prided themselves as being one of the biggest sports companies in the world. In late 2016, the Ferreita brothers sold the UFC to WME-IMG for an astounding $4 billion. WME is one of the largest Hollywood talent agencies representing a plethora of A-list stars – a nice bit of synergy, as reportedly more than 19 A-list personalities and Hollywood stars have shares in the UFC.

In an effort to keep the momentum going with Randy's promotional activities, I was heading to see him in his home city – jetting off to Sin City less than two weeks after the New York trip. I had never visited this desert city in Nevada, but I had heard quite a bit about this place famed for its vibrant nightlife, and as a hub for gambling and combat sports.

I was quite surprised that downtown didn't look as big as I had expected. It's nothing like Los Angeles or New York – two truly huge cities. The world-famous MGM Grand Garden Arena Caesars Palace is one of the main attractions. This is where the big boxing fights take place. Being there transported me back to being a kid, watching Marvin Hagler and Sugar Ray Leonard on TV – the classic fight at Caesars Palace. Now, of course, it is the home of the UFC and many big UFC fights events seem to have taken over. I feel UFC couldn't have picked a better place than Vegas.

Although I was more acclimatised to Los Angeles, the city I mainly frequented, I felt at home in Vegas. I was there as Brock Lesnar and the Dutch sensation Alistair Overeem were headlining UFC 141, an event which marked Brock's return to the sport after being out for a year due to an injury. Brock had defeated Randy in Vegas three years earlier at UFC 91 but then lost the title to Cain Velasquez. Many believed that his return against Alistair was premature and market driven. Nevertheless the bout garnered over a million pay-per-view buys. UFC fans wanted to see this giant fight and the former pro-wrestling star filled arenas. Proving many people right, the Dutch giant beat the former WWE superstar with a first-round knockout.

While in Vegas, I had a chance encounter with a familiar face, bumping into Kerry Kayes and his wife who were over on a trip from Manchester. Kerry, the former conditioning coach of Ricky Hatton, Rampage Jackson and Mark Coleman, is a former bodybuilder and a thoroughly nice guy. He recognised me immediately because I had met him several times before. We exchanged pleasantries and had a quick chat.

Next, I accompanied Randy to a gun store. Yes, a gun store. He was meeting fans there, far from an unusual event in a country that's obsessed with firearms. It was quite weird seeing the staff at the store wearing guns and pistols as they served customers. In America, not only were the police armed but many security guards, too. In the United Kingdom, gun crime is very low and even the police don't carry guns. If there's a firearms incident near where I live, the closest armed response unit is 12 miles away, back at police headquarters. American gun culture is crazy. Shopkeepers have big guns under the counter, so if they get robbed they are ready to defend themselves. It's quite a culture shock when you're coming in from another country such as mine.

It was a good event, but the one thing I regret is not having a go at shooting when I was there. Although I had shot rounds overseas on firearms training, I had never fired a gun elsewhere. I needed to focus, though. I had arranged to meet Rasheda Ali, Muhammad Ali's daughter, who also resides in Las Vegas. I had interviewed her once before on the phone, but I had never met her. And so, when Randy left, I stayed behind, sending a text message to her to let her know I was waiting.

Eventually, Rasheda pulled up in her four-wheel drive. When I got a glimpse of her for the first time as she walked towards me and we greeted each other, I was mesmerised. My first impression was, *What a wonderful smile, jovial personality and happy-go-lucky person.* I could barely contain my enthusiasm. There was a classroom in the gun store where we sat down to have a long conversation, and it felt like I had known her for eternity. Rasheda is the fastest friend I have made as far as public figures are concerned. I couldn't believe I was in the presence of Muhammad Ali's daughter. I rarely get star-struck as my work involves meeting many well-known people, but suddenly I was transported back to the feeling of being a young teenager. I was awestruck. Over the years I have interviewed many personalities, but if you were to ask me who has been the most mesmerising person I've met, I would say Rasheda Ali has a serious shot somewhere near the top spot.

As we sat there for more than an hour or so chatting away during and after the interview, Rasheda told me about the gun culture in America. Anyone could have access to a gun, she told me. And gun violence and its effects and consequences were something that she had witnessed first-hand while growing up in the city of Chicago. Her cousin was shot as an innocent bystander during an event in 1997, and other people had suffered their own losses in this mad culture. Finally, the interview was wrapping up and I told Rasheda that I was going to be with Randy at his gym the following day and that she should come. Not only did she show up, but she brought her husband, Robert Walsh, and her two kids, Baggio and Nico. I introduced her to Randy, and we had a great day.

* * *

That wasn't the end of the party in Vegas, either. Randy had invited me to his house for New Year's Eve, and so I asked him if it was OK if I asked Rasheda to come, too. He said it was fine, so I phoned her and invited her and her family to join us in our celebrations.

Randy lived in a gated suburb community on the outskirts of Foothills at Southern Highlands, in a million-dollar home he bought a few days after his victory at UFC 68 on 3 March 2007, when he dispatched Tim Sylvia to take yet another title. This 3,700 sq ft mansion place had four bedrooms, five bathrooms and a swimming pool. After I'd taken it all in, Randy introduced me to his partner, Annie, who was gregarious and had a very extroverted personality. A couple of MMA and UFC fighters were in attendance, including lightweight title contender Tyson Griffin. We made ourselves feel at home and chatted away in the kitchen and living room with Randy and others and helped ourselves to the food.

It wasn't all fun, however. Being paranoid and having a rather strong tendency to be suspicious – the result of a couple of fallouts with prominent American personalities – I tried to elude one individual who was a businessman at the party, having a gut feeling that he knew a former notorious, well-known champion that I had fallen out with years before. I was rather apprehensive and didn't really want to attract undue attention. Perhaps nothing would have gone wrong, but sometimes it's better to be safe than sorry.

Anyway, as the night wore on we did end up conversing together and although I felt somewhat anxious, I kept my cool. Later, our genial hosts, my two companions and I checked out some hardware in the garage with Randy and Annie. It turned out that Randy had an extraordinary collection of guns of all shapes and sizes. Randy had been in the American Armed Forces and had been stationed in Germany among other countries. I wasn't all that familiar with all the technical jargon, but one of my companions was, and said that Randy knew his stuff. Randy, clearly, was living the good life. He had made a name for himself around the world, been the best fighter on the planet, and was making a great living as a professional sportsman. Yet, I never did see any of the fame get to his head.

By the time we'd finished checking out the guns, the house was quite full. Rasheda, her husband Bob and their two kids arrived late. I found her kids to be shy and reserved but well-mannered. One thing that I shared with Rasheda's family was that I didn't drink because of my religion – neither did they, so we stuck to soft drinks. I was curious about American Muslims, so I asked Rasheda about her thoughts on Islam and on bringing up her two boys in a Western country. She told me that she was often judged because she didn't wear a headscarf, but that she still endeavoured to go to the mosque for her Friday prayers. In an effort to console her, I told her there will always be criticism and people judging others, and commended her for her faith. She had grown up in the windy city of Chicago, and her mother, Belinda, was not a convert; she was a born Muslim. So Rasheda, her twin sister Jamillah, and her other siblings Maryum and Muhammad Ali Jnr were all born Muslims.

I had a long conversation with Rasheda and couldn't pass up the opportunity to ask her what her famous dad was like when she was growing up. Ali's swagger in and outside the ring made him a larger-than-life sportsman. I asked if she had any intriguing anecdotes from home life.

'We visited him every summer,' she told me. 'We were driving around in California one year when my dad ran across a family who had lost their home and didn't have a place to stay. My dad brought them home with him, and fed them and gave them money.' Ali was known for this kind of act, for helping random strangers, and often gave money to the poor and homeless, something he continued doing to the end of his life. 'We were all frightened at the time, of course,' said Rasheda, 'Because we were like, *Oh, you don't know these people.* But my dad didn't have a care in the world.'

For her part, Ali's daughter has done her bit for charity by promoting awareness of Parkinsons disease and by doing other charity work on the public-speaking circuit. 'I think my father did what most people should do with their celebrity status: help certain causes,' she told me. 'He has helped fight against obesity, illiteracy, racism. One of his legacies has to be the gift of giving.'

That wasn't all we talked about, however. Rasheda had shocked me when she told me that, when she was younger, she wanted to be a professional wrestler. Her brother, Muhammad Ali Jnr., had also revealed to me his affinity for professional wrestling when I talked to him. It seemed like the Ali family were huge wrestling fans. Ali Senior's fascination for professional wrestling fuelled his career. He famously got the idea of being a big mouth and braggart after seeing Gorgeous George wrestle in Las Vegas, and realising that people would pay to see a loudmouth being shut up. Of course, in time, Ali became known as much for his antics outside the ring as his boxing brilliance. Ali Jnr. actually told me that his hero was Hulk Hogan. Hogan was somebody that I also watched and somewhat admired when I was a kid, but I grew out of it and no longer had an interest in WWE and its antics as an adult.

Years later over lunch in Las Vegas, I asked Rasheda about the hard time Muslims were having in America. Of course, it's never been popular to be a Muslim in the land of the free. 'My Dad always told us whether it's about terrorist attacks or something else, the world will always have misconceptions about Muslims,' she told me. 'But he also told me that true Muslims aren't terrorists. Our religion is a religion of peace – that's what it means, peace.' Ali, for his part, never stopped propagating this fact. Intelligent people have the capacity to understand this about Islam, but there's a small percentage of people, just as with any other religion, who take whatever scriptures they read and distort them. Unfortunately, in the religion of Islam there are clearly some bad apples and sometimes it feels that the whole world is showcasing the religion as a bad one. So, Rasheda told me, it's our job to do the best we can to be great representations of true Islam, and inform people that if you are intelligent and read about it, you will come to the realisation that it's a religion of peace.

'Most people really don't want to believe that, or may not have done their research,' she told me. 'They rely on the internet and they'll believe the worst from the media. So I think those people need to take time and learn about not just Islam but other religions they may not be familiar with.' She proudly told me that her dad loved everyone regardless of their race, creed or religion and taught his kids to love everyone regardless of their affiliation or group. Ali wasn't perfect, but I think for the most part he was sincere and he did showcase the great values the Muslim religion teaches.

Undeniably, we are living in critical times right now. Rasheda's mom and brother were stopped by air travel security officers as they were returning home to Deerfield Beach, Florida from attending a Black History Month event in Jamaica in 2017. 'The officers interrogated my mom and brother separately for nearly two hours, asking illegal questions like, "Where did you get your name? Are you Muslim?"' Rasheda told me. Their passports were in order and verified, and no questions relating to documentation were asked, according to Rasheda. 'I feel that our new appointed US leader has taken us back nearly 100 years.'

Rasheda believes that if her dad was here today, as difficult as it was for him to speak in his final years, he would go on national TV to let people know that what's happening to us is horrible, and that the Muslim religion is one of peace. In his time, the three-time heavyweight champion was quick to inform the public of the misconceptions about his religion, and constantly spoke against bigotry and racism in America. We should all remember that today.

CHAPTER TWENTY-FIVE

CANADA: MMA MAD

I HAD set up another trip overseas to accompany Randy Couture, this time to Canada, but first we had another American city to jet off to. The annual wrestling event and expo was taking place in St Louis, Missouri, so we negotiated with the organisers to bring Randy over as a special guest. In March 2012, I flew over to St Louis, and after a brief stop we flew to Toronto. At border control I was hit by a barrage of questions, but honestly, compared with what I was used to in the USA, it almost seemed like a reprieve.

The Canadian MMA scene is huge. Canada's population is only a tenth of what American's is (and half of the United Kingdom's), and yet at one point, Canada boasted two of the largest attendances in UFC history. Randy had fought in Toronto at the Rogers Centre at UFC 129 on 30 April 2011, breaking the attendance and gate records as over 55,000 fans witnessed him being knocked out by Lyoto Machida via a *Karate Kid*-style jumping front kick to the face. The gate was $11 million, while the pay-per-view buy rate cleared the 800,000 mark. Supposedly, Steven Seagal had worked with Lyoto, after the action movie star and aikido specialist had associated himself with Anderson Silva. How much he actually contributed to their victories is questionable, but if these Octagon warriors are happy to be associated with him, I guess that's fine by me.

Back in New York I had asked Mike Garrow of Fight Network TV why MMA was so big in Canada, and bigger than in the USA. It was beyond my comprehension – was I missing something? He told me it was simple: Canadians love ice hockey; in ice hockey fights always break out, and Canadians just love to see fights and brawls. Well, I wasn't sure about that, but I guess it was a reasonable explanation, and it would certainly be foolish for any serious MMA business or UFC athlete to ignore the Canadian market. It had the buying power to be considered one of the powerhouses of the sport and exploiting it was crucial. And so with this in mind I made sure Randy was contracted to doing appearances in Canada as part of his promotional obligations with the company I owned.

One can't talk about the sport or the UFC in Canada without mentioning the name GSP. He was the biggest name to come out of Canada, a gentleman and a scholar who also happens to be one of the most dominant champions ever to grace the Octagon. After great success in smaller MMA events, GSP made his UFC debut in January 2004 at UFC 46 at the Mandalay Bay Event Center in Las Vegas, then went on to have a string of victories over some of the best fighters in his division, including dominant wins over then-champion Matt Hughes and the highly regarded BJ Penn. After brutally avenging his only losses and remaining undefeated as champ, then returning to take the middleweight belt from Mike Bisping years later, the former UFC welterweight champion is considered by some to be the greatest of all time. He made it look pretty easy as he destroyed every opponent put in front of him, but his route to the top was anything but simple.

'There was a time in my life when I was studying in school and working three jobs at the same time,' GSP told me in an interview. 'I was bouncing in a nightclub, working in a floor roofing place and in a government programme for teenagers at school.' At the Montreal nightclub, he was working with guys who were imposing and strong, most of them happy to put their fists up at the first sign of trouble, but the softly spoken fighter never resorted to violence if he could help it.

CANADA: MMA MAD

He told me, 'I always thought the best way to take care of the problem was talking, so that's what I did most of the time to sort out problems.'

Like many at the time, GSP's knowledge of the sport of MMA was limited. In Canada, hardly anyone knew what Brazilian jiu-jitsu was because it had just emerged. Seeing the early UFCs, GSP pursued the art doggedly. He had always been very good on his feet because of his Kyokushin karate training, and after adding Brazilain jiu-jitsu at 16 he progressed quickly. His knowledge of ground fighting was limited of course, but he was very strong so he would often power out of submission attempts from his opponents on the mat. It's also interesting to note that at the time the sport was illegal in Canada. He was competing in secret no-holds-barred competitions, which permitted open-hand strikes on the ground. GSP had four amateur fights, prevailing in every single bout. This teenager was fighting adults before he made a transition to fighting on a professional level.

GSP revealed to me that he's not one of those competitors who fights because he has no choice. He fights because he loves to fight. If he wanted to pursue a professional career doing a nine-to-five job, he told me, he could have gone in another direction because he has a diploma to fall back on. 'The morning I wake up and I'm not happy with my job, then I'm going to do something else,' he said. 'If I didn't fight in MMA I could have been a professional trainer.' That, of course, would have been a huge loss to the sport of MMA.

* * *

Back on our schedule, Randy had a three-city tour to do, including stops at the Xtreme Couture gym in Toronto, and another gym owned by a former UFC fighter Jeff Joslin, in Hamilton. Our third port of call was to be in Quebec, another part of Canada, where the trainer hosting Randy had already hosted GSP, among other prominent names. Randy and I were welcomed by the owners of Xtreme Couture, a franchise Randy had started, who seemed like nice people who simply loved MMA. The Xtreme Couture gym was massive, and dozens of fans came to the meet-and-greet. Something that caught my eye was an Asian – when I say Asian I mean Indian – girl fan. I was like, *Am I seeing this for real? What would an Asian girl in Canada be doing in a MMA gym?* One thing I've learned about MMA is that it attracts a huge variety of people.

After the Xtreme Couture appearance we made our way to Hamilton, where there were 130 people all eager to meet Randy in a restaurant. We had a lot of fun and everyone seemed to be enjoying themselves, in a great night of entertainment with food and music. After an extensive Q&A with Randy, he posed for pictures and signed autographs. The whole event lasted two long hours. Again, Randy was a trooper. He was on his feet meeting fans for two hours without taking a break, and, moreover, he would pause and smile for a picture with every single fan. He was very conscious about representing his image in the best way possible, and the fans meant everything to him.

The atmosphere was relaxed and I was elated with our reception despite the fact that exhaustion had set in. For fighters and athletes, travelling the world and experiencing different cultures is one of the best parts of the sport, and it was a privilege to be in the same position as a sportswriter and member of the media.

After the event, a black limousine was waiting for us, and Jeff, Randy, I and several others jumped in with more drinks and pizzas for the ride. It was great to be treated well. Not that we had demanded special privileges, but Jeff was amicable and made us comfortable. I had been a fan of America all my life, but now I was converting into a Canada-lover.

I was going to head back home, while Randy was flying out to Quebec for the final leg of his promotional tour. The feedback from the host and Randy himself was that it went well and Randy enjoyed it. I had made it clear to the promoter that the remaining money had to be wired over to me before Randy could make the appearance, telling him that if he didn't comply, Randy wouldn't show. Knowing the risks associated with requesting payments after an event, I had made it clear to Randy that he should make sure the promoter deposited the money into my account, but the promoter promised that he'd pay me afterwards, leaving the situation precarious. Nevertheless, I decided to trust the guy. Boy, was I naive.

* * *

When I got back home, disaster struck. By now I was used having problems squeezing money out of most of these promoters, but we had fulfilled our obligations, made appearances and they had used Randy's name to get people in. Yet, when it came to fulfilling their part of the bargain, false promises were made, resulting in non-payments.

I was, to a great degree, to blame. I had to stop breaking my own rules; I had to keep the mindset of an astute businessman. I understand that putting on events is not easy, but good promoters will succeed if they do their job well. Most agents and managers demand to be paid in advance in most cases, on the understanding that if promoter wish to host a big name, they should have the capacity to make it a success. Marketing, advertising and power to get the crowds in is the promoter's responsibility. If you can't do the job, you don't take on the task. Famous athletes and their agents don't care whether you get 100 people or 1,000. Essentially, the fee is fixed in most cases. I've had promoters approach me asking if they could have Randy at their place and give any revenue they generate to the fighter. That's not how it works, I told these guys. Why would a star name risk that? The promoter gets a famous name at their event so it's a win-win situation for them and their kudos, but what if nobody shows? Sports and entertainment personalities are commodity, and a value is placed on them, which they need to keep. If it was that easy then everybody would be doing it – no risk attached.

I was furious and stunned when two of the promoters decided to hold back the remaining money they owed. Jeff had paid me but the other two were the problem. They were cheating me and the UFC champion. When I told them in no uncertain terms that my legal team as well as Randy's would need to be involved, as the promoters were also withholding from him, one promoter vowed payments would be made in several instalments. In the event, both of the promoters that were in breach sent some money, but not the pledged amount, so the disputes remain unsettled in my view. The mishap taught me a salient lesson: always make sure the payment hits your account, every single cent, well before an appearance. And never listen to a promise made by the other party.

Sensing no payment was readily forthcoming, I wrote to Randy's PA. 'Just want to check what your relationship is with this gym in Canada. I want to let you know that their behaviour has been unacceptable. They promised me numerous times that they'd make the final payment, but the organisation then completely ignored my requests and emails. It's somewhat embarrassing that they would do this. The reason for this email is to merely inform you, not for you to deal with the matter, which is a matter I'm dealing with.' Randy had done events at this gym before, I knew, but I continued, 'Have you had money problems with them in the past? I had a feeling you may have. Because they have not paid, this is something you should take into account in the future if you decide to do anything with them, otherwise it's sending the wrong message. And they may feel it's no big deal. Remember, it's not just about stealing from me but stealing from Randy.' I was absolutely stunned by the whole fiasco. It never crossed my mind that a reputable well-known gym which had ties with my client would even dream of ripping us off. Of course, what you see is not always what you get. It only takes a second for a person to show their true colours.

Not digressing, but I could not believe that Tyrone Woodley, who at the time was actually represented by Randy's management and went on to win the UFC welterweight title years later, had the nerve to short-change me also – not paying all of what was owed in relation to an event Randy took part in. I let it slide after requesting a full and prompt payment, which I quickly realised was never going to make

CANADA: MMA MAD

its way into my account. I didn't even bring it to the management's attention. It was embarrassing and it would have been discomfiting for them. Again, never did I think I would be ripped off. Furthermore, a couple of promoters in Britain had, months before the Canadian experience, also ripped us off.

The sad fact is, these problems are standard. I have heard countless stories about athletes or entertainment celebrities having problems with squeezing money out of a studio or a promoter. When you're the unfortunate victim, you may think you're the only one, but when it comes to money, believe me, you quickly see how people's colours change and how they deviate. They're so engrossed in the paper we call 'money' that they will intentionally do whatever they can get away with. After all, it's only money. It comes and goes. And so when it came to money, I sometimes just let it slide. When most businessmen would do everything in their power to get their hands on those pieces of paper, I'm often prepared to just let it go. Now, on one or two occasions, I've been on the other side of the table, but I've never intentionally short-changed anyone.

All in all the Canadian experience was great, other than the fact that two promoters ripped us off. Maybe fortunately for me, I was oblivious to what lay ahead. Another fiasco was on the cards. It was none other than the former BAMMA employee who would be responsible for this next bizarre episode.

CHAPTER TWENTY-SIX

THE MASSIVE MMA FIASCO

WHILE I was in Canada, a massive MMA Expo, the Mixed Martial Arts Show Live, was being organised in the United Kingdom by the same former BAMMA staff member, Liam Fisher, that I had already encountered. He had partnered with Paul Clifton, a man who promoted a martial arts expo annually, and who eventually ended up in prison for fraud.

I wasn't keen. The chaos and commotion I had experienced six months earlier, relating to Randy Couture's appearance at BAMMA, left a rather sour taste in my mouth. Then again, the show promised to be an unforgettable experience dedicated to the sport of MMA. The show's advertising boasted that they were bringing 40 fighters and MMA personalities from around the globe to the United Kingdom, including a mix of fan favourites, legends of the sport, champions and stars, as well as athletes who were making a name for themselves. All were set to congregate under one roof in May 2012. This was the big one! Well, that's what the promoters were claiming.

The organisers had approached Randy via his management, offering him a package deal that was enticing and hard to refuse. I had spoken to and advised Randy's PA, Valerie, emphasising that Randy should make an appearance at the Seni show instead, a combat sports show which was taking place a month later, in Birmingham. I knew and had worked with the promoters of Seni before, but now the UFC legend was being offered a lucrative deal and his people – his legal and management team – were drawn to it like a moth to a light bulb. Consequently, my advice was dismissed. So what do you do when plan A goes down the drain? You activate plan B, of course. I always have a backup plan; it can steer you out of a mess. It occurred to me that maybe we could tie something in with the MMA Expo, even though I wasn't personally keen on working with the promoters.

So, I liaised with Valerie and also the Mixed Martial Arts Live Show's Liam Fisher. The idea was to tie in a slot at the show for Randy to promote himself and his product, an idea I floated with the promoter. I was acting in good faith, so I was stunned when Liam took things out of context and apparently tried to drive a wedge between me and Randy's management. Basically, he went behind my back, giving Randy's management the impression that I was interfering with matters. This was bullshit. I was on the edge now and very distressed. But in situations such as this, it's imperative to have self control. So I composed myself.

I never really dealt with Randy's lawyer and manager; I dealt with Randy directly and with his PA and his literary agent, and had only dealt with his lawyer six months before when all the commotion and chaos linked with BAMMA was going on. Randy's lawyer succinctly told me that they were being offered a large sum of money and that they didn't want the deal to be jeopardised. Essentially, he was saying that I could potentially put a dent in a good deal. Sensing the whole thing could spiral out of control, I left it to both parties to negotiate, but I voiced my concerns to Valerie, advising her to request an upfront payment if Randy was going to make an appearance.

Shockingly, at least to some people, five days before the show, the expo was abruptly postponed. The official website of the show changed to include a press release saying that the show had been postponed till 20–21 October due to circumstances beyond the organisers' control. Now, a whole host of MMA athletes had been scheduled and advertised to appear at this so-called massive expo, and what's most bizarre is that many fighters' reps said they had found out about the cancellation online. Following this, they attempted to make contact with the organisers, but, again, the response they received concerning the unexpected U-turn was unacceptable. When some of the managers and lawyers demanded answers and a logical explanation from Paul, the promoter came out with feeble excuses and basically apologised for his ineptness.

'We would like to apologise to any fans we've disappointed for postponing the show and we would like to thank everyone for their support and understanding, as we are deeply disappointed at having to make this decision,' the press release read. Understanding? No one could understand these culprits who, it turned out, had been misleading a lot of people.

As speculation about what was happening was mounting, certain individuals who had been duped felt the promoters were holding back information, because they simply had no valid explanation. Valerie told me that she was trying to work things out with the promoter, who had asked Randy's legal team to bear with the organisers while they came up with an amicable resolution. Not convinced, I made it clear to Valerie that she should make sure the promoter flew Randy over, regardless, as I had Randy's itinerary planned out to promote the second leg of his European tour. I also said that if the promoters had already paid Randy the negotiated fee in advance, he should hold on to it tightly and have them fulfil their obligations. Inevitably many of the lawyers who managed and represented some of the top MMA fighters set to appear were now seeking damages for breach of contract as things started to further spiral out of control. One manager, who had negotiated for a bevy of fighters to appear, said that the promoters had deceived him – and everyone else for that matter. The show's promoters had not only left the athletes and thousands of eager fans out of pocket, but had put everyone's schedules in chaos. Some fighters, no doubt, had refused other work due to their calendar being full.

THE MASSIVE MMA FIASCO

Randy was to be paid his appearance fee a week before the show, but it didn't materialise, so there was nothing he could do other than wait to see how things unfolded. Clearly, there was no money to pay the fighters. My guess was that the promoters had gambled that, with all the top MMA stars, the show would attract major sponsorships and ticket sales, which would generate a huge amount of revenue, and were oblivious to the prospect of their plans failing. They were risking everything by guaranteeing large sums of money to fighters, not knowing, or perhaps not caring, that it wasn't guaranteed to work. It soon came to light that they were banking on securing a sponsorship from the film production company Lionsgate, the company behind *The Expendables II*, through Randy's lawyer, as Randy was one of the stars of the movie. The problem is, assuming can often put you in a lot of trouble. And, boy, they were in trouble and only providence could save them now.

Figures kept deflating. Things felt futile. To further illustrate the scale of the deceit, one of the promoters had apparently called Randy's lawyer, boasting that the show had already sold around 24,000 tickets, and that they were expecting that number to increase by 25 per cent by the time the week ended. These are huge numbers for an expo. If I hit those numbers, I'd be filthy rich. Liam also bragged to one MMA manager that the major sponsors they had been pursuing were now on board, which was another blatant lie. 'They were front-loading this event and they were looking to bring in a sponsor,' one disgruntled manager reportedly said. 'My belief is that they didn't have the funds.'

I think it was clever of the promoters to declare that the show was postponed because of unforeseen circumstances, even though they knew very well there wasn't going to be a show at all. It was just a feeble excuse to save their asses. The fact is, it was doomed from the word go – or so I believe. Not surprisingly, Liam once again blamed his co-promoter, in this case Paul Clifton. He always blamed someone else for his mishaps. The latter, according to him, had sent out a press release without Liam's approval. Finger-pointing, which Liam could have held a PhD in, was a bad habit of his. 'I was assured Paul and his team were going to speak to every fighter, manager, member of staff and exhibitor involved before the press release went out,' this guy wrote in his statement. When I read that, the anger started to boil up inside me. This was the same guy who had played the finger-pointing game with me more than once. I was furious, but endeavoured to retain some shred of sanity.

Looking for a way out, Liam next claimed he had no final say in the postponement of the event, and that his own company worked in partnership with Paul's company. The excuse was that a major contractor had pulled out, which made it impossible for the show to proceed, according to the promoters. What left people incensed, though, was the fact that no specific details were given. The collective thinking was that the promoters simply didn't have the ability to run an event of this magnitude. With the amount of money the organisers were promising the big stars, as I said, it wasn't going to be easy to generate the required sum. It was beyond their capacity. To my dismay, Liam had put us into another fine mess. I had warned Randy's team, but they hadn't listened to me, perhaps because they were seeing dollar signs. I felt the event organiser had taken the piss, misleading people with nonsense and trying to create friction in existing relationships. In the end, though, we all saw who was right and who was wrong.

It was time to implement plan B. I was still hoping to get Randy over to the Seni show. Unfortunately, after several discussions, it didn't pan out because of a conflict of schedule. Randy always had a hectic timetable, as he was filming and making appearances all over the place. So we never did nail another date or recover from that fine mess. From then on, it was a downward spiral for me, ruining any hopes of returning to normality.

CHAPTER TWENTY-SEVEN

I'M NO TERRORIST

AFTER THE MMA expo fiasco, my life took a turn which included me becoming involved with a few charitable causes. These days, I see charity events taking place, everywhere I turn, but until relatively recently I never had a soft spot for charity or got involved to any degree. I was always of the notion that it was hard enough for most people to survive these days, and so throwing money at charities was beyond my comprehension. Besides, some of the people who work for, or run, some charities get rich off others' money as it's not uncommon to exploit the situation. It wasn't until I attended a musical event in December 2010, coinciding with the release of a musician's debut single, that I got a real taste of charity work. The experience I had changed my perception about charity, and a seed was planted in my head that has stayed with me ever since.

The event was raising funds for Palestine and Syria, and I was able to help as a professional writer. It gave me a platform to promote the icons of sports that impacted pop culture at most of these events. Since then, I've come across many events raising funds, particularly for the Middle East, but also for Africa or other good causes, and I'll often take part. I am by no means a political activist, but if I can help raise money and awareness for humanity, then great.

I've never really been inclined to have political views, and I was never an ardent or casual follower of any political cause. The Palestine and the Middle East situations have been going on for longer than we all care to remember, and I doubt they'll be resolved in my lifetime. And yet, over the years, I was, along with so many others, exposed to the outpouring of sorrow via the medium of not just the media but people directly affected by these issues. There was a period when my naiveté lead me to believe that the Palestinians were unfairly attacking innocent people. Since then, I've learned that the truth is a little more complicated.

What first got me pondering was an incident when I was in Los Angeles many years prior to the musical event. I was being picked up by a representative of a notorious, but retired, fighter who I was negotiating with. This woman, who was obviously aware of my background as a Muslim, wasted no time in expressing venomous anger directed at me in the car as her husband drove. 'How can these Palestinians launch bombs in Israel and blow people up!?' she asked, angrily. The rage pouring out of her mouth like volcanic lava gripped me by surprise. Bemused, I thought, *Why is she ranting at me? What's that got to do with me?* It wasn't till later that I realised she was an American with links to Israel via her heritage. Apparently she had already put me on her hit list because of the fact I was a Muslim. This woman was painting everyone with the same brush, but she needed to change her brush or her target. I was no threat, nor was I responsible for these atrocities. At the time I was still of the opinion that what was happening in Palestine was wrong, but I barely knew anything about the issue.

Like I said, even though I'm not one for having strong political views, I will say this now: injustice is being done in certain parts of the world, and when the media shows only one side of the story, it doesn't help. As a matter of fact, it's a dangerous thing to do. It seems that when one party does something horrific there's an outrage, but when part of the mighty West kills millions of people who are more or less innocent, this doesn't register on many people's radars. Double standards are rife. It took me a long time to comprehend this, but now it's fully sunk in.

Anyway, this woman kept on raving and ranting while I sat there composedly listening to her bullshit. I eventually realised that I had made one of the biggest mistakes of my life in getting involved with her. She was the typical 'can never get on with' type, vying for control and totally money-mad it seemed – no surprise considering her background. So, this little episode planted a small seed, which eventually grew in my brain.

What astounded me more, though, was when one day I had a visit from the United Kingdom's Special Branch. I was out for the day, and when I came home I was told two plain clothes police officers had paid a visit and left a message, saying they would be back. I was left with my imagination flying all over the place. *What could this be all about?* I thought. Later that day there was a knock on the door and two typical-looking plain clothes officers were standing right there in front of me as I opened it. They asked me if I was Fiaz Rafiq. I confirmed my identity. They politely asked if they could step in to have a chat with me. Trying ever so hard to keep my demeanour intact, I let them in. Well, what choice did I have?

Bear in mind at the time that the situation in the Middle East was precarious to say the least. A certain Middle Eastern embassy in London and the British Government had received ongoing bomb threats from terrorists, and things were hitting fever pitch. These days, the word 'terrorists' has apparently become synonymous with us Muslims, but back then I was curious about what this was all about and a sense of agitation set in. I hadn't robbed anyone, so what were these men doing in my house? Dismayed at the prospect of being locked up for something I hadn't done, I sat on the edge of my seat waiting for the worst to unfold. 'It's nothing to worry about,' one of the officers assured me. 'It's just about a phone call.' I thought to myself, *What the hell is going on?* 'You made a phone call five months ago enquiring about firearms training,' he continued. 'The individual you contacted is an ex-police officer and he was suspicious and reported you.'

I let out a loud laugh, slouching back on the couch. Oh, God, was I relieved. I wanted to jump up and down. The fear that had gripped me left my body faster than it had arrived. I told the officers that I was a professional working in the media, a sports journalist who wrote for the number-one martial arts publication in the United Kingdom, and that I had a bodyguard qualification, also known as Close Protection and Executive Protection. I showed the officers my Close Protection credentials and copies of my work in various magazines. I proceeded to explain that I had been, at the time, scouting for bodyguard courses, which had firearms training as part of the syllabus – planning to add an additional qualification to my resume. I already possessed a Close Protection licence.

I was no terrorist. And I wasn't going to be called one, hell, no! What I found amusing was the fact that, years earlier, I had been one of the Close Protection operative assigned to the Middle Eastern embassy in London, working for a country that was an ally of the West. I had been one of two Close Protection operatives at the embassy when it was on a code red alert and receiving bomb threats from terrorists, and now I was being accused of being a potential terrorist. To be perfectly honest, even though I had been fairly composed while carrying out my duties, which included surveillance, naturally there was a twinge of fear running through me. It had been Christmas time – the perfect time to target – and the chances of getting blown up were pretty high. You ask yourself, *Is it worth risking your life?* I don't think so. But that was my first Close Protection assignment, so there was no way I was going to bypass the offer. Getting your foot in the game is hard enough and to decline an operation could be career suicide – no pun intended. So I had no hesitation in accepting the assignment, even if it meant putting my life on the line. Given the fact I had taken risks throughout my life, one more risk wasn't going to make much difference. Besides, sometimes in life you have to pursue adrenaline-pumping situations for the sake of the thrill.

Anyway, the two officers apologised and left, convinced of my innocence. I can't remember if I offered them tea, but I don't think they deserved a glass of water, never mind a nice cuppa after what they had come to accuse me of. However, I wasn't quite rid of Mr Columbo and his sidekick. Several months later I got a visit from the same officers. This time they wanted me to come aboard. They were looking to make a new 'friend', and asked if I would work for law enforcement as an 'interpreter'. Interpreter, my arse! Apparently what they were really saying was, would I be willing to spy on people for them? I wasn't game, nor was I ready to play James Bond. If I wanted to, I could play 007 by protecting foreign royal families, celebrities or businessmen instead.

I politely declined, saying I doubt I could accept the 'interpreter' role because I was inundated with my media work. Still, one of the cops left his card and said if I changed my mind then I should call him. I never did. I was quite flattered, though. Months earlier I had been suspected of criminal activity, but now the same law enforcement organisation wanted me to be a part of the 'team'. Nah, no thanks! You do your own dirty work.

* * *

Government authorities like that never got off my back. They were stuck to me like a magnet – especially the Americans. Whenever I visited America, without exception, I would get stopped and harassed for up to three hours, which made my life hell. Los Angeles, New York, Las Vegas, wherever and whenever I landed I would be victimised like a potential terrorist. The bastards hadn't done their homework – or maybe they had. Perhaps it wasn't surprising considering the low IQ level I encountered as early as my first ever visit to America.

Apparently, I was on the American Homeland Security's 'list'. Homeland Security, in case you aren't aware, is a department of the

USA federal government with responsibility for public security. Every time my passport was scanned or my name fed into their system, alarm bells rang, which meant I needed extra security checks. I had proved my identity time after time, which confirmed that I was a professional working in the media. Not only was I working for a national sports magazine, but I was working with high-profile martial arts and UFC personalities from the USA and had a track record of doing it. Moreover, I got into the habit of carrying two of my old expired passports with me, along with the current valid one, just to prove my ID. But, no, these idiots just had to waste my time and treat me like shit. On a couple of occasions, it did cross my mind to make the staff at the airport aware that I would be more than happy to write about my mistreatment – after all, I was a journalist.

The first time I got pulled up in America was when I was on my second trip to Los Angeles in 1998. They spent hours detaining me. These idiots finally told me I had overstayed a week on my first visit two years previously and that I now automatically required a visa. I was beckoned towards an area where they grilled you with extra questions, and one immigration officer kept looking at me and the picture in my passport. He kept on asking if it was me in the picture, which annoyed me more and more. I wanted to scream at him. This prick was hoping I would trip up, but how could I trip up when I had nothing to conceal? I later learned that this officer had been on a TV show about immigration departments at American airports. While all this drama was going on, a couple of officers joked to me that he was the guy who dealt with the case of a Chinese woman who married an old white guy. No wonder he looked familiar.

Anyway, my interrogation continued. I got talking to one of the officers, who looked like Tom Selleck, about martial arts, and he seemed friendly enough. Next, I got frisked and had my finger prints taken, and was eventually handcuffed.

Never had I experienced this type of humiliation before. I felt like a piece of shit. I went through the standard interview procedure, where they try to extract as much information as possible and employ trick tactics in the process. No tactic was going to trip me up because I was genuine, even though my demeanour probably made me look guilty as hell. Nervousness was all over my face. I hadn't mastered the art of confidence in these situations yet. Now I know that officers are happy to make you sit there while they probe your background, obtaining information from whatever source or means they can. Then they question you again, the same questions over and over, hoping you'll crumble or misremember an answer you've given. In my case, the boredom and the fact I'd been on a flight for 12 hours made this exhausting. The experience was deplorable.

I didn't get the worst of it, though. Several feet away, was a tall, skinny, dark-skinned guy with a tanned blonde woman who was his partner. They were returning from Australia and were having problems with the authorities, just as I was. Unfortunately, the guy got a little hostile as things got worse, and several security immigration officers, who actually carried guns, had a standoff with him. The officer in charge had a remarkable resemblance to Dan Lee, one of Bruce Lee's original students. I seem to always come across look-alikes whenever I'm in America. This officer had his hand on his gun ready to draw, like you see in Westerns before a shootout. This guy was ready for action. After some raving, ranting, shouting and commotion, things calmed down. Thank God no one was shot. It suddenly dawned on me that this was America where even security personnel carried firearms. It was quite terrifying, especially for someone from Britain where the police officers don't carry guns.

After similar treatment was repeated on more visits to the so-called land of opportunity, the country I had admired all my life but was starting to have reservations about, I decided to pay a visit to my local member of parliament. He was associated with a family friend who was a local councillor. He wrote an endorsement letter on his letter-headed paper, and so on my next trip, when I landed at the airport in America, I figured I could shove this official endorsement from the British Government up the immigration officer's ass, after he read it of course. *That has to be good enough for them*, I thought. I'm afraid I was wrong. By now I had developed the sort of guilty look cops will always pounce on.

As I approached the counter on my next trip to America, I handed over my passport and shoved the golden letter on the desk right under the immigration officer's nose. 'Every time I come here they stop me for hours!' I sarcastically remarked with added venom in my tone. 'Here's a letter from my MP.' This was a letter from the British Government. Surely, I'd be taken seriously now. After the guy checked me out on his screen, he beckoned me to move to the side as he handed me the card we fill out on the plane for immigration. So, now I was back to the routine of waiting in the 'special' room, a routine I was more than familiar with. After hours of waiting, my name was called and I walked up to the desk. Again, more questions were fired at me. In the end, the ordeal would waste at least three hours of my time. I learned that day that immigration is a government department and that no matter who you are, they will treat you like shit if they want to.

The only time I didn't get stopped was on my first trip to Las Vegas. When I got to the immigration desk in Sin City, the officer was surprisingly OK. I told him who I was and what I was doing there – working with UFC star Randy Couture. This was UFC city and UFC and fighters were now in the consciousness of the general public. I told him that I got stopped every time at the American airports, and he stamped my card and consoled me telling me it wasn't going to happen this time. I had just broken my record. I couldn't believe it.

* * *

I'd had enough of this terrorist-list bullshit but things came to a head when my American visa expired in 2012 and I went to the American Embassy in London to renew it. The visa was for ten years, and the procedure was always the same: you paid a hefty application fee, drove for four hours to London, waited all day and felt like crap, as if you had done a 12-hour shift of hard labour. When it was my turn I went into the designated room and at the other end of the counter an American staff member who looked like Mark Wahlberg appeared. I told this Wahlberg lookalike that I was going on a business trip to a UFC event in Las Vegas with Randy Couture. 'In 2006, you threatened the US Embassy,' this guy fired back at me, taking me by complete surprise. He said he had the emails there with him.

Unfortunately, I did write to the embassy expressing my disdain but I did not threaten the embassy. When I had applied for a media category visa in 2006, I made it clear that I had interviews lined up in mid-September for a Bruce Lee documentary I was working on, so I would want a decision well before then. And so when I received the visa about five weeks late, it really pissed me off. I basically said in my follow-up email that a lot of Americans lacked a great deal in the way of IQ and always had the impression that they were the best at everything, I also said that their armed forces were not even the number one in the world – something I think Americans are a little sensitive about. Well, apparently they decided that I really hated America and its armed forces and that I was a potential threat to the security of this proud nation, or maybe even a potential bomber.

'You do not threaten a US government institution,' my interviewer boomed at me. Suddenly it dawned on me that this was the reason I was on their list and getting detained every time at the airports. Now, I was pissed off with this American guy, but I tried ever so hard to keep myself composed. This guy was a twat, but you could tell he was a proud American. Anyway, after more waiting he called me up to the counter again, told me that I would be hearing from the US Embassy and would be able to send the passport to get it stamped. Needless to say, I left the embassy dismayed.

Six months later, nothing. I chased it up via email only to be told they had asked for my passport five weeks after the application, and since I didn't send it in, I had to now reapply and go through the whole process again. Needless to say, I wasn't pleased at all but made a conscious oath not to express my anger at the American Embassy if I ever wanted to step into the country again. In the end, I had to send my friends Seyfi and Tash to Las Vegas to represent me with Randy. Of course, Seyfi loved it as he was getting an all-expenses-paid trip.

In the end, all this hassle about being on the list was, because I had a mark on my name for overstaying, and because, according to the Americans, I had threatened their embassy in London and was on the 'potential danger list'. The funny thing is, as I said, I had protected their allies's embassy in London when they were getting bomb threats many years earlier, when I was forging a Close Protection career. How about checking that out? But all I got was crap in return. And, no, I did not threaten any embassy, as I said. All I did was explain some facts about Americans. Talk about freedom of speech. As much as I have been influenced by America all my life, these experiences left a rather bitter taste.

Even without the Americans, I was cursed with airport problems ever since I broke the golden rule of overstaying on my first trip. When I was flying out to St Louis to join Randy Couture at a wrestling event, I encountered armed police at Manchester airport. When I got to the airport I walked over to the counter, but there was no queue. As I approached the attendant I was told I had missed the check-in deadline. I had to be there at least an hour before flight time and I was ten minutes late. I protested that I was only a little late and that the flight had not even left, but the staff would just not budge. Next, I explained the importance of my trip, explaining that it was a business trip and not a vacation, and that I had to be there for the next day otherwise there would be dire consequences. The attendant wouldn't comply, so I had no choice but to go into gear seven and get a little hostile. A security guard walked over, and to my further dismay I was told that I had to change the ticket and fly out the next day.

That was out of order, but what came next was worse. After seeing my 'hostile' behaviour and deciding I was capable of employing desperate measures, armed police made their way over to me. It was a couple of officers with the kind of machine guns that you usually see patrolling when there's a terror alert. One calmly attempted to reason with me while the other stood back glued to his big machine gun like Rambo. I explained that I was a combat sports journalist. I was no terrorist and I felt that all this intervention was unnecessary. I was no real threat to the staff or people around me.

Still extremely upset, I pleaded once more, emphasising the importance of my trip. The desk clerks proceeded to check their system for flights that would get me to my destination, even if it meant they had to send me on a different route. The lady finally found a flight that would leave the same day. But it would take me into another city where I'd wait for seven hours, and maybe I could put my head down before jumping on a flight that would get me into St Louis. My hotel accommodation had all been sorted out, all paid for by the organisers, as was my flight. Now, though, I had to pay extra money because of the change made to the original ticket.

On my return I came to learn that the police had checked me out because, when I returned, Bob Sykes, the editor of the martial arts magazine, had a good laugh with me. 'What have you been up to, Fiaz?' he laughed, needling me as he often did. He told me the police had been in touch with the magazine. Bob loved chaos and commotion and wasn't going to let this hiccup pass without taking the piss. So, the authorities in America and back at home have been on my back forever, but I'll never let it stop me.

* * *

Ever since I can remember I've been interested in pursuing something different as far as a career is concerned. I have always been ambitious, and I wasn't really going to settle for a normal job. Before I ultimately became a professional writer, a profession that had intrigued me was that of a bodyguard. Another profession that invoked my interest and one which I would have liked to pursue was Hollywood stuntman.

TO THE TOP

My friend Peter Consterdine, who was a leading authority in Close Protection in the United Kingdom, and who had some high-profile clients, was the man I turned to back then. Peter, a former national karate team member and advocate of realistic self-defence, advised and encouraged me to do some training courses, to give me the relevant qualifications to pursue a career in this highly competitive industry. Peter had run these courses long before I came on the scene, and was active on the Close Protection circuit. So, as a young man I endeavoured to take this path with the intention of carving out a career, in a field that most people perceive as being glamorous. If you're as old as me or older, you will remember Kevin Costner's 1992 movie *Bodyguard*, which was a glossed-up Hollywood portrayal of a celebrity protection officer. Shortly after it hit cinemas, young men flocked to training courses in the vain hope of becoming the next Kevin Costner. I did the courses many years later, and by then the students were from a diverse background, including a couple with an armed forces background. A lot of these men had no martial arts experience, something that left me stupefied.

Some years later, major changes came into play which meant that everyone working in any type of security, be it security, doorman or bodyguard, had to be licenced again, this time by the SIA (Security Industry Authority) – security and door supervisors in the past had never really had to train or hold a qualification, while bodyguards had had to be trained at the highest level, qualify and be certified. With the new government-stipulated rules, I had to retrain, so I redid my training and received my qualification again. As part of the course we flew to Sweden for basic firearms training. We landed in Denmark, at Copenhagen airport, and took a tram into Sweden. This was the first time I had seen my place of birth because I had left Denmark when I was only a couple of years old so couldn't remember anything about it. Sweden was cold as fuck and the snow blanketed the place. The food was crap, and I missed home, and my comfy bed and home-cooked food, not forgetting my daily routine that I was all too familiar with.

I'M NO TERRORIST

Worst was yet to come though. We were going to be walking through hell and only providence could save us. One of the students, who apparently had mental health problems, had broken up with his partner when he was on the course and was struggling to get over the split. This guy was not in the right frame of mind to be on the shooting range. He needed help. We were put up in a camp which was like the ones you see in old black-and-white films about the war and the wooden huts built for POWs. Each room housed two students, and this nutcase was in mine. Yes, of course, it had to be me. Back in the United Kingdom during our unarmed combat training, I had pissed him off a little because in our self-defence training on the ground I would add extra pinning moves. At the time, this resulted in a bit of a scuffle, but nothing serious. The way I saw it, I was merely injecting a bit of reality into the training. This guy was slim and about my weight, but pretty tough and solid, so I knew he could look after himself. I could feel his energy. A lot of the times these skinny-looking individuals are the most dangerous ones. Never underestimate them, believe me, or you'll be in for a nasty surprise.

Anyway, some of the students were refusing to come on to the shooting range. *What if the guy goes berserk and starts shooting everyone?* was the question in our heads. The three instructors, Matt, Gary and Johan, congregated into a room for an emergency meeting. On the range there was some fear of the unknown. We felt that our lives were being put on the line and some even had second thoughts about staying for the rest of the course. We've all heard of crazy lunatics in America going berserk, shooting random people in schools and shopping malls, and now I wondered if I was going to be experiencing this for real right there in ice-cold Sweden. The snow was taking the piss, so was the food, and to have the thought of being potentially gunned down was just too damn terrifying. I'd rather live on water and bread than leave this world young. The group made it known to the instructors that it was for the best if 'Mr Lunatic' sat out the gun training part of the course. Take into account that this guy had handled firearms before when he'd been in the armed forces. We were using Glock 18 guns, so we knew he'd have plenty of bullets.

After much discussion, the instructors decided that our 'friend' would be allowed to take part on the range. This, of course, made the rest of us furious. We were being put up to be slaughtered. Well, we knew who would be responsible for any potential bloodshed, but dead men can't complain afterwards. I've never been shot but have friends who have, and I wasn't planning on getting live rounds in me just yet. Thank God, things went smoothly. The instructors had marked out their man, and were keeping a very close eye on him. It was a relief to complete the firearms training.

In the Close Protection world it is very hard to carve out a career. What you have to remember is, you're applying for the same jobs that hundreds of other CPOs are, and in the industry, who you know often helps. Most of the work is in the capital. One friend of mine, who did the course with me, immersed himself in Close Protection on a full time basis. He's now worked in over 30 countries. From America and France to Russia and Nigeria, you name it, he's been there. Whenever I'd phone him he'd be somewhere on the other side of the world, and he'd tell me when he was back so we could catch up. It seemed like a great career, travelling the world, wearing nice smart suits, driving nice cars, being at massive mansions, protecting foreign royal family members, dignitaries and high-profile businessmen. It's one of the dream jobs if you can make it work. He trained in kickboxing, but more importantly is a very pleasant guy, and well-spoken.

It is very lucrative, too. At one point, there were contracts popping up paying a lot of money. Paying £500 a day, which would amount to £14,000 a month, to go to Iraq and Afghanistan wasn't unusual. Back then, a lot of people didn't even make that much money in a year, never mind a month. I was tempted, but decided not to pursue it further. You could do three or six months and make your money, but then again you could be blasted to kingdom come on your first day. Taking risks in life is something I'm an advocate of – believe me I've taken my fair share – but there are times when you have to gravitate towards doing the sensible thing, weigh up everything and look at things from the perspective of the long term. So that idea went out of the window. On the bright side, I could eliminate the fear of being shot or bombed. It wasn't a bad deal after all.

Anyhow, I had a prestigious professional qualification under my belt, which is always great to fall back on. I did eventually go on to forge a professional career in this field, protecting one of the top sportsmen and his family, which was fun, and taking care of some other individuals.

Protecting celebrities wasn't something that particularly invoked my interest as I matured. Taking care of multi-millionaire executives and foreign royals and dignitaries is something that was ideally right up my road. Now that I have been working in the media and dealt with so many sport and entertainment figures, I'm not interested in associating myself with a celebrity just because of who they are. Depending on who you protect, you could be in for trouble, too. My friend Ron Balicki was a bodyguard to Steven Seagal, Will Smith and the rap group Public Enemy, and Ron told me that once in a nightclub he had to draw his gun on a guy. Because the rap stars were wild and would often look for trouble in nightspots, taking care of them was a major headache, he warned me. Like I said, there's big money in it, but often you must be able to travel around the globe if you seriously want to pursue it as a career. Long hours, staying away from home, following protocol and having the ability to get the job done are all part and parcel of Close Protection. It was interesting to learn that UFC icon, Ken Shamrock, once went into bodyguarding and 50 Cent was one of his clients. We had more than one thing in common.

CHAPTER TWENTY-EIGHT

FROM RACISM TO ROAD RAGE

IN LIFE you sometimes cross paths with people who become a regular fixture, popping up throughout your life. For me, Ronnie Green is one such person. Nicknamed 'The Machine Gun' because of his rapid machine gun style combinations, the five-time world Thai-boxing champion is a revered member of the martial arts fraternity. Ronnie is widely regarded as the greatest Thai-boxing fighter and champion Britain has produced in the history of this brutal contact sport. Not only is he a tremendous fighter, he is one of the most self-effacing guys you will ever meet. Ronnie's master is the famed Thai-boxing coach Master Toddy. Ronnie was his number-one disciple. Master Toddy later moved to Las Vegas, where he coached numerous famous MMA champions including Gina Carrano, Randy Couture, Tito Ortiz, Forrest Griffin and GSP.

Growing up in the Moss Side area of Manchester Ronnie often experienced racism, which left an indelible mark on his life. I often meet up with him just to hang out, go for a coffee or grab a bite to eat and talk about martial arts. As much as Ronnie became known for his lethal and brutal fists and feet, he is equally famous for his big mouth. When I say this, I don't mean he is a loudmouth – far from it. It's just that when he starts talking you have to literally kill him to stop him, and believe me it's not going to be an easy task.

But Ronnie has a big mouth for the right reasons. With his focus on giving positive role models to the community his vision has always been to work with the young generation to get them off the streets and involved in the martial arts. He was always trying to get me involved in school programmes. Getting involved in inspirational talks for kids in schools and colleges because of my sports journalism background was something he really pushed me towards. Our friend Esmond Francis had a brother who was a victim of knife crime and lost his life, and he now works tirelessly to spread the message, helping the youngsters to see the light and steer clear from gang life. Tottenham, an area of north London with large African and Turkish communities, is a knife crime infested area. The police force is under increased pressure to clamp down on knife crime after a surge in the number of teenagers stabbed to death over recent years. Whenever I stayed with my friend Elbiz, in London, whether it was being on a film set or interviewing someone, I often got off the tube there late at night, and although I never became a victim of a crime, it's always there in the back of your mind. In America gun crime is high, but on this side of the Atlantic the knife rules.

In this spirit, Ronnie and I were both invited to a community event in Tottenham, as special guests of Esmond. At the event, a documentary film, *One Mile Away*, was screened. It highlighted the historic feud between Birmingham's prominent Burger Bar Boys and Johnson Crew. Among the special guests were gang members from London and Birmingham, who were on a mission to tackle the evils of gang culture. The speakers voiced their concerns about gang life. Making a positive change in young peoples' lives was the overarching message.

Ronnie has always espoused the philosophy of bringing people of all colours, creeds and cultures together. In the long, thought-provoking conversations we've had, he's always stuck to this. I feel he is doing his bit for the human race and community through the medium of martial arts. On this occasion the event kicked off with a kickboxing demo from Esmond's students. The Mayor of Tottenham was in attendance and was given a platform to voice her opinions. 'We need education to claw ourselves out of the pit,' she addressed the audience. 'I like the fact that you have people here who are working so hard with young people to bring them up and show them the right way.' As the mayor continued with her edification, some members of the audience, which was 95 per cent black, were in despair. The mayor went on to speak about occasions in the past when the black race had been treated wrongly, and of the white man's injustice towards the black man. Next, the audience voiced their opinions, arguing that racism was still prevalent in today's society. Suddenly I witnessed a change in atmosphere as outbursts continued and the mayor's comments were derided by the attendees. Her head was turning from side to side in disagreement with the unruly crowd

Things were getting tense. For as long as I can remember I had the impression that we, Asians from the subcontinent, were more likely to be victims of racism than the blacks now. Yes, the black community had been subjected to horrendous treatment well before us, but now I thought they were accepted more than us. Black music and entertainers had won the hearts and minds of the Western world, I believed, and white people had changed. But I was wrong. Perhaps things have improved since the civil rights movements, but the disease of racism is far from beaten.

I witnessed something in the crowd's eyes that day that I will never forget. Being exposed to more African-American history really put things into perspective, and was disturbing to me. I was stunned to learn how black Americans were treated in the slave-trade period.

Eventually, everyone settled down. Ronnie was up next as guest speaker and MC, broaching the subject of role models and how we could be inspired by men like Muhammad Ali and Bruce Lee. Both men, he pointed out – one Chinese and the other black – made a difference and stood up for their beliefs and their people who'd experienced prejudice.

FROM RACISM TO ROAD RAGE

I refrained from making a speech that day, as I've never enjoyed public speaking. Once I was in Barcelona, Spain as a special guest speaker at an official Bruce Lee event. Frightened by the prospect of public speaking, a part of me was experiencing fight-or-flight syndrome as I sat onstage. I think it can be traced back to my early childhood, when I would feel a twinge of nerves whenever I had to stand up and talk about myself in the classroom. I was never good at that, and my accent only added to the problem. Now, though, it was my turn to enlighten the audience and share my knowledge. After all, I was an authority and encyclopaedia on the late martial arts master. I had an interpreter, which actually made me a lot more comfortable because I find it a lot easier talking to one person than talking to 100 people at once. I mean, who are you supposed to look at? As all eyes were glued to me, I managed to get through my speech, eradicating any nerves that would cause embarrassment. I even received rapturous applause at the end. On the second day I was set to deliver another speech but I was feeling a little uncomfortable, again. But this time the host was my interpreter. Again, this put me at ease. I was feeling very calm and confidence made its way into my soul as nervous energy made its way out. So I did well. Furthermore, what I can say is that whenever I did book signings with crowds waiting in line, I never felt any sort of shyness whatsoever. I was always very comfortable, in control and enjoyed talking to people.

* * *

Ronnie made his mark in the fight world himself proving in the ring against the best. Outside the ring he is a gentleman with impeccable manners and he kept his cool at the event. But once when I was in his company, he almost got into an altercation in the street with a motorist. A former UFC champion friend of mine from the USA was on a seminar tour, so I rang him to tell him that I'd make it down to Steve Marsden's place in Sheffield for a quick catch up. The Marsdens is a nice family and I was always happy to see them. I rang Ronnie, who I had introduced to this UFC champion years ago. Ronnie picked me up and we set off to Sheffield, which is a pain to get to. Well, at least I've always thought so. West Yorkshire is direct and easy, but South Yorkshire is just a hurdle so I always try to avoid it.

We were in our lane and this guy was horning and suddenly overtook us. Ronnie, the personification of calmness, the epitome of niceness, love and peace, suddenly changed into Superman as the situation got the better of him. The car was in fifth gear and so was the adrenaline of one of my best friend's. He hit the accelerator hard, tailing this guy. The guy clocked on, pulled over in front of us, got out of the car and sprinted towards us. This guy was in his late 20s, was tall and looked fairly solid. Ronnie was old enough to be his dad. Ronnie and I got out of the car and Ronnie started racing towards the guy. I ran behind him with a smirk etched across my face, trying to keep up. An argument started and this guy was shouting, raving and ranting arguing that Ronnie is in the wrong. Both parties are having a bit of a domestic. As they got closer I intervened and warned the guy that Ronnie was a five-time world Thai-boxing champion, to try to defuse the situation. As soon as these words hit the young man's ears, he immediately put himself into reverse gear. 'I'm not going to fight him in front of people,' he countered, losing his bottle.

I couldn't stop laughing throughout this bizarre episode as both men were roaring that they would rip each other's heads off. This was the first time I'd seen Ronnie really furious. I felt sorry for the other guy. I thought if Ronnie's light is lit, the other guy would get it and get it real hard as if a firework had hit him. I thought I was going to see a world champion – the greatest kick-boxer Britain ever produced in this brutal bone-crushing sport who had knocked out champions all around the globe – in a live altercation right in front of my own eyes. Within seconds they both calmed down and Ronnie transitioned into the calm caring man I knew and gave the other driver a hug, which the guy accepted. The situation was defused.

Ronnie may have hung up his gloves 15 years before, but his reflexes, power, speed and accuracy were so phenomenal that even the current crop of fighters would have a hard time prevailing. Not only had I seen his fight footage, but I had see him move live. And, boy, he could move fast and hit hard and hit you many times before you even knew what what was going on. Some fighters have a mouth, but can't back it up. With Ronnie, it was the opposite.

Back in the comfort of our warm and cosy car I could not stop laughing. Sensing the lighter side of this whole episode, my friend joined in. Despite what I had witnessed, I can say with great conviction that my friend embodies the true spirit of kindness and a non-violent approach to finding a solution to a problem. In fact, Ronnie has often told me that in the gym and when he was fighting in the ring, some people used to say that he wasn't aggressive enough, that he often held back – even though he was beating everyone up and winning. Once in the ring when Ronnie caught his opponent with a devastating elbow to the face, which caused severe damage, he made a pledge to himself never to employ elbows to the face again. He had the capacity to do real serious damage. Although he was a dangerous and powerful fighter, he was compelled to hold back. I feel he has a natural tendency, despite being a world champion fighter, to feel empathy for others. Call it a weakness or whatever, but his power is something he has been unable to diffuse within.

CHAPTER TWENTY-NINE

MR ROCKY

JOURNALISM IS one of the only professions in which you are paid to learn. There are a slew of opportunities you can take advantage of as a journalist. One of the many merits of being in this position is that it allows you to meet a wide array of public and famous figures. Often you can spend quality time getting to know those individuals during an interview. Depending on the press exposure, they usually welcome your presence – particularly if you work for a high-profile establishment. And who would say no to free drinks and access to the VIP section at events and ringside seats at sporting events? It truly is a dream job. I have been fortunate enough to be able to do what I love.

Although I had rubbed shoulders with the Hollywood elite on movie sets, there was nothing better than actually interviewing the stars or meeting them in a professional setting. So, when major action stars were in town, who made a name for themselves playing prize fighters, how many would bypass the opportunity to meet them? When Sylvester Stallone was over for two exclusive events in London and Manchester in August 2014, I grasped the opportunity. A friend's birthday party was on the same day so I had a bit of a dilemma. In fact, he was vexed when I made my choice, complaining that Stallone was more important to me than him. Consoling him I told him that I'd make it up to him.

Sports figures, particularly boxers, have been on the after-dinner speaking circuit for years now, but for A-list Hollywood stars to resort to this was unheard of. Hollywood is out of reach for most. The glitz and glamour, fame and fortune are the major attractions. Fame is the state of being known or talked about by many people, especially on account of notable achievements. Personally, the star-struck syndrome has worn off because, after all, it is a job that I've been doing for a long time. But people are obsessed with celebrity now more than ever. Big stars are unreachable in a physical sense, unapproachable by all but an inner circle. Sports fans get to see their favourite athlete in the confines of an arena or stadium. Others have to content themselves with seeing the star's image on TV, the worldwide web, in magazines and newspapers. Today, sports and entertainment megastars have immense commercial reach, with modern technology firing their image to every corner of the globe.

I wasted no time in getting in touch with the promoters flashing my media credentials which resulted in obtaining two access all areas passes. Obsessive fans were forking out up to £1,600 for VIP tickets. Compare this to a £200 VIP boxing dinner event ticket with the likes of Mike Tyson. Despite the fact that punters seem more than willing to pay hefty sums for admission, what kind of a message does this send? It clearly indicates that these stars are commodities who are valuable and have their worth, which can be sold to the highest bidder. It takes the shine off them if they're willing to do a Q&A for that kind of money and allow such access. It feels far from glamorous. If I'm totally honest, I was aghast at the idea of someone of the calibre of Stallone resorting to such a medium. It was astounding.

Anyway, this was a rare opportunity for me to meet the action hero. My friend Ronnie Green and I arrived at the MEN Arena early. It was packed with over 3,500 noisy fans – with one media outlet reporting a figure near the 4,500 mark. We were escorted to the VIP area where some major TV actors were in attendance. After mingling with VIPs and celebrities, some of whom I knew, and an actor friend of mine who is a cast member of the most popular TV show filmed in the same city, it was time for the show to kick off in the arena. In what is considered to be true superstar fashion, Stallone arrived late after being stuck in traffic for four hours. The Hollywood heavyweight entered the arena to deafening fanfares and an ovation escorted by the military with the *Rocky* tune blasting away. The general vibe, I sensed, was hero worship. Onstage the audience was treated to a Q&A with Stallone. The crowd was extra exuberant, with one man clambering onstage requesting a hug from Mr Rambo, only to be manhandled off by Stallone's bodyguard.

Listening to the star talk about the barriers he had faced in life was inspirational and empowering for many, although for me it was merely a repeat of what I already knew. The *Rocky* star had huge obstacles shoved in his face. He is another actor whose background can be traced to combat sports and bodybuilding. His mother was a wrestling promoter. As a young teenager, Steve Reeves, the Hercules movies star and bodybuilding icon of the 1950s and 1960s, became the young man's inspiration. Stallone was a weakling teenager so in his quest to build his muscles he started lifting weights, and anything else he could find, inspired by the bodybuilding legend. He would eventually sculpt one of the best physiques in cinematic history. His speech impediments, which led to him being bullied, made him less of a candidate for transforming himself into an alpha male. His speech problem was the result of an unfortunate accident left his face paralysed. Nutritional deficiencies in early childhood exacerbated the problem.

Stallone's story is one of the most inspirational in the history of Hollywood. His upbringing as a kid in contrast to becoming Hollywood's top action star with blockbuster hits is phenomenal. Like Arnold Schwarzenegger's father, Stallone's father never believed in him and always put him down. This, I'm sure motivated him to prevail against overwhelming odds.

He further opened up to the audience. A struggling actor, he churned out the *Rocky* script in a matter of three weeks after watching the Muhammad Ali–Chuck Wepner fight on cable TV in 1975. Related to this, I came to learn something very interesting when I was researching Ali's life. One of Ali's training partners at Deer Lake revealed to me that Stallone was among the boxers who spent time at the camp before anyone ever knew who he was. He said, 'He came, yes. He stayed in the bunkhouse, he had nowhere to sleep. This was a year before *Rocky*. He wrote *Rocky* on yellow tab paper in the bunkhouse. He was a normal guy but he was a boxer.' Boxers were welcomed at Deer Lake and Ali would be accommodating. He'd give you tasks to do. He'd find somebody for you to spar with. He would spar you. The training partner added, 'Stallone was eating in the kitchen, staying at the bunk house, boxing. I think he sparred with Sugar Ray Leonard early on. Ali was trying to get him work. I think it was Ali who was the one who introduced him to the guy who made the movie *Rocky*. I did remember him. There were a lot of people there they were coming and going. It was full of people.' All this was a pleasant surprise to me. This individual told me to talk to Eddie Mustafa Muhammad, who spent time at the camp and became the WBA light-heavyweight champion. But when I asked Eddie, who lives in Las Vegas now, to verify the story, he said he didn't remember Stallone being at the camp.

The aspiring actor and scriptwriter tried to sell the script and got offered $125,000. But he was adamant that he would star in the film. The studio refused because they wanted a bona fide star, they told him. A couple of weeks later they offered the broke actor double the amount – $250,000, then increased the offer to £350,000 but he still refused to accept. Would you refuse that kind of money if you were broke with only $50 in your bank account and nothing to your name? Some would take the money and run. Finally the deal stipulated that he'd receive only $35,000 for the script but get to star in the film. As we know, the *Rocky* franchise became one of the most iconic in cinematic history catapulting Sylvester Stallone to superstardom.

TO THE TOP

Fast forward to 2020 when I interviewed Irwin Winkler, the producer of all the *Rocky* films. I was curious about this widely circulated story in the public domain of how the then unknown actor convinced the studio to take a gamble on him. I asked, 'Irwin, what can you tell me about the first *Rocky* movie and how Sylvester Stallone convinced you to do the movie with a then unknown?' He said, 'Well, the thing which is interesting is he came to me but he was an unknown actor. And I didn't have a role for him for another film. But as he was leaving the office, he said to me, "Oh, by the way, I'm a writer."' Irwin was dubious and told me that he didn't sound like a writer nor did he look like a writer. Stallone, refusing to take no for an answer, enthusiastically tried to pitch another idea to the producer, 'I have a script that I'd like you to read.' And he gave the script to the producer and actually thought it was well written. Yet, Irwin wasn't interested in pursuing it any further. Consoling Stallone, he said, 'Look, I think you're a good writer but I don't like to do a movie on it.' Stallone had another plan, which I would refer to as plan B, up his sleeve. As he was about to leave, he said, 'I have another idea.' And he proceeded to pitch the idea of *Rocky*. As I mentioned earlier, it was based on the underdog Chuck Wepner, whose boxing heroics had inspired Stallone to churn out the script in a matter of weeks. So, originally, Stallone had visited the producer to pitch something else.

Stallone said something that Irwin found very thought-provoking and which very few people would ever be willing to do. He said, 'Look, I don't have any money,' – which was true – 'and I will write the script for you but you don't have to pay me. No money! One thing you have to do is once I write the script you don't have to pay me, but you have to give me the starring role in this movie.' This impressed Irwin and he felt it was very unique. This unknown actor had won over the Hollywood producer, and the rest, as they say, is history.

I asked Irwin whether the film was an idea for the kung fu films that had caught the attention of the public several years earlier. 'No, not at all,' the producer said. 'The thing is we never considered it as a fight movie; we always considered it as a love story between him and Adriane. The fighting was just an opportunity for him to show that he could make something better out of himself.' This, I must admit, was a complete surprise to me. You learn something new in my game. The movie was a huge success and the unknown macho man instantly rocketed to international prominence and fame. For Irwin it was a very proud moment when he received the Oscar at the Academy Awards. You see, back then, traditionally, the only people to accept the movie-specific production awards were the producers, but as Irwin and director John Avildsen (who later went on to to direct *Karate Kid*) went onstage to collect the award, Irwin grabbed Stallone and practically forced him to come up onstage to accept the award with them.

Subsequently, Stallone went on to write all the *Rocky* movies and directed *Rocky II, III and IV,* and *Rocky Balboa*. So, he directed four of the movies and wrote all the scripts. Now, what they then did was turn the writing and directing to a stranger Ryan Coogler. Stallone was very gracious about it, very, very encouraging to Coogler, Irwin told me. He was very determined to pass the baton on to this young filmmaker. 'What surprised me most in my career was we made this movie with a then-unknown Sylvester Stallone and it won an Academy Award,' Irwin said. 'It became a world phenomenon. And 40 odd years later we're making *Creed III*, which will be the ninth version of *Rocky*. It's quite an accomplishment going from 1976 to 2020 still making *Rocky*. The only one I think which has a longer history is the James Bond franchise.'

Widely considered the hard man of Hollywood with a heart of gold, Stallone slept in the bus station in New York for three days while homeless when he was at his lowest. He was unable to pay his rent or buy food. We're talking about America here, not a third world country. Determination and willpower and clasping on to your dreams were the messages Stallone empowered us with that day.

* * *

After the Q&A session and rapturous applause, the VIP's congregated in the VIP area for a meet-and-greet and professional photo. The fanatics had paid a hefty price to shake the hand of an icon. Stallone walked in with his rep and event promoter from the south. I was sitting at my table and as Stallone passed, he pointed out to an Arnold Schwarzenegger item on the table and picked it up smirking as we shared pleasantries.

Suddenly his official said, 'No, we can't have this.' It seemed that although Arnold and Stallone are on friendly terms now and even collaborating, the rep didn't want an Arnold product being promoted at a Sly event. *Here we go*, I thought. It dawned on me that the clash of egos between the two action stars was still prevalent. The rep went over to confer with the promoter, but soon found that she was wasting her time. The Americans seem to make things difficult for everyone. The control and power that agents and publicists have is phenomenal. In this case Arnold seemed to be in direct conflict with this action-alpha male; that's how it seemed to me at the time. Ronnie and I were quite stunned as we thought both long-time competitors had left their differences behind and moved on. But, no, apparently both men seem to be vying for control and the crown of best action star in Hollywood.

After he finished posing for photos Stallone walked passed again and stopped by my table. We shook hands and had a quick chat. I tried handing him a copy of UFC champion Randy Couture's autobiography which prompted a perceptible change in his behaviour. I felt his ego surfacing which manifested as, *I'm the best and I'm not interested in anyone else.* I felt perplexed, because when promoting *The Expendables,* Stallone, who is now one of the celebrities who owns shares in the UFC, had praised Randy on *The Late Show* with David Letterman. 'You put all these tough guys, Dolph Lundgren, Jet Li, in a room together, who comes out?' the Hollywood action star had proudly said. 'If you walked in ten minutes later, you'd see Randy Couture sitting on top of us having a chocolate fudge sundae.'

MR ROCKY

I was aware of the reverence he had for the UFC legend, so was quite puzzled by his reaction when I tried to shove Randy in his face. After a quick chat with me his bodyguard, who looked like this British drama actor who was in *Coronation Street* many years ago – I can't recall his name – whisked him out leaving many VIPs rather bemused.

Apparently Stallone was tired. After being forced to smile for 100 rich fans he'd got fed up and left, leaving punters disappointed. Those who never got their promised photos with him got refunds apparently. I could see the promoter running around like a headless chicken. He had disappointed VIPs who had missed their once-in-a-life time chance to mingle and be pictured with the actor. So the meet-and-greet went out of the window. There was some bitterness and chaotic scenes followed but all in all it was a great day for the many who had this rare opportunity to see the man in the flesh.

Now, his brother Frank Stallone, I am no fan of. I had requested an interview with him in my early years, when I got in touch with his publicist in New York. An interview was being arranged, but because of some unforeseeable circumstances it didn't materialise. Years later I got in touch with him directly in the vain hope of securing an interview. He said he'd do it. I sent him material of some other action stars I had interviewed for the magazine. Suddenly he gave me the silent treatment. It was obvious. I had fallen out with a personality who worked in Hollywood, who happened to be a friend of his, and realised who I was so I was on his blacklist. I thought *if that's the attitude, then so be it*. No disrespect, but Frank is no Sly. Frank, a musician and actor, also dabbled in boxing, but never really made it big in the entertainment world. Instead he's been living in the shadows of his older brother who I found to be quite funny and an affable character. Following this event, the same promoters flew over Stallone's former nemesis, Arnold Schwarzenegger, for an exclusive black-tie dinner. And both have made repeat visits since.

* * *

I had the opportunity to attend the European red carpet premiere of *Creed II*. It was a dark rainy night and the stars walking the carpet included Michael B. Jordan and Dolph Lundgren to Tessa Thompson and Brigitte Nielsen. Numerous world champion boxers were also at the star-studded event. But I think it was Tessa Thompson who was the queen of the night. She dazzled the audience with her confidence and style and wore her Valentino Haute Couture dress with such grace and ease. I grabbed a quick interview with Dolph, who was gracious enough to give me a few minutes on the red carpet before his handlers whisked him inside. 'What's the most fascinating thing about working with Stallone on the *Rocky* franchise and on *Creed II*?' I asked the Swede, who himself at one point had a dream of pursing a boxing career, something he had revealed to me in a conversation a decade earlier, before he became an actor. 'Well, I think the *Rocky* movies are very special for me because it's not only entertaining and about sport, but it's about life, it's about family, it's about things you love, what you want to fight for,' he said 'It's about some deep issues that touch many people around the world, and even if you don't know anything about boxing you can resonate with it. It's really changed my life and now, almost 35 years later, it has changed my life a little bit again. I think because this film was a great chance for me to play a dramatic role. I had some good reviews the first time I worked on *Rocky* with Stallone, and I'm very pleased and I want to thank Stallone to have given me the opportunity again by transporting me back into the franchise. I never thought I'd do this role again.'

I soon learned that, in addition to specific brief questions, certain questions which are generic in nature often bring out some compelling anecdotes and revelation. These include: What's the most thought-provoking conversation you've ever had in relation to your life or career? The darkest time? The most fascinating thing that ever happened in your career? The most bizarre experience you've ever had? I asked him, 'Can you give me a funny anecdote with Stallone while working on *Creed II*?'

MR ROCKY

'One thing I won't forget is that we both look older in the film,' he said. 'We both are wearing makeup, we've actually got grey hair and wrinkles in real life, and we – the characters – do interviews in the movie and Stallone keeps wiping his makeup off. Then in the end he goes, "You tell the people back home this is just make up, we don't look like this."' I have to say, Stallone looks in way better shape than Arnold Schwarzenegger, judging by images and videos that have surfaced in the last several years. And the man is in his early 70s now. But his motivation to keep in the best shape possible has never wained.

CHAPTER THIRTY

BRUCE LEE: ENTER THE RING

THE BEAUTY of Bruce Lee is how he transcends and has a crossover appeal. Numerous boxing champions that I have interviewed over the years were not shy to concur that this 135-pound Chinese man left an indelible impression on them. I painstakingly researched a piece relating to Bruce Lee's Western boxing connection, aptly titled 'Bruce Lee: The Western Boxing Connection', and submitted this feature to an editor at a leading boxing magazine in November 2015. The piece reflected on how and who in the sweet science game the martial arts master inspired, what and who influenced him and his art and whether he would have triumphed in the squared ring. If you're well read on the subject of Bruce Lee, it won't come as a surprise that boxing theories and concepts were an integral part of the personal form of combat he devised, which he labelled jeet kune do. The great pugilist champions I had personally spoken to, and others I had seen quoted, adulated this lightweight fighter. These men actually fought at the highest level in the squared ring. These were world champions, fighters whose life revolved around a competitive arena.

However, if I thought the boxing editor was going to embrace my opinions with open arms then I was gravely mistaken. The piece drew sharp criticism from the editor via his assistant. 'Fiaz says that the 135-pound Lee could hit harder than a man twice his size due to the speed of his punch,' the editor wrote in his response message. 'How does Fiaz know this? Pure conjecture! So, Lee hit harder than the 160-pound Gennady Golovkin; the 175-pound Sergey Kovalev; the 225-pound Mike Tyson; the 190-pound Jack Dempsey; the 195-pound Joe Louis? Really? I can't get my brain around that one.' Maybe this editor had been hit far too many times in the head. Perhaps he was in need of edification. Well, those were my immediate thoughts.

I also advocate that had Bruce turned to boxing on a professional level, he would at the absolute least have been an overwhelming force in his weight division. This was a viewpoint shared by Bruce's closest training partner and a man who has widely been acknowledged as the world's greatest martial artist, Dan Inosanto. 'At the absolute least, really?' the editor responded, 'Up against lightweight champs such as Roberto Duran, Alexis Arguello and Esteban DeJesus?' Speaking of training partners, there was a period in Bruce's life when he was surrounded by boxers and street fighters who were his personal students, who admitted that Bruce would tie them in knots and that they couldn't touch him. 'The last paragraph of Fiaz's piece quotes Ricky Hatton,' he continued, in his assault. 'I've interviewed Ricky and the quote just doesn't sound like Ricky talking. I'm not flat out saying Ricky never used the words used in the quote, but that's another quote I'd like to see backed up.' Well, I had interviewed Ricky myself, twice, once for the martial arts magazine and the other time for the documentary on Bruce Lee.

Furthermore, Ricky, in his autobiography, revealed the influence the late, great martial arts master had had on him. Maybe the editor needed to do his own homework in terms of acquiring opinions from some of the best boxers. I'm sure he would have been in a state of shock by the response. 'To me, there were too many loose ends, plus conjecture and inaccuracies in the piece,' the editor wrote. 'I respect Fiaz's knowledge of martial arts, but the Bruce Lee piece, to me, doesn't quite make the transition. We can't be publishing pieces that would have the pugilist-specialist readers shaking their heads. It's a piece that could work, but not quite in its present form.'

On a more constructive note, he admitted that the Muay Thai fighters often did very well in Western-style boxing and that some had even won titles very early in their boxing careers. He said these fighters used a lot of punching in their Muay Thai bouts, and were accustomed to bruising, punishing and bone-on-bone contact. But he wasn't sure that Bruce, who was a wonderful athlete and skilled fighter, had that sort of hard-grinding background. After this verbal assault, I happened to mention the situation to my good friend Ronnie Green, the five-time world Thai-boxing champion. This man had beaten the champions of the sport in Thailand and is the pioneer of Thai-boxing in the United Kingdom. Needles to say, Ronnie, who I feel has a better grasp on reality, couldn't get his head around the editor's opinions.

Certainly, boxers experience full-contact blows and are able to dish out and absorb punishment. It's a full-contact sport just as wrestling is a body-contact sport. But based on the fact Bruce was a lightweight and so would've been unlikely to have been a force to be reckoned with in the ring is debatable. Be that as it may, when you look at lighter-weight champions who've prevailed, you would think that had Bruce pursued boxing then it is quite plausible he could have triumphed. Having said this, there are ambiguous suggestions that he didn't spar full contact all-out, according to some, while others claim that he emphasised full-contact sparring. Being the intelligent man he was, he implemented realistic training methods according to his personal students. Let's get one thing straight here: to make it in boxing on a professional level or even amateur level, I feel you have to train in pure boxing. Otherwise it's like trying to become a 100-metre runner by playing soccer or being in the NFL just because a lot of running is involved. One must comprehend the clear distinction between the two.

Personally, having been a student of the martial arts – particularly grappling, with any striking devoid of full-contact sparring – I never did get a taste for pure boxing until many years later when I entered a boxing gym in the hope of acclimatising myself to sparring in the ring. This was the sole reason. It didn't take long to grasp reality as the urge for 'flight' was really strong. The heavy bag combinations that you mastered for many years just fly out of the window as you struggle to find your target, and there's overwhelming tendency to flinch as you are bombarded with big bombs. In the process you're being outsmarted, in my case by skinny teenagers who had been boxing for some time and looked thin as a stick. Much to my surprise their ability to hit me and not get hit was both embarrassing and frustrating. Although the punches didn't hurt nor knock me down, it taught me a lesson; a reality check was in order. Besides, I always had a glove phobia and found it extremely uncomfortable with pillowcases on my hands trying to punch and move.

Once you clear that first monster hurdle, you begin to feel more confident. So, learning a martial art, which within its framework doesn't implement full-contact sparring, is one thing, and getting in the boxing ring is a completely a different experience. The sweet science allows you to experience the brutality of a fight, the rawness, in a controlled environment. I think any serious martial artist should experience, to a fair degree, some sort of boxing sparring to really appreciate getting hit and experience full contact on the move. Otherwise you will never know the reality of your limitations – and true potential. At one of the gyms I visited for a while, the coaches seemed to lack a code of ethics, a code I was used to at martial arts gyms. But you know what? These boxers wouldn't last in a grappling gym. It's befitting to mention that Bruce's only real experience in the confines of a boxing ring was when he laced up gloves in Hong Kong and competed in the Inter Boxing Competition as a teenager. He knocked out Gary Elmes to win the championship. I was told by his best friend, William Cheung, he had used wing chun straight punches in the fight.

Anyway, after taking in criticism, which was, by the way, hard to swallow, and contemplating it, I came to terms with the fact that the critic had several valid points. Yes, 'several'. And to be fair to him, he had the right to his opinion, albeit not every right. I later came to value his critical feedback, even though I did not agree with most parts. However, we have a problem. Some of the biggest names in boxing had shared their opinions, which I valued, and they matched my own. The champions Sugar Ray Leonard – who gorged his passion on the likes of Muhammad Ali and Bruce Lee – Evander Holyfield, Ricky Hatton, even the great George Foreman – the latter always happy to speak to me whenever I ring him – all great fighters that I had interviewed, seemed to share my view. Countless other world boxing champions seemed to be running on the same track – not only did they revere Bruce for his iconic status, but also for his fighting ability. If these fighters thought Bruce was not a great fighter, or had the potential to triumph in the ring should he have pursued this avenue, they wouldn't have gone on record offering colossal praise. 'He influenced a lot of people and showed that size didn't matter,' Evander Holyfield told me once. Even heavyweights were intrigued by this 135-pound fighter of a diminutive stature. 'I don't know anybody that was better,' Holyfield added. 'He was very technical.'

I had done my homework and research well. What these champions had to say about a skinny 5ft 7in man were more valuable opinions than those of anyone else. Moreover, one legend in the fight world whose opinion I value more than most is 'Iron' Mike Tyson. I met him once. 'Bruce Lee had an awesome philosophy of life, which blew me away,' Tyson openly declared in a Roots of Fight promo video. 'Bruce Lee is a killer! You do as much damage as you can and get out without being hurt, less damage to yourself as possible. I have so much respect for his philosophy.' When you've managed to influence the most ferocious fighter in the boxing game, you know you've done something right.

'Bruce Lee, he didn't believe in fighting in tournaments and stuff,' Tyson said. 'He basically believed in, "Let's do it right now." But Bruce Lee was really a street fighter, like an MMA fighter for real.' Tyson himself built a notorious reputation for being a ferocious fighter in and out of the ring. Tyson and I have a mutual friend, Joe Egan. They lived and trained together for two years when they were teenagers in New York, at the famous Catskill training camp before we witnessed the jam-packed arenas Tyson fought his fiercest foes. I got a thrill when Joe used to tell me how both of them used to watch Bruce Lee movies at the house where they lived. Both teenagers would try to mimic Bruce, replicating the sounds that he became famous for. Tyson was a huge fan of kung fu classics and would fork out thousands of dollars on kung fu flicks. He went as far as watching *Enter the Dragon* to learn explosiveness. And we all know how explosive Tyson became – he was dynamite!

Tyson is a man who loves all styles of combat. He is a huge fan of the UFC and it is his belief that Bruce was a real-life ferocious fighter. 'No one talked about MMA before that, or grappling,' Tyson said of Bruce's innovative approach in an interview with *MAXIM* in 2016. 'He said, "I don't believe in grappling because I equate grappling with being on the floor and I equate being on the floor with being stomped on." And they said, "What do you mean?" And he said, "One guy maybe, but I'm fighting five or six guys, but I can't be on the floor wrestling around." Is that deep or what? That just totally opened my head. We talk about killing, not any championship.' Tyson understood that Bruce's approach was not fighting to see who is better, but fighting for survival in a street encounter.

Bruce has had more than his fair share of critics, but equally he has garnered profound respect from some of the toughest combatants. But the boxing editor had his own opinions. Then again, an opinion is an opinion. Needles to say, the piece didn't make it into the publication and neither did I want to deal with this editor again.

CHAPTER THIRTY-ONE

ENTER THE OCTAGON

AROUND THE same time, I was talking to an editor of a martial arts magazine in Sweden. I had dealt with this individual in the past, but didn't find him very instrumental at all. By then I had ventured into working with magazines around the globe, in America, Australia, Dubai and Europe, while still holding the position of columnist for the martial arts magazine domestically. On a personal level, being recognised for your work around the world and promoting the sports and athletes gave me a great sense of achievement. I had made it on to the international platform with ease.

I had submitted a piece on Bruce Lee, reflecting on his influence on a new brutal sport and his impact on the MMA scene. I didn't hear back from this individual, so I was prompted to pick up the phone and resort to the old fashioned approach. I was oblivious to what lay in wait. Well, I was in for another unexpected shock. This time an editor of MMA press was vilifying the greatest martial arts exponent of the century. His argument was that he wanted to promote 'real' fighters. He wasn't keen on even giving coverage to movie martial artists. Basically, he was making it clear that Bruce Lee wasn't good enough to be in his magazine. What? Almost five decades after his demise, this icon continues to grace the covers of magazines all over the world, from specialist magazines to more major mainstream periodicals such as *TIME*.

ENTER THE OCTAGON

He went on and on as I listened to his criticism, keeping composed. This magazine had transitioned into a publication based on MMA and a more practical street form of martial arts after years of focusing on traditional martial arts. Bruce, according to this individual, was merely a movie actor. There still persists a vague notion that the kung fu star was merely an actor, martial arts mythology apparently had taken root. Some feel it twists every fact to turn Bruce Lee into a fantasy legendary figurehead. Bruce didn't compete nor prove himself, but the MMA fighters had proved themselves, he further added. 'The UFC tried to do something with Bruce Lee's image and promote him,' he said. I wasn't oblivious to this. Well, I wasn't thrilled at what I was hearing.

I tried to refrain from letting my personal feelings take over. Controlling my emotions I clung on to my professional attitude. But inside my stomach was turning faster than a washing machine on its final cycle. Again, I felt that he was entitled to his opinion. I had to be fair and think with a rational mind. However, we had another problem. Yes, the same problem that we had with the boxing authority. Let's look at this free from undue bias or preconceived opinions. I had spoken with a plethora of top UFC fighters and champions who had a very different take on the martial arts innovator. With the advent of the UFC, a whole new generation of hybrid fighters rose to prominence. Randy Couture, Rashad Evans, Ken Shamrock, Jon Jones and Conor McGregor, to name a few, were all influenced by the late martial arts exponent. When I met Rickson Gracie at his academy in west Los Angeles in 2002, I was dying to chuck the Bruce Lee question at him. With his humble yet dignified bearing, Rickson acknowledged Bruce as being the greatest martial artist of our time. When it comes to fighting, Rickson knows what he's talking about, believe me. He has this aura about him; when you're in his presence you feel this gigantic energy like Samson.

Now, MMA is no Mickey Mouse sport; it's one of the toughest sports around. So I valued the opinions of the gladiators who fought in the Octagon more so than most. These men's achievements and experience of fighting in a brutal sport was admirable. Again, on the surface someone may feel, because of Bruce's rather diminutive stature, he may have been butchered in an MMA setting. McGregor (Bruce's weight) is a perfect example of a light fighter who managed to rule the UFC. It's interesting to note that his strength is in striking and there are plenty of fighters who are more experienced in submission grappling than he is. You have lighter divisions. 'I think he could have competed in the 145-pound weight class,' Randy once told me when I was researching the life and legacy of the late fighter and movie star. 'Sure, he could have got himself in that weight class and done well, there's no doubt about it.'

I feel that, as part of the argument, it's vital to go to the original source – grappling masters, martial arts champions and personal students who trained with the man himself. Essentially they are the only ones who really witnessed Bruce's true abilities, to whatever degree, first-hand. During his lifetime Bruce did work out with several world-class grappling experts, notably jiu-jitsu master, Wally Jay, and Pan-American judo champion, Hayward Nishioka, who slot into this category very nicely. So it's crucial to take their opinions on board. After all, these men were world-class grappling competitors and champions. These individuals witnessed Bruce's skills and potential first-hand. Hayward and Wally were impressed by Bruce's martial arts abilities. They told me that Bruce could demonstrate judo throws. However, he didn't do enough, which is understandable because his art was evolving and much of the focus at the time lay on striking, but they were in awe of his striking skills and overall pedigree.

Original Seattle student, Patrick Strong, who now lives in Los Angeles, where he teaches a style more reflecting the wing chun system but which integrates Brazilian jiu-jitsu into the overall spectrum, actually said to me that had Bruce lived he would have become best friends with the Gracies. I believe that. In his lifetime Bruce was close friends with and worked with some of the top martial arts masters, including some very prominent and notorious grapplers. The Gracies opened the eyes of the world and Bruce would've been intrigued. Adding to this argument, I must mention that another notorious grappler back in the era often had the inclination to put down Bruce's prowess. He had worked with Bruce for a while, exchanging skills. He claimed to have taught Bruce, but that is often disputed by some who were close to the late martial arts master. His argument was that Bruce never fought competitively.

Furthermore – and this is the crucial point – when assessing Bruce's ability most people, including even some modern-day MMA champions and boxers, can't come to grips with the fact that you have to separate the theatrical art from reality. A lot of people's perception is based on what they see on celluloid – good or bad. Most view Bruce as the fighter beating up 20 men on screen and coming out unscathed. Speaking of which, the unforgettable opening scene from *Enter the Dragon* epitomises true MMA. This scene accurately captures the true essence of MMA in action. It projected exactly what MMA is based on: two competitors attempting to defeat each other by potentially utilising a variety of techniques ranging from striking vertical to ground grappling. Bruce is wearing fingerless gloves, which became the precursor of UFC, and black underpants. It's a testament to Bruce's innovative genius which would go on to influence a plethora of UFC champions

Very few would doubt that Bruce was revolutionary in bringing not just the fighting arts into the spotlight in the West but accentuating the need for adaptability and a more realistic training approach. As Bruce embraced American culture and Western combat sports, he kicked the martial arts tradition into smithereens in pursuit of devising the ultimate fighting art. His hybrid style encapsulated a composite of techniques and methods, which at the time received criticism from the traditionalists. This approach made him something of an outcast in the martial arts fraternity. In modern-day martial arts, we have seen cross training being embraced and advocated. The MMA movement has catapulted the martial arts to the forefront of combat.

The golden question remains to be answered: could Bruce have emerged victorious if he had locked horns with the likes of Royce Gracie or Conor McGregor? I had thought long and hard about how he would have fared in today's MMA environment. I personally believe that if a frail-looking Royce Gracie can tear through no-holds-barred competitions with his technical supremacy, it is plausible that Bruce could've whooped asses with his devastating kicks, chokes, strangles and ground-and-pound provided he spent an inordinate amount of time with a good coach. This is my honest opinion. It goes without saying that he would have had to attain a high level of grappling skills, including groundwork, which Bruce's art was completely devoid of, given his assiduous approach.

According to one of Bruce's personal training partners, 'As far as no-holds-barred tournaments like the Ultimate Fighting Championship, I don't think Bruce would enter something like that.' However, all this talk is speculative at best. What is apparent is that his popularity continues to grow. He is the fighter that has been chosen more than any other UFC fighter in the EA Sport's UFC game, 3.41 million times in the games first month of availability. This is an accomplishment because Bruce never fought in the UFC, nor did he compete competitively. GSP and Jon Jones have, both been played 3.4 million times; and from there it's a big drop off. This is an opportunity to live off a fight fantasy.

Based on the response from a plethora of UFC champions and warriors, as well as boxers, it's safe to conclude that Bruce had the potential – and I emphasise the word 'potential' – to become a force to be reckoned with in the squared ring or Octagon. In conclusion, there's not ample evidence to substantiate this, and by the same token, there's little to disprove it. There are just too many variables involved to make any meaningful prediction. This debate will always be surrounded by great criticism and speculation. The critics will continue with their assaults. On the other end of the spectrum, ardent followers and fighters continue to adulate the fighting legend. If only he had lived, arguably he would be proud of the MMA scene. Many credit Bruce Lee with being the godfather of this movement, while others are, understandably, reticent about handing this 'title' to the late master. About the piece? Needless to say it never got into the Swedish magazine. I didn't like the editor, anyway. Instead I wrote it for *Fighters Only* magazine.

CHAPTER THIRTY-TWO

OLD SCHOOL MEETS NEW

ROYCE GRACIE was fighting his old nemesis, Ken Shamrock. I was shocked to hear this. I immediately got on the phone to Royce to get this validated and also conduct an interview with him. 'Mr Gracie the Great, do you want to do a quick interview pertaining to your upcoming Shamrock fight?' I messaged him. 'Let me know what time LA time I can ring you.' I received a prompt reply, 'Call me here on WhatsApp in 20 minutes.' It was always great to talk to Royce and have a laugh with him. He had given me the nickname 'Taliban', referring to me as a terrorist, because of my Muslim background. And he would always joke and ask me how many planes had I and my 'brothers' blown up – it was hilarious. Ken had tasted defeat at the hands of UFC's first ever champion in the first ever tournament, when the Brazilian choked him out in just 50 seconds. Following this, in their second outing at UFC 5 in the super-fight, both men fought to a draw, a fight that lasted 30 minutes. The famous rivalry began. Ken was always so eager to avenge his defeats and had long desired to add another chapter to their rivalry.

I said to Royce that I was surprised to hear about his upcoming fight. I asked him why he was stepping into the arena again given that he had retired years ago. He didn't need to fight any more. This man had started a revolution in combat sports and made a name globally

OLD SCHOOL MEETS NEW

when he sent shockwaves across the fight world, paving the way for promising MMA fighters. Every man wants to be the toughest guy. It's an alpha male thing and a subconscious dream whether we admit to it or not. Royce had become a global phenomenon. He had the world at his feet, had fame and fortune in abundance. So why return to fight in the world's most brutal sport and put everything on the line when you can stay within your comfort zone? Well, it was time to find out from the man himself.

According to Royce his nemesis kept pestering Scott Coker, promoter of Bellator. 'Man, he wants to fight you, he wants you,' Scott told the Brazilian. Royce thought to himself, *Man, I'm a fighter, let's do it – might as well.* When you're a professional fighter and have fought for so many years at the highest level, fighting is in your blood. It's hard to blank it out. When you've dedicated your whole life to something, a cause or a craft, once you retire you're missing that element of contentment in your life that gave you that buzz, a meaning to life and that surge of urge. Personalities such as, let's say, Arnold Schwarzenegger, even though they're retired in their respective sports, in some capacity continue to be linked to their sports. Arnold continued to promote his beloved sport of bodybuilding even after he became the governor of California.

After Muhammad Ali hung up his gloves for good he also went through this syndrome. George Kalinsky, the famous American sports photographer who worked with Ali numerous times, once shared an anecdote with me. 'At one time in the early 80s, at the first WrestleMania, which was at Madison Square Garden with Hulk Hogan, prior to the build-up for WrestleMania, they had a lot of celebrities that were honorary referees,' the photographer told me. 'They had people like Pete Rose, a diverse group of people. And Ali was one of the referees. I was looking at him and it was the first time that I realised – it was a couple of years after his final fight – and feeling sad because you could see he wasn't the Ali that I was used to seeing. I felt really bad. I remember back when Ali said to me that the ring is his life and everything and the ring is his opportunity to be famous. Here he is in the ring but not necessarily the star. Hulk Hogan was the star that day and Ali was just one of the supporting athletes.' Once you've been in the public limelight but then fade into obscurity, you're sometimes itching to be adulated again. It's a drug.

Still, for Royce I think, like I said, fighting is in his blood and not because he craves to be in the limelight. Royce told me that people put age on things and that age dictates things to them, but that has never been his mentality. Being a professional athlete, he doesn't drink or smoke, is in very good health and watches his diet. 'A guy like him who is 220 pounds, and a guy like me who is 176 pounds, he still can't understand, I guess,' Royce said of Ken's fresh challenge. 'He's been losing sleep in the last 20 years.'

Ken was bigger than Royce and in pretty good shape with rippled muscles. Royce was planning on avoiding getting hit in the fight. 'He's still a good grappler,' Royce admitted. 'He finished a lot of his fights so he's dangerous.' I thought Ken's versatility might be a threat to Royce. Ken had boasted to the media that his long-time nemesis was living in the past because the sport had evolved and advanced. He broached the subject of being a versatile fighter in the modern-day MMA arena. Having remained resolute in his original fighting philosophy, Royce explained that the Helio Gracie system of self-defence advocates that a small person can overcome somebody who is bigger and stronger. And this is what he had proved to the world when he sliced through his bigger, stronger adversaries when in his prime. This tenacious man was sticking to his original fighting style when almost all professional MMA fighters were shrewd enough to evolve.

I had seen Ken fight before at an event. Although I had perceived Ken to be passed his prime, which he was, his physical presence could still intimidate many. But no man could intimidate the Brazilian, no matter how big or muscular. I guess Royce had already sussed his foe out – either that or he was taking a huge risk this time, putting his reputation on the line. His status was on the brink of being potentially tarnished, I feared. At the same time, if Ken lost, this would further tarnish his own status, which already had taken a severe beating after tallying up a considerable number of losses in the last few years. Both men had pioneered the sport and were holding on to their reputations. But Royce is one of the most confident fighters I have ever known. I've known him for more than 24 years and I don't think I've seen fear in him. I don't think he's ever been scared of a fighter.

This was like the classic Ali–Frazier rivalry of MMA – outing number three – and Ken would find redemption if he triumphed. Personally, I thought it could go either way. As our conversation progressed I was inclined to ask Royce about training preparations. 'What kind of training are you going to do to prepare yourself?' I asked the UFC Hall of Famer. 'I can't tell you about my training, man, you're going to be telling Ken,' he joked. That's the last thing I would be doing. I wanted Ken to be choked right out. As it happens, Royce wasn't going to be applying any of his trademark chokes that night; he'd be shocking everyone.

As we wrapped up our conversation, he told me to fly over to Houston to the fight. The magazine wasn't going to finance the trip I told him. Many years earlier when he was fighting in Japan, he had invited me to join him in the Land of the Rising Sun. I was flattered. I envisaged being in Royce's corner, picturing the cheering crowds in the packed-out stadium and all the flash photography. It was appealing to say the least. But I had other commitments so couldn't fly to Japan, a country where Royce packed out arenas with up to 90,000 fans.

The fight took place on 19 February 2016. In the morning, as soon as my eye lids opened, the first thing I did was check the result on my phone. I'm lying there in my bed with my phone as a nervous tremor of emotion ran through me. And as soon as I read the headline, ROYCE GRACIE STOPS KEN SHAMROCK, BUT NOT WITHOUT CONTROVERSY, a sense of relief shot through my body. I felt vicarious excitement coursing through my veins.

During the bout Royce had allegedly kneed his opponent in the groin. It was hilarious when Ken protested in anger, pointing to his victor in the ring after he recovered. 'You did this on purpose!' he barked several times. Ken was pissed off and I guess a little embarrassed, so resorted to desperate measures. The Brazilian jiu-jitsu pioneer had locked into a clinch midway through the first round and traded knees before he took Ken down, following up with a series of hammer fists to his floored opponent's face. This was the first ever knockout of his professional career. You just couldn't picture Royce knocking someone out with his fists. But, hey, he had been training in kickboxing for some years. I guess it had paid off.

After the commercial break when the beaten fighter was interviewed, he said, 'I got upset. I was wrong for getting upset because it wasn't Royce's fault.' Yet, after the fight Ken sent an open letter in which he strongly urged Royce to 'do the right thing'. But ironically, later, Ken failed the drug test, which made the whole episode even more interesting and fuelled further speculation. How can you say Royce cheated when you yourself were cheating in the first place? Regardless, I was over the moon at Royce emerging victorious. The Gracie–Shamrock feud would now be put to bed at last and the defeat plunged Ken into despair. Gracie's record was two wins and one draw. Considering his time off and ring rust, Royce had proved himself. In my pre-fight conversation I had asked him if he had any future fight plans. He had a tendency to sign one fight at a time but said that after this fight anything was possible.

* * *

The year had started with a big bang. The first ever UFC champion had come out of retirement after nine years to prove he still had it in him at age 49 to compete again. Royce was like Pele – he endeared himself to previous and current champions. But 'The Notorious' Conor McGregor was the biggest name in the UFC. McGregor was establishing himself as a global superstar and has taken the sport that

Royce had brought to our attention to another level. No contemporary MMA fighter impinged so much on the consciousnesses of the MMA fans and of those beyond but it is incontestable that Royce's legacy has made him the most influential figure in the sport's history, however notorious any past or current fighter is. Royce was fighting in the organisation that essentially began life as a way to settle the age-old argument over which style of fighting would prevail in a style-versus-style fight.

McGregor was preparing for UFC 196 where he was going to be facing Nate Diaz. He pulled up in his Rolls Royce and was looking forward to a training session at Nano's Hapkido, a small gym run by Royce's friend in Hermosa Beach in Los Angeles. Royce, who was fresh from his win less than two weeks before, happened to be there that day. Would Royce melt away under the glow of UFC's biggest champion, given the latter's current star power? No. 'The Notorious' was somewhat speechless when both fighters crossed paths. The Irish sensation, usually boisterous, seemed star-struck, struggling to find words as the two men conversed.

The name Conor McGregor has become synonymous with multi-million dollars. He is one of the biggest sports superstars and is known for his neat, tailor-made suits, his brash talk and for looking great dishing out the pain in the Octagon. Now, this Irishman was talking big money. He'd been broaching the idea of how he was on the verge of accumulating $100 million in the UFC. At first, I must admit, I thought it was all speculative talk. *How can you make $100 million as a UFC fighter?* I thought to myself. It soon dawned on me that this was plausible, but only something that McGregor could pull off. The whole game has changed. Gone were the days when smaller entities were the only potential sponsors inclined to get involved in a brutal spectacle sport. The UFC had been breaking pay-per-view records for some years. This is where the big money rolls in. Where did you think boxing accumulated all those millions from? Major sponsors and the medium of pay-per-view played a pivotal role.

TO THE TOP

I remember many years earlier some top boxing fight purses were $300,000, topped off with a $1.5 million TV deal. So that's $1.8 million right there. Then some went on to make a lot more per fight, reportedly earning a $3-million purse, and pocketing a career-best of $13 million taking into account TV and sponsorship deals. UFC has not only caught up but has eclipsed boxing in a certain respect, and McGregor is responsible to a large degree for this. As far as comparing pay-per-view figures for the two sports, when Ronda Rousey fought Bethe Correia at UFC 190, the pay-per-view buys hit the 900,000 mark. Furthermore the UFC had eight events in that time which hit the one-million mark. Of course, the Mayweather–Pacquiao fight is an exception, and reportedly generated 4.4 million pay-per-view buys and a revenue of $400 million.

At UFC 194 McGregor had beaten Jose Aldo knocking him out in 13 seconds and earning $500,000. Adding to that the 1.2 million pay-per-view buys he reportedly banked $8 million in total. In the much anticipated UFC 196 when he was facing Nate Diaz, pay-per-view revenues poured in, a million and half buys, totally eclipsing the UFC 194 numbers. McGregor became the first ever UFC fighter to earn a million-dollar purse. According to sources $5-plus for each buy he received reportedly earned him over $8 million in total for the bout. Each buy was sold at $50 or $55. Something else that needs to be taken into account, as far as the financial figures are concerned, is that certain sponsorships and post-fight bonuses, are not publicly disclosed. I had always heard Dana White talking robustly about how the UFC broke the record. 'We just broke the record,' he would announce ebulliently at post-fight press conferences. Without a question his savvy marketing skills has contributed to the organisation's immense success.

Just as stars Randy Couture and Chuck Liddell had helped propel the sport into the mainstream prior to McGregor's emergence, this UFC champion was now the new superstar surpassing his predecessors. Every now and again someone comes in to a sport and

OLD SCHOOL MEETS NEW

changes things for the better, stands out from the rest and is just intoxicating to watch. McGregor has done something that no other UFC fighter has done. This fighter was asking for a stake in the UFC now. He generated millions of dollars for this sports organisation, so much money that he, being an astute businessman, felt he should have a cut of the profits. Undeniably McGregor had taken the whole sport into another dimension.

At UFC 196 at the MGM Grand Garden Arena McGregor, on a 15-fight winning streak, faced one of the biggest tests of his career. For Nate this was his biggest fight at that point of time. Nate tried countering McGregor at every opportunity. McGregor was aggressive from the word go and looked strong. With forty seconds left in the first round, Nate took McGregor down by catching his leg as McGregor shot a right kick to the midsection. However McGregor got into the guard position quickly and tried to get some ground-and-pound in as his opponent was by the fence, before the round ended. In round two McGregor, throughout the aggressor, continued with his explosive spinning back kicks as he did with his fists. Nate's eye had blood running down as his adversary's shots scored, busting open the cut. He was keeping busy with his jabs and the rear hand cross while sneaking in uppercuts when he could – particularly the left-hand uppercut. Also using various kicks and front hand bate it to try to close the distance. McGregor used good head movement. With two minutes and 20 seconds to go, Nate caught him with a left straight to the face, hurting him, and a couple of effective punches, eventually getting into the clinch on the fence. Then, as the fighters broke away, both connected showing aggression. McGregor shot for a double-leg takedown. Nate defended with a sprawl. Both fighters on the ground, Nate managed to get on top mounting 'The Notorious'. After several left-rights ground-and-pound, which forced McGregor to turn over leaving his back open prone to a submission, Nate had an opportunity – a smooth transition – to apply the classic choke with 48 seconds left on the clock. 'The Notorious' tasted his first ever defeat in the UFC.

TO THE TOP

In the post-fight interview McGregor was humble in defeat. 'I'm humble in victory or defeat, I respect Nate came in and took the fight at short notice and came in at 170 (pounds) and done the job. He was efficient, I wasn't efficient, that's how I feel.' He said he'd face it like a man and come back and do it again by prevailing. He admitted that his adversary could take a hell of a shot, and both brothers can take shots and persevere. 'I was relishing the opportunity to step into there and fight Nate.' Nate felt he was the superior striker, martial artist and jiu-jitsu specialist. He had access to some of the top sparring partners in all aspects of the game.

McGregor's defeat to Nate was perceived as a catastrophe for the UFC promotion. It sent shockwaves. I, along with countless others, started to wonder if the defeat would have a disastrous effect on box-office takings at the UFC. McGregor engaged in two epic battles with Nate Diaz. As the much anticipated rematch at UFC 202 approached, McGregor's wallet was to get a lot fatter. This time around he would be pulling in a record purse of $3 million, taking his total earnings for this bout to $10 million, taking into account the 1.2 to 1.5 million pay-per-view buys. He was back!

CHAPTER THIRTY-THREE

CHALLENGING CONOR McGREGOR

THESE DAYS, Conor McGregor is such a massive name that any fighter who attaches his name to 'The Notorious' naturally attracts attention. Challenges to him weren't surprising, but one in particular caught my attention. A month ahead of McGregor's rematch with Nate Diaz on 20 August 2016, the boxing sensation Amir Khan threw a challenge out stating that he would be willing to face the UFC champion in the Octagon. When asked about how he would do against McGregor and whether he was serious, he told one interviewer, 'I was serious about that MMA fight ... going into MMA for me would not be a problem.' He continued his claims in another interview, boasting that, 'A good boxer will always win an MMA fight. I've always said that.' It was a sentiment that I, and many others, didn't share.

Ever since the advent of the UFC, I've been interested in how boxing champions perceive the UFC and its warriors. After Amir won the Olympic silver medal and turned professional, he borrowed my Royce Gracie DVDs through a mutual friend, including the first five UFCs when Royce fought back in the 1990s and there were no gloves, rules, time limits or weight divisions. The feedback I received was that Amir immensely enjoyed watching Royce and the early UFC fights. I was sceptical at first, but my contact was insistent.

Many years later, I sent Amir a video of Mike Tyson paying homage to the Gracies. This time, it was my way of shoving Royce in his face. 'I am a chairman of SFL – the Super Fight League,' he messaged me back. He went on to explain that he was part owner of an MMA organisation in India, claiming it was the third largest MMA promotion after the UFC and Bellator. 'We do shows in India, Dubai and are now signing a deal in USA – 50-plus events in the year,' the boxer enthusiastically bragged. Sure enough, SFL is an MMA fight promotion headed by a business tycoon, Bill Dosanjh, who Amir partnered up with in 2012. Its primary intent is to give MMA fighters in India a platform to compete, in addition to attracting fighters from other parts of the globe.

At first I was somewhat surprised that Amir would be promoting MMA or getting involved. But since he seemed to have embraced the 'enemy' sport, I asked him if I should ask my friend Royce Gracie if the UFC icon would be interested in making appearances in India. It would be a great way to promote SFL and MMA, I told him, and Amir essentially said OK.

I rang Royce, and he was enthusiastic, but I wasn't going to stop there. I advised Amir that for the league to really prosper, it was imperative to bring in some of the biggest names from America, such as Randy Couture, Royce and others, as brand ambassadors. These were UFC champions who had pioneered the sport, and were readily recognisable, despite some of them being retired. I felt that if the league promoted itself with globally recognised names and pioneers of the sport from America, then his MMA adventure had a prospect of really making waves. Sadly, it turned out that this would go into one ear and out of the other. Sometimes I don't know why I even bother.

I sense that Amir's interest in MMA gravitates towards the financial side of things. He's been ramping up his business interests, and, like astute professional athletes, he's going the right way about it as his career wanes. Bankruptcy is not an uncommon scenario for world champion boxers – or other sports and entertainment personalities – who retire only to find themselves in dire financial straits. At the highest level, boxers can earn millions in a fight and accumulate tens of millions during the course of their career, and in the case of Mike Tyson several hundred million; Mayweather is on the south side of a billion. But these men are the exception, and even some of them find themselves in trouble with the taxman as their earning power fades.

Thomas Hearns is among the many world champions who have walked the bankruptcy route. Once I left a message for him to call me, and later I was out with some friends in the car and my phone rang. The 'Hitman' was on the other end of the line. I told him I wanted to interview him for the magazine, but since I was out I'd call him back at a better time. I don't think he was doing much with the media because of his financial situation, and I felt bad for him.

I'm a firm advocate of sports athletes and entertainment artistes investing in business ventures. It is estimated that 78 per cent of NFL players end up broke within two years of retirement, and 60 per cent of NBA players end up broke within five years of retirement. Financial difficulties can force athletes to resort to desperate measures. I'm familiar with both the risks and rewards, as over the years some ill-fated choices and a bit of bad luck have put me in dire financial straits. I invested in a couple of diverse business ventures as sidelines while I continued to focus on my combat sports business and professional writing career, and unfortunately the sideline businesses failed after a couple of years.

Let me make this clear, India runs on large numbers. Its movie industry thrives because the country has over 1.3 billion people, so if you make a popular film you're going to sell a ton of tickets. With this in mind, it's my belief that Amir the entrepreneur couldn't refuse a lucrative offer to set-up shop there. I can assure you that if India had, let's say, a population of 70 million, its movie industry would never have taken off to the extent it has in terms of popularity. It's a poor country but numbers and masses make up for it.

Still, it was perfect timing for Amir because even Bollywood took a shine to MMA. Actor Akshay Kumar had recently starred in a movie called *Brothers*, which became the first Bollywood MMA movie. This was a huge platform to really promote MMA and the public's awareness of this controversial sport. Akshay has been a long-life martial arts exponent, and before venturing into acting he actually taught martial arts.

After conferring with Amir, I phoned his management team to have a chat about the SFL and see if I could possibly be of assistance. But I was, I felt, snubbed in my efforts to offer guidance. After a phone call to his management, we were going nowhere. This individual told me that the SFL fights in India and Dubai were, in his own words, 'crap'. Not surprisingly, I was never provided with a contact for the main man behind this MMA promotion. Eventually I made contact myself, but there was no response. These guys were running an MMA league, but I wondered if they were going the right way about it. I was merely trying to help out, because of my vast behind-the-scenes experience in the MMA world. But sometimes if someone doesn't want your help, you have to step back, and step back I did.

Nevertheless, I decided to do a short profile piece in *MMA Uncaged* magazine about the SFL. I sent it to Amir when it hit the newsstands and he thanked me for the piece. Amir has never granted me an interview, nor did the management ever arrange one. Once, I messaged Amir explaining that someone who was working on one of his projects wanted me to see if I could interview him to promote his own project. I was reluctant to request an interview, but proceeded nevertheless because the individual who had asked me is actually a friend. I was stunned when Amir gave me the silent treatment. I just couldn't put my finger on what I had done, if anything, because I had never made disparaging comments about him in the press. In fact, I never did any press with him or on him. Having said that, I went on to conduct pre-fight interviews with some of his opponents – Phil Greco, Samuel Vargas and Terence Crawford – but Amir Khan the man never seemed to give me access. From that debacle on, I just kept my distance.

What does Amir think of the sport of MMA? My friend Sandy Holt, a former Thai-boxing champion, told me that Amir had come down into his gym and done a session on the pads and even the warm-up that the others were doing. Sandy was impressed with Amir's use of Thai pads using combination punches, and his accuracy was phenomenal despite not having really used this type of pad before. Amir had always said that he was first and foremost a boxer and that MMA was another game.

Anyway, following the SFL situation, Amir floated a potential crossover to MMA by challenging McGregor. When I first heard this 'shocking' news, I instantly knew it was contrived, nothing but a way to drum up publicity for his MMA League in India. It was a desperate scramble, I believe, to breathe back some life into his venture. It's all part of a trend – recently combat sports have gravitated towards WWE-style promotion and have become circuses. It's a tired old routine. The fighters know that they are never going to fight each other, but resort to bullshit hype anyway, sending the media and fans in to a frenzy, and deceiving the fans.

Anyway, I wasted no time in picking up the phone and speaking to Royce – always readily available to me – to get his views surrounding this latest round of hype, which, frankly, I had had enough of. 'Recently it's been in the news that Amir Khan, the boxer, is willing to face Conor McGregor in the Octagon,' I said to Royce. 'Do you feel it's merely another publicity stunt?' Royce, surprisingly, was in favour of the boxer pursuing the sport he had pioneered. 'I'm glad that Amir Khan is thinking about the transition,' Royce said. 'And if he learns some grappling – he's got very good hands and power – then he can do it. Anybody can do MMA, you just have to train for it.'

Next, I asked Royce how long it would take for someone of Amir's calibre to prevail, because grappling is very intricate – you can't pick it up in three months. What advice was he willing to give the boxer on a quest to capitalise on MMA? 'If there is a good teacher out there that can teach him, he's a professional athlete, he could pick it up very fast,' he replied. 'So if he puts his mind into it, he can do it. It's hard to give a timeframe but it's doable.' Despite Royce's optimistic views, he said that, although in a boxing match he'd put his money on Amir against McGregor, in an MMA fight it would be a totally different ball game. 'Amir Khan right now wouldn't stand a chance against McGregor, sorry,' the Brazilian jiu-jitsu legend told me. 'Not in an MMA match. But, having said that, anything can happen; there's only one way to find out.'

Once again, Royce emphasised that there is a big difference between these two sports. 'If you make a karate fighter fight tae kwon do rules or fight boxing rules, or a boxer fight tae kwon do rules, it's totally different, man.' Was it beyond the realm of possibility that Amir would really face someone like McGregor? Well, I knew Amir would never step into the Octagon. Nevertheless the boxing champion achieved his objective, linking his name with the number-one UFC star.

* * *

I remember watching the 2004 Olympics, one of the first times a Pakistani athlete from Britain was given great media exposure. At 17, Amir was the only boxer representing his nation. Not only did this kid qualify for the Olympics, but he was fighting adults and beating them up. Seventeen is a relatively very young age. You're still at transitioning into an adult, and don't always have the strength, power and the maturity you'll develop as soon as you leave your teens. So I thought that was a brave thing to do. And, of course, no Asian in Britain ever imagined that we would have an Asian athlete who would rise to prominence and be catapulted to fame. After he won a silver medal, the exposure and media attention he garnered was absolutely phenomenal.

As a young British Asian, like many other Asian kids in the community, I grew up dreaming about doing something unexpected and making it big in life. Watching boxers, action movie actors, sportsmen and footballers, I was inspired. I remember watching boxing and soccer on *Sports Night* and *Midweek Sports Special*, seeing the careers of classic fighters like Dennis Andries, Barry McGuigan, Frank Bruno, Terry Marsh, and of course Mike Tyson, gracing my TV screen. Little did I suspect that a young man who grew up with social links to an Asian community, would dedicate himself so relentlessly to the brutal sport that any of us can only dream of prevailing in. Soon he was fighting in MEN Arena, 02 and eventually the MGM in Las Vegas, The Staples Centre in Los Angeles and Madison Square Garden in New York. It was surreal. While most young Asians were acting tough, some being hard-men wannabe gangsters influenced by rap stars fulfilling their own fantasies, Amir was fighting for real in the ring with some of the best in the professional arena. Boxing is a hardcore contact sport. If you merely have a big mouth, you won't cut it in the ring. You need to be able to do the business and leave the talking outside.

I guess it's inevitable that when someone such as Amir prevails, some people from his own community will resort to making derogatory comments. That's human nature. Unfortunately, Asians seem willing to take it to the next level. These armchair experts couldn't get into the ring to save their lives, but they were willing to talk down to an Olympic hero. Well, talk is cheap, we can all talk and we love to criticise others, especially those are better than us, who have made it and who are adored – but I can't condone it. It's a sad fact of life.

If you grew up as an Asian in the United Kingdom, you could probably relate to the sport Amir triumphed in – fighting. He had pursued something diligently, instead of sitting at home in front of his friends acting tough and trying to be Mr Popular, and made the best of himself. Stepping out of that comfort zone and competing with people in the real, the big world, is something that most people are afraid of. And so, I strongly believe that Amir has influenced the Asian community in his country. The interest that the Asian community has in boxing has grown because of this athlete. Now, you have young boys who visit the boxing gyms and aspire to become boxers. They watch and follow the sport more. He catapulted the whole thing to new heights.

What also impressed me about Amir is the fact that he is a very humble and down-to-earth individual. As I learned in life, the road to success humbles the top champions and Amir epitomises this – contrary to some people's perception of his public persona. As a journalist who has worked with professional athletes, I have the ability to switch on a kind of 'attitude radar'. I've worked with enough famous people to discern their personalities. Many people apparently get the wrong impression of Amir, but trust me when I say he hasn't let fame get to his head. This is essentially my impression of him. I always say that if you were in that position, you'd be subjected to the same negativity chucked at you like dirty mud, too. No one talks about a nobody; everyone talks about someone who is a somebody. From what I have seen, by and large, Amir has endeavoured to be accommodating when it comes to his fans. He rarely refuses to have a photo taken and is a very approachable guy. Actually, comparatively, he's more accessible than most celebrities. But some from the Asian public expect him to come up to all of them like he owes them something. He doesn't owe you anything.

I would like to state, by the way, that Amir is not a friend of mine and never has been, unlike some top personalities in the combat sports world. Despite the fact I'm a sports journalist, I don't feel he owes me anything, either. The key is to control your ego.

* * *

While McGregor was being needled by a boxer for all the wrong reasons, 'The Notorious' had more serious things to contend to – like his own fighting career. Before his upcoming rematch with Nate Diaz I approached McGregor via his representative to talk to him about the fight and the Irish sensation's life so far. 'At the moment we are not doing much media with him but I'll keep pushing for you,' was the reply I received from Zach, who was handling the press for McGregor.

Several days before the fight, I thought I'd see if I could still nail things down. Zach got back to me saying, 'Fiaz, I really have no good timeline for you. Conor is in fight mode and I won't approach him about media considerations [given] the amount of obligations he already has with the UFC. What I might try is getting you on one of the international media calls he has to do this week. Could that work?' It was understandable. A star of his calibre was certain to be inundated with requests, but fight night was round the corner and it's crucial for a fighter to keep his mind on the job at hand. I told Zach, 'I totally understand and I think since Conor is in fight mode let's leave it until sometime after the fight when he's more relaxed and the fight is out of the way.' It wasn't till several years later that I connected directly with McGregor's agent Audie, who, I must admit, is a very friendly individual – despite managing one of the biggest sports stars, he makes time for me.

Since I was already thinking about talking to some of the big UFC names, and McGregor wasn't available, Daniel Cormier was the next guy that came to mind. He is managed by agents who I had dealt with for many years, who represented Chuck Liddell and Forrest Griffin. Heidi was always nice and happy to sort out interviews out for me with her star talent, so I got in touch and soon enough she had me on the phone to the UFC light-heavyweight champion. He had earned a decision over Anderson Silva five months earlier, and was happy to talk. 'How do you control fear being a professional fighter when you step in to the Octagon?' I asked once we were into the swing of the conversation, mindful of the terrifying adversaries he'd faced.

'I wouldn't necessarily call it "fear",' he replied. 'I would call it "nerves".' In fact, Daniel proclaimed that he feared nothing and no one. 'When it comes to another human being, I don't fear any man. It makes no difference.' Sometimes, for sure, a fighter feels too relaxed. Any combatant needs to feel some nerves because it's a natural human instinct. Indeed, when the fighter is in the dressing room getting ready to fight, in psych-up mode, his hairs start to stand up, and he's cognisant that he's nervous because he's ready to compete. But when Daniel walks into the Octagon, he says, it's an opportunity to represent his team, his coaches, his management, his family and everybody that has invested in his long, up to 12-week, training camp. 'It's a relief when I walk up those steps,' he told me. 'I do get those competitive nerves and if I don't then I start to worry a little bit. But I've never really felt fear.'

In the fight game a lot goes on behind the scenes that the audience is oblivious to. Certain fighters, be it for personal reasons to drum up publicity for a fight or just plain disdain for each other, do get into verbal and on rare occasions physical altercations. Daniel's not immune to this, so I asked him if he was willing to share any behind-the-scenes stories about things escalating. 'You know, I work not only as a fighter but also in the broadcast side of things,' he told me, before going on to say that he gets to watch and see a lot of things behind the scenes that most of us know nothing about. As it happened, he explained, Dominick Cruz and Cody Garbrandt, who were to fight at the end of the year, ran into each other when Cody was about to fight Takeya Mizugaki at UFC 202 in Las Vegas. Daniel and Dominick were actually doing co-commentary right next to the Octagon, and both Dominick and Cody came face to face as the latter walked passed. 'Cody is in a nice suit and Dominick is in a nice suit,' Daniel told me. 'And these guys are in each other's faces now. All of our bosses from the UFC and the TV bosses are there, but no one knew what to do. Everyone just kind of stood back because it escalated to the point that I had to get in the middle and go there and separate those two guys.' If it wasn't for Daniel at UFC 202, Dominick and Cody would've fought in August, according to Daniel, because none of the UFC bosses and TV crew were willing to actually get in the middle of these two 135-pound men with their adrenaline pumping. 'I thought that was funny because these aren't little guys back there backstage,' Daniel told me. 'But they all stood there with their hands in their pockets not sure how to break it up and stop the fight. And I ended up stopping it. I actually made them wait for UFC 207.'

An aside here: several months after I spoke to Daniel, I had dinner with Dominick when I was in Las Vegas to discuss potentially working with him. I found him to be a very intelligent fighter, very articulate. He was very inquisitive, and you had to have the right answers for him, or he'd pull you up on what you said. He isn't an easy one to convince. He knows what he wants and how to go and get it. Is he a little hot-headed? Sure. But he's no idiot.

I asked Daniel about his own rivalry with Jon Jones. 'Obviously between you and Jon Jones there has been a well-publicised feud,' I said. 'Do you feel you can hang on to the belt until you retire or is your worst nightmare coming for you?' Daniel was brimming with confidence. 'Sure, Jon will be coming to fight me to try to claim the championship, but I'm going to be here afterwards,' he said. 'I'm champion until I retire and then correct the wrong from the 3rd of January 2015.' He told me with great conviction that he would retire as champion, but also that it wasn't a pre-requisite to beat Jon Jones to be content with what he'd achieved. Nevertheless, Daniel felt he needed to be there as the champion when his nemesis returned, and was planning on beating him.

Another interviewer had asked Jon if competing in a grappling match with Daniel would be of interest, but Jon remarked that he wouldn't entertain such an opportunity, that he would rather meet Daniel in the Octagon where he could punish him for real. 'Would you ever consider a grappling match with Jones?' I asked Daniel, curious as to his take. 'I would prefer to fight him in a cage,' he said. 'I would grapple him. I would wrestle him. I would play basketball against him. I will swim against him. I will play baseball against him, it does not matter. I just want the opportunity to beat him in every sense and in every thing, in every competitive field there is in this world. So, I'll wrestle him, I'll fight him, box him, kickbox him. I would do all that. Every competition avenue there is. I want to beat him in every single aspect of life.'

Another thing fans will know about Daniel is that he looks more on the chubby side than a typical UFC champion. 'How important is endurance and stamina for an MMA athlete?' I asked him, with the hope of him revealing his training regime. Cardio, he told me, is the most important element of his preparation, and he doesn't care how he looks. 'You can look like an Adonis, but if you cannot endure the pain in the ring then you're going to get dropped,' he said. 'I mean, a number of guys that I've fought they were aesthetically better than I am, but when it's time to fight I've got the cardio. I can push. I'm durable and I can actually take those guys into deep water where they fall. So cardio and endurance are the most important things.' Much of Daniel's training, then, is based around cardio. Even if he was unable to develop an admirable physique, his entire team was focused on getting him to the Octagon in perfect shape to fight. He is a guy some can't help but admire.

CHAPTER THIRTY-FOUR

TOUGH MAN TALES

AT THE end of 2016, there was another huge fight on my calendar. Dan Henderson, who I had met when I was at an event with Randy Couture in St Louis, was set to fight Mike Bisping at UFC 204 on 9 October. Dan came across as a nice guy and a man of few words, but he was a veteran of the Pride Fighting Championships, and a veteran of the sport, and used to taking on tough opponents outside his weight class. Everyone knew it would be good.

The fight was taking place at the MEN Arena in Manchester. I attended the media press conference, where we had the opportunity to interview the fighters. I bumped into my friend Karl Tanswell, who had a fighter on the card. I've always done exclusive interviews, but this time I didn't get the opportunity. Instead, I asked Mike several questions as other journalists flocked around him. The media day was OK, and more of a day out than anything. I was looking forward to being ringside. Press conferences are often fairly interesting, but at other times, if I'm honest, can be mundane.

The night of the fight, the arena was absolutely packed with a raucous crowd, most of them cheering on the home favourite as he came in to his signature theme music. Dan had looked solid as a fighter in his training, and looked focused on his walk to the ring. He is a classic wrestler, forged over years of arduous training and conditioning and thousands of rounds on the mat, but he's also a dangerous striker with one killer weapon. His favourite attack, where he would lead with a left low round kick and immediately follow up with the heavy right hand he was known for – all pretty much in one motion – was dubbed the 'H-bomb' by fans, as if you were hit with it, you were probably done. Dan's hands were as dangerous as any other fighter, and it goes without saying that the calibre of his wrestling was Olympic level. He was a dangerous fighter and Mike knew it.

Mike wanted to avenge his crushing defeat at UFC 100 when Dan had scored a devastating knockout using that big right hand, followed up with a diving forearm to the unconscious Bisping that the ref was too late to stop. The rivalry had never really stopped, as people never failed to send video clips of the knockout to Mike on social media. Now their rivalry had reached fever pitch and it was a fight the fans craved. It was also a very important fight for Mike because he was going to be defending his belt – a title which had eluded him for a long time – in the highly anticipated rematch. This was an opportunity for the Brit to prove that he could prevail against his former nemesis in the Octagon. Mike never needed motivation to come in top shape, but for this fight I knew he'd thrown himself whole-heartedly into his training, to ensure no stone was left unturned in the preparation process.

Thinking about it now I recall the electricity of the arena, which kept me on my toes as I sat and then stood ringside waiting to see how the fight would unfold. I, of course, was gunning for Mike, personally speaking. You can't applaud or root for either fighter out loud in the UFC press box, but I knew who I was hoping would win.

Dan was booed on his entrance, but came out looking strong. Every time Dan resorted to his low kick-right hand strategy, which I'm sure Mike had well scouted out, I felt a twinge of nerves. Hendo landed his trademark H-bomb in the very first round, sending Mike to the canvas and bringing the crowd to its feet in support, as Mike somehow managed to get up. Mike already had a bad eye from a previous fight, and now the other eye was severely swollen, something that seemed to be affecting his vision. Still, he put on a show, outpointing the wrestler despite being cracked with another H-bomb later in the bout. Dan started to look gassed. He hadn't fought beyond a third round in five years, and this was a five-round title fight, and when he was accidentally hit with a low blow, took the opportunity to recover. The fight was gritty and both men put on a show that would be entrenched in my head forever as one of my best experiences ringside at a UFC fight.

Dan lost a decision, but I think it could've gone either way, to be honest. Both men had put on a superb performance. Mike's face was bruised up and bloodied, while his adversary's face was more or less intact, but the Brit was victorious. Gracious in victory, the champ told the crowd to give it up for his adversary and sure enough a chant of 'Hendo!' for the retiring all-time great nearly lifted the roof off the arena. It was the best possible end to an all-time rivalry.

* * *

Working in the world of sports, I have been extremely fortunate to make some lifelong friends – from the martial arts world in particular. One of my good friends is 'Big' Joe Egan. In case you aren't aware of Joe, his claim to fame is he was Mike Tyson's sparring partner for two years, and all that time Tyson never was able to knock him down – not once. This is when Tyson was up and coming and before he was crowned the heavyweight champion of the world in the mid-1980s. Joe, a former Golden Gloves Champion, had left Ireland to live at the famous Catskill training camp with the then young Tyson in New York in 1983. That's more than 37 years of friendship there. And I'm not surprised that they got on for so long. One thing that strikes you instantly about this Irishman is his amazingly affable personality; you just can't help but instantly develop an affinity for him.

Before I met Joe for the first time in 2010, I wasn't sure how approachable this monster of a man was going to be. He had a frame wider than most big men and when you set your eyes on him you were instantly in awe. His figure resembled the body of the bare-knuckle street-fighting legend Lenny McLean, but, as they say, appearances can be deceiving. Well, when we met, Joe greeted me like he had known me all his life. His welcoming attitude put me at ease immediately. I thought, *What a great guy.* He had loads of charisma, charm by the bucket load, and was polite from the off. We had swapped numbers and have been good friends ever since.

Apart from the fact that this larger-than-life character makes you feel on top of the world, he is extremely humble. If you ask anyone who knows him, you'd be hard pressed to find anyone murmur a bad word about him. But you'll also be hard pressed to hear him say anything derogatory about anyone else. A man so completely devoid of ego, any hidden agendas or negative energy, seems like he should be more or less non-existent, but there he is, larger than life. As a mark of how well liked he is, when Joe released his autobiography, Tyson, who wrote the foreword, personally took time out from his busy schedule and jetted into the United Kingdom to support his friend in front of 5,000 people at Canary Wharf.

Not surprisingly, Joe has a profound passion for combat sports, including the UFC and martial arts. 'I like to see two men get in the ring and fight,' he once told me. 'But I like them to be trained fighters.' Joe's not an advocate of violence outside the ring. Like many of the toughest men and longest-lived world champions in the professional fight game, Joe is a good role model. Fighting, Joe believes, first and foremost gives you self respect and it gives you respect for your opponent. You can play soccer, basketball or tennis, but you don't play fighting; fighting isn't a game. He admires courage, and it takes a lot of courage to get into an organised fight, no matter what discipline you choose. It's not like having a cheap pop at someone in a bar or the street. In the Octagon, of course, there's a combination of all forms of fighting, which Joe loves. 'Years ago a question that always got thrown around was, "Can a kick-boxer beat the boxer? Can the judo man beat the karate man?" Joe said to me, once. 'And now, all forms of fighting have come together to make the complete fighter.'

Of course, I wanted to pick Joe's brain and learn more about his vicious sparring partner – whether he ever saw fear in his eyes, for example, as I had heard that Tyson used to be very fearful in the dressing room before a bout, and as their boxing coach Cus D'Amato used to say, 'There's a very fine line between the coward and the hero.' That walk to the ring and the waiting around before you get into the ring is very daunting for any fighter. Once the bell goes, sure, the fear leaves you because it's time to fight. But the build-up, the walk to the cage or ring? It's very, very emotional, because you have all sorts of thoughts going on in your head. You don't think about losing; you just don't want to let yourself down. You want to give a good performance. If you give your best and you lose, then you've done all you can. Tyson, Joe told me, felt this way as much as anyone. 'He'd say, "Did I do enough? Have I done enough? Has my opponent done more?"' Joe told me. 'Mike's a human being, he's not a machine. He had the same emotions that his opponent had.'

What Tyson did have over his opponents was the fear factor he carried, based on his apparent invincibility and devastating power. When you've got the concussive power in your punch, everyone's afraid of you, and Tyson had that aura of destructiveness about him throughout his early career. He would fix you with an unwavering stare in the ring, and not everyone could cope. There are two ways to look at the word FEAR, Joe told me: you can 'Face Everything And Rise', or you can 'Forget Everything And Run'.

Frank Bruno was once asked about his first ever experience with Tyson, and his answer stuck with me: 'I remember Mike being a savage, aggressive and violent animal, attacking me in the ring.' He was referring to when he first sparred with the notorious heavyweight, when Tyson was only 15 and Frank was 20. Both men went on to battle it out for real in the ring twice, and Tyson was just too much for Frank, beating him on both occasions. As for Joe, he has been humble enough to admit that the heavyweight champion made him cry often. Their sparring sessions were brutal and barbaric. Tyson, apparently, could often reduce grown men to tears. I once asked Joe what strategy he would implement against the ferocious Tyson when sparring. He said you had to keep your hands up, if you dropped your guard Tyson was so rapid he would take advantage of the smallest opening and nail you with his terrifying combinations.

Hearing Joe talking, I had a newfound admiration for Tyson, but also for his sparring partner, who'd got in the ring with this most feared of fighters on multiple occasions. I thought I was hungry, motivated and crazy, but having known Joe for many years I think he beat me to the gold medal for being crazily ambitious. His drive and motivation are second to none. These days, Joe's phonebook is full of famous celebrity friends from the sports, acting and entertainment worlds. Now he's an actor, with credits including *Sherlock Holmes I* and *II*, and is having a great life.

* * *

In the late 1980s and 1990s Joe and Tyson had the pleasure of spending some time with Donald Trump. Trump, of course, owned casinos in Atlantic City where he put on a lot of boxing events – he enjoyed attending bouts, and has many friends from the boxing fraternity. Joe first met Trump in New York, where Tyson had an apartment in Trump Tower, on Fifth Avenue in Manhattan.

On the many occasions that Joe was in the company of Trump, he found him to be very personable, he told me. 'I'm Irish and he had a lot of time for the Irish because he believes that the Irish contributed immensely to building America,' he said. 'The Irish were the forefathers of early American settlers. They came in boat loads and they built America. There were lots of other white Americans – Germans, English and others – but the Irish, in particular, were people that Donald seemed to have an affinity towards. I had a few conversations with him about this because I'm Irish.' Trump was well aware of the Irish history of the boxers, too. Ireland has always had a history of producing great fighters and Trump was familiar with some of the Irish greats. They spoke about Barry McGuigan. 'Mike Tyson was a big fan of Barry, too,' Joe recalled. 'I spoke to Donald about Barry because Barry was renowned all over the world. He was an ambassador for Ireland in boxing. Irish boxers are legendary because we wear our heart on our sleeves.'

He said Trump had an absolutely delightful personality. There were no airs and graces about him. Despite being a billionaire, Joe said Trump didn't have that aura so typical of rich men, *Oh, no, you can't approach me because I'm so rich and powerful.* 'I'm sure, him landing the job of president of America he'd still have the same attitude that he had every time that I was in his company,' Joe told me. 'He'll enjoy shaking hands with ordinary people, people who voted for him and even those who voted against him.' Joe said with great conviction that Trump would be successful in his quest to make America great.

I wanted to discover if Trump's and Tyson's relationship was merely business related or personal. Unfortunately Joe wasn't privy to any business talk between the two. Most of the times that Joe was in the company of Trump there was, he said, fun and laughter. 'Mike was a young man and Donald was young at heart,' he said. 'I think he has an awful lot of affection for Mike Tyson as a friend.'

Trump, of course, has made headlines ever since coming into the political spotlight. His derogatory remarks about Muslims even prompted Muhammad Ali's family to respond with a statement, which I mentioned in an earlier chapter and discussed with Ali's daughter. Speaking with Joe, I wondered aloud if the public's perception – and even the media's – of the president was somewhat distorted. 'Let me tell you something now,' Joe said. 'I've got a lot of Muslim friends – you're my good friend. It's like the Irish: you can't judge the Irish on the IRA. The IRA is a small minority of the Irish. It's same with the ISIS and the Taliban, who are a very small minority of the Muslim population.'

Joe went on to say that you can't tar all Muslim people with the same brush. There are a lot of wonderful Muslim people. 'I'm sure Donald's got a lot of Muslim friends as well. It's just unfortunate that his views are over a minority of Muslim people America is at war with.'

Trump would have sanctioned the UFC after it first debuted in America, according to Joe, when it was abhorred by the political fraternity. Trump enjoys the sweet science, so Joe doesn't see any reason why he wouldn't have enjoyed the UFC back then, and done his best to make it legal and a legitimate sport. Personally, I feel he would have had a big fight on his hands in the bare-knuckle days – but who knows? Let's put it this way: Trump would have sanctioned UFC much earlier than it eventually got embraced.

'He's a man!' Joe said of Trump. 'He's been a fighter all his life, you know, in business. So he admires the physical prowess of fighters as well.' Trump's great resilience is apparent in business, Joe said, and the fact that he ignored those people who dismissed him when he put himself forward for president of America shows you the strength of character and willpower of this man who fought all the way to the White House.

Being an ardent fan of the sweet science, Trump actually went as far as to get involved in MMA by having a hand in the now-defunct Affliction MMA promotion, a direct competitor to the UFC. At the time, Trump declared, 'It's really something that I'm doing because I enjoy doing it. If we make money, that's great. I think we will. I think it will be successful.' On the flipside, Trump, who had a significant equity stake in the business, once went on Howard Stern's radio show only to embarrass himself by exposing his lack of knowledge about the game. He didn't even know the surname of the organisation's number-one fighter Fedor Emalianenko, who was widely considered the greatest MMA fighter. All this talk was, of course, just before Trump became president and caused turmoil.

CHAPTER THIRTY-FIVE

NOTORIOUS

BEFORE THE UFC gladiators first graced the Octagon, back in the early 1990s, another violent phenomenon had emerged from obscurity in the form of bare-knuckle boxing. With the mainstream press suddenly offering exposure to this underground movement, the street-fighting brawlers who participated in its bouts became instant celebrities. Suddenly the life stories of these once-unknown fighters were on bookshelves, and the men themselves were doing interviews and appearing in films. Notorious figures Lenny McLean, Roy Shaw, and other hard men, many associated with true crime, unexpectedly found themselves on the *Sunday Times* bestseller list.

What was so striking about these men? What was the appeal and interest? *The Guv'nor* by Lenny McLean, an autobiography released in 1998, was one of the first of its kind, kicking off a whole new genre and meeting with resounding success. It told the life story of Britain's hardest man, an unlicensed bare-knuckle boxing fighter, or should I say 'street fighter' – who once fought and beat the New York Mob's best fighter – then went on to carve a meaningful career in TV and Hollywood films. Though Lenny died around the time of the book's release, the media frenzy was in full force and it was no surprise that it landed on the number-one spot. It reminded me of when Bruce Lee died. After all, Bruce's glossy epic *Enter the*

Dragon was released five weeks after he died and made a global star out of him.

It was fascinating to see how Lenny met with mass appeal – a non-professional fighter who fought in front of a couple of hundred people at a time, not in big arenas with millions more watching on TV. It's safe to say that it was beyond the scope of even Lenny's imagination just how infamous he would become. For me, it would've been a major sin to ignore this movement, given my interest in combat. The careers of these lethal street fighters were something I couldn't ignore.

In the early days of the boom, I remember talking to a major freelance newspaper journalist who had exploited some of these characters, including Lenny, in prominent tabloids. He told me that the editor of a certain red-top giant had great relish for these men and their gritty stories, which was why he ran these articles in the paper. I would soon come to realise that when it came to getting a story or client in the press, a lot of the times it depended on the editor's taste and interest, as well as the level of interest from the public. No matter how much you felt a story was compelling, you could hit a brick wall if the editor wasn't interested. But if you could find one who shared your passion for combat and the martial arts, you could do great things. Personally, I respected martial artists and professional fighters who had their heads screwed on straight. The kind who exuded respect in and out of the ring, abiding by an unwritten code of ethics, and downplaying their hard-man image, were humble and not labelled 'gangsters' as some of the notorious men from the bare-knuckle arena were. But, like everyone else, I was also intrigued by these violent street fighters.

In June 2017 a film, *My Name Is Lenny*, based on Lenny's life was released. And before it, I had the opportunity to interview Lenny's only son Jamie, who offered some rare and compelling insights into his late father and who had been involved in casting the lead before the director came on board. Personally, I actually felt Joe Egan had the perfect size and build to play Lenny, and I'm sure he could've pulled the cockney accent off. Still, the Australian actor by the name of Josh Helman played Lenny and, I must admit, did a commendable job. Josh looked every inch the menacing man Lenny was, pulling off his mannerisms and little nuances to a tee.

Another familiar face played Lenny's most famous rival, Roy 'Pretty Boy' Shaw. Mike Bisping, who had landed roles in several top Hollywood movies, had contacted the producers personally because he wanted to play the part of Lenny's well-known nemesis. Jamie, for his part, was oblivious to the fact that the UFC star had done any acting before. The producers, along with Jamie, sat down and talked about it and scanned some pictures of Roy when he was younger. The resemblance between the two was pretty remarkable, it was concluded.

Another thing in Mike's favour was that he is very comfortable in front of the camera. When the cameras started rolling he was doing 15-hour-day shoots in really unbearable heat, and he manned up and took it. He perfectly brought out the brutality of the character in front of the camera, and did a great job, with only one moment of concern coming when an on-set accident occurred. He had a big fight coming up. Worryingly, Mike was playing the drums in the film's dream sequence scene and cut his finger in the process. Luckily the damage wasn't too bad.

I was very curious to learn about Jamie's take on his father's thoughts on the UFC. It was something that, I believe, would definitely have appealed to the big brawler. When Lenny died, the UFC had been going for almost five years. Of course, it was bare-knuckle and with minimal rules back then. 'Back in those days I think he would probably have struggled,' Jamie said, when I asked him how his father would have done in the Octagon. 'But if it was completely a stand-up game and bare-knuckle he would have done really well.' Lenny was in his mid-40s then, but maybe if he was in his 20s when the sport began he may have taken up the offer to enter the Octagon. At the time, Lenny wasn't that big. He weighed 15st, so he wasn't the huge monster of a man that everyone saw in *Lock, Stock &*

Two Smoking Barrels, when he was over 20st. And despite his heavy frame, Lenny was very fast. His hand speed was just phenomenal. I remember watching a documentary in which he was dressed up in a nice light grey suit in a car showroom and he demonstrated to an up-and-coming bare-knuckle fighter his hand skills, with added head butts thrown in for good measure. He was absolutely terrifying.

'Yeah, he liked it,' Jamie continued. 'We used to watch it on the old VHS tapes when it came out after 1993.' Furthermore, Lenny told his son that UFC was going to be massive as long as they marketed it right. Well, he was right about that.

Would the British brawler have been inclined to learn a more sophisticated art form in the form of grappling? After all, the street fighting he was accustomed to was fairly simple. 'No, I don't think he would have because I can't see him grappling,' Jamie said. 'I think he was very sort of hard to control. I don't think he had the patience to learn the grappling skills; it's a long process.' Lenny had a great tendency to get things over and done with, Jamie told me, his raw physicality and aggression being his greatest assets. Lenny was well aware of the Gracies, though, and I learned that Jamie is cognisant of their history in Brazil. 'Their family was involved in no-holds-barred fighting, but also in learning an art form,' he said. 'Where my dad grew up, it was a very rough place to survive and you didn't have time to learn, you had to learn on the street.'

Coincidently, just over two months earlier, I had asked Royce Gracie his views on how someone such as Lenny, or any other bare-knuckle street brawler, for that matter, would fare in the Octagon he once ruled. Royce said he had never heard of Lenny nor seen his fight, but proceeded to explain, 'If a guy is just a brawler without technique, they wouldn't last long. Sorry, you're comparing a street footballer playing on the pro team. Just because he's great on the street game kicking coconuts and balls around, it doesn't mean he's going to do great on the soccer field. Yes, he's tough, he plays barefoot on the street but that's no way to build the technique to play with the big boys on the main field. The same goes with the street fighter – a guy who is a big street fighter with no technique he might win one or two brawls, but he's not going to stay on the top for a long time.'

Lenny, in later years after he stopped fighting, turned his hands to acting and was a natural, which saw him get paid for belting men onscreen instead. Before *My Name Is Lenny* ever saw daylight, there were plans to make another film with Jason Statham in the lead. It was a potential project with a £10-million budget assigned to it. Jason was really eager to play the part and he had contacted Lenny's son, but the production company went into liquidation, so the deal fell apart. It was five years later that Lenny's life story finally made it on to the big screen. 'My friend was driving Liam Neeson the other day and he was talking about the documentary we did last year,' Jamie told me. 'He told him he was a big fan of my dad's and that he wanted to play the lead in *My Name Is Lenny*.' What these people admire is that Lenny was born on the wrong side of town, and he didn't have an education; he just had to fight for survival. He didn't win the heavyweight title of the world; he won one from the street. He was a unique personality and real-life character.

I was at the red carpet premiere for the movie on 9 June 2017, accompanied by a friend of mine from north London. My friend Mike Bisping was kind enough to do a quick interview with me on the red carpet, as was the lead Josh Helman. Lenny's brother had flown in, all the way from Australia. The actor Nick Moran of *Harry Potter* fame, who was one of the co-stars, I found a little peculiar. When we were having a photograph taken he was giving me odd looks. It was as if he knew me from somewhere, which wasn't possible. He probably mistook me for someone else he may have had a run-in with.

As everyone congregated inside the theatre, I was paying close attention to the crowd. With East End gangsters in their sharp suits, and women dolled up to the nines it was like being at a speakeasy. As for the film, although I enjoyed it, it would've revived Lenny's legacy further had a major studio produced it. A bigger budget and bigger noise would have definitely done Lenny's life the justice he deserved. It's an amazing story of an incredible man. Nevertheless, Lenny McLean is now a legend, with a massive fan base and a cult following. Not bad for a guy who made his name in the underground arena.

* * *

The year 2017 was also one when sporting history was made, as the two biggest stars in combat sports inked a deal to rumble. Conor McGregor had challenged Floyd Mayweather to a super-fight, during a back and forth war of words that had quickly escalated. In the summer I started writing for *The Sun*, becoming a contributing boxing and UFC writer as well as covering showbiz. I also started to contribute to most of the other national papers – the *Sunday Mirror, Daily Star Sunday, Sunday Express, Mail on Sunday, The Independent* – and developed a working relationship with *The Sun*'s sister paper, the *Sunday Times*. I spoke to my sports editor at *The Sun* and threw some names associated with McGregor around to secure some pre-fight exclusives. At this point, I happened to be focusing more on boxing than the UFC. Just before the two went head to head in Las Vegas in August, I had locked down several sparring partners from Team McGregor who were preparing the UFC star for the biggest test of his life. Among them was an Irish boxer by the name of Jay Byrne, who I thought I'd prod for some answers to get an indication of just how McGregor was progressing in his secret training camp.

I asked Jay about the sparring sessions and how the UFC star was transitioning to a hands-only game – whether he was finding it a challenge or naturally adjusting.

'I can't give an awful lot away because we signed a form saying that information will not be dispensed,' Jay told me. I reassured him that I understood, and he revealed that McGregor's most interesting quirk was his ability to throw shots from different angles. That was no secret, but it was interesting to hear it from a sparring partner.

Apparently, McGregor would throw very unorthodox punches, and had a tendency to change his stance an awful lot. Jay also told me that his partner was brimming with confidence in the ring at the training facility, but then, again, confidence is McGregor's middle name. Another distinctive quality McGregor possessed was his conditioning. The man is a pristine athlete, and his conditioning was typically top notch, Jay told me. He was also looking very strong in the gym. McGregor, apparently, wasn't going to cut any corners in his training, though many people expected him to be outclassed. It was an interesting fight. Being primarily a striker McGregor prevailed in fights largely because of his crisp boxing, though he did use kicks to change distance, and was of course used to small gloves. Grappling isn't something he uses a lot, but it's a threat that all strikers have to take seriously. So how hard would it be for him to conquer the square ring?

To investigate further, I managed to lockdown another sparring partner of McGregor's. I asked professional boxer Louis Adolphe what impressed him the most about the UFC champion. 'I like his movement, he's unorthodox and the way he can get behind you,' he told me. 'He had quite a bit of weight behind his hands, a lot more weight behind his hands than I expected, due to his bodyweight being higher than it used to be.' He further went on to compare 'The Notorious' to one of the most famous soccer superstars as far as both status and work ethic goes. 'He's the Cristiano Ronaldo of the fight world, there's no question about it,' Louis told me. 'He doesn't cut corners.'

McGregor was certainly mentally prepared. He has always believed in himself. If you don't believe in yourself then you don't get anywhere in life, and he's the living embodiment of this philosophy. He believes in everything he's going to do. I was told by multiple people that he was certain of the notion that he would beat Floyd Mayweather. Louis, however, backed up a little, conceding, 'He may not, but he believes he's going to do it.'

Perhaps strangely, 'The Notorious' had insisted on not using a boxing coach when preparing for his first ever boxing bout. I was perplexed, but his sparring partner explained the reasoning: Mayweather had fought and beaten Olympic gold medallists, numerous world champions and hall of famers and guys who have been boxing since they were kids, who nobody could really beat. With this in mind, McGregor's preparation for the fight had to be unconventional – a boxing coach would have tried to mould him into a different fighter, tried to teach him to box for ten weeks. McGregor had no delusions about what would happen if he tried to beat Mayweather at his own game. Instead, what McGregor brought to the table was a vision of what he was going to do and a fresh game plan in his mind. The game plan wasn't to outbox Mayweather; McGregor's game plan was do whatever it took, whatever he felt he had to do to beat him. He was ready to rough up the champ, make it into a brawl, and hit him from every angle. When McGregor got into the ring he was hoping not to go 12 rounds. He was going into battle with a great conviction that he could knock Mayweather out well before it reached that point.

Still, for me, it was hard to digest how a man with only MMA experience, even of the calibre of McGregor, would prevail boxing against such a phenomenal pugilist with a spotless record. The only person I spoke to who was really positive about McGregor's chances was revered pugilist Evander Holyfield. Although he conceded that Mayweather was the overwhelming favourite, he also said that McGregor could shock the boxing world. He explained, 'The only way he can have a chance of winning is, for example, if it's a dull fight and Mayweather loses his cool and both swing at the same time and McGregor knocks him down.' When you get in the ring, he told me, one lucky punch is always a possibility.

* * *

Before I made my final prediction, I felt the views of a UFC fighter who had shared the Octagon with McGregor were important to take into account and I found the perfect subject. Eddie Alvarez had fought and lost to McGregor nine months earlier in the historic Madison Square Garden arena at UFC 205. Not only that, but McGregor had put on a boxing clinic against the man who was sometimes known as the 'King of the Underground', at one point putting his hands behind his back to taunt Eddie into throwing a punch.

'Conor has this Muhammad Ali persona, where what he does outside the ring is all part of the show,' I said to him. 'What can you tell me about the experience of fighting him?'

'I think some people think they're not in a fight – they don't treat it as a fight until the day when the actual fight happens,' Eddie said to me. 'For Conor the fight actually begins the first time you meet, whether it's on a press tour or week of the fight; that's when fight will actually begin then for him. All confrontation and the bickering, it will begin the minute he meets you, not in the cage. If you're new to the sport or you don't really understand or you don't deal with the bickering stuff then it can go bad for you. Most of Conor's fights begin way before he enters the ring.'

This made sense, and was reflected in the way McGregor was trash-talking and taunting his opponent – and in its popularity. The McGregor–Mayweather road show caught the attention of the media and public alike. Billed as the biggest fight in history, it generated 4.3 million pay-per-view buys, and $600 million overall. This was no fight, it was an event. As I was doing my own thing surrounding this fight, I remember watching pre-fight press conferences as part of a city to city tour, and, let me tell you, it was cringeworthy – two men trying to upstage each other with Oscar-winning performances. Not surprisingly the public bought it, but I wasn't enamoured with the pre-fight spiel. I know that McGregor's an entertainer, and his trash-talk, psychological warfare and pre-match predictions have often led to comparisons with the late Muhammad Ali. Yes, his success is due in substantial part to his big mouth, and it's an identity he relishes. But will McGregor ever take a political stand in the way Ali has? Time will tell, but I doubt it.

Did the fight live up to the hype? Some certainly think McGregor acquitted himself well, and I think he left many fans surprised. He asserted his physicality landing a few punches on Mayweather in the early rounds, including one uppercut that landed clean. Sure, he lost after gassing out, but the majority of the UFC fans knew the loss wouldn't put a dent in the UFC organisation nor, by and large, McGregor's reputation as a fighter. After all, it wasn't an MMA-rules fight, nor was it a title fight. But there were others who weren't exactly impressed with McGregor's punching ability, and some believed his adversary could have gone for an early knockout had he so desired. I think most commentators knew the fight had been arranged merely for financial gain for both parties, and to fatten the bank accounts of anyone else associated with the event. Had Mayweather lost then that would have been the end of boxing, but I don't think there was a real risk of that happening.

I remember speaking to Muhammad Ali's associates about when he fought the wrestler Antonio Inoki, and how it left a bad taste in the mouth of almost everyone involved. The WBC president actually divulged to me once that he had warned Ali about going ahead with his crazy idea because it would be bad for boxing if he was defeated. Well, that fight was a pantomime, but at least this one seemed real.

Both superstar athletes laughed all the way to the bank, earning huges amounts of money, while a few fans were left dismayed. McGregor, meanwhile, received a mixed response from the fighting fraternity. While some former boxing champions commended him for enduring ten rounds, others had less favourable opinions to offer. What was most frustrating was when the teams tried to start talking up a rematch. It wasn't a fight, I felt, that people would want to watch again. We had seen it all – everything that both men had to offer. These days, I feel the whole thing about a boxer fighting a UFC champion is absurd now – we know that both athletes will triumph in their own arenas. What we learned from this was that such a bout isn't necessarily going to be interesting, unless you want to watch someone be outclassed.

This highly hyped sporting event, something that I had previously thought might not even manifest into reality, undeniably further catapult the UFC superstar's name beyond the confines of the combat sports sphere. Suddenly your average person on the street was aware of Conor McGregor's existence, and this could only be a good sign for the UFC. I've lost count of the number of UFC champions who have since then called out boxers. And even boxers are not shy to get in on the act. But my personal opinion? *No thanks! Never again.*

CHAPTER THIRTY-SIX

MEETING WITH AN UNDERWORLD FIGURE

TALES ABOUT people overcoming insurmountable odds, growing up amid crime or poverty, or having had to fight and finding light at the end of the tunnel are stories that can be deeply personal, candid and shocking at the same time. It's a category many UFC fighters fit perfectly into. Tamer Hassan, an actor with a portfolio of Hollywood blockbusters, is one of those characters, as I learned several months after the McGregor–Mayweather fight. Tamer has appeared on a number of high-profile TV shows, including *Game of Thrones*, which he told me was probably the toughest job he had done. The actor had been used to doing movies in which the talent was treated like luxury, where it was more relaxed and the stars had privileges, but on *Game of Thrones* it was an absolute nightmare. He was half naked, he told me, constantly shooting without even time to have lunch. It was all work, work, work, he said, not only for the actors but for the crew. Furthermore, the writer would be writing as the scenes were being shot. It was just constant, non-stop action. Nevertheless, it was a joy for the hard-man-turned-actor to be part of this series with an ensemble cast; he loved every minute of it.

Tamer's credits are quite impressive, and include an appearance alongside Curtis '50 Cent' Jackson in the crime comedy *Dead Man*

MEETING WITH AN UNDERWORLD FIGURE

Running, and action film *Blood Out,* which starred Val Kilmer and Luke Goss. It was in *Dead Man Running* that Tamer and '50 Cent' first collaborated. '50 Cent', of course, is a music icon, an ex-gangster who started dealing in drugs before he turned a teenager during the 1980s crack epidemic. The man has obviously been through the mill. I mean, he's been shot, he's from the street – all things Tamer could relate to.

Before the music star turned up on set, Alex, the director, flew to New York to meet him to pitch the project and explain his role. It was kind of the beginning of his acting career, and he was very happy to do this gangster flick. Tamer expected him to be hard-spoken, tough, very to the point, very demanding. However, when '50 Cent' turned up and greeted Tamer, shaking hands for the first time, Tamer immediately found the former gangster to be very softly spoken, very in control, very generous and sincere to a fault. A friendship between the two quickly ensued. The Grammy Award-winning musician, according to Tamer, is always willing to learn, doesn't have any ego and is an absolutely wonderful human being.

I'm always up for being treated to interesting anecdotes when it comes to major stars. Besides, '50 Cent's' passion for combat sports is no secret, so I find him fascinating. When he was younger he was a frequent visitor to a boxing gym where he learned the sweet science, and after dabbling in boxing promotion when his career took off, '50 Cent' got involved with MMA. He's currently involved with the second biggest MMA promotion in the world, Bellator. Tamer was brought up and fought on the streets and I asked him what he thought of no-holds-barred fighting and the UFC. 'To be fair with you, being a boxer, I hated the UFC,' he told me. 'Back when I first watched it, it was kind of an undisciplined gladiatorial street fight. And I kind of still have certain reservations about it. For me, to have someone's head on the ground and you're ground-and-pounding them into the canvas, and they can't move – that's not a safe sport.' I was somewhat surprised with the response, but he conceded he now had huge respect for UFC and MMA fighters – especially after the rules changed to make it safer.

The Cypriot was born in the late 1960s in London, so he grew up over the 1970s and 1980s. Back then, London wasn't like it is today – one of the world's most cosmopolitan and culturally diverse cities. It was a very racist society, especially in inner-city areas where the Hassan family grew up, in a tower block council flat. If you were black, Turkish or Irish in those days you were subjected to immense racial abuse.

'I'm 6ft 3in now but back then I was a very short and tubby little Turk kid,' Tamer said. 'The bullying, the racial and physical abuse that we'd get for just walking down the street was horrendous. No one wanted to be your friend.' At the time, there weren't a lot of Turks living in southwest London, so life was isolated for Tamer and his brother and they would get it all the time. The brothers were never fearful, but they weren't big enough to defend themselves as older kids and grown men were nasty to them. For Tamer it was worse, as his own brother used to bully him, too, he told me.

Getting a broken nose, black eye or cut on the arm or leg, was not unusual for Tamer. So to try to change things he had to find his own path. First, his mother encouraged him to take up martial arts. He first took up judo and did well, but it wasn't enough for him to defend himself. He found that it's very difficult to grab someone on their lapel and arm and throw them over your shoulder when you are getting abuse. Next, his mother introduced her young son to a dear friend of hers, who became a kind of second dad to her children. This gentleman took the young boy and his brother under his wing, and both youngsters then pursued boxing by attending All Saint's Boxing Gym in a church hall in New Cross. 'I ended up breaking my brother's nose on the first day there,' recalls Tamer. His new father figure saw potential in the young man and disciplined him, educating him about life and being there for the family as a pillar of support.

MEETING WITH AN UNDERWORLD FIGURE

When he started boxing, little did he know how it would change his life for the better. He recalls the moment he came to understand how respect was earned. 'I won my first fight, then won the second,' Tamer told me. 'As soon as I had several fights and was winning, people started leaving me alone. It was quite funny because in my day all the girls liked the boxers. It was kind of cool to be a boxer at the time.'

It wasn't long before Tamer started building a reputation for himself. Eventually, the bullying and the abuse faded away altogether. 'Those who verbally or physically abuse you, they're actually cowards,' he told me. 'They have a problem with themselves, and I learned that quite quickly because once I started to become a boxer, people showed you respect and became afraid of you.' After a year to 18 months of boxing and competing, there was no more bullying. Quite a lesson for a young man to learn.

* * *

Unlike the gangsters in movies, the real life gangster fraternity, who had an insatiable appetite for violence, had never invoked my interest nor influenced me – especially when a generation of youths seemed to be heavily influenced by such characters. Money, fame, power, sure, these elements are synonymous with gangsters, but I've never been interested in them. In fact, when the movie *Gotti*, based on New York mobster and crime boss John Gotti and starring John Travolta, was released, an interview with Gotti Jnr was arranged for me. I was looking forward to it but it didn't materialise in the end.

There was an exception, though. When a documentary based on the godfather of British crime was set for release I received a message from the same publicist who was responsible for *My Name Is Lenny*, and I was interested to take the interview he suggested. The next thing I knew, I was on a train bound for the capital to meet and chat with the underworld's Freddie Foreman, famous for being the Kray twins' enforcer and hitman. This was going to be an interesting meeting and experience, I thought. Just how interesting, I'd soon find out.

In April 2018 I met the publicist and we rushed to Freddie's flat. The publicist said Freddie would be impressed by the fact I had made an effort to look good in a suit – a good sign, I thought. Freddie, a bespectacled short man, had a cream-coloured short-sleeve polo shirt on, was very welcoming, and greeted me with a warm smile and a handshake. Although in his mid-80s, he looked pretty solid – he looked as good if not better than *Coronation Street* star William Roache who I had the pleasure to interview once, who also looks great despite in his late-80s.

We sat down and Freddie made me feel comfortable. I casually opened up the conversation with the topic of martial arts and UFC. Freddie, I learned, had been a boxer back in the 1940s and 1950s. He talked me through some photos that adorned the wall, including a shot of him as a boxer, and showed me some shorts that actor Stuart Granger had given him with initials engraved on them. He even dined with the Queen Mother back in the day, I was surprised to learn.

Here I was with one of the most feared and notorious men who had been at the heart of London's underworld, and yet you couldn't have found a more perfect gentleman. This was a man who had allegedly been involved with murder and some of the most brutal criminals of his era, but you'd never have known it to look at him. I had always perceived Lenny McLean as kind of mean – his stern demeanour made you tremble in your boots just looking at a photograph of him. I once heard Lenny say that if you're nice to someone, let's say, if you're telling a group of young men, 'Please don't do that', they will take that approach as a weakness. Lenny would always use the hard-nosed approach. I then came to realise why he used the rough approach instead of a milder one, and I think his philosophy was spot on.

With this in mind, I asked Freddie for his take on niceness, and his answer somewhat surprised me. 'Civility costs nothing. My parents taught me to be polite and well-mannered. It doesn't mean you're weak

MEETING WITH AN UNDERWORLD FIGURE

or you're not strong just because you're polite and you treat people fairly and you don't cause any trouble – whether it's business or at home or wherever you are.' Bullies and ignorant people might make the mistake of thinking you are soft, he said, because you're polite, but you can deal with bullies. Old courtesy, Freddie felt, seemed to be going out of the window. The Kray twins, who were behind plenty of nefarious activity in their time, had been amateur and professional boxers in their youth, I knew. They even entertained Sonny Liston at one time. Since their story had been done to death, I asked Freddie if he had anything to share with me that he hadn't revealed before. He told me a story that was brand new to me. Apparently, the twins would send out four of their firm's guys to round up anyone they wanted to speak with. These men were 20-stone giants, and they used to go out and pick up – kidnap might be the correct term – certain people that Ronnie wanted to meet and fetch them back to him. Well, one of these people was Cliff Richard. The Krays sent out three guys to pick him up and bring back the music star for a chat. Fortunately for Sir Cliff, the crew didn't go through with it. 'He was appearing at a theatre nearby, but these three henchmen didn't have the heart to do it so they never bothered,' Freddie revealed. 'If they had done I don't know how it would've turned out, but it wouldn't have been very pleasant for Cliff for sure. It wasn't fair on him.' As a result Ronnie got very annoyed.

The key story that emerged from my captivating conversation with this ageing underworld figure was of how he had turned his life around, even if he left it a little late. 'I want to tell the youth of today, don't miss out on your education,' he conceded. 'I missed out because I was an evacuee. Schools were closed down, they didn't even open them in the war because of the bombing.' You've got to go out and get a decent job and make a living, and you have to have the knowledge and intelligence, he told me. Otherwise you're going to end up doing heavy labour all your life – scaffolding, meat poultry, hard labour jobs, all of which he had gone through – or be plunged into a life of crime. It's harder and harder to commit crime now, or at least to get away with it, with all these cameras in the streets everywhere in the city, he told me. Some of the criminal activities Freddie took part in the old days you simply couldn't get away with now, and you'd be throwing your life away the first time you tried.

Next, Freddie said something that stunned me. This reformed character revealed he was proud of the fact that none of the people he dealt with ever went to hospital or was injured badly. He was apparently always treated fairly and carefully, and not injured in any way. In contrast, he told me, with all these stabbings now among the young people it's a complete waste of life and one just can't see where it's leading.

Another interesting thing Freddie shared with me was that he had been the technical advisor to Tom Hardy for the film *Legend,* directed by American director Brian Helgeland. Tom, who played both Kray twins, told Freddie it was one of his most difficult roles because the two twins were so alike yet different, and the only way you could separate and portray the two characters was with little mannerisms and patterns of speech. Freddie, of course, knew this more than most. According to the ex-gangster, out of the two, Ronnie was the nuttiest – but he preferred him, since Ronnie was more true to his word than Reggie. Reggie used to sit on the fence and see which way it went before he decided what he was going to agree with, who he'd side with. With Ronnie, Freddie revealed, if he was with you he'd be with you regardless. Reggie had a quizzical look on his face all the time. You could tell that all sorts of thoughts were swirling around in his head when you were talking to him. He wasn't listening to you but his mind was elsewhere. If you asked him, 'Did you get what I said?' He'd say, 'Oh, yeah, yeah.' But with Ronnie he'd listen to you and was more genuine as a person. That's what Freddie brought to Tom's attention: a simple way to separate the two of them in the way he played the two characters.

According to Freddie he was the only non-crew person invited on set by Tom Hardy because it was a closed set, which means there

MEETING WITH AN UNDERWORLD FIGURE

are restrictions in terms of who can be present. 'Tom wanted to speak to me about how he was portraying the Krays,' Freddie told me. 'I was there to guide him personally. He felt I was the one person who could really offer him a true insight into the characters.' These days Hollywood actors keep in touch with the former Kray enforcer. Freddie had already helped Tom, who also starred in the MMA sports drama *Warrior*, get his role in the *Bronson* movie. 'I recommended him for that movie,' he told me. 'I met the producers and director of that film in the Punch Bowl pub.'

It was refreshing meeting this man who is part of criminal history. I left that day not only with great insights into the workings of the underworld but a new-found respect for a man who I had only heard of from afar, a notorious figure who once ruled the streets of a convicted criminal associated with murders. Once again, preconceived perceptions of people often don't tell you the full story.

Later, the publicist told me that Freddie had liked me. I was invited by one of the producers of the documentary to the premiere, but it was Ramadan, the month of fasting, and I just couldn't make it to London's Soho, so I regretfully declined. It would've been an experience to see which characters showed up.

CHAPTER THIRTY-SEVEN

THE PERILS OF SPORTS FAME

ALTHOUGH MY forte is combat sports and entertainment, I'm not unwilling to cross over into other territory on rare occasions – as long as it doesn't become a habit and it's an area I find interesting or the individual I'm interviewing is a high-profile personality. I have interviewed athletes ranging from Olympic track and field and swimming to NFL and NBA superstars. Soccer is the world's most popular sport and its popularity, both in participation and interest, in the USA has increased. According to a survey almost 25 million people play soccer in USA. It is the third most watched team sport behind American football and basketball. Also, according to an ESPN poll soccer is the second most popular sport in the USA among 12-to-24-year olds.

So, as I looked for more interview opportunities, it was the natural place to start. George Best was top of my list. Sometimes known as the 'Fifth Beatle', treated like a pop icon and a pin-up, he was an emblematic figure, the first true celebrity soccer player at a time well before the emergence of David Beckham. I had long admired the soccer sensation – alongside Pele, he was my favourite player – and he had crossed over to the States himself. He was one of the first soccer stars to come to the USA in the 1970s, joining the Los Angeles Aztecs. But it was after years of trying to persuade Pele to join the

North American Soccer League (NASL) that George became the focus. Pele signed a three-year $7 million contract with the New York Cosmos to help promote the sport in the USA. More recently I got in touch with Pele's daughter who resides in Florida. I sent her a WhatsApp message because she was working on a documentary focusing on women's soccer, which is now a global phenomenon. FIFA ranked its national team number one in the world after its back-to-back World Cup victory in 2015 and 2019.

I learned more about George from his ex-wife, Angie Best, who had had a rollercoaster of a life with the alcoholic. I spoke to Angie after she became a reality TV star in 2017 – not that she wasn't well known previously. What intrigued me about George was his antics off the pitch, as well as his dazzling skills on it. He epitomised the football superstar.

'You see, that's the problem, that's the difference between George and everyone else,' Angie told me when I asked her about her ex-husband's party life and the glitz and glamour that have been attached to his name. 'He hated celebrities. He didn't hang out.'

I was astounded. I, like everyone else, had always perceived the soccer player as a party monster, a real reveller. On the contrary, apparently George and Angie didn't frequent any fancy restaurants or attend any parties when they were residing in Los Angeles. They lived in Hermosa Beach – a place where I had on several occasions trained with a UFC champion friend of mine more than two decades later – where they had a modest apartment. 'We weren't grandiose, we didn't have fancy cars,' Angie recalled. 'We had each other and his soccer. And, of course, his Bestie's Bar, which was the only thing he was interested in. So the parties and all those things didn't exist in George's life. He wasn't that kind of a person.'

Much of the time, it emerged, George was a very subdued individual and kept himself to himself. When he did party, it was with some of his close friends down the pub or in his bar by himself. Angie had lived with Cher before she moved in with George and she and Cher would frequent parties but George would snub them. Once, Cher took her to the Playboy Mansion for Sunday lunch. An array of celebrities were invited. 'We didn't go in the jacuzzis or wear bikinis,' she recalls. 'We just had lunch, watched a movie and left. For me it was quite nice, it was completely normal. There were a lot of people there but I didn't know who they were.' That was the only time she went to the mansion.

George was reticent about opening up about anything and it was really very difficult to get anything out of him, Angie told me. 'But he used to say to me that it was enough that he knew he was the best. He didn't talk about being George. I think the George that the public knew was the George that he put out there for them. But the real George was a completely different person. He was a shy, sweet, intelligent, humorous drunk.'

I asked her whether she could compare David Beckham, who became a superstar beyond the confines of the pitch and a pop culture icon, to George off the pitch.

'Let me say something before I forget,' she proceeded to tell me. 'That was all about timing and people managing the player. If George had been managed properly and had had a proper agent and manager, he would have been able to make millions and he would have been looked after.' David was not quite the player George was, in Angie's opinion – far from it – but he had a team of handlers behind him. They groomed him, looked after him, went to great measures to make sure he didn't derail himself and went down the right path. They secured lucrative sponsorship deals and took care of his financial affairs. 'And he was treated the way celebrities and stars should be treated,' Angie said. 'George wasn't. Because George was the first of his kind, and people didn't know how to manage him, they didn't know what to do. Then of course if you had tried to tell George anything, what to do, he would have just laughed in your face.'

Angie, a long-time fitness fanatic, was a personal trainer to the stars in Hollywood. Aside from working with Cher, and at one point Darryl Hannah, she was later invited to train Sharon Stone. However, the relationship was short-lived because the day after she was hired Angie received some unexpected news. The actress had had an accident and therefore wouldn't be training for three months. Angie never heard from her again.

Nevertheless, Angie kept busy by working with a lot of what she calls 'R and Fs' – the Rich and Famous – in Hollywood and Malibu, including wives of the stars and female directors.

When George and Angie returned to England George started drinking again. Angie had left America and her job there to come home to England with George when he started to play for an English club again, and his drinking left her feeling dispirited. 'I was very unhappy with him because he would go with Tim Adams – his agent – and Billy Connelly out boozing,' remembers Angie. 'I would be really unhappy because I'd be left at home doing my needle point. I had my own flat, so I left his place.' One evening Cher called Angie, saying, 'Angie, please come back I'm going back on the road and I need you. There's a ticket for you at the airport.' On hearing the good news, Angie went to see George in the hospital – he had had an accident outside Harrods while driving drunk – to tell him she was going back to America. 'I walked into his room and some girl, a random stranger or a nurse probably, was pleasuring George,' recalls Angie. 'I was horrified and rushed straight out. I took off and got on the plane to America. I got ready to go on tour with Cher there and I was staying at her house.' While staying with Cher, she was inundated with calls from her mother, who would call Cher's house to try to persuade her daughter to call George. He didn't know where Angie was staying. 'He didn't have Cher's number,' Angie recalls. 'We didn't have mobile numbers in those days so my mum used to call me and say to me, "Darling, you must call this boy. He calls every day. Have you spoken to him?" Eventually, after two months of this nonsense I said OK. I got on the phone to him, "Hi George," and he said, "Don't hang up! Will you marry me?" I said yes. This was in the late 70s.'

The marriage, sadly, didn't flourish. George drifted into depression. When Angie was with him she didn't know anything about depression. In the 1970s and early 1980s, it wasn't talked about openly like as it is today. She came to the conclusion that he just needed somebody to settle him down, cook him dinner, have a nice house and keep him happy. She made the effort and tried all that, but years later when she looked back on their life together and how things evolved, she saw what had happened. 'I would see George go very quiet,' she told me. 'He'd sleep late. He'd start to grow a beard and he'd eat food that was full of sugar. That would happen for a couple of weeks before he went on a bender. Now, when I look back on it, I can see how the picture evolved. But at the time I was clueless about his depression.'

George left his mark on both English and US soccer, changing the landscape of the game. Americans first fell in love with the world's most popular sport back when he and Pele were playing there. He would open the gates for future Manchester United superstars who would, at the end of their careers, play and promote the game across the Atlantic. It's a shame he wasn't able to enjoy the fruits of his labours himself.

* * *

A later soccer star who also became the subject of controversy and often appeared in newspaper headlines for all the wrong reasons is former Manchester United star Wayne Rooney, who would follow in the footsteps of George Best and team-mate David Beckham by going over to the USA to play for D.C. United. Wayne had a connection with a couple of my interviewees – Joe Egan once told me that, when Mike Tyson was in the United Kingdom, he wanted to meet Wayne. According to Joe, Tyson had a great deal of admiration for the soccer player, who, much like Tyson himself, had been catapulted to fame at a young age. 'Iron Mike' had a lot of respect and concern for Wayne because the former heavyweight champion was cognisant

THE PERILS OF SPORTS FAME

of the pressure on his young shoulders. So, when the notorious boxer was over for an after-dinner speech in Manchester, Joe planned to introduce him to the young star. In fact it was Joe and our mutual friend Charlie Hale who first suggested Tyson do these dinner events. At this particular event, a table that had been reserved for the Manchester United team was given to the Carrington training ground staff because the team was stuck in traffic after an away match. On another table was Wayne's wife, Coleen, and her family. Tyson had prepared a presentation for Wayne, but he presented it to Coleen's brother – Wayne's brother-in-law – instead.

Despite Wayne and the team not making it to the event, Joe introduced the soccer sensation to Tyson in a restaurant in Manchester called Lounge Ten later that night. This place has a high-profile clientele and a pedigree of attracting the region's celebrities, including many A-list sports stars. As it happened, a mutual friend of Wayne's and Tyson owned this restaurant, and hosted a private, intimate dinner for the former heavyweight champion.

'Wayne was over the moon to meet Mike and the latter was over the moon to meet Wayne,' Joe told me. 'An ex-boxer himself, Wayne loves and follows the sport of boxing and he's a very good fighter himself. Because they're both superstars, Mike wanted to speak to Wayne about the perils of global fame, pitfalls and the problems that all young superstars encounter. Mike imparted a little bit of advice and gave him some inside knowledge on things to watch out for when you're a rising superstar.'

Wayne, I'm told, really appreciated Tyson's advice and concern. Everybody's aware of what's happened in Tyson's life, the pitfalls he's faced and the people who took liberties with him during and after his career. Lawsuits, thieving promoters, personal and social problems in life spiralling out of control, multiple trials and bad investments, Tyson has experienced it all. Although he enjoyed a legendary career, he battled bankruptcy after a frivolous lifestyle that culminated in his downfall. Wayne, who used to box as an amateur, has been around boxers all his life and some of his best friends are pugilists. All three men talked about boxing as the evening unfolded.

Since then, Wayne has apparently managed to keep his head screwed on as far as his finances are concerned, though how much of an affect the former heavyweight champion had on him is anyone's guess. Tyson continues to do multiple gigs to rake in money, from his Las Vegas show to autograph signings to offering personalised birthday messages for fans willing to part with their hard-earned money for a celebrity messaging service. I think it's cheap, celebrities resorting to this medium. Wayne doesn't have to resort to such things. Still, Tyson may have lost it all, but what he achieved one can only envy. And he still has time to become rich again, in more ways than one.

CHAPTER THIRTY-EIGHT

MICHAEL, MATT & MARTIAL ARTS

WHEN IT comes to musical royalty you can't get bigger than Michael Jackson. The late pop star's life was plagued with controversy, but even since his demise Michael Jackson continues to make headlines and front-page news. So, naturally, when I heard his brother Tito Jackson was going to be visiting the United Kingdom, I jumped at the chance to meet and interview the former Jackson Five member, a founding member of a group which has sold over 100 million records, making it one of the best-selling of all time. I had one special motivation in mind – finding out more about his brother's interest in martial arts.

When we first sat down to chat, Tito seemed very down to earth. He had been coming to the United Kingdom since the early 1970s, and he easily recalled the very first time the band was on tour on these shores. Heathrow airport, he told me, was swamped with 10,000 fans there to welcome the Jacksons. They followed the brothers to their hotel, bringing traffic to a standstill, and singing Jackson Five songs in the street. This was the beginning of a special relationship, almost a marriage, between the Jacksons and the devoted fans across the pond. Tito told me that ever since then the United Kingdom has been in the band's corner, as fans in the United Kingdom seem to, as he put it, 'get it'.

TO THE TOP

The dedication, love and support these fans gave the Jacksons are the main reason Tito has continued to show a lot of love and dedication to them also, he told me – to try to give back the same feeling. The United Kingdom, to him, is a country that is a beautiful place.

'In America, sometimes you can be a little sceptical about certain situations,' he told me. 'With policemen in America, you feel inferior to them. It's that kind of place.' It sounds simple, but in the United Kingdom, the policemen are nice, he said, they talk to you properly and so does everyone else. At the time, I didn't quiz him on whether he had experienced police brutality. Perhaps he had because African-Americans often are victims of racism, and despite their fame I knew that back in the old days the Jacksons also suffered racism in its ugliest form.

Michael's relationship with Tito was great. They could talk to each other about literally anything. They had a special love for each other. 'I always felt that he was there for me and I was there for him,' Tito said. 'We talked about everything from when we were children to when we grew into adults. However, Michael wasn't a sports person so we didn't talk about sports or things of that nature.' Tito was a little different to all the other brothers, because he enjoyed working on cars, or making furniture – getting his hands dirty. Michael appreciated those types of qualities. He often showed interest in them although he didn't get involved in them practically.

It was a fairly clear day when I interviewed Tito, and we were sitting outside a countryside hotel. Our chat continued as the light breeze turned to a rather stronger one. I changed the subject slightly as I wanted to slip in a question pertaining to something that, I would say, had been something of a closely-guarded secret, something one of Michael's friends had divulged to me: the fact that I had been told Michael wanted to marry Bruce Lee's daughter. *How can I pass on a golden opportunity like this – after all, it's Michael's close family member*, I thought. I was desperate to dispense with any speculation and discern just how much substance this claim held. So, I worked my way up to the question gradually, because I felt if I started to probe into deeply personal matters about his brother, it could derail the whole interview. It was, I felt, too much of a risk to take. One thing I've learned over the years is if you have a controversial or personal question for your subject that you feel could upset the person, then you leave it right to the end of an interview. Still, if I approached things delicately, with a little humour thrown in for good measure, I felt I could squeeze something out of Tito.

'It's interesting that Michael did martial arts and you did, too,' I said, to warm him up a little before hitting him with the big knockout blow.

'Yes, there was a time when we all took up kung fu – starting back in the 70s – for a little while with a gentleman called Kam Yeun,' Tito said. 'Michael was very good at it.'

Despite the Jacksons' interest in martial arts they were unable to continue because of the simple fact they were constantly travelling around the world. Despite that, Tito said, it was a great time in their lives. 'We all loved Bruce Lee,' he continued. 'He's one of our heroes. Michael had conversations about him all the time with us. When I watched *Enter the Dragon*, what I noticed about his style was it was so different and unique. He had just so much "style". He's just a hero.' Tito went on to tell me that all the Jackson brothers wanted to have the Bruce Lee body, like many other kids of the time.

Well, this was my opening. Still hesitant, I felt another warm-up question was required before the final assault. I asked if he felt Bruce influenced Michael as far as his mastery of body movement and dancing went.

'I wouldn't say he owes his style to Bruce Lee,' he explained. 'But I would give Bruce Lee credit for some of the attitude that Michael had and came to embrace.' Well, I felt that now was the perfect time to chuck in the golden question. Whether it would catch him off-guard or not, I wasn't sure, but I could no longer hold back.

'Is it true that Michael wanted to meet Bruce Lee's daughter Shannon Lee and marry her?' The question was sprung on him and a smile crept across my face. Tito seemed a little apprehensive, but he didn't walk away.

'Probably, knowing Michael, yeah, he probably did want to marry her,' he said. 'We all wanted to meet Bruce Lee, he was our hero. I don't know if Michael ever got the opportunity to meet Bruce or his daughter, but it would've been a great situation for that to have happened.'

Now, Matt Fiddes, who never fails to astonish me, had told me this a year before. Matt was Michael's bodyguard for ten years, and is a friend of mine who claims to be the owner of the biggest martial arts franchise schools in the world. A friendship between Matt and I ensued a couple of years before I met Tito. Matt once disclosed to me that at every music store they went to Michael would purchase the whole Bruce Lee film collection. Michael was a Bruce Lee fanatic, he told me, adding that Michael had begged him to connect him to Shannon Lee and Bruce's widow. Yes, begged him! According to Matt, this was the late pop star's dream.

Michael had also given Matt some advice on business matters. I had once quizzed Matt on how he managed to build what he claims was a £30-million empire with just £100 to his name when he started out. 'What happened was, Fiaz, if it was not for [Michael] I would just have five martial arts schools now,' he proceeded to explain. As much as Michael was an extremely gifted musician and an exceptional dancer, Matt told me, he was also a very shrewd businessman, very intelligent – people forget that. They see him as the man behind the makeup, the mask and all that fake stuff, but behind all that there was a lot of intelligence.

'Michael once said to me, "How's business?"' Matt told me. 'I said, "Good, Michael, but, I've gone as far as I can go." He said, "What do you mean?" I said. "Well, I've got five schools and the next town is 50 miles away." He said, "Oh, poor you. If I can sell albums all around the world and have the biggest albums and be a billionaire," – which he was on paper because of The Beatles catalogue and his other assets

– "you can find a way to get someone to travel 50 miles to open a school. I'm going to call you every week from wherever I am in the world."' According to Matt, that's exactly what Michael did. Using a napkin, he wrote down a list of things for Matt to do, starting with the basics. Look for an instructor. Plan this out. Do this by this day.

Michael would call Matt up to check on his progress. The conversation, Matt told me, would often be funny. 'Matt, how many schools have you opened lately?' Michael would ask. Matt would say, 'Four, Michael. What have you been up to?' He'd say, 'I've just closed a deal for $80 million.' Matt would feel like crap. It was another level. During one conversation, the pop star revealed something to his friend that would change the young man's life for the better. He said, 'There's a thing called franchising. That's what you need.' Matt's response was less than enthusiastic, he said, 'Well, no one has done this before in martial arts.' Michael said, 'Well, that's exactly what you've got to do.' And that stuck in Matt's head. No one had done it before, especially in the United Kingdom, as far as martial arts schools were concerned. But, amazingly enough, a year later the martial arts entrepreneur allegedly had 600 martial arts schools to his name.

* * *

I learned a lot from Matt about Michael Jackson – revelations about the world's greatest entertainer in all his complexity, his passions, unhealthy obsessions, eccentricities, flawed personal life, his failed ventures and personal relationships. Matt had not only travelled with the late pop star whenever he visited the United Kingdom, but around the world, including staying over at Neverland in California.

From the way Matt told it, it sometimes seemed that Michael wanted to marry literally every famous woman. Before he pursued the daughter of the world's greatest martial artist, he had another woman on his mind. Matt revealed to me that Michael wanted to marry Princess Diana, and was absolutely besotted with her. 'He was always telling me that Diana would be his ideal wife, but they [the

Establishment] wouldn't let him meet her again,' he said. 'I think in his head there were two things swirling around. Firstly, it was a way to be bigger than the King of Pop. He would have a royal connection. Secondly, he also wanted to be a father to her children. He did that with Lisa Presley's kids wonderfully and he desperately wanted children at the time. I think with Princess Diana, he was just in love with her completely. I mean, they both were very similar people. He always told me she was his ideal wife. He said to me, "I wish she was alive so I would've tried harder, we belong together."'

Above all, the one thing the pop star shared with Matt that stuck with him forever is that when Diana was part of the royal family, she might have been the only person in the world who could understand his life. Michael was the most misunderstood person Matt had ever met, my friend said. No amount of fame or stardom can act as a replacement for healthy relationships, but perhaps these two misunderstood souls really were made for each other. A caring, compassionate, wonderful person, Diana endeared herself to the pop star by her elevated character and indefatigable benevolence. Michael spent hours and hours talking on the phone with the late princess, spending thousands and thousands of dollars on phone bills as they spent all night on the phone. After she died, Michael cancelled all of his upcoming concerts. He was actually very distressed that he wasn't invited to the funeral. Then again, he understood that if he had attended it would have turned into a media circus; the focus, perhaps, would have turned on him. Still, Cliff Richard was there, so were George Michael and Elton John, and so he felt he should've been at least invited. Instead, he watched it on TV.

The media has long served as an organ for exposing and embarrassing famous personalities. In today's media-saturated environment, no story gains traction quite so rapidly as one that tears down a well-known public figure. And Michael wasn't immune. He certainly had the ability to say some outrageous things on TV shows. When Michael married Lisa-Marie Presley, one of the first things he did was a TV chat show with her to put the record straight, and the world tuned in. So Michael was of the opinion that Charles saw him as a threat, according to Matt, and the late-night phone calls Michael and Diana shared would allegedly aggravate Charles. Diana had revealed a great deal to her friend during their phone sessions, but Matt refrained from divulging everything to me. What he did tell me, though, was that the King of Pop and the princess had developed the kind of trust that enabled them to talk about anything and everything.

Michael also wasn't against using the media. 'He would take advantage of the paparazzi and tip them off when he stayed in hotels,' Matt said. 'He had a couple of fans he was very close to, and we'd use them and he'd say, "Hey, can you tell them I'm going to be at this hotel."' Sure enough, the press would turn up. On other occasions, Michael got banned from hotels because the fans resorted to spraying graffiti on the walls, tipped off about his presence by the press. Essentially, Michael had a love-hate relationship with the press. He would be deeply upset if he was in public and no paparazzi turned up, just like Diana. Then again, when he wanted his private space, he would stay at the actor Mark Lester's house, where they would do deals with fans to help create publicity.

The King of Pop never really endeared himself to me. But I'm under no illusions about the magnitude of his global popularity and his story is definitely a complex but fascinating one. As for Tito, well, I was left stunned when his representative informed me that Tito wasn't happy that I had asked him personal questions about his late brother. Win some, lose some.

CHAPTER THIRTY-NINE

A NEW DIRECTION: NEW WORLD

WHILE I was mingling with pop royalty, things were reaching fever pitch on the political front. On 26 July 2018, I met Reham Khan, the ex-wife of former sportsman and current prime minister of Pakistan Imran Khan. If I'm honest, I had ambivalent feelings about interviewing her, as I felt it could have deplorable consequences. Yet, I didn't want to pass on the opportunity, either. If anything, I wanted to have an experience to take away with me, and so eventually I did agree to meet her.

The conversation leaned towards her motives for writing her highly controversial self-titled memoir, which had garnered publicity and notoriety. I said to her that it was alleged certain individuals, the opposition party, had offered her lots of money to actually put together a book to defame Imran Khan. Dismissing the rumours, Reham claimed she had a very different viewpoint as to why she needed to tell her story.

'For example, I've got 18 things happening in my life and the chances are that someone from your family or you yourself will have experienced some of them,' she said. 'I've led a very interesting and challenging life and I've experienced many different lifestyles, cultures, and continents. People who don't know who I am.'

A NEW DIRECTION: NEW WORLD

Reham told me with great conviction that she isn't the sort of a person who can be derailed; she makes her own decisions as a strong-minded woman.

'Nobody can bully me,' she continued. 'A lot of people have tried to contain me and a lot of people have tried to bully me. I'm a very free-spirited person who pretty much cannot be dictated to. People try, but I'm not going to let them change my mind.' It was apparent that she was on a mission to pursue her objective despite claiming that death threats lay at her doorstep.

I must make it explicitly clear that there had already been countless derogatory stories relating to Imran Khan floating around at the time. I wanted to get her to shed light on her own views and be able to discern the validity of these other claims.

'Can you clear up the allegations that you wanted to take over the party?' I asked. 'When they say I want to be part of the party, I say there's nothing wrong with being ambitious.' Reham said. 'But being a British national I couldn't take a risk of leaving my British nationality because I have kids here.' Her prime responsibility was and is with her children from her first marriage, in which she suffered extreme domestic abuse. 'I came here because of the death threats in Pakistan. How can I give up my nationality? When they started these accusations, which were in September before the wedding was announced, I didn't pay too much attention to them.' This woman couldn't have in a hundred years imagined that these were serious – that's what she told me. According to her she didn't attend the meetings that she was rumoured to have spoken at and claimed that she was being framed well before the wedding. Some regarded her as a bad influence on the sportsman-turned-politician who ran the country, but she told me differently. If you are not facilitating their agenda, she said, they get rid of you in that government.

The never-ending string of rumours and salacious allegations surrounding Reham, which I had ambiguous feelings about, left me somewhat perturbed. They painted the prime minister in a very bad light. I had, as I mentioned before, avoided the sensationalist journalism route as I had spent the bulk of my career in sports and it wasn't something that I gravitated towards. Then again, writing about Hollywood definitely opens you up to the sensationalist showbiz world, and I must admit, to an extent it has rubbed off on me. Having said this, I endeavour to avoid sensationalism. Anyway, any attempts to derail her ex-husband were certainly a failure as he was embraced by the public, and the media essentially refused to entertain the allegations.

Reham seemed very approachable, confident and intelligent. She spoke about her time at the BBC, and said she wanted to get involved with community programmes in which martial arts helped young women with self-defence. My friend, a martial arts instructor, was present that day, so they talked about that further, but nothing came of it.

None of the conversations I had with Reham ever made it into the papers. Needless to say, I was relieved as I had no intention of vilifying Prime Minister Imran Khan, who is perceived by most in his country as a hero, and has done more for his country than any prime minister before him.

* * *

When I was done with hobnobbing with the wives of prime ministers, talking politics and having to sit through sordid revelations, it was time to get back to focusing on my forte – combat sports. Deontay Wilder was facing Tyson Fury in what was going to be Tyson's meal ticket into America and the consciousness of American fans. The fight was to take place on 1 December 2018 at The Staples Center in Los Angeles, and I spoke to Deontay on 17 October.

I learned, for a start, that he was a late starter as far as boxing is concerned. So why was he inclined to pursue a bloody sport when there are less dangerous vocations? Some fighters get into boxing or martial arts because of being bullied when they were growing up – it's pretty common – but for Deontay, the reason he pursued the sport so relentlessly was none other than his young daughter. She had been diagnosed with life-threatening spina bifida, which is a condition affecting the baby's spine, and he was fighting for her.

'My daughter inspires me to come to the gym,' he told me. 'She inspired me to change my profession. I was just a guy in college, on the basketball team. It was a job. I'd do it all over again if I had to for my daughter.'

The heavyweight was willing to do whatever it took to take care of his child. Deontay had pledged to his daughter that Daddy would be a world champion one day, and be able to support her. Well, the 'Brown Bomber' did just that as he swept the heavyweight division, undefeated for 40 fights. He further added that he did this not only for his daughter, but for all his children. 'It's such a great motivation and a blessing to have those little ones in my life,' Deontay said. 'They're so intelligent and amazing. I just love them.' *Very touching, indeed, a softer side to the big giant*, I thought.

Before I hit him with any questions about his upcoming fight, I asked, 'Will we see you fight Anthony Joshua before both of you retire?'

'Anything can happen, especially with a potential Joshua fight,' was the reply. Even so, he said that the biggest fight in the world right now was with Tyson Fury, a hulking 6ft 9in boxing beast. His mind was focused on the 'Gypsy King', but the AJ fight was certainly something that had his interest, he made it clear.

According to Deontay, AJ's team had their reservations. And that the only way the fight could materialise was if the fans were vocal enough.

'And stop all the bullshit that Eddie Hearn always keeps on talking about,' Deontay said. 'If this continues then there won't be a Joshua–Wilder fight. You will never see he and I getting in the ring together. They will never see me knock Joshua out.' He claimed the reason behind the reluctance from AJ's end was that his team feared Deontay, the most dangerous man in the boxing game. 'It's one of those fights that it might one day happen or maybe it never will,' he concluded. 'It's uncertain. Not because of Deontay Wilder but because of the other side.'

Two years later, I asked promoter Eddie Hearn what his thoughts were on Deontay's comments. 'Those comments look silly now, because all we ever received was an email from Deontay Wilder's hotmail account asking about numbers,' he said to me. 'We asked for contract details but they were never sent. But Wilder and his team are showing their true colours. He fought Tyson Fury and lost his belts. So he's now irrelevant to our picture.'

Taking Deontay in another direction, I said to him that certain boxers are fans of the UFC and MMA.

'What's your opinion on Khabib wanting to fight Mayweather?' I asked. Khabib had beaten his bitter rival Conor McGregor in their classic UFC 229 fight exactly a year earlier. 'Do you think this crossover from UFC champions wanting to test themselves with boxing's best has gone too far?' Deontay confirmed that, yes, he feels everyone should definitely stay in their own lane. Yet he added, 'But I also feel that if it makes a lot of money then yes. If people want to see such a fight, then it should happen. People love seeing fantasy matchups, those fight that make you think, *Man, that would be amazing.* That's why people do it.'

With Khabib challenging Mayweather, the former, he stated, could make a lot of money out of the bout. If people wanted to see such a matchup, if there was great interest in it, then, there would be no stopping anyone. Money was a great motivator. 'I'd do [a crossover fight] one day if it makes money,' Deontay conceded. 'At the end of the day whether it's boxing, MMA or UFC, whatever you want to call it, it's all combat sports.' Deontay has some friends who fight in MMA, but his focus has been on boxing, a sport that has always taken control of everything for him. MMA fighters work just as hard as anyone else, he admitted to me, and he wished them all well and said he hoped they'd make as much money as possible.

A NEW DIRECTION: NEW WORLD

Going back to his opponent, Tyson had been subjected to harsh criticism ever since he became the world champion. His views were often perceived as abhorrent, and everything that came out of his mouth seemed to attract the wrong kind of attention. Consequently, he became so disillusioned that he once announced he was going to move to Los Angeles where the public and fans treated their sports stars with great reverence. I asked Deontay if he felt Tyson hadn't received the respect he deserved in the boxing world.

'People are just weird sometimes, and will make certain remarks that I just don't understand,' he said of Tyson. 'But I do understand Fury. Currently he's only getting negative feedback and people are like that because he's fighting me. They say, "He needs more warm-up fights if Fury wants to fight Deontay Wilder." You would not hear that he needs more time to fight, he's out of shape, and so on, if he wasn't fighting me.'

Deontay also added that when people come back from a dark situation to perform, some people will always want to see them fail again. 'There are a lot of things that people want to say, that they really have nothing good to say but just want to discredit you.' People didn't want Deontay to succeed, either, he told me, they didn't want him to prevail and do the things that he said he'd accomplish. 'I think I'm also a victim in that people give me a lot of criticism, especially right now. The only reason they give me criticism is because they don't want me to succeed.'

Next, Deontay revealed his strategy: he was going for a knockout. He was confident, and with good reason. Known for his heavy fists he had given many an opponent the beating of a lifetime. When fans go out to watch a boxing match at an arena, he explained, they don't want to be there all night and they certainly don't want to sit around watching the fight go the distance. The fans, he told me, want the thrill of seeing someone get knocked out, so they can go about their business and enjoy their night out. That's what the 'Brown Bomber' had made his name doing, and was what he planned to do again.

TO THE TOP

As you probably know by now, the fight ended up a draw – though it was one of the most exciting draws the world had ever seen. It was inevitable it would lead to a rematch, which would once again generate millions for all concerned. The 'Gypsy King' went on to beat the 'Brown Bomber' in their rematch just over a year later, which solidified his status on the worldwide stage. What irritated me, however, was when Tyson's new promoter Bob Arum, a veteran in the game, kept on incessantly hyping his fighter by making comparisons with Muhammad Ali. All I could see was money. Bob was using Ali's name to do what he was good at, and that is to 'sell' a product. Still, credit to Bob, Tyson has become a household name and the American public has embraced him, and the heavyweight champion's charity donations have been truly inspiring. Tyson's appeal has gone beyond the confines of the ring – his struggles with mental health and defiance of the odds is something that resonates with the wider public.

* * *

While the 'Gypsy King' was in the limelight, so was the world's most famous royal family. Princess Meghan Markle was the talk of the town and her estranged family garnered endless public attention from the moment it was revealed that the Hollywood actress was going to wed Prince Harry.

One of the most bizarre characters I have ever come across and interviewed for the papers is Meghan Markle's estranged brother, Thomas Markle Jnr. No introduction required there – he's probably more famous now by association than some A-listers. I got him through an avenue that suited my skill – my research led to a man named Dan, a boxing promoter, in Pennsylvania. Thomas was fighting in a celebrity boxing match promoted by Dan and Dan put me in touch with him directly.

It wasn't long before I was speaking to the brother of a princess. He had just fought in the ring, and was fairly chatty. He had been scheduled to fight Mark Wahlberg's best friend Henry 'Nachco'

A NEW DIRECTION: NEW WORLD

Luan at the Showboat Casino in Atlantic City, New Jersey but Luan failed to show up. Nevertheless, a fight went ahead and Thomas was awarded a decision over a boxing radio host. During our conversation, though, he suddenly claimed that his promoter had short changed him and he had a story that I should run, disparaging the promoter. Alarm bells started ringing. Thomas had a reputation for bad behaviour – run-ins with the law and general drunken behaviour. I wasn't going to get into this. Thomas, who looked overweight, has long been a fan of boxing and the martial arts and enjoyed the training, so instead we discussed some of the boxers of the 1980s and 1990s. He had followed the sport with a close eye, I could tell, even if on a casual level.

He also wanted money to be interviewed for *The Sun*, which didn't surprise me because Dan had warned that Thomas would only talk if he got paid. Well, the number of people I've interviewed over the years who have asked for payment for granting me an interview, I can count on one hand – and I've interviewed hundreds of famous personalities over the years. Anyway, I told him that I'd have to confer with my editor, and got in touch with my showbiz contact. She emailed me back: if the story makes a spread then we will pay £2,000, if it's a lead then £800 and if it's a splash then we could pay more like £3,000. She said they would only pay him if the story went to print and that payment would be delivered two weeks after the date of publication.

OK, I thought, great. Once Meghan's brother was convinced and satisfied with the sum being offered, he wasn't hesitant to talk. And, oh, boy, did he rip into Meghan. His disdain for her was all too apparent. Still, we got off to a civil enough start.

'How did you and your father perceive Meghan's future had she not met and married Prince Harry?' I asked.

'She was on her way to being a successful actress' he said. 'Being in *Suits* was a big stepping stone for her.' 'It was a good move on her part, but I think if for some reason her career failed and she'd never met Prince Harry she would still have a family – us.'

Since the courtship, though, the rift between Meghan and her father and other family members has deepened, and her brother's detachment was all too apparent. To add further conflict, Meghan didn't visit her father when he was hospitalised after he suffered a heart attack.

'What would your feelings be should your father pass away or find himself in a critical condition and Meghan never gets to see or speak to him?' I asked.

'That's a good question, actually,' Thomas replied. 'I thought about this the other day. That would probably be the saddest thing on the planet. If something critical happens to our father, would she show up? I honestly don't think she would. Would it be too late at that point? The thing about this is, God forbid she's not that heartless, because she would have to live with that her entire life.' He felt nobody could live like that or carry that burden on their shoulders for the rest of their life.

'Do you think the royal family is finding all this quite bizarre?' I asked, referring to Meghan's rift with her family.

'I think any normal family would find it bizarre that you ignore your entire family and don't give a real explanation,' Thomas said, further adding that it didn't matter if you're royal family or just a run-of-the-mill family anywhere. 'I don't know if they're just siding with Meghan or giving Meghan what she wants. I'm sure they've opened their arms to Meghan, but they must be wondering, *What kind of family is this? Why won't she talk to them?* I'm sure it's come up in their conversation.' Thomas believes that Hollywood changes people. Being an actress and starring in a show, you become psychologically programmed to believe that you are better than other people, he said. Some people let it get to their heads, while it doesn't affect others, he told me. 'And Meghan let it get to her head that she's better than everyone else, and that she's better than her family and her friends.' 'That's pretty obvious to me.'

Thomas wasn't shy about expressing his disdain for Meghan. In fact, that was the whole point of him speaking to the press. He thrived

A NEW DIRECTION: NEW WORLD

on it. I soon realised that, for him – and for some of his other family members – it was a mechanism for making money. I mean, there was no class. There was no dignity. Ever since Meghan's relationship with Harry was announced, Thomas had been hounded by the press, and yet, he has used the press for his own financial gain. I ended up interviewing Thomas three times and it wasn't unusual to receive a message from him asking when he was getting paid by the newspaper. Despite being aware of the process, he was always anxious. He would invariably say that he was in desperate need of money, he was going to get evicted, or he had bills pilling up. He also apparently had arthritis issues come up the year before, which had had hit him pretty hard. It was very bizarre.

Soon it became apparent that he had, by and large, virtually nothing new to disclose: the record was always the same, Meghan needs to make amends with their father, and she's abandoned the family. I mean, if you truthfully have sincere intentions and want to express something, make a point, but your motivation is money and you're only willing to do media if you get paid, then your true intentions are clear. Indeed, I felt that the only real reason some members of Meghan's family wanted to be embraced by her was because she was a member of the royal family, and they were on a quest to squeeze whatever they could out of her. It raises the question of just how close some of the family members were to Meghan, and even raises doubts about the credibility of some of the allegations. Of course her father had spent a lot of time with Meghan and was close to her, but as for the other family members, who knows? I recall that when Muhammad Ali died, several women came forward claiming he was their father. It was bizarre but this sort of thing happens with celebrities.

On 2 October 2019 I spoke to Thomas again. This time, his sentiments hadn't changed and he did everything he could to defame Meghan, again. I thought, *Here we go again.* I often stressed I needed new material in order to convince the editors to pay him, and although he had some generic stories of Meghan's childhood, I was somewhat dubious as to just how much time he actually spent with his sister in adulthood. What I found disturbing is that he would sometimes tell me to add my own depth and colour to the feature with a half-hearted laugh, saying, 'Make it a really interesting piece.' That just validated my suspicions of his true motives. Again, he messaged me from his cell phone: *I could really use the money.*

Thomas next told me that nobody in his family recognised the Meghan they used to know. She's pretending to be something she's not, was his argument. Meghan's father had invested hundreds of thousands of dollars in her, he told me. Growing up, Meghan had been pampered with everything she'd ever asked for from her father – clothes, cars, money and love. Whatever she wanted, she apparently received. Thomas told me that their father has the receipts to prove it. Soon enough, what Thomas had to say dried up and the papers were less enthusiastic about speaking to him.

In the meantime, I had spoken to my agent about a memoir idea – a collaboration with Meghan's father. In fact, when I first got in touch with Thomas Markle Jnr my intention was to see if he or his father would be interested in collaborating with me to tell the Meghan Markle story to the world. My agent, who was rather dubious about the whole idea, advised me against it. He was being prudent. I took his advice, realising that he was right. Although a book on a prominent royal family member by her father would have been monumental, I feel that getting involved with that family feud would not necessarily have been a good move. The most famous royal biographer, Andrew Moreton, was somebody I admired and he influenced me when he wrote the groundbreaking book on Princess Diana in 1992. I had interviewed him about Meghan before her wedding to Prince Harry.

CHAPTER FORTY

FLYING HIGH

IN EARLY 2018, I finally managed to make a start on one of my dream projects – collaborating with Muhammad Ali's brother, Rahaman Ali, on the definitive biography of the great fighter. No one knew 'The Greatest' better than his only sibling. There existed an unbreakable bond between the two, with Ali's death leaving his brother bereft. Not only was Rahaman the family member Ali was closest to, but he was his best friend, best sparring partner, and a constant companion to Ali on his travels all over the world. They dined together with presidents, rubbed shoulders with celebrities, you name it. This monumental memoir/biography, I felt, would be arguably the most important perspective on one of the 20th century's most iconic figures.

In October 2019, I visited Rahaman in his hometown of Louisville, Kentucky. I had also arranged to meet up with his manager Ron Brashear, who flew over from Atlanta the next morning. Ron and I had other plans. After two nights in Louisville we would fly to Los Angeles and then to Sin City, Las Vegas. Ron picked me up in the late morning to drive me to Rahaman's home. I could hardly wait, as I was really looking forward to meeting Ali's brother. We arrived at the house and Rahaman, whose health had deteriorated considerably, was dressed up in a sharp dark navy suit, and looked very smart indeed. He had on his trademark hat.

TO THE TOP

He was feeling elated and was in good spirits, which was, to be honest, a great relief and solace. I expected him to take things lightly, but apparently he has a somewhat serious side, too. Anyway, we all drove to the Ali Center including his wife.

'Your home is my home,' Rahaman said to me. 'Come visit me often.' Now, Louisville is out of my way and hardly on my radar whenever I visit the USA. I routinely hit the West Coast and Los Angeles, where I have several well-known friends, and I endeavour to see Rahaman's niece Rasheda in Las Vegas. And if I fancy the East Coast then New York is to my taste. Nevertheless, I had to make this trip to Ali's hometown and meet his closest family member. Besides, we had co-written a book so it was imperative we met before one of us left this earth.

Several years before I met Rahaman, I had plans to meet Ali himself. I was going to call Ali's daughter who I have been friends with for many years and we'd go to the Arizona home, with several of my close friends. That was the big plan. Unfortunately, since my visa had expired and with other things going on, I didn't get around to renewing the visa on time. To my great regret, Ali passed away before I could make good on my plan, and I never was able to achieve my goal. When I later revealed to his daughter about the plan, she said her father would've liked me and would've even done an interview with me.

Anyway, when we got to the historical Ali Center, Ron had arranged to do a short advance announcement about our landmark project. After lunch at a restaurant we settled in back at the house where we spent some quality time with Rahaman. This man had had it all – money, cars, homes – but now all that had vanished. Ali had taken care of his only sibling when they were together, but when Ali's health deteriorated in later years in his ripe old age, something of a wedge grew between various Ali family members.

I felt wretched about the state of affairs. There is no doubt that had Ali been in charge of his senses he would never have neglected his own brother who he had grown up with and loved as much as their parents. There had been rumours circling for years about the family feud. Ali's family had certainly garnered some negative press, something that I refrained from involving myself in, despite being a journalist who typically has considerable latitude in criticising public figures. Sure, a few family members had been in the spotlight prior to and after Ali's passing, but family problems are nothing unusual. We all experience them one time or another in our lives. Ali's family had their own share of problems and inner battles to contend with, but I didn't want to get involved. If anything disparaging was attached to any press that I was doing, I would never want to attach my name to it. I simply would never want to get involved.

Ron gave some copies of the book to Rahaman to sign for some very distinguished personalities. He signed copies for Bill Clinton, Barack Obama, Will Smith, and Clint Eastwood, to name just a few. Speaking of Clinton, he had actually been approached by us to write a foreword. The former president acknowledged our request and said he'd do anything to help and support Ali's brother, and that Ali was a good friend of his and he loved him. Rahaman had actually met the former president. Unfortunately, Clinton's agreement with his literally agent prevented him from endorsing a third party's book in the form of a foreword. Needless to say, we were disappointed. Will Smith was another personality we had spoken to. His people made noises about coming aboard, but nothing materialised in the end. Anyhow, NFL great, Jim Brown, a man who, of course, had been a close friend of the three-time heavyweight champion, wasted no time in stepping up.

* * *

We arrived in Los Angeles a few days later. The morning after landing, we had arranged to drop by Will Smith's office in Calabasas. Will was away promoting *Gemini Man*, but we left a gift for the actor in his absence. I rang Paul Heller, who produced *Enter the Dragon*, and Ron and I went to see him at his home in Beverly Hills. Paul had been an executive at Warner Bros studios and had worked with the likes of Clint Eastwood and Elizabeth Taylor. I had a short discussion about his thoughts in relation to Hollywood producing a new Ali biopic – after Will Smith's portrayal almost 20 years earlier didn't quite hit the mark. I told Paul that the ultimate goal would be to have a major Hollywood movie made based on our book. Paul said with great conviction that it was perfect timing, even suggesting Robert De Niro as being the ideal man to potentially produce such a film. 'I think De Niro is your man,' Paul said. 'He understands boxing. He's done *Raging Bull*.' The producer showed a lot of optimism, and given his stature and experience in Hollywood it was advice that I would be embracing seriously.

I've had the pleasure of interviewing Paul twice, including two years earlier when I first visited him at his home – a nice bungalow tucked away in a quiet street. Sitting down with the man who was pretty much responsible for catapulting Bruce Lee to superstardom on a global level was a great experience. Paul, who is one of the most affable people I've ever met, was 92 but looked well for his age. It was wonderful to be treated to some fascinating anecdotes by this Hollywood legend, and I was rather impressed by the fact his memory hadn't lapsed at all. He told me that *Enter the Dragon* originally had a modest budget of $250,000 assigned to it, which then went up to $400,000, but once they were done it was inflated to $800,000, including costs for music, and so on. Nevertheless, it became one of the most profitable movies in the history of cinema as far as budget-to-profit ratio goes.

Paul told me that Bruce would often visit him at the house and once sent him flying with his famous one-inch punch in the same room we were sitting in. I learned how the producer, of all people, would paint the famous red scars on Bruce's body because the Hong Kong makeup artists didn't quite grasp the importance of continuity, leaving the American producer to take up the task himself. I asked him what Bruce was like. He said, 'I've never met anyone in my life who wanted to become a star more than him.' After our conversation he showed me some photos, but what I really wanted to get my hands on was the original script for *Enter the Dragon,* so I asked, 'Do you have the original script?' He showed me one, saying, 'It's not the original but it's my copy.' Well, it was one of the original ones. Maybe I'm wrong, but I felt maybe he didn't want to reveal this as the original in case we came back to steal it. Anyway, I was reluctant to further probe him. That day I was in a rush as I had arranged to meet up with Muhammad Ali's son in law, Kevin Casey – an MMA fighter who fought in the UFC – otherwise I'd have enjoyed spending more time with Paul.

One of the highlights of this trip to Los Angeles was going to be meeting an American sporting legend who, although he had retired many decades earlier, is still a massive name – the one and only Jim Brown. The running back and hall of famer held several NFL records, and is lauded by many as the greatest American football player in history. Besides an illustrious sports career, in the late 1960s he pursued a movie career, appearing in several cult classics. Moreover, we were going to meet him at his home in Hollywood Hills. We drove up to Jim's house, passing some very nice homes. We were greeted by Jim and his lovely wife Monique, who were welcoming. All of us congregated in their beautiful living room where everything was cream-coloured. *Very nice,* I thought to myself. Through the glass doors you could see the swimming pool. And there it was: the balcony, where you had the best view of Los Angeles and Hollywood I could have imagined.

Jim had been living in the four-bedroom, four-bathroom home for many years. His health had deteriorated and he used a walking stick, but one glance at this 83-year-old athlete's face and you'd think he wasn't a day older than 49. He must be the youngest-looking 83-year-old I have ever seen in my life. One thing that did not escape my notice was the sheer size of his forearms. They were like grabbing a massive baseball. These guns were as huge as a bodybuilder's forearm.

TO THE TOP

Anyway, we gathered in the room which Jim used as his office because the lights were too dim in the living room. Having a casual chat with NFL's greatest was an experience I'll forever cherish. I found him to be very approachable, and humility radiated from him. Despite his fame, this is a man who has his feet firmly on the ground. I said to him he was humble considering his status.

'We, me and Monique, we don't do the bullshit,' he said. Jim is someone who, even though he's a superstar who's rubbed shoulders with the biggest names, disliked attending certain events where egos were running around loosely where it was all about who sat in the big chair and all that eccentric stuff Hollywood is known for. He spoke to you as if he had known you for a good while, as if you weren't a stranger.

Jim's friendship with Ali can be traced back to the mid-1960s. Both men were top of their respective sports and had something else in common: acquiring justice and equality for African-Americans. Jim had spent an inordinate amount of time with Ali and Rahaman in the 1960s and 1970s, and a deep friendship had ensued, especially between Muhammad and Jim. Ali's brother had always taken a back seat, being in the shadow while Ali's polar-opposite brash personality won over millions. Jim said that Ali's brother deserved success and acknowledgement, and that he was the ideal person to tell the Muhammad Ali story.

Of course, being an MMA journalist, naturally the conversation was going to gravitate towards the UFC for me. This isn't known by some modern-day UFC fans, but Jim was involved with the UFC after its creator Rorion Gracie – both men were friends – approached him in the early 1990s to come on board. After Chuck Norris and John Saxon declined work as commentators because they felt the event was just too raw, too gritty, for them to be involved with, Jim was easier to persuade and ended up ringside co-commentating.

Naturally, I wanted to ask Jim what his thoughts were on those two diminutive-looking men, Royce Gracie and Bruce Lee, who had revolutionised the martial arts world in two different eras. 'Those two unique individuals are both awesome,' he said. 'Bruce was very unique and very effective in movies, but Royce was the real deal! They don't say "cut" in the UFC.' Ron let out a laugh.

'Royce was a great, great person, unbelievable fighter,' the NFL legend said. 'He was fully responsible for the whole mixed martial arts thing being recognised by the whole world. He was not a big guy, but he could beat big men and he was a champion fighter and a nice human being.'

I said, 'He changed the world of fighting in a sense. They had been doing no-holds-barred in Brazil, and it then took off in America, the whole concept, but people were shocked. Yet now it's a sport.' Jim replied, 'For me I look at it this way: to me he was a scientist. He could beat people twice his size. He knew and understood what I might call "martial arts", and he had an attitude that nobody in the world could beat him. Boxers can only use their fists, but in the sport that Royce excelled in you had to know how to do all these other things (grappling and ground fighting) that were strange in this country at the time. He was a pioneer, in my opinion. He created a whole way of inspiring fighters and size didn't matter. It didn't matter if you were a lightweight or heavyweight, you could be as heavy as you wanted but this guy could whoop you.' Jim laughed, adding, 'He was the most influential fighter and he presented himself in a certain way. And at the time I think the promoters understood the value of his style of fighting. It was amazing for me, sitting ringside and commentating. I'm looking at this little guy, so slender. The least-tough-looking guy. I had so much respect for his style, people would go,' he tapped his hand three times on the desk, 'I give up,' and that would be it.' Again he let out a laugh.

I had interviewed Jim nine years earlier over the phone, but this was even better. I mean, a man of his calibre who has had a stellar multi-dimensional career? You don't get bigger than Jim Brown in the world of American sport. It was a moment I still savour.

TO THE TOP

* * *

In Las Vegas, we had a meeting lined up with one of Muhammad Ali's closest entourage members from his heyday. Now, I have met many people in the fame game, and experienced some outlandish situations, but meeting this particular individual, who I shall refer to as 'Mr BS', was going to be a repulsive experience. I had an inkling he wasn't the most affable of people, but this experience would forever be entrenched in my head. This guy, in his late 70s, had been right by Ali's side primarily throughout the 1970s. He had been part of sporting history by association. Now he was living a modest life. He was on welfare amounting $30,000 a year, he told me, but he was content.

Well, problems started from the word go with this idiot. He's an associate of Ron's and had given Ron the address of a diner where he suggested we convene, but when we arrived there was no sign of this man. Ron rang him, only to have 'Mr BS' bark back at him, 'You can't take simple instructions!' As it happens the diner he was waiting at was a different branch, about ten minutes away.

Anyway, we finally managed to get there. We walked in and there were hardly any customers. It was so quiet you could hear a pin drop, a far cry from the ambience of a prestigious place. And inside, here was a bulldog-faced giant of an old man with his fat ass sat digging into his sweet pudding. My first impression was that he was a miserable-looking man with a demeanour that would put you off for the rest of your life. There was no welcome, nothing. Well, that set the tone for the day – the signs were bleak. Next thing you know, our guest chucked a tirade of abuse Ron's way, which I found perplexing. I mean, we were all grown men and professionals. I had even interviewed this man a couple of years earlier over the phone, and so I had experienced his aggressive approach before. I had a sense of what to expect, but it was beyond my comprehension how things would unfold.

One of the most amusing things that happened that sunny afternoon was that I nearly choked to death when I was sipping water.

I was sitting directly in front of 'Mr BS' when he made a sudden derogatory remark about Ron's little camera that was parked on the table. I burst out laughing while sipping water from a glass, which prompted me to jump up and swiftly move several feet away because I didn't want to give 'Mr BS' the impression I was laughing at him – worst still piss him off. This guy didn't even blink. If I'm honest, I thought I was going to fall over on the floor laughing and make a real scene. Eventually I sat down, still out of breath and, believe me, I was trying so hard to settle myself. Trying to keep a serious face hiding the smirk I was breathing heavily. 'Mr BS' asked, as if he was concerned, 'Are you OK?' Gasping I said, 'Yes, I just …' I almost choked on water.

This man didn't seem to have a nice word to say about anyone. Yes, that's right, anyone. He was just a constant naysayer who tried to cast gloom on everything. His ego was larger than a whale; he was one of the most narcissistic people I had come across in my whole life.

Next, for some reason, this guy wanted us to accompany him to Floyd Mayweather's gym. Ron and I thought, *What are we going there for?* Unless Mayweather was going to be there himself, we didn't care to visit the gym. Anyway, we agreed to go with him, and while there we could both see him drip with deceit as his ego ballooned up. He wanted to give us the impression that he had garnered respect at the gym. We came to learn that numerous people had parted ways with this Ali entourage member over the years. It wasn't surprising, because his attitude was absolutely abhorrent. He's the kind of guy you'd be guaranteed to part ways with if you were ever to deal with him on a professional or personal basis.

Why were we there to meet him? Ron had set up a meeting with this man primarily to discuss business. Being an inner-circle member of Ali's team in the old days, he'd had dealings with many important and famous individuals. His contact list, no doubt, must have been a who's who of the celebrity world. He had convinced Ron to meet because he said that he would not only ask but 'make' Clint Eastwood

TO THE TOP

produce a movie based on Rahaman and my new book. To me, if I'm honest, the idea seemed far-fetched and I soon realised it was completely out of the question.

When Ron and I got back to our hotel, next thing you know 'Mr BS' was phoning Ron on his cell phone and screaming like a little boy throwing his toys out of the pram. This guy had a problem with a certain individual who had trained with Ali who had been given substantial coverage. It was preposterous. So, the next day we met up with 'Mr BS' again. Yes, at the same diner. It was going to be round two.

Ron sat directly in front of 'Mr BS' this time with me to his right. The day before, I had actually asked 'Mr BS' if Muhammad Ali had ever met Bruce Lee. I mean, I already knew the answer to the question. I knew with absolute certainty that the two legends had never crossed paths. After all, I'm a biographer of both. Still, I just couldn't help kill my curiosity because 'Mr BS' had met literally everyone Ali had met. It struck me as rather odd, actually left me stunned, when he said, 'Yes, we met him.' I countered his comment, 'They never met.' My response was met by an incensed glare as he barked, 'Yes, we did! He was a very nice man.' I was disorientated. For a split-second he almost had me doubting myself. Next, I revealed to him that I'm a close friend of Bruce Lee's goddaughter, who I'd known for many years, to give him a little taste of the fact I knew what I was talking about. Suddenly his face fell but he stuck to his guns refusing to backtrack. He'd been caught out red-handed and I think deep inside he knew it – either that or he was one of those deranged individuals who believes their own lies – you know the type one sometimes comes across.

I had interviewed and spoken with countless individuals who were around Bruce and close to him – and I think I told him this – and I had put the same question to several. Not one said Bruce had met Ali. Not even Bruce's immediate family have been documented on saying this, ever! Bruce's daughter Shannon Lee said to me a year later in

October 2020 in an interview, 'I think my father was and would have continued to be a huge fan of Muhammad Ali's, and so are we. There are two names that are mentioned together in the same breath often. I think that's wonderful, it's a beautiful thing.' In fact no human on earth has come forward proclaiming both legends ever met. Moreover, I had questioned several people who had been friends of both Bruce Lee and Muhammad Ali. One particular individual, the same person 'Mr BS' abhorred for some reason, tried to connect the two icons but Bruce died in 1973. 'Mr BS', I quickly came to realise, seemed like a pathological liar. First, I couldn't understand why such a man in his position would resort to such a shameless act. Despite the fact he had met the most prominent personalities in the world. What was the motive? I have no idea. Then, again, I had come across several famous personalities in the combat sports world who had sugar coated the truth in terms of their association or friendship with other celebrities, when they had no reason to apparently, while others had a tendency to resort to such tactics to inflate their own prestige and position.

The fact of the matter is, nowhere will you find anything whatsoever documented that even remotely confirms that Ali and Bruce ever met. Still, I thought maybe 'Mr BS' and Ali met one of the Bruce Lee impersonators in the 1970s, as there were imposters cashing in on the name with cheesy movies at the heart of the kung fu boom after Bruce's untimely demise. That would explain it. This was the only plausible answer. Then, again, 'Mr BS' must have been so thick he thought this was the real Bruce Lee. But, after meeting 'Mr BS', it could be a straight-out lie.

Now, 'Mr BS' claimed he was Ali's best friend and looked me right in the eyes, very tensed up with his fist clenched on the table, making it clear that no one knew Ali better than him. He complained I should have interviewed him about Ali when I was doing my research. Sure, he was around Ali as one of the more prominent members of his team, but it was clearly stretching it to make the claim of being his 'best friend'. I can't remember what I said, but I triggered something and he suddenly clenched both his fists in a fit of rage screaming at me as he tried to grab me. Giving a roar of rage, he barked, 'Don't put words in my mouth!' If that table hadn't been in the way, which was the 'no man's land', he would have virtually gone for my throat. 'Mr BS's' hands were huge – the biggest hands I have ever seen in my life. His face was like a big Frankenstein. For a second it felt a little disquieting, I must admit, when the adrenaline rush switched on and the panic button started flashing in my head. Just to let him know, I said, 'I'm not scared of anything. I'm not scared of anyone.' He soon settled down.

He claimed there were people loyal to him who would do anything for him. I don't think this statement had much substance either. I felt that he was blustering. Name dropping and lying were this guy's full-time profession and he was convincing, very convincing indeed. I don't think he had the power he made out that he had anymore. 'Mr BS' was a washed-up guy living a miserable existence. I thought, *Is this guy involved with the Mafia or something*. In fact, it's a question I later put to Ron. After all, it was Las Vegas and he had been a connected man, and allegedly was still connected. One thing that did take me back was that this guy reminded me of one of the most dangerous fighters in the world who I had a business problem with over 16 years earlier.

Speaking of ego, the day before, 'Mr BS' had his own little digital camera with him and had taken photos of us with him posing as if he was a celebrity. On the table was a cream-coloured A4 envelope. He opened this and took out two enlarged photos. I asked, 'Is this for us?' He calmly said, 'Yes.' Next thing he's personally autographing both photos to Ron and I. *What an egotistical man*, I thought to myself. He had gone to all that trouble to take photographs and then autograph them so apparently we can go away with a souvenir and hang his mug in our home or office. During our conversation he rang someone – or someone rang him, I can't remember now – and after the call ended he proceeded to brag to us that it was one of the Kennedys. 'Mr BS' told us this family member of the Kennedys was visiting Vegas soon and he'd be spending time with him hanging out. It was all etched across his face. How could one miss that inflated ego? Not a chance.

What further stunned me was despite claiming to be Ali's best friend he bad mouthed the heavyweight champion on several occasions in my presence. According to 'Mr BS', Ali's close relative had made derogatory comments to Ali in front of all those present at the Louisville home when Ali's mother was on her death bed. Ali's wife allegedly said it would make sense to have the doctors turn the life support-machine off. It's not something you divulge to others, especially someone you've just met for the first time. One of Ali family member, who is a good friend of mine, brought to my attention that 'Mr BS' on numerous occasions had talked trash even in front of strangers divulging to them how Ali's family didn't help Ali's brother, etc. This really put everything into perspective for me. I came to a conclusion, as a clearer picture of this man emerged. I detested him with venom now because of the fact he would go to a shameful level, talking about Ali and his family in derogatory terms in front of strangers. My impulse was to knock his head off. But what would that accomplish and going down an unprofessional route wasn't something that would be regarded as the right thing to do for a man of my professional standing.

Meeting this old man is an experience I would never forget. Despite the fact the experience was far from amicable, however, it was an experience regardless – he was an interesting character whose name is forever carved in sporting history. Exactly a year later I interviewed former chat-show host Michael Parkinson. Personally I got the vibe he didn't particularly like Ali although he found him to be extraordinary. He had had Ali on his show four times. Ali went into a rant on air accusing the host of trying to trap him. I found his response strange when I said that I'd seen a clip of him at Ali's house in 1973 chatting, with Ali's tiny son there. 'I don't think any journalists, apart from American journalists, went to Muhammad

TO THE TOP

Ali's house,' he told me. 'I never did.' I was totally perplexed. I was scratching my head.

While in Vegas, Ron and I had lunch with Floyd Mayweather Snr, who is a friend of Ron's. Anytime Ron's in Las Vegas he stays at his home. Mayweather Snr, I found affable, a down-to-earth guy always up for a laugh and joke. Also, visiting Vegas and not having lunch or dinner with my good friend Rasheda Ali is never going to happen. I had dinner with her accompanied by Ron. It was a pleasant evening and I brought up my horrific experience with one of her father's close entourage members.

CHAPTER FORTY-ONE

A TUMULTUOUS YEAR

THE YEAR 2020 was total chaos. From March onwards, as the whole world battled Covid-19, our world was turned upside down. The crisis has, of course, had a dramatic effect on how we live our lives and on the economy, on every industry from tourism to the theatre and the cinema, with the world forced to socially distance. The combat sports world was hit as hard as almost any other industry, with fights being cancelled, some promotional companies thrown into financial trouble, and fans left disappointed.

There was, however, the hope of a comeback for the world's biggest MMA organisation. As the pandemic gripped entire nations, UFC president Dana White insisted the UFC would overcome the forces that had slammed the brakes on virtually every other sporting league and event. As the USA locked down, he begun negotiations to buy an island in international waters that could host fights without legal repercussions; it was like something from *Enter the Dragon*. Despite the demands of social distancing, professional fighters started to get back to training and fighting, though their cornermen would have to wear masks and the crowds couldn't attend fights.

Meanwhile, it was an incredibly exciting time for UFC. Stepping up to welterweight for the third time in his career, Conor McGregor had emerged victorious against Donald 'Cowboy' Cerrone at UFC

246, which took place on 18 January, before most people were aware of the seriousness of Covid. It only took 'The Notorious' a mere 40 seconds to dispatch his foe, using a blistering array of techniques. After sprawling from a flying knee, McGregor landed some surprisingly effective shoulder whips from the clinch, wobbling his opponent before finishing him with pin point striking and ground-and-pound. While McGregor was laughing all the way to the bank, UFC fans were left hoping to see a rematch with McGregor's old adversary Khabib, though the latter was to face another opponent – Tony Ferguson – at UFC 249 on 18 April at the Barclays Center in Brooklyn, New York. In the event, Covid struck again. With Khabib under quarantine in his home country, the event was pushed forward to 9 May in Florida, and Khabib was replaced by Justin Gaethje.

Nevertheless, Khabib – at the time lightweight champion and the dominant force in the division – would finally defend his crown against Justin – crowned the interim champion – at UFC 254 on 24 October on Yas Island in Abu Dhabi, for the UFC lightweight championship unification bout. In Russia, the fight was aired on REN TV and drew almost 11 million viewers in the country, though interestingly, it only garnered 675,000 pay-per-view buys.

It's incontestable that Khabib is an awesome fighter. He is a draw, no doubt. Still, had this been a rematch with McGregor, it's my belief that the pay-per-view figures would have skyrocketed. McGregor's fights will always attract bigger pay-per-view buys. This is only likely to change if the star gets derailed to a point at which he is no longer relevant; and his performance against Cerrone had many convinced that he was a better fighter than ever. Still, Khabib pocketed a McGregor-sized pay packet of his own on that occasion, earning a staggering £4.6 million excluding bonuses.

It was a fight that some people thought would be one-sided. Typically, Justin is a big hitter, using chopping leg kicks and tight boxing to turn every bout into a brawl. He's not against getting up close and taking punishment, something that many thought would play into Khabib's hands, as Khabib is something of a pressure fighter who wants nothing more than to drag you to the mat and punch you until you make a mistake.

In the event, though, Justin had improved his game and was mobile from the start, making himself a moving target as opposed to a stationary one. Khabib, meanwhile put pressure on his adversary, showcasing his punching skills. He still managed to take Justin down, and though Justin fought admirably, the gap in skills on the ground was clear. In round two, Khabib slapped on a triangle choke forcing Dustin to tap out in one minute 34 seconds.

After the fight, during the traditional post-bout interview in the Octagon, Khabib shocked the MMA world as he announced his retirement from the sport. He had tallied up a 29-0 professional MMA record. His father, who was also his long-time coach, had passed away from Covid-19 in July, at the age of only 57, which had left him bereft. He made an oath to his mother, he explained, that he would never fight again after his final title defence, and he was going to follow through with his promise. The UFC's latest big commodity was leaving the sport that had spread his name around the globe after coming to prominence just two and half years earlier when he won the UFC lightweight belt in April 2018. It was six months after winning the title that Khabib would come to be known by virtually every combat sports fan, after a bout with McGregor that had been clouded by controversy. The war of words had escalated into a series of real-life assaults, with McGregor attacking a bus that Khabib was on after Khabib confronted his team-mate Artem.

Nevertheless, Ever since beating 'The Notorious', Khabib garnered a much bigger following, especially from the Muslim world, while McGregor was treated with disdain by many. I always stayed impartial as certain people and fans continued their vilification of the Irish sensation, but when he was accused of making anti-Muslim remarks after talking about Khabib's religion and his wife, I wasn't thrilled, too. Still, what many people seem to be oblivious to is the fact that

McGregor's agent is a Muslim. And so I believe that, in spite of McGregor overstepping the line with Khabib and making some extremely personal remarks, he is not a racist. Yes, he uses tactics to get into his opponent's head and sell a fight that I don't always approve of, something I mentioned a lot earlier. Indeed, I think the man should have refrained from making such derogatory comments to Khabib. But I think McGregor had no idea that it would lead to dire consequences, and he probably didn't think his comments through. For him, it was just another day at the office. Khabib, however, seemed to take it all very personally.

Khabib leaves an impressive legacy. He will forever be remembered as a UFC great, one of very few fighters to never taste defeat. Among MMA fans you will always have differences of opinion as far as the GOAT [greatest of all time] is concerned, but he's certainly in contention. Jon Jones, for his part, was quick to respond when many gave Khabib the accolade, going on a rant that seemed a little unworthy of him. 'I'm talking to all you Khabib fans out there,' Jones said, smirking. 'I have 15 world title defences. Your guy has four.' He went on to say that if the fans were talking about who was the best fighter ever, then they must be joking if they brought up Khabib. 'The only person who can really come back and challenge my record in the UFC is possibly Georges St-Pierre.' Then again, the latter would have to win two championship fights to tie with him. Jones also made it clear that he hadn't retired yet, and has a whole new chapter to go through before his legacy could be decided. Just 33 years old, he also said that Khabib had just started to fight in elite level competition. It's something to consider, but Khabib fought everyone he could, and beat them all, mostly with ease. I think his name should certainly be in the conversation. I had spoken to Khabib's manager several times about working with the UFC champion, but nothing came to fruition.

Khabib may have retired, but there was another fighting legend who had been at the forefront of the sporting press. And I was going to be taking note. I was busy, juggling publicity demands and promoting a couple of biographies I had released. I was going on prominent radio stations – Talk Sport, Talk radio in the United Kingdom and a radio station in the New York area – on both sides of the Atlantic, and packing in media interviews talking about my favourite subjects: Muhammad Ali and Bruce Lee. I wasn't going to be side-tracked I filled my diary with famous personalities to interview for the newspaper. Michael Parkinson, David Arquette – who had had a stint with professional wrestling amidst his Hollywood career – Terrence Crawford, Eddie Hearn and Shannon Lee were all on my list, and I was working flat out. The pandemic really affected even the papers I write for, with most staff working from home, to mention budget cuts.

* * *

So, who was making these headlines? Amid the pandemic, it was Mike Tyson who was splashed across the sports pages. Though 'Iron' Mike was in his 50s, rumours started to circulate that the former heavyweight champion was making a comeback and ready for the ring. He was training with a Brazilian MMA coach, Rafael Cordeiro, at Kings MMA – the well-established Huntington Beach MMA gym. But he wasn't planning on entering the Octagon, not at all. It was rumoured that the retired boxing champion was coming out of retirement to face a potential former champion. Soon enough, the sporting press was in a frenzy. Several years earlier I had been assigned by the *Sunday Times* to interview Tyson in Las Vegas. Although I made the trip – I had other meetings and people to see there – I was disappointed that the chat with Tyson didn't materialise. Now, of course, a plan quickly formed in my mind. I was going to reach out to former champions myself to ask what their thoughts were, and whether Tyson was doing the right thing.

One of the first names that cropped up was Evander 'The Real Deal' Holyfield, who had beaten Tyson in their two high-profile fights. I had always found Evander affable. Even now, I often call him directly if I want to interview him for the newspaper sports pages, and he always obliges with no hesitation whatsoever.

I had two conversations with Evander, both relating to a potential comeback fight with his old foe. Our first conversation took place in May. I asked him, 'Recently you've announced a comeback, are you doing this because Mike Tyson's announced a comeback?' Evander replied, 'No, no, no. My whole thing is doing something for my Foundation. Exhibition fights even with people who don't even box. That's the idea.' He made it clear that he had already contemplated pursuing an exhibition fight before Tyson announced his return. Tyson wasn't the one who invoked his interest in lacing up the gloves again, he said.

I asked, 'Would you be interested in fighting Mike Tyson for a charity?' He said, 'I would do that! Yes, I want to fight Mike Tyson. My whole thing is I'm open. And I know that I want to do well for myself at age 57. The thing is, I can protect myself well, I know that. I can definitely handle him.' I probed him further, arguing that he was 57 years old and asking if his age would not be a factor in the risk of getting badly hurt. He told me that he was taking care of his body, regularly hitting the gym. Next, I asked him to tell me what kind of training regime he would go through if he was seriously contemplating a comeback. He was already in good physical condition, judging by the images that were circulating online. 'I know my reflexes aren't as good as they used to be,' he conceded. 'But it depends who I go against, and if I'm to go three rounds of two to three minutes a round.'

A third fight between the two legendary pugilists would, without a doubt, provoke immense interest. It's something that I would be interested in, for sure. Tyson has captured the world's imagination for over 35 years and I believe fans will always be drawn to him far more than any other boxer alive – active or inactive. I was somewhat surprised at what he told me next, though. 'We have to come up with something that explains that this is not a knock-out grudge match,' Evander told me, with a mild laugh. 'It's not about who can beat who, but to show people we were some of the greatest fighters in our era and we've come together as men to do something for others now. Not, "I'm still mad at you! I'm still this, I'm still that."' He continued, 'I can still shoot the jab. I can still shoot the shots, but not like a killing thing, *I'm going to hurt you, I'm going to show you that I can knock him out.*' I wasn't sure that keeping things safe and sanitised would be the right attitude if the potential fight was to leave an indelible impact on the fans. But that's Evander for you, a gentle giant with an affable personality. How can you not like the guy? He was aware of how sharp Tyson was looking, but insisted he was also in very good condition physically and mentally.

Tyson had suddenly been inundated with offers after he had initially released a clip of himself hitting the pads with ferocious power. It was almost a throwback to the prime Mike Tyson as he literally ripped the pads out of the coach's hands. Bear in mind Tyson had been inactive for 15-plus years, during which he had essentially turned his back on any boxing training. Now, everyone wanted a shot at the former champ. In fact, I also managed to speak to Tito Ortiz, who in the past had also been coached by Mike's current trainer, who had jumped on the bandwagon to try and entice the boxer into fighting him in a boxing match and not MMA rules. 'Since we have both announced a comeback, a fight between me and Mike would definitely be the fight people want to see,' Evander said. 'I don't have anything against Mike personally. The thing is, I think it would be good for the sport, and even though boxing is a rough sport, we can show people we come together.'

But Evander's idea was shattered. It was Roy Jones Jnr who, eventually, Tyson would be locking horns with. When I spoke to Evander again, as the date of that fight neared, I wondered if he had given up all hope of facing his foe one final time. I asked whether, if they offered him and Tyson the right money, regardless of whether Tyson won or lost against Roy Jones Jnr, he would still fight? Would Tyson want to really face Evander again, and be willing to get in the ring for the third time with the man who gave him so much trouble in their previous legendary encounters? Evander was adamant, saying that, while he was open to fighting him, Tyson would really want to do it as well. I asked 'The Real Deal', 'Why did Mike choose to accept a fight with Roy Jones Jnr, while there were a lot of other fighters lining up offers including you?' I think some felt Tyson had a better chance of beating Roy Jones Jnr, and so he accepted the easier fight instead of facing the likes of Evander Holyfield, and I wanted to get Evander's opinion and see if he felt Tyson was ducking him. 'Of course that's the whole point of asking yourself, when you're going into something, how comfortable you want to be,' he answered. 'If you fight somebody on your level then you both stand a chance to lose, but I don't go in with that mentality nor plan on losing.' Evander would never fight anyone if he felt he was going to lose, but he respected Tyson's decision to fight Roy. 'It's a decision Mike made,' he told me. That was enough.

I did learn something else from Evander. He was on a mission to help boxers and youngsters, alike. As far as boxing went he had plans to help the sport and the fighters, who put their lives on the line in what is a brutal sport, for the long-term health of its participants. 'What I'd like to say about boxing is it's one of the only sports that don't have a pension plan for participants when they get older,' he said, diverting his attention from all the Mike Tyson talk. 'So, a few have ideas about how I can help other fighters who become champions when their boxing careers are over, to help them decide what kind of plan are they going to have to take care of themselves, including health-wise.' Evander, who had made a staggering $300 million in his career, didn't have problems personally. Despite losing most of his wealth, he'd taken care of himself and made a lot of money back, but he understood that a lot of fighters out there didn't take care of themselves. 'So people like Mike, myself and some other people, we should look at how do we make this game better for these younger people who are doing the same thing career-wise that we did. People

Fiaz Rafiq

19 May 1993

Dear Fiaz

Thank you for letting me see a copy of your article on Bruce Lee.

Sadly, it is not suitable for publication on this occasion, and I am therefore returning it to you in the hope that you will meet with success elsewhere.

Again, thank you for getting in touch.

Yours sincerely

Roger Collier
Features Editor

First rejection letter dated 1993 from the *Daily Mirror*

October 1, 1998

Dear Fiaz:

Thank you very much for sending us your manuscript about "Understanding the Two Principle Components of Training" for consideration. Unfortunately, this particular one does not fit our current editorial needs. We feel that the story is too general. Perhaps you could rewrite it with more of a Bruce Lee focus.

We depend on our freelance writers, so please feel free to submit other ideas via a query letter at your convenience.

We wish you continued success and hope to hear from you again.

Sincerely,

Rodney Ley
Assistant Editor, *Black Belt*

Black Belt, the world's greatest martial arts magazine, acceptance letters dated 1998

February 17, 1998

Thank you for your article for *Black Belt* magazine. We have decided to accept your article entitled "Bruce Lee—The Searcher" for publication in the "Dragon Spirit" column in the June 1998 issue. This issue will be available on newsstands in April 1998. In the meantime, please sign the enclosed writer's agreement. Keep one copy for yourself and return the other copy to us as soon as possible.

If you wish to order bulk quantities of the issue, please call Becky at the above number before March 10, 1998. Quantity orders are sold for 40 percent off the cover price and need to be prepaid.

Thank you for your interest in our magazine. We hope to hear more from you in the future.

Sincerely,

Rodney Ley
Assistant Editor, *Black Belt*

Warner Bros studios letter, 1997/98

Archive interview recordings of UFC, boxing, martial arts, Hollywood and entertainment stars

THE SUNDAY TIMES

Dear Fiaz,

I am writing to confirm that we would like you to interview Mike Tyson for a "Life in the Day" feature for The Sunday Times Magazine.

For "LIDO" we interview a person about their daily routine and ask them to weave in insights, witticisms and anecdotes from their lives.

Past interviewees include Nelson Mandela, Muhammad Ali, the Dalai Lama, Andy Warhol and Sir Paul McCartney.

It might be helpful for Mike's team to know The Sunday Times is by far Britain's biggest Sunday newspaper with 3 million readers nationwide.

We have a reputation for producing some of the world's best journalism and would be delighted to run an interview with Mike.

Best wishes,

Gabriel

1 London Bridge Street, London SE1 9GF
T: 020 7782 8000
Registered Office: Times Newspapers Limited, 1 London Bridge Street, London SE1 9GF
Registered Number: 894646 England & Wales

Sunday Times assignment letter to interview Mike Tyson in 2017

WILLIAM JEFFERSON CLINTON

December 5, 2019

Rahaman Ali

Dear Rahaman:

Thank you for sending me a copy of your new book about your brother. As you know, I loved him very much, and I'm looking forward to reading it.

All my best wishes to you.

Sincerely,

Bill Clinton

Thanks too for the inscription

Personal letter in 2020 from President Bill Clinton to Rahaman Ali for a copy of the internationally acclaimed Muhammad Ali biography co-written by Fiaz Rafiq

Some of the author's press passes: Randy Couture Canadian tour, Mike Bisping V Dan Henderson UFC 204, Arnold Schwarzenegger exclusive event, *Creed II* movie premiere

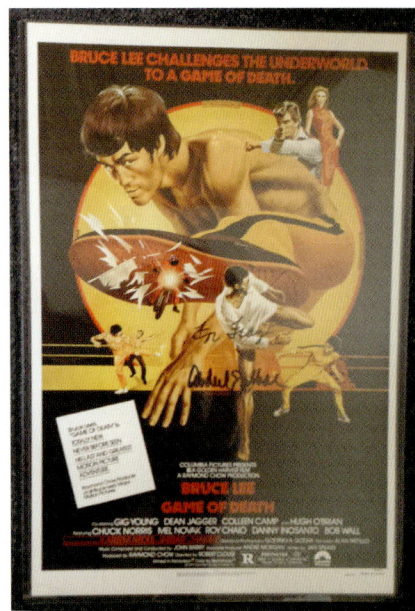

Personally signed poster gift from NBA legend and co-star of Bruce Lee's *Game of Death*, Kareem Abdul-Jabbar, given to the author before an interview in Los Angeles for a documentary in 2006

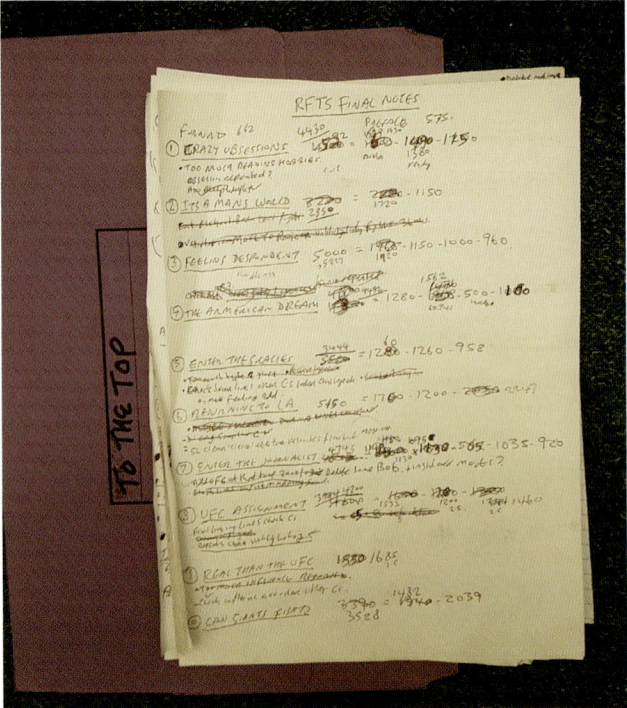

Personal hand-written notes by the author for his memoir

Part of the author's personal home library

who came up like us in life who didn't have other avenues to do real well other than pursuing boxing.'

These days, the former heavyweight champion is on a mission to motivate youngsters so they can have a platform for success. His message is: you live a full life and you'll get old too, so become successful and then you are able to help others. He's interested in creating motivational tools for the next group of people – a new generation. 'It's something that my mom said to me, pretty much,' he said. 'She said to me that each generation are supposed to get better because people who were good, or great, you pass it on to others in the next generation, and they pass it on to the next.'

On 29 November Tyson and Roy Jones Jnr fought for eight two-minute rounds in an empty arena, sharing an engaging draw. Several days before the fight, rules were made public which basically stipulated the following: no knockouts, no winners or losers, and no betting on the exhibition fight. Some fans were infuriated, thinking that the pair should have fought to the finish, and others were confused, placing bets with companies who were later forced to refund them. Still, it was a great bout. Tyson looked in good shape as he used his physicality and forward pressure. He landed with lots of body shots and power, but I think he was holding back somewhat. His opponent was being cautious, and Roy looked a little out of shape, trying to keep Tyson away with the jab but not looking as fast on his feet as he did during the prime of his career.

After the fight, the presenter asked Tyson if he was happy with the decision. He asked him, 'Mr Tyson, what do you think about that?' Tyson, without hesitation blurted out, 'I'm good with that.' Then he was asked, 'Do you think you won the fight?' He responded, 'I'm good with the draw.' The presenter asked, 'Why?' Tyson said, 'Because I entertained the crowd. The crowd was happy with it.'

Mike Tyson was back, UFC's superstar Khabib had retired, and a tumultuous year was coming to an end. I was working on a compilation of interviews with some of the top UFC champions in history. From the pioneers of the sport, and hall of famers to current champions who have captured the hearts and minds of the millions making the UFC a dominant force and the biggest sports company in the world, I wanted to talk to the people who made it happen. I feel that these challenging times have given people a chance to reflect, and the sports world will continue to flourish and mesmerise fans who crave seeing skilled men put all their skill on the line, whether it's beating the living daylights out of each other or appreciating the little nuances of a grappling match. The future is bright for fighting, and I can't wait to see it.

EPILOGUE

I CAN recall, on more than one occasion, my close friend, the editor at the martial arts magazine, saying to me, 'We are lucky to be doing what we love. We could've been working in a factory or somewhere.' He was right. In life, if an individual is fortunate enough to have a hobby manifest into a professional career then, believe me, it's one of the greatest feelings in the world. There is some contention regarding transitioning a hobby into a profitable enterprise. Well, that doesn't apply to me. For me, earning a living doing something you relish in a professional capacity, whether you're a fighter, an actor, musician, writer, sports athlete, agent or manager of an artist, is a dream come true.

You have to savour what you do. I have, almost without exception, immensely enjoyed my work over the years. It has, by and large, felt like playing instead of working. And, whenever I feel dejected, I look back on the good times in my profession – a beacon of hope, status, something to fall back on and give solace in my darkest days. It has been an absolute pleasure being part of diverse, interlinked fields, in a behind-the-scenes capacity, seeing things other people can't, and meeting people who many would treasure the chance to just say hello to. In hindsight, it was a constant progression up the ladder. I reached a point where I always knew, in the back of my mind, that any goal I set, I would achieve it. There would no longer be doubt clouding my mind.

TO THE TOP

Recently it dawned on me that further goals are still waiting to be achieved. When you've ticked off your goals, where do you go from there? You can either fade away into obscurity, or put your motivational cap back on and set new challenges. Well, my love affair with sport and the Hollywood fraternity is far from over. I'm too obsessed to call it a day. I plan on being part of this for a long time. In early January 2021, as I was finishing writing this memoir, my agent – who also represents Rahaman Ali – started pitching to Hollywood arguably the most intimate biography ever written on Muhammad Ali, the greatest sportsman and one of the most adulated figures of the last century, in our quest to nail down a deal with a major Hollywood studio, potentially to have them produce a biopic film based on our book. This, if it sees daylight, will be monumental.

Life is what you make it. I have been reaching for the stars ever since I was a small boy. And when I reached to the top, I learned a lot about people and life. Despite the immense obstacles I've encountered, they will never dispel the memory of the enjoyment of the journey and the ultimate contentment and experiences.

If I could tell anyone reading this one thing, it's this: have high ambitions because the sky is the limit. I always say there are three vital ingredients that are the backbone of anyone's success, indeed my own success: cultivate an obsession, have immense motivation and be tenacious. Like all successful people who had hurdles to overcome, you have to defy the odds and prevail.

AFTERWORD

AUTHOR'S NOTE

Looking back on my life, some of my most awkward moments have come from trying to explain and convince members in the community (people that I know or met for the first time) of my profession in the literary world. Finding it something of a taboo, I had a tendency to be reticent in broaching the subject. When we are growing up and maturing, we often are inclined to boast or sugar-coat our achievements. But, for most people, this mentality soon fades when you become a bona fide professional. Indeed, humility sets in and you no longer feel the need to prove yourself or crave validation.

As I mentioned earlier in the book, *Sunday Times* bestselling author, martial arts innovator and former doorman Geoff Thompson, who left school with no qualifications, was told that people like him don't write books. People like us are destined for the factory floor, according to many people, but Geoff would partly dispel this myth for me. I can also vividly recall Eunice Huthart, the martial artist who parlayed her success into a lucrative stunt career in Hollywood, saying how she had a hard time convincing other mothers that what she said she did for a living was true. When picking up her kids from school, the martial arts champion would have to stand there for 20 minutes explaining to parents what she did for a career. I could understand her struggle, even though I had little interest in convincing outsiders of my worth at the time.

One afternoon when I was at my sibling's house, we had visitors – family friends that we had known for decades – and I decided to break my oath. The man of the family, several years older than me, who I had known almost all my life, a nice guy, had somehow got on the wrong side of me. This guy had this neck twitch problem. We sat there chatting and I couldn't help but notice his constant twitch. Every five seconds he was in action. I tried my best not to burst out laughing and held it all in, but he was Premier League. I swear I was on the verge of dropping to the floor, bursting out laughing. Well, during our small talk he asked me what I did for a living. Oh, yeah, this was the golden question.

Now, me, I had ventured into an unconventional career. So simply explaining myself, as I said earlier, always put me in dilemma. Who in their right mind, where you grew up, is going to believe that you're a professional writer and author? After all, you're an Asian. Taking into account that I had left school with no real qualifications and that on the surface I was devoid of any impressive exterior, I felt like the lie detector would come out with the vain hope of tripping me up, because this had happened countless times before. Often I got the impression that some people thought I was either lying or just sugar-coating what I did for work. Now, I always had a robust attitude towards my work, and if someone else is unable to appreciate the value of something, how can that individual even possess the capacity to achieve it himself? What does valuing a person or something actually mean? It means that you appreciate a person, you see how amazing they are, for example, in their job, and their qualities, and you find them of high worth. Appreciation is to recognise the full worth of someone or something. Respecting someone means you have a feeling of deep admiration for that individual, elicited by their qualities, abilities or achievements – and due regard for others. It's that simple. If you are unable to discern this then you're devoid of basic common sense.

Anyway, my intuition would turn out to be spot on. I told this man that I was a writer and had written several biographies on high-profile

AFTERWORD

personalities, one being Muhammad Ali. Suddenly, this guy went into deaf mode. I realised I was talking to myself, as his interest in listening to me faded faster than you could blink. Indeed, the blank-out syndrome kicked in. It was as if I was now talking in a foreign language that didn't register with his arrogant brain. Consequently, I sometimes stopped explaining myself when I realised people only understood from their level of perception. Indeed, I never really vocalised my opinions back then, even though I felt a deep resentment.

Truth be told, I had run-ins with a lot of idiots. When I initially embarked on my first literary adventure at the tender age of 21, freshly back from my first trip to America – having fulfilled my initial dream of training with an original student of Bruce Lee and Royce Gracie – I was ready to start another chapter in my life, looking to penetrate the combat sports world via the medium that involved the mighty pen. On this occasion, another associate of our family, who was visiting our home, tried to mock me for the sheer pleasure of it. The conversation shifted to me, as it typically would in these social gatherings. 'You write books?' this guy sarcastically questioned with the typical evil smirk that I was only too familiar with. I could sense this man's sarcasm pouring out in abundance. Ironically, it was one of his family members who had first taped the movie *Enter the Dragon* which I had watched as a kid at someone else's house and which had been the introduction to Bruce Lee that planted a seed for all the success that followed. Well, this guy shot himself in the foot, but he had his two minutes of fun at my expense as I sat there listening to his bullshit. Boy, did I want to wipe that smile off his face.

In my early years I had to learn the trade while making mistakes. I can relate to controversial film director Quentin Tarantino in more than one way. The movie buff's first film was shot on a camcorder. Working in a video rental store, he was very passionate about making a film. The only difference between the director and I was that I wanted to convey my message via the medium of print, while he wanted to utilise celluloid. A lot of people who make it professionally as artists, actors, writers and musicians look back at their first attempts – the initial amateur phase – and they cringe. Years later, when I achieved the status of a professional writer, a bona fide authority, I realised it was acceptable to go through the amateur learning phase that I went through, and it wasn't just me who had sunk into the trap. In fact, the editor of the number-one martial arts magazine once told me that he didn't think much of the first issue he edited.

I'm a firm believer in the philosophy 'if you want to learn to swim you must get into the water'. First you will learn to drown. Then you will hold your own. Eventually you will learn to swim. And if you're persistent and unleash your potential, you'll become a champion swimmer. This example perfectly resonates with most things we pursue in life. I went through the swimming pool scenario myself in my quest to prevail in my career, getting wet in the pool, almost drowning. But no way was I going to drown and dig my own grave. If you think you can sail through life perfectly, you're not venturing into life but merely existing. Soon I developed a fastidious approach as I learned from my mistakes. I also had eagerly speculated how much impact this would have on the future if a future did exist.

Still, the negative mindset of those around me left an indelible stain on me. This breed has a problem with every solution, and their corrosive attitude will affect you. I have, by and large, endeavoured to be a positive person, but I have grown up with both positive and negative people, and the latter will always drag you down if you let them.

Psychology is a subject that has always, consciously or subconsciously, invoked my interest. It was something I even pondered studying formally. It's something that we humans can all relate to. I think a lot of people have a delusional mindset and their perception of themselves and others is far from reality. I think people should look within before embarking on a critical analysis of others. A lot of people these days define other people in the most derogatory manner. I feel this attitude often stems from insecurity. Having a basic

AFTERWORD

appreciation for psychology allows you to understand these negative individuals and to get to know yourself also. I learned a lot about myself and others.

Being defined wrongly and having people telling me my worth was a constant battle. Firstly, when people I knew took a pot shot disguised as light banter which I would laugh off, they equated it to weakness. Secondly, because of my friendly, unpretentious and warm exterior, this more often than not gave idiots artillery as they relegated me to the 'unimposing' category. There's a saying: 'don't mistake kindness for weakness'. Unfortunately, it's beyond the majority of peoples' comprehension. It took me several decades to consciously come to terms with these facts, concluding: in life, if you keep your hands down, you're going to get hit. You have to keep your hands up as a defensive mechanism. Imagine leaving yourself open in a boxing ring or the UFC Octagon, you're inviting your partner to tag you in the face. Eventually, I came to the realisation that in life your parents are the only ones who won't think they're better than you, and maybe your siblings. Terms and conditions apply.

I can attest to the fact that the most pessimistic individuals, in most cases, are the 'talkers', and to make themselves feel better they have to drag down the 'achievers', regardless of whatever endeavour they're in. The contrast between the two, the person defining and the person being defined, may be worlds apart. Another saying I like is: 'opinion is really the lowest form of human knowledge'. It requires no accountability and no understanding necessarily. I have found that the most dangerous 'talker' is the one who will make you believe you're worthless. This is the type who will wrongly tell you your self-worth. No matter who you are, narcissistic people will have a negative thing to say about you. Having achieved hardly anything worth mentioning all their lives, this breed is the first to judge all others. In all honesty, I got to a stage where I welcome peoples' disparaging sentiments, but only if they are better individuals than those they are criticising – because these types can hardly back themselves up.

TO THE TOP

Experts say that negative people have a vested interest in seeing themselves as decent, competent and somewhat better, or that an element of denial exists. They're not just evil or inept. When it comes to traits that matter to their self-esteem, they tend to have positive delusions – meaning, on these dimensions, that others see them more accurately than they see themselves. Well, it always seemed to be the judgemental non-achievers who had an infectious habit of negativity in my experience. Unfortunately, you can't change everybody. In fact, it dawned on me that a lot of people are not ready for a change and wouldn't want it if it was offered. Moreover, I earned a platform in that I write for the newspapers which gave me opportunities to criticise and express my views, but essentially I refrained from pigeonholing people who I personally know outside of the professional arena.

In contrast to these people, I've always found that professional personalities, well-educated individuals and essentially those who have gone on to achieve things in life are less prone to having a negative aura about them. I have always been held in high esteem by friends and associates who are professionals. One of my friends, Lance Lewis, who actually is, to an extent, one of the inspirations behind me writing my memoir, was the first non-American member of legendary Thomas Hearns' world-famous boxing gym in Detroit. Lance had joined the gym at a relatively young age. He had boxed professionally and could have gone on to carve out a lucrative career in the sport, but there was a scandal which prevented him from continuing his boxing career, even if he did win the world title in kickboxing. Lance's encouragement of me was optimistic. He told me that I was an Asian of a Pakistani decent growing up in a Western country, and that maybe I didn't make it in education, but that my drive, passion and determination propelled me to achieve what I ultimately did. People in communities are often of the notion that it can't happen to people like us, but you have to defy the odds and grab your dreams. Lance said it's an inspiring story. The encouragement he offered certainly got me thinking.

AFTERWORD

We are fighting all our lives. Whether it's for a new job, more money, recognition, acceptance, power or whatever, life is a constant fight. It's a daily fight for survival for some. That said, you have to recognise that the biggest adversary in your life is you. Yes, that's right: you are your biggest opponent. I learned early in my own life that the mind is the most powerful tool. Martial arts teach you about life and tackling problems, overcoming hurdles and developing certain character traits. They made me into the man I became, teaching me to master myself – and even if I nowhere near pursued them to the extent my interviewees and subjects have as far as the physical level is concerned, I'll always be grateful to them for that as I learned more as a professional journalist.

Now, I try not to crave validation from anyone. I stepped outside my comfort zone and went into the real world, a world where you competed with other high calibre professionals, and soon I was working with some of the top men in combat sports. So, if you are someone who wakes up in the morning and 'talked' your way through the day, your fulltime profession being criticising everyone, then your viewpoints are nullified. I'm not the one sitting on the fence or the edge of the swimming pool, not wanting to get wet. I went to an average school, came from a non-descript area, had a normal family background. If I can rise, so can anyone who has or is willing to cultivate their talent, unleash their potential and keep going till they triumph.

ACKNOWLEDGEMENTS

A HUGE thank you to the staff of *Martial Arts Illustrated* and *Impact* magazines: Moira, Martin, Neal, John, Roy and especially editor Bob Sykes, for giving me the opportunity and embracing me early on my writing career. Our 15-year working relationship was a lot of fun. Another thank you to all my editors at the magazines and national newspapers whose help and support have contributed to my success in my professional writing career. Also, I would like to thank the personalities I have interviewed over the years from the sports and entertainment worlds – you were, of course, an integral part of my success.

I would like to thank my long-time personal friends Diana Lee Inosanto, Royce Gracie, Rasheda Ali, Ron Balicki, Bob Sykes, Ronnie Green, Lance Lewis, Seyfi Shevket, Joe Egan and Peter Consterdine for their countless years of support and encouragement.

I would also like to thank Muhammad Ali's brother, Rahaman Ali, who gave me the opportunity to make history. I would like to thank my agent Charlie Brotherstone. I would like to thank Joel Snape for editing the manuscript.

I would like to thank my friends in the industry, both in the USA and United Kingdom, who have enriched my life and supported me.

I must mention some of those who have influenced me as a writer. Some of my earliest influences, first and foremost, included Bruce Lee

ACKNOWLEDGEMENTS

biographer John Little. Considered to be one of the world's foremost authorities on Bruce Lee, he was selected by the Lee family to review the entirety of Lee's personal notes, sketches and reading annotations and compile books on the late icon including the philosophies of Lee. He inspired me profoundly which culminated in me being selected by Muhammad Ali's closest family member to collaborate on the definitive biography on 'The Greatest'. Other inspirations include bestselling author Geoff Thompson, who had an indelible influence on me as a writer. I was inspired by his story of becoming a writer after leaving school with no qualifications. Davis Miller – a Bruce Lee and Muhammad Ali biographer whose part-biography-part-memoirs received acclaim, and Matthew Polly – another Bruce Lee biographer who also wrote his own memoirs on Shaolin kung fu and MMA. When I was a lot younger, the Canadian bodybuilding writer Robert Kennedy also inspired me.

In life we strive to elevate ourselves. Some of us take our passion to the extreme and become totally consumed by it. Of course to succeed and realise our dreams, we must endeavour to pursue our passion wholeheartedly and be dedicated. Achievements and accolades and acclaim are all great, of course, but sooner or later we may, or should, realise that the core happiness and meaning of life lies not in merely fulfilling our ambitions and achievements, but in cherishing those who are close to us and appreciating the simple things in life. This enables us to achieve contentment.

Also available at all good book stores

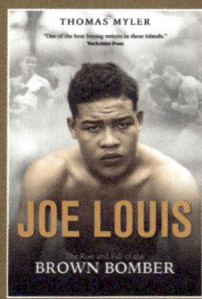
9781785315367

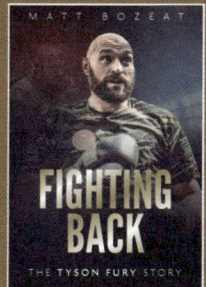
9781785315527

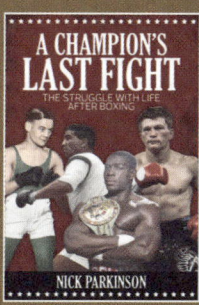
9781785311642

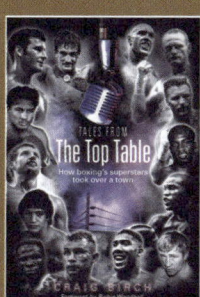
9781785315374

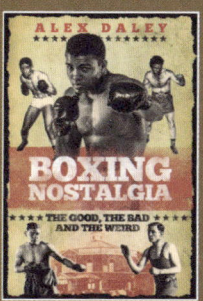
9781785314551

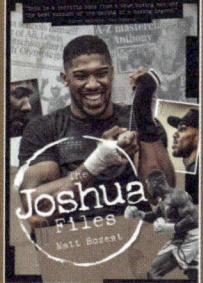
9781785313912

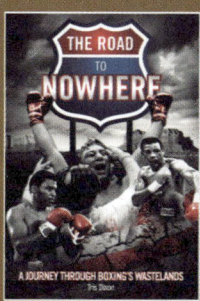
9781785311437

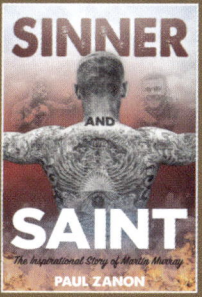
9781785313851

9781785313196